CAROLINAS

GETTING STARTED GARDEN GUIDE

Grow the Best Flowers, Shrubs, Trees, Vines & Groundcovers

D1088509

First published in 2015 by Cool Springs Press, an imprint of Quarto Publishing Group USA Inc., 400 First Avenue North, Suite 400, Minneapolis, MN 55401

The information in this book is true and complete to the best of our knowledge. All recommendations are made without any guarantee on the part of the author or Publisher, who also disclaims any liability incurred in connection with the use of this data or specific details.

Cool Springs Press titles are also available at discounts in bulk quantity for industrial or sales-promotional use. For details write to Special Sales Manager at Quarto Publishing Group USA Inc., 400 First Avenue North, Suite 400, Minneapolis, MN 55401 USA. To find out more about our books, visit us online at www.coolspringspress.com.

Library of Congress Cataloging-in-Publication Data

Bost, Toby, author.
  Carolinas getting started garden guide : grow the best flowers, shrubs, trees, vines & groundcovers / Toby Bost.
     pages cm
Includes bibliographical references and index.
ISBN 978-1-59186-900-9 (sc)
1. Gardening--North Carolina. 2. Gardening--South Carolina. I. Title.

SB453.2.N8B67 2015
635.09756--dc23

2014039035

Acquisitions Editor: Billie Brownell
Design Manager: Cindy Samargia Laun
Layout: Kim Winscher

Printed in China
10 9 8 7 6 5 4 3 2 1

CAROLINAS

GETTING STARTED GARDEN GUIDE

Grow the Best Flowers, Shrubs, Trees, Vines & Groundcovers

Toby Bost

COOL SPRINGS PRESS
Home and Garden Experts™

MINNEAPOLIS, MINNESOTA

DEDICATION AND ACKNOWLEDGMENTS

To my children and their spouses, Brandon and Lauren Bost, and Alex and Terri Moy, who have new homes of their own and who will find this book helpful for many years to come. Much success with the plants you grow and the love you know.

A work of this kind would not be possible without the help and support of many people. I cannot thank everyone enough for all they have done. Even though this book is dedicated to my children who are getting started with new homes and gardens, I want to give special thanks to my wife, Becky, for her constant support and understanding of my commitment to this writing project.

Also, Cool Springs Press is long overdue recognition. Their contemporary state and regional books meet the diverse needs of gardeners throughout the country who face various geographic challenges in their search for outstanding plants. Their books guide gardeners toward the results they desire and in turn a lifelong love for gardening. Further, I would like to thank my editor, Billie Brownell. Her expertise and commitment helped make this book accurate and beautiful. Without her guidance this work would not be the accessible, friendly tool for gardeners throughout the Carolinas. Many thanks to the rest of the Cool Springs Press team, especially Tracy Stanley.

The following people have helped me gather information and prioritize plant lists so that Carolina gardeners could have more tools in their toolbox. Landscape professionals are most generous with the cutting-edge plant knowledge they share when asked. I would like to acknowledge the individuals who graciously provided me with technical information to update the manuscript as I worked through each chapter, often during their busiest time of year—Adrienne Roethling, horticulturist at the Paul J. Ciener Botanical Garden for contributing bulb and perennial text; Scott Welborn, Extension Agent, edited the lawn section; and, P.J. Gartin, garden writer/Master Gardener helped organize the plant list. Others offered plant variety and cultural advice—Mike Garner, Sedge Garden Nursery; Jimmy Speas, Winston-Salem Rose Society rosarian; Frank Sink, Frank's Perennial Border; Mark Abee, AB Seed Garden Center; John Hoffman, Hoffman Nursery; Doug Chapman, Plantworks Nursery; and Tony Avent, Plant Delights Nursery. Finally, I appreciate the help from various green industry business websites and returned telephone calls from staff employees of Park Seed Company, Tinga Nursery; Hawksridge Farm, Piedmont Carolina Nursery, Wayside Nursery, Monrovia Nursery, L.A. Reynolds Garden Showcase, Lowes Company, Home Depot, Nurseries Caroliniana, and Riverbanks Botanical Gardens. You guys were great!

With the death in 2011 of legendary gardener Jim Wilson, I consider his gardening wisdom passed along to me as coauthor of *Carolinas Gardener's Guide*, a gift that I will always cherish. Hopefully, readers will appreciate the richness of a new edition, in *Carolinas Getting Started Garden Guide*. After much scrutiny, I have attempted to highlight the very best ornamental plants and grasses, both native and nursery-introduced, that flourish in Carolina landscapes with minimal care for establishment.

Considering all the talk in the scientific community about global warming and sustainability, it is my humble prediction that new plant selections will continue arriving at the current rate of more than 350 cultivars annually. Landscape gardeners in the future will have no shortage of plant materials to fill the spaces they have available to naturalize woodlots, beautify homes, and design formal gardens.

Happy landscape gardening!

CONTENTS

WELCOME TO GARDENING

IN THE CAROLINAS

There is precedent for combining North and South Carolina into one book about gardening. After all, they share the same hardiness and heat zones and generally the same soil types. Prevailing southwest to northeast winds warm both states and hurricanes brush both shores. Both South and North Carolina have three geographic regions: Mountains, Piedmont, and Coastal. A strong cadre of knowledgeable nursery owners, landscape professionals, and garden center operators can be found in every region. Thankfully, gardeners are not far from a ready source of plant information. The Cooperative Extension, a marvelous public service in every county, overwhelmingly supports lawn and garden activities in both Carolinas.

The land area in the two Carolinas is considerable in size. From Boone, North Carolina, in the northwest mountains of North Carolina to the sunny beaches of Charleston, South Carolina, the topography and microclimates are significant to successful gardening. Mount Mitchell in North Carolina at 6,680 feet is the highest peak east of the Mississippi River. Gardening at that altitude presents a set of challenges totally unlike the challenges experienced while planting the sandy soils at sea level in Brookgreen Gardens, Pawleys Island, South Carolina. Coastal gardens, whether located in the tidewater or farther inland, have unique concerns with salt spray and high water tables. On any summer day in the Carolinas the average daytime temperature can vary 20 degrees. Plant establishment, growth, and sustainability are impacted greatly by winter weather and summer night temperatures. Unfortunately, the weather can change quickly in the South, and the four seasons, as glorious as they are, may not be constant from year to year.

During much of the 20th century, it is fair to say that only two of the four seasons were fully utilized by flower gardeners in the Carolinas. They had azaleas, dogwoods, and rhododendrons in the spring, camellias in the fall, and a long stretch of green in between. The spring and fall seasons also brought food gardening. That's all changing now. Thanks to heat- and humidity-resistant flowers, landscapes can glow with color during the summer. New woody shrub and tree introductions have fewer pest problems and dwarf forms are available for numerous species. Rock-hardy winter annuals can brighten the dark winter days. Ornamental grasses are appearing to add interest and motion to otherwise static borders. Herbs and edibles planted in raised beds are making all-season food gardening not only enjoyable but gratifyingly productive.

But let's be honest about gardening in the Carolinas. Except high in the mountains, summertime gardening is an early morning and late evening activity. Midday gardening is not fun; the risk of dehydration, heat stroke, and skin cancer is real. That's why experienced Carolina gardeners plant shade trees as a first order of business. They know from trial and error that when books say, "grow in full sun," that plants will grow just as well with afternoon shade, and that the same shade is a great place for a comfortable seat and a glass of sweet tea.

Though the sun can be your enemy, you can make it your gardening friend, unlike some pesky critters. Dog and deer ticks lurk on plants waiting for you to come along; stinging caterpillars take refuge under tattered foliage; yellow jackets bore holes in inconvenient places. Slather repellent from head to toe before venturing into your summer garden to deter the ticks. Wear leather gloves in perennial gardens in late summer to protect your hands from stinging caterpillars. Products with DEET® repel mosquitoes. And a hornet-wasp killer aerosol sprayed into their entrance at dusk will prevent unsuspecting passersby a lot of pain. Well, you didn't really expect four seasons of good gardening weather to come without a downside, did you?

Once you get into the swing of gardening in the Carolinas, you can make the trying weather and intractable soil your servant. Gardeners moving to the Carolinas from up north often complain about the sun "not being in the right place for the time of day." Summer days in the Carolinas are shorter, nighttime comes with a rush, and winter days are significantly longer. And they complain about "that awful clay." Give it a chance and it will grow beautiful plants when adequately modified with soil conditioners.

When you study this book, filled with years of experience, gardening will become more enjoyable and productive. You will look forward to spending time in your garden rather than dreading the prospect. With each passing year you will gain skill and confidence. You could even become that person that all the neighbors turn to for advice—a "master gardener."

Getting Started
The Benefits of Organic Matter

Organic matter is a component that increases a soil's water-holding capability while giving it a dark, earthy appearance. It is found in manure, compost, aged leaves, sawdust, and decomposing mulch.

Peat moss is readily available to gardeners and is suitable for amending sandy soils and for use in container gardening. In the Piedmont's clay soils, finely ground composted pine bark is one of the best amendments. (Its general particle size should be ½ inch or smaller.) Tight clay soils can be improved if 20 to 30 percent (by volume) of pine-bark soil conditioner is tilled into the garden (spread a 2-inch layer over the bed and spade or till 6 inches in depth). Other good amendments are leaf compost, granite screening, small pea gravel, and Perma-Till™. Hardwood bark should not be

used as a soil conditioner; however, aged hardwood bark makes a fine landscaping mulch.

Making "Black Gold"

Compost is biologically active organic matter that can be made at home by nature (humus or "woods dirt"). No gardener should be without a compost bin. Stir a little compost into the top few inches of soil, and your plants will flourish. (Compost does for plants what steroids do for athletes—but safely,

Grass clippings and leaves combine well for composting.

of course!) Gardeners gloat over their compost. Some even call it "black gold." The billions of living creatures found in compost help plant roots absorb water and nutrients. Organic gardeners know that you feed the soil, not the plants.

Making compost is simple. Just layer "green and brown" organic yard wastes, maintain moisture content, and turn the pile a few times. In six months to a year, you will have a high-quality organic material that can be used as a soil amendment. A simple compost recipe calls for two trash bags of shredded hardwood leaves combined with one bag of grass clippings. There are numerous recipes and instructions for composting available at any Cooperative Extension office or public library. You will need 2 cubic feet of compost for every 8 square feet of garden bed you plan to amend.

How to Prepare a Bed

Poorly drained clay soils are the norm throughout much of the Carolinas. When preparing a new bed for planting, several tricks will help you avoid "wet feet" and subsequent root rot. The simplest method is to borrow topsoil from one area and add it to the new bed. Rototill the bed and rake it smooth. Adding a few inches of topsoil can have a profound influence on whether a plant lives or flounders.

Landscape timbers or ties, rock retaining walls, and steel edging materials are frequently used to facilitate bed preparation. Or you can create berms for planting, using another technique that involves sculpting high mounds of amended native soils that serve a dual purpose as planting bed and privacy screen. If sand is used in clay soil to improve drainage, the volume of sand must exceed 70 percent.

Finally, where soil drainage is questionable, install a "French drain." This project is best performed using a backhoe. Lay slotted drain tile in the bottom of a 2-foot-deep trench that has a 2-percent slope to daylight. Surround the drain pipe with a bed of crushed stone and then backfill with a loose soil mix. This is the method often used for preparing beds for roses and rhododendrons.

After all is said and done about bed preparation, many gardeners will continue to dig a planting hole and throw a few inches of gravel into the bottom. Though

Add compost and soil amendments to new beds.

they may feel good about this effort, it is a total waste of time and will more than likely worsen soil drainage. Digging a hole in a poorly drained site is something like constructing a pool or creating an in-ground aquarium—only riparian plants thrive under such conditions.

When in doubt, check soil drainage before planting. You can do this with a post-hole digger or shovel and a bucket of water. Dig a hole 1 foot deep and fill it with water. Let it drain cleanly, then refill with water. If the water is still there the next day, don't plant until you install drain tiles or create berms.

Fertilizing: Just a Numbers Game

1. Type of fertilizer. "Ready to use" means that you can directly apply according to the instructions. Fertilizer marked as "concentrated" has to be mixed with water before spreading on plants.

2. The fertilizer brand name. There are different brands of fertilizer, just like there are different brands of clothes.

3. Intended use. This tells you which plants the fertilizer is for. Use different fertilizers for grass, vegetables, and flowers.

4. Fertilizer analysis. Every fertilizer has three numbers on the bag, separated by dashes. This is called the analysis, or sometimes the N-P-K number. The first number is the percentage of nitrogen in the fertilizer, the second number is the percentage of phosphorus, and the third number is the percentage of potassium. This number is also a ratio. For example, a fertilizer with analysis 10-10-10 has a ratio of 1:1:1; in other words, the same percentage of available nitrogen, phosphorus, and potassium in the fertilizer. A 12-4-8 fertilizer has three parts nitrogen to one part phosphorus and two parts potassium.

5. Nitrogen content. This number indicates the percentage of nitrogen in the contents of the package. In this example, a 4-pound bag with 12 percent nitrogen has .48 pounds of nitrogen.

6. Phosphorus content. This shows the amount of phosphorus in the fertilizer.

7. Potassium content. This number shows the amount of potassium in the fertilizer. This fertilizer example has .32 pounds of potassium in a 4-pound bag. If you need to apply 2 pounds of potassium per 1,000 square feet, you would need 6.25 bags of this fertilizer.

8. Nutrients other than N-P-K. These are micronutrients, other nutrients that plants need in smaller amounts than nitrogen, phosphorus, and potassium.

9. Other ingredients. Other ingredients make the fertilizer easier to spread.

Although seventeen essential nutrients are required for plant growth and development, only three are important to remember when gardening in the Carolinas. A healthy plant will consume the largest amounts of three nutrients, nitrogen (N), phosphorus (P), and potassium (K). These elements are the main ingredients in fertilizer and are expressed in terms of a percentage weight. For example, a general garden fertilizer labeled 10-10-10 contains 10 percent nitrogen, 10 percent phosphorus, and 10 percent potassium. The other 70 percent is filler or clay.

Each nutrient serves a function in the overall health of a plant. Nitrogen promotes vegetative or foliar growth; higher nitrogen percentages in a bag are beneficial for lawns or evergreen plants. Phosphorus enhances root and flower development; "starter" fertilizers and "bloom-boosters" are rich in this nutrient. Potassium is important for the overall health of a plant; "winterizer" fertilizers have a high percentage of potassium and may help a plant tolerate drought, cold, or disease. (A general rule of thumb when applying garden fertilizers is to use 1 pound of actual nitrogen per 1,000 square feet. That's equivalent to 1 gallon of 10-10-10 for every 1,000 square feet of garden area.)

The soil's pH determines the availability of the nutrients to the plants; acidic soils starve plants by locking up vital nutrients, thus creating deficiencies. Monitor the soil pH with soil testing. Limestone neutralizes acidic soils and helps fertilizers work. Acidic soils can waste more than half the nitrogen fertilizer applied, and wasted fertilizers are an environmental hazard.

Although selecting the right fertilizer can be a bit frustrating, it's really just a numbers game. Compare the costs of fertilizer products by the amount you are paying for each pound of nitrogen or other dominant nutrients in the package. Controlled-release fertilizers (CRF) generally cost more, but they have some distinct advantages over common garden fertilizers. They slowly release nutrients to plants and are less likely to burn roots from high salt concentrates. For best results, apply a fertilizer with at least 40 to 50 percent of its nitrogen in the ammoniacal or urea form. "Slow-release" fertilizers are an ecologically sound way to supply nutrients since excess nutrients will not leave the garden after a heavy rain. It is prudent to clean up after granular fertilizer and pesticide applications. Sweep hard surfaces, like drives and walks, to keep these materials from entering storm drains and polluting our water. Last but not least, fertilizers need not be applied more often than once or twice each season, freeing the gardener for more important tasks.

The Importance of a Soil Test

When it comes to soil-testing kits, you get what you pay for. The inexpensive chemical kits and probes are acceptable for a "ball park" analysis. If you test this way, we still recommend the services of a professional laboratory every few years, especially for major garden installations. In the Carolinas, either the Department of Agriculture's Agronomic Services will analyze your soil or you can contact a Cooperative Extension office for a free soil test kit. Many large farm-supply stores offer their customers a similar service.

No amount of fertilizer will compensate for a soil pH that is out of kilter. More than half the problems identified by the Plant Disease Clinic at North Carolina State University were caused by fertilizers—too much, in most cases. The optimum pH for most lawns and gardens is 5.5 to 6.5. (Remember that a pH below 6.9 is acidic and a pH above 7 is considered alkaline.) The addition of limestone reduces the acidity of soil and raises the soil pH. How much limestone you need depends on the type of soil, amount of organic matter, residual nutrients, and the limestone product purchased.

The Best Defense Against Pests

The conditions that make our gardens flourish also make for a happy homeland for insect and disease pests. Mild winters and wet, humid summers favor healthy populations of bugs and blights each growing season. Quarantines for gypsy moths, emerald ash borers, and fire ants are currently in place. Gardeners and homeowners are holding their breath in hopes that these and other garden pests will not become widespread throughout North and South Carolina. A prudent axiom to garden by is "The best defense against pests is a healthy plant." Most garden plants can tolerate moderate amounts of leaf injury before a pest-control strategy should be implemented. Natural predators often lurk on the garden fringes, waiting to help when problems arise. Second only to a vigorously growing plant is variety selection. The strength of this book is in its plant variety recommendations. The industry has made great strides over the last three decades in the selection and breeding of genetically superior plant varieties. Choose these plants, and you will have an ally in the fight against pests.

Integrated Pest Management

Our approach to pest control in the lawn and garden incorporates the principles of Integrated Pest Management (IPM). Proper identification of the pest and of the host plant is of paramount importance in the IPM system. This may appear to be a slow, painstaking course of action, but it does make more sense than the "Spray and Pray" philosophy of some gardeners today. In one situation, pruning a diseased twig may solve the problem. In another case, a fungicide application may be justified. Removal of a certain plant variety may be required in another situation. IPM is here to stay— learn more about it.

Weed Control

Ask any gardener what he or she dislikes most about gardening, and nine out of ten times the response will be "weeding." Gardeners and professionals alike go to great lengths to keep weeds under control.

The most ecologically sound approach to weed control is mulching landscape beds and gardens. Organic materials such as bark, compost, and pine needles are good choices for mulch. On steep banks and slopes, use shredded hardwood bark or pine needles; on flat surfaces, use bark nuggets that won't float off in a rainstorm. The rule for mulches is to apply to a depth of 1 to 3 inches, and don't heap the mulch up against the trunks of trees. Landscape fabrics can be useful in areas where irrigation is not an option.

Use a hard rake or a four-tine claw to rake the mulch around the bed.

After spreading the mulch in the landscape bed, pull the mulch slightly away from plant stems and leaves.

There are some excellent pre-emergent herbicides for keeping crabgrass out of beds; apply these in late February or March. To get the grassy weeds out of shrub and perennial borders, hand weed or apply a grass killer that contains sethoxydim. Nonselective herbicide containing glyphosate is excellent for clearing a new bed prior to planting. If you spot-spray with any glyphosate product, be sure it doesn't contact the green tissues of any garden plant because it systemically kills everything green.

The Need for Water

Unless you incorporate drought-tolerant plants into your garden design, irrigation will be necessary. There is no substitute for water in gardening! Plants cannot produce their own food via photosynthesis without sufficient water.

While lawns consume a lot of water, herbs and groundcovers prefer drier conditions by virtue of their native habitats. Most regions of the Carolinas receive 35 inches of rainfall each year, and some have twice this amount. The wet periods are interspersed with dry seasons, and supplemental irrigation can play a vital role in garden survival.

Most plants in our gardens need at least 1 inch of water a week, whether measured with a rain gauge or a tuna fish can. That's the equivalent of 600 gallons of water a week for a 25- by 50-foot garden. It would take several hours to apply this amount with a handheld garden hose, so it is best to buy sprinklers of some type.

Supplemental watering is a must during the first season. With the use of sprinklers, hand-watering, or more elaborate permanent systems that have time clocks, the garden can be kept in good health. In clay soils where soils absorb water slowly, drip irrigation in combination with mulch is the preferred method for watering woody ornamentals. An inexpensive water timer and a few soaker hoses can be the gardener's best friends.

Use a watering wand to water at the base of your plants.

Many gardeners prefer to water "on demand," especially in established gardens. Given time and experience, even the novice can take this approach. You must learn to recognize the symptoms of water stress before irreparable harm is done to the garden because of negligence or oversight.

Sunlight Requirements

For the best results, plants need to be placed where they will receive the proper amount of sunlight. The amount of sunlight suitable for each plant's growing requirements featured in this book is noted with "symbols" for suggested light exposure.

Hardiness Zones

Zone maps rate how much cold a plant can endure, giving an idea of its survivability at low winter temperatures. The most common map in current use is the United States Department of Agriculture (USDA) Plant Hardiness Zone Map. Each 10-degree drop in average minimum winter temperature places a region in the hardiness zone with the next lower number. In North Carolina, gardeners in the mountain regions are in Zone 6, while gardeners near Charleston and farther south live in Zone 8b.

Remember that these are averages, and seasonal extremes of cold will limit what grows in your garden. Another map available from Rutgers University accounts for rainfall and sunshine, two other important climatological factors that determine a plant's hardiness in the garden. The newest map developed by the American Horticultural Society (AHS) determines which plants will survive summer's hottest days. The AHS Plant Heat-Zone Map divides the country into twelve zones; each zone corresponds to the average number of days each year with temperatures over 86 degrees Fahrenheit. The Piedmont region is in Heat Zone 7 and averages sixty to ninety days above this temperature.

What's in a Name?

Although common names are easier to remember and pronounce, a scientific or botanical name allows you to communicate with a gardener in China or a horticulturist in Brazil. The new world opening up to us via the Internet makes knowledge of plant nomenclature even more essential.

Both common and botanical names are used throughout this book. A plant's botanical name consists of a genus and a species epithet, both italicized. For example,

Ilex x meserveae 'Blue Girl'   *Ilex crenata* 'Compacta'

all hollies belong to the genus *Ilex*. The epithet identifies a specific kind of holly: *Ilex cornuta* is a Chinese holly. To identify a plant even more closely, a cultivar name describes a special feature or tells the name of the person who selected the plant. The cultivar name is set off by single quotation marks. For example, the needlepoint holly's botanical name is *Ilex cornuta* 'Needlepoint'. Some plants that occur naturally in the wild may be denoted with the abbreviation "var." and another word following the epithet.

Knowing these straightforward rules of taxonomy will be of use as you search catalogs and websites for new and interesting garden varieties.

Gardening Made Simpler

The turfgrasses and garden plants described in this book are time-tested and durable in Carolina gardens. Many are cultivars of native plants, and most are appropriate for sustainable landscape gardens. These plant lists are by no means complete. It was necessary to exclude some fine ornamentals, but the plants on these pages are readily available at the major wholesale and retail nurseries in our states. Landscape professionals will recognize most of the plants from the required plant lists provided by their trade associations for the Contractor's exam and other certification credentials. Certainly the list is a good starting point for creating a new garden or revitalizing an existing one in the Carolinas.

Gardening is America's number one "leisure" activity—it should not be drudgery. Gardening books should be enjoyable to read and motivate one to try new plants.

I hope the *Carolinas Getting Started Garden Guide* will accomplish its goal of taking the mystery out of gardening in our states. This book offers a wealth of information gathered through networking with home gardeners and professionals alike. It contains the latest research findings on plant varieties, practical gardening techniques, and "how-to" suggestions set in an easy-to-read format.

Good luck with your Carolina garden!

How to Use This Book

The information in this book can be applied throughout both states. Each entry in this guide provides you with information about a plant's particular characteristics, its habits, and its basic requirements for vigorous growth as well as my personal experience and knowledge of it. Hopefully, the information you need to realize each plant's potential is found with its profile. Only when a plant performs at its best can one appreciate it fully. You will find such pertinent information as mature height and spread, bloom period and seasonal colors (if any), sun and soil preferences, planting tips, water requirements, fertilizing needs, pruning and care, and pest information. Each section is clearly marked for easy reference.

Sun Preferences

For quick reference, symbols represent the range of sunlight suitable for each plant. "Full Sun" means a site receiving eight or more hours of direct sun daily. "Part Sun" means a site that receives direct afternoon sun for six hours a day, or partial sun all day. "Part Shade" means a site that receives morning sun/afternoon shade. "Shade" means a site that is in dappled or even in deep shade all day. Some plants grow successfully in more than one sun exposure, which will be indicated by more than one sun symbol. Note: Afternoon sun is stronger than morning sun, and this exposure is more apt to stress certain plants.

Full Sun   Part Sun   Part Shade   Shade

Additional Benefits

Many plants offer benefits that further enhance their appeal. The following symbols indicate some of the more notable additional benefits:

 Native: these plants are indigenous to the United States

 Drought tolerant: after establishment, these survive on rainfall or minimal watering

 Attracts hummingbirds: their flower color and nectar will attract hummers

 Deer & rabbit resistant: these are not attractive to deer or rabbits

 Fall foliage: these have seasonal color or variegation, in addition to spring flowers.

 Attracts beneficials: includes honey bees, butterflies, and pollinating insects

 Edibles: bears fruit/flowers/leaves edible for people or birds

Companion Planting and Design

This section provides suggestions for companion plantings and different ways to showcase your plants. This is where many people find the most enjoyment from gardening.

Try These

This section describes those specific cultivars or varieties found to be particularly note-worthy. Or, sometimes other species that are also good choices. Give them a try . . . or perhaps you'll find your own personal favorite online or a new release.

USDA Hardiness Zone Map

The United States Department of Agriculture (USDA) developed the cold-hardiness zone designations. They are based on the minimum average temperatures all over the country. Each variation of 10 degrees Fahrenheit represents a different zone, indicated by colored bands on a zone map. Because perennial plants, whose roots survive winter, vary in their tolerance for cold, it is important to choose plants that are suitable for the zone of your region. Consult this map to learn in which zone you live. Most of the plants in this book will perform well throughout the area. Although a plant may grow in zones other than its recommended cold-hardiness zone, it is best to select plants labeled for your zone.

Note that all featured plants are appropriate for gardens across the Carolinas unless they're flagged with a specific ZONE subhead as noted with the added benefit symbols. For example, Zone 8 plants will struggle with the low winter temperatures found in Zone 6.

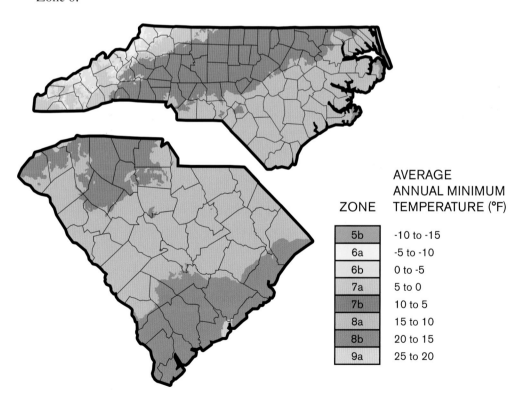

ZONE	AVERAGE ANNUAL MINIMUM TEMPERATURE (°F)
5b	-10 to -15
6a	-5 to -10
6b	0 to -5
7a	5 to 0
7b	10 to 5
8a	15 to 10
8b	20 to 15
9a	25 to 20

USDA Plant Hardiness Zone Map, 2012. Agricultural Research Service, U.S. Department of Agriculture. Accessed from http://planthardiness.ars.usda.gov.

ANNUALS

FOR THE CAROLINAS

Annuals complete their life cycles in one growing season. These jewels, also called bedding plants, are cheerful workhorses of the landscape. They transform uninteresting spaces into colorful flowerbeds. Many bloom continuously from spring until a hard frost in autumn ends the bedding plant season. Annuals are the backbone of the summer garden and are important for supplying early color in perennial beds. They are easy to plug into otherwise bleak gardens that are just waking up from their winter dormancy. Many dazzle your eye with lovely colors. Most are sun lovers, though a few are appropriate for lightly shaded landscapes.

The Versatility of Annuals

Most gardeners buy seedlings in pots or cell-packs from garden centers for planting after danger of frost has passed. Many quick-sprouting annuals lend themselves to direct-seeding in the garden. New gardeners may feel uncomfortable with seed germination at first, so it may be better for them to stick with the greenhouse-grown transplants. For more experienced gardeners, starting the newest annual introductions from seeds in February can provide a diversion from the winter doldrums.

Annuals can be massed in beds for color impact. Some gardeners find monochromatic plantings effective, such as a "white garden" that consists of white periwinkle, white petunias, and white fan flower or white zinnias. Most Southerners like to celebrate with garden color and find it difficult to stay with a single color scheme. Stylish color combinations are seen along every residential street, but you will seldom see the stereotypical "petunias in old tire planters." Heat-resistant annuals in containers as large as half-barrels provide fabulous color accents.

Gardeners with a sharp eye for color tend to look at the color of their house and garden accessories before choosing flower colors. Dark-colored homes in green surroundings may look somber and can benefit from bright flower colors. Light colors will make a small garden space appear larger.

Annuals Are Hard to Beat

For the display of color you will get for your expenditure and effort, annuals are hard to beat. Keep in mind the two groups of annuals. The ones with tiny seeds should be sown indoors eight to ten weeks before the planting season in order for them to develop and flower on time. This is especially important where short growing seasons prevail, such as in the mountains. Also, the quick-sprouting annuals will bloom rapidly from direct-seeding in the garden. Some of these will "self-sow," which can be a blessing or a curse. For me, 'Flamingo Feather' celosia became a nuisance, providing far too many seedlings in my flower bed. However, volunteer seedlings of impatiens and globe amaranth can be useful every year as filler flowers in borders.

The Possibilities Are Endless

Hundreds of annual varieties are available, and there is no shortage of opportunities for creating stunning beds. Some annuals, such as snapdragons, cosmos, and sunflowers, are perfect for cutting gardens. Peruse seed catalogs for

Many annuals, such as these impatiens, are sold in cell-packs ready for planting.

the newest flower selections for sowing at home or buy healthy, compact transplants at a garden shop each spring. Tall, long-stemmed varieties for cutting are easier to find in seed catalogs than in displays at garden centers. Homegrown seedlings can be planted out in the garden in April or May after the chance of late frost is past. Annuals are easy to grow and require attention only to routine fertilizing, irrigation during dry periods, and control of weeds that can spoil the floral display.

Planting Tips

Most kinds of annual flowers with freshly opened blooms are offered for sale as bedding plants. Some are in tiny, 2-inch cells; others are in 3- or 4-inch pots. A few may be for sale in larger pots but at much steeper prices. Consequently, many gardeners buy flats of three to six dozen individual colors in cell-packs, while others with smaller gardens settle for six-packs or individual pots.

Some gardeners, having experienced mediocre success transplanting small plants of annuals directly to the garden, routinely pot up small annuals into 4-inch pots and grow them for two or three weeks before setting them into the garden. In good potting soil, the plants develop more substantial root systems and survive the rigors of transplanting with little loss of momentum.

Whether you transplant small annuals directly to a flowerbed or container, or grow them in a larger pot, consider "butterflying" their rootballs. Root systems can become so congested that they encase the rootball in a solid mat of rootlets that are reluctant to foray out into the surrounding soil once set into a flower bed. This condition is described as "potbound." Butterflying the rootball consists of pushing or tapping the rootball out of the cell or pot, grasping it with both hands, and, with your fingertips across the bottom of the root system, cracking the rootball. New feeder roots will grow out of the crack and into the surrounding soil to take up water and nutrients.

Before butterflying or shifting annuals to larger pots, prepare your soil. Ideally, you will have submitted a soil sample to your county Cooperative Extension office for testing. If you lack test results, liming is called for on all Carolinas soil types except a few near the coast. As a general rule, incorporate limestome into the soil prior to planting. On sandy soils apply ½ pound per 10 square feet. On clay soils, apply 1 pound per 10 square feet. Use pelletized dolomitic limestone that supplies both calcium and magnesium, and work it in thoroughly. Liming soils helps in two ways: it counteracts excessive acidity in the soil releasing mineralized nutrients, and builds soil structure for improved drainage and aeration. It's money well spent.

Spade or till the soil before spreading limestone. Remove roots of perennial grasses or weeds. For consistency of coverage, divide the recommended application of limestone into two parts. Broadcast half walking in one direction and the other half while walking across your initial path. This is a good opportunity to add organic soil conditioner as well-aged, ground pine bark, mushroom compost, or composted manures, and so forth. Spread a 2-inch layer. Finally, spread fertilizer to add the major plant nutrients nitrogen, phosphorus, and potassium. A controlled-release fertilizer will do the best job; it will feed annuals through most of the growing season. Spade or till these amendments into the soil.

Read the label that came with your plants. If it calls for full sun all day, you can be assured that the plant will benefit from afternoon shade, especially in Zones 8b to 9.

Most sun-loving annuals can endure full sun all day, but they need more frequent watering. If the label calls for shade, set your plants where they will get light or high shade during much of the day. Few flowering annuals do well in moderate to deep shade;

Geranium, million bells, and sweet potato vine combine in this elegant container planting.

foliage plants fare better because their broad leaves trap the limited light that bounces into shaded areas. Follow the plant spacings recommended on the label. On large flowerbeds, leave "sneak paths" behind two or three rows of plants. Run the path across the line of sight and make it just wide enough to traverse without stepping on plants.

Now you can "set out" your plants into your flowerbed or into a container that's at least 7 gallons. Use inexpensive white plastic labels to temporarily mark where each plant is to go. Keep a filled watering can handy; don't add water-soluble fertilizer to the initial watering. Dig individual holes with a trowel and butterfly the rootballs just prior to transplanting. Position the plant so that the top of the rootball is level with or slightly above the surface of the surrounding soil. Pull the excavated soil (backfill) around the rootball and firm it slightly with your hands. Water the plant before moving on to the next. Collect the marker labels as you go.

Don't pinch the tops out of annuals when planting. This outdated practice is a holdover from the days when most annuals grew tall. Now, most are bred as compact forms. Seedlings need all their leaves to establish quickly. After planting, water the entire bed. Let a sprinkler run for an hour, or long enough to saturate a bed without runoff. Leave it in place because you will need to water your new flowers every morning for three or four days. Once they begin looking happy, reduce watering to every three days; then taper off to a weekly and as-needed basis.

Now What?

If you build a flowerbed, weeds will come. Keeping beds weed-free is important. The best way to minimize weeding is to spread a 2-inch layer of mulch. Pine or hardwood bark works well. Don't pull the mulch up close to the stems of annuals; it can hold moisture and cause plants to rot. Pine straw is difficult to work in between annuals and is usually reserved for larger perennials and shrubs.

Broadleaf weeds and grass will find a way to emerge. Take a dandelion digger with you to pry out the entire root system with minimum soil disturbance. Collect the weeds and dump them in your compost heap. If you recognize the terrible weeds called Florida betony and mugwort, take a spray bottle of a nonselective herbicide with you. Set a tin can or plastic milk jug (bottom removed) over the weed before spraying, to avoid spray drift. These weeds try to regrow; respray in three or four weeks. Any aggressive perennial spreaders, such as chameleon plant or culinary mint, can be eradicated this way.

Drip irrigation is the easiest, most responsible, and efficient way to water a bed during dry periods. Flowers like about 1 inch of water per week, twice that on sandy soils, which tend to dry out faster. "Leaky hose" is the simplest drip irrigation system. Weave the porous hose through the flowerbed so that no plant is more than 9 to 12 inches from the hose. Connect the leaky hose to a water faucet and let it run for an hour twice a week during dry weather. Some gardeners object to the look of leaky hoses and conceal them beneath mulch. That can lead to damaging the hose with a hoe or dandelion digger. If you leave the hose on the surface, annuals will soon cover it.

Removing old flower heads, called "deadheading," can be a dreaded task or a way to calm your mind while doing no-brainer work. Either way, deadheading leads to a second flush of color and to neater-looking flower beds. A few annuals such as coreopsis, sunflower, and cosmos can provide food for finches and are often allowed to go to seed.

Starting Annuals from Seeds

If you have a sunny south- or west-facing windowsill, you can sprout seeds of annuals successfully and grow them to transplant size. Even better is a fluorescent light fixture that can be lowered to within 2 inches of the tops of seed pans. Some gardeners use metal halide lamps that come closest to imitating the full spectrum of sunlight and can deliver the footcandles needed by plants when placed farther away than fluorescent tubes.

Most flower seeds will sprout (germinate) at soil temperatures of 60 to 65 degrees Fahrenheit. Some species that have a tropical provenance sprout more rapidly at 70 to 80 degrees Fahrenheit. Such warm temperatures can be produced atop a hot water heater or by using an electrical heating mat with an adjustable thermostat. It is important that you move the seed pan to a somewhat cooler area just as soon as you green seedlings emerge. Some gardeners cover seed pans with clear plastic wrap to maintain high humidity; remove covers promptly when green seed leaves appear.

Plastic meat trays about 3 inches deep make good seed pans. Use an ice pick or a large nail to punch six to eight drainage holes. Fill pans to within ½ inch of the rim with "seed starting mix," which is formulated from fine Canadian sphagnum peat moss and fine particles of vermiculite or perlite. Use a short length of board to firm and level the mix. Moisten the starter mix by setting the filled pan in a tray of warm water. Capillarity will pull water up into the mix and saturate it.

Gardeners usually plant the contents of a standard seed packet in a single seed pan. Some prefer to scatter the seeds evenly over the surface; others prefer to plant seeds in three or four straight lines or "drills." The best topping to cover seeds is "milled sphagnum moss," which is produced by grinding the ropy moss from the surface of peat bogs. It has biological properties that greatly reduce the incidence of "damping-off," an infection that kills seedlings at ground level. A very thin topping of seed starter mix will work nearly as well. Certain species require light to sprout, but enough light can penetrate a thin topping to initiate germination.

Gardeners usually start seeds six to eight weeks prior to the spring frost-free date, earlier on species that can tolerate light frosts and later on fast-sprouting, fast-growing species. The initial bottom-watering should suffice to sprout the seeds, especially if the seed pan is covered with clear plastic wrap. Overwatering seed pans is a fast track to damping off, especially if the germinating area cools to 50 to 60 degrees Fahrenheit at night.

The rate of growth of seedlings depends greatly on the seed size. Large seeds produce robust seedlings with enough stored carbohydrates to nourish them for up to three weeks. If they're given adequate light and the proper range of heat, you can almost hear them grow. Tiny seeds produce seedlings almost too small to see. They grow excruciatingly slowly until they produce enough foliage surface area to trap a significant amount of light.

When seedlings develop four to six leaves, transplant to individual 2- to 3-inch pots filled with high quality potting soil formulated for bedding plants. They can be "pricked out" (pried out) of seed pans with a Popsicle stick

Dusty miller adds needed contrast in flower gardens and containers.

or a similar tool. Hold seedlings by their leaves, not by their stems, to avoid crushing tender stem tissues.

Poke a planting hole in the center of the filled pot and lower the seedling into it so that the top of the root system is level with the surface of the soil. Firm the potting soil around the root system. Set the potted plant aside for bottom-watering when all the seedlings have been transplanted. Certain species such as lobelia and begonia have such tiny seedlings that they are customarily transplanted in small clumps, grown for a few weeks, then divided into individual plants for transplanting into pots.

Invariably, first-time seed starters are surprised, even overwhelmed, by the geometric increase in space needed at transplanting. You can go from fifty seedlings in a small pan to fifty individual pots of 2- to 4-inches in diameter. All of a sudden, the area lighted by two 48-inch fluorescent tubes must strain to hold the plants from one seed pan. Many gardeners keep a "coldframe" handy, lighted by the sun and perhaps warmed with grounded electric light bulbs, to handle the overflow of plants.

You may ask, "Why bother?" If you like to try the very newest annuals, you can usually buy seeds a year or two before started plants become widely available. Also, tall varieties of annuals that are preferred for cutting gardens are rarely available as started plants because they take too long to show color and grow too tall in the process. Neither growers nor retailers like to handle them. Starting from seeds gives gardeners a way to propagate heirloom varieties that are no longer grown by seed companies and to produce plants at a lower unit cost. Last but not least, starting plants from seed teaches patience, a virtue that is common among seasoned gardeners.

Ageratum

Ageratum houstonianum

Botanical Pronunciation
a-jer-AY-tum hyous-tone-e-AY-num

Other Name
Floss flower

Bloom Period and Seasonal Color
Spring to fall blooms in blue, lavender, pink, and white

Mature Height × Spread
6 to 18 inches × 6 to 30 inches

When the Olympic Festival debuted in North Carolina some years ago, patriotic flower gardens were planted in the Triangle region in anticipation of international guests. The annual of choice to represent blue color in the red-white-blue design scheme was ageratum. This compact, mounding plant is used to provide vivid contrast in color beds and dress up a walkway where it is used for edging. Its blue or white furry blooms are held in tight clusters above medium green foliage. When this small plant is hit by drought and extreme heat, there is no struggle to survive. Ageratum combines well with other annual flowers in planter boxes and containers. You will not be disappointed with a plant that has blooms when it goes into the ground and its willingness to bloom until frost.

When, Where, and How to Plant
Wait until all danger of frost is past to set out potted plants. Pull off your socks, and if the ground is warm to your bare feet, it is prime time for planting heat-loving annuals. Planting can continue into summer. Few gardeners start ageratum from seeds because they require two months from seed to garden-ready plants. It needs well-drained soil and warmth. This chapter's introduction will advise on soil preparation and planting. Space 1 foot apart or slightly closer when planting in clusters for the best display. Full to part sun (in coastal areas or sandhills) is fine. Water thoroughly after planting.

Growing Tips
Ageratum is popular because of its ease in growing. For optimum bloom and dark foliage color, apply all-purpose liquid fertilizer monthly (twice monthly in containers), or work controlled-release fertilizer into the soil prior to planting. Feed sparingly, or you will lose blooms. Water once weekly during dry spells or when leaves appear limp in afternoon. A thin layer of mulch can trap water so that it soaks in rather than running off. This annual is native to Central America; don't overwater when getting it established. Pamper it in late summer to get it energized for late-season flowers.

Regional Advice and Care
Perennial ageratum is occasionally spotted on the roadside. It is a different species but evidence that this plant can fend for itself with little interference. If you give ageratum average loamy soil and good drainage, when the summer rains descend it should not wither away from root rot due to the extra moisture. Snip off spent flower clusters when the flowering slows and a light haircut to ready it for a late summer growth spurt. Few pests bother ageratum.

Companion Planting and Design
The blazing reds of annual scarlet sage and blue salvia beg for blue or white ageratum. It's traditionally used as an edging or pattern plant with companions dusty miller, verbena, periwinkle, marigold, and coreopsis. Interplant in containers with Dragon Wing™ begonia for contrast. Enjoy its wonderful mounding habit with *no pruning required*.

Try These
Award-winning 'Blue Danube' and 'Aloha Blue Hybrid' are great for color gardens. 'Blue Horizon' grows to 30 inches, a vigorous triploid on stiff stems, suitable for cutting.

Alternanthera

Alternanthera ficoidea

Botanical Pronunciation
all-ter-NAN-ther-ah fi-COID-ee-ah

Other Name
Joseph's coat

Bloom Period and Seasonal Color
Flowers insignificant; grown for its multicolored foliage

Mature Height × Spread
5 to 24 inches × 6 to 30 inches

Beautiful foliage in a plethora of color tones is what makes the *Alternanthera* family so special. Among the most ornate species is the one that Southerners call Joseph's coat. This heirloom plant was popular in the Victorian era in formal gardens and is being installed in increasing numbers by professional gardeners to edge color beds. Chartreuse alternanthera has eye-catching yellow-green foliage, compact growth, and nonstop color from spring until frost. Its irregularly shaped leaves are thin and soft to touch. Most available varieties are herbaceous perennials and range in leaf color from purple to pink. Tall selections add contrast in less formal, sunny beds of annual and perennial flowers. Get a lot of bang for the buck with alternanthera as the foliage is the main feature, not sporadic blooms.

When, Where, and How to Plant
Add potted plants in spring and throughout the growing season. Leaf color is best in full sun, but color is decent in a half-day of direct light. Plant in containers and in annual flowerbeds for immediate color. Alternanthera does best in moist, well-drained soils. Prepare annual beds by incorporating limestone, continuously feeding flower fertilizer and pine bark soil conditioner into beds. Use a rototiller for large areas for loose, well-aerated soil. Hand plant and lightly firm; water thoroughly to remove air pockets. Mulch beds and keep them irrigated for quick establishment.

Growing Tips
Pay attention to watering and fertilization. These foliage plants have made their way by way of Mexico and have proven durable in our Carolinas heat. They tolerate moderate drought but appreciate moisture and routine watering in the late summer and fall. During summer heat, monitor in the afternoon for wilting; allow soil to dry between waterings. Apply slow-release fertilizer to the soil's surface several times during the growing season per product directions, or on eight-week intervals. Maintain a 2-inch mulch layer, such as leaf compost or shredded hardwood bark.

Regional Advice and Care
Lightly shearing or pinching new growth is the secret to a compact plant. Poor drainage during rainy Julys can increase root rots and leaf diseases. Site as you would rose gardens for maximum sunlight and air circulation. For formal gardens, pruning shears are your closest friend. Alternanthera will not shy away from occasional pruning for size control.

Companion Planting and Design
Alternanthera enhances or echoes other colors, making them appear more vibrant. Use as a filler in mixed container plantings, or use a single selection as the main attraction. Landscape professionals choose this tender plant to define annual color beds, frequently as a facing plant on the perimeter. Add to hide the ankles of taller flowers. Add to jazz up a bed of rudbeckia, dusty miller, or lantana.

Try These
Chartreuse alternanthera is a sunny warrior. 'Red Threads' and 'Calico Form' are dark cherry to pink. *A. dentata* 'Purple Knight' mounds to 3 feet for outstanding contrast.

Angel Flower

Angelonia angustifolia

Botanical Pronunciation
an-ja-LONE-e-ah an-GUS-ta-fol-e-ah

Other Name Summer snapdragon

Bloom Period and Seasonal Color
Summer through fall, deep violet blue, white, pink, lavender, and bicolors

Mature Height × Spread 16 to 24 inches × 16 to 24 inches (half that in dwarf varieties)

Although known in botanical gardens for many years, angel flower plants only began to appear in garden centers fairly recently. Now it has become a major player in the South. In semi-tropical countries, angelonia grows as a perennial, but in the Carolinas its sensitivity to frost means growing it as an annual. Heat and humidity don't faze it. Angelonia gets its common name because it begins blooming when snapdragons take a summer break. Its medium-length, curving spikes are somewhat reminiscent of snaps. Seed breeders have expanded the color choices to include pastel shades and bicolors and are developing dwarf strains that stand up to beating rain. Angelonia is gaining popularity for container gardens and for flower arrangements. It will bloom reliably, if somewhat late, in relatively cool, upper elevations.

When, Where, and How to Plant
Wait until two weeks after the spring frost-free date before setting out transplants. Grow in fertile, moist soil. Angelonia thrives in full sun. Near the coast or on hot, sandy land, it thrives in afternoon shade. Refer to page 19 in the introduction for soil preparation and planting instructions. Space 18 inches apart, wider if you intend to intersperse filler flowers. If you need lots of plants at low cost, start seeds indoors eight to ten weeks before the frost-free date.

Growing Tips
Drip irrigation works best for angelonia; watering with a sprinkler can beat down its flower spikes. Although angelonia has narrow leaves that give it

drought resistance, its bloom production suffers without weekly water. Mulching reduces soil-splash, which can mar flower spikes. Mix an extended-release fertilizer with the backfill at planting to feed for most of the season. For a faster response, use a water-soluble plant food formulated for flowers.

Regional Advice and Care
Deadhead spent spikes when they begin to look shabby. In late summer, shear back all the plants to half-height and drench the soil with a shot of 1-2-2 ratio water-soluble fertilizer. Angelonia is by nature a bit "floppy;" some of its branches tend to recline, then straighten up, making them an asset to flower arrangers. Harvest spikes frequently for flower arrangements; new flowers will form quickly. Angelonia is still new to the Carolinas, so insects and diseases are limited.

Companion Planting and Design
Use it to fill beds between low edgers and tall background flowers such as cleome. Or try enclosing a bed of mixed color angelonia and blue sage between an edging of dusty miller or curry plant for the calming influence of silver. A background of mandevilla vines on low trellises looks good with lavender or purple angel flower. When mixing angelonia colors in beds, use only one bicolored variety with perhaps three separate colors to highlight the show-stopping bicolor blooms.

Try These
The original deep violet blue and 'AngelMist Light Pink' are my favorites.

Dragon Wing® Begonia

Begonia × hybrida Dragon Wing®

Botanical Pronunciation
bee-GOHN-e-ah HI-bred-da

Bloom Period and Seasonal Color
Spring to fall in red or pink

Mature Height × Spread
2 to 2 ½ feet × 2 ½ to 3 feet

A re you ready for a blaze of color in a partially shaded location? Dragon Wing® begonia grows with a vengeance where it has moist soil and a half-day of sun. Large clusters of red or pink blooms are set atop lustrous green foliage. Flowers are continuous until it succumbs to a killing frost by autumn. Gardeners have found this annual to be both a terrific bedding plant and filler for mixed containers. Distinctive, wing-shaped leaves add lushness to gardens. This medium height annual is a good foil for smaller mound-forming flowers used as an edging in color beds. Dragon Wing® is a crowd-pleaser and will hold its own in a garden that is starved for a little pizzazz.

When, Where, and How to Plant

Plant potted Dragon Wing® begonias after the soil warms in spring, and continue planting in the growing season. It prefers part-sun to part-shade sites, and grows in evenly moist soils that are well drained. A half-day of morning sun is an ideal location for this annual. Too much direct afternoon sun can scorch tender foliage and predispose to leaf disease during wet summers. Give them plenty of room to expand by spacing 2 feet as they grow huge by fall. Enrich the soil with organic matter; spade or work the soil to facilitate root development. Begonia has fine roots and will need close attention to watering after planting

Growing Tips

Be diligent with watering for several weeks after planting; develop an irrigation schedule to keep Dragon Wing® actively growing in the warmer months. Mulch plantings as needed to keep the soil moist. Keep mulch back a few inches from stems. Once established, apply a slow-release continuous feeding fertilizer. Fertilizers should not touch the stems.

Regional Advice and Care

Dragon Wing® begonia has gained in popularity throughout the Carolinas for its ease in culture. This selection will not take the extreme sun exposure like the wax begonia. Give them partial shade, mulch, and water and they will be "happy, happy, happy"! In containers or where space is limited they can be cut in summer to control their size. Good response can be achieved from bimonthly soluble plant fertilizer applications. In late fall, be prepared to toss a bed sheet over them when light frosts are predicted.

Companion Planting and Design

A large container brimming with Dragon Wing® begonias is a delightful accent on a patio or entranceway. In mixed containers, interplant with dwarf dahlias, blue salvia, and myriad spiller plants of grays and blues. In large borders, plant it with a backdrop of Persian shield, plumbago, Japanese anemone, or standard dahlias. Pink begonia is best appreciated in a hanging basket.

Try These

Potted Dragon Wing® begonia is a vigorous selection for many gardening applications. Seeds can be found for Dragon Wing® Pink; it is ideal for baskets and window boxes.

Dusty Miller

Senecio cineraria

Botanical Pronunciation
sah-NEE-sec-oh sin-err-AIR-ee-ah

Bloom Period and Seasonal Color
Silver foliage all season, until winter

Mature Height × Spread
Artemisia stellarana: 2 feet × spreading
Other species: 12 to 18 inches × 24 inches

Four different genera are called "dusty miller": chiefly *Senecio cineraria*, but also *Chrysanthemum ptarmiciflorum*, *Centaurea gymnocarpa*, and *Artemisia stellariana*. These silver plants are so popular that garden centers often sell out of them early. While the many forms of dusty miller are usually grown as annuals in the Carolinas, some species will overwinter in well-drained soil. You can choose dusty millers with lacy, ferny, deeply cut, or ruffled leaves. Some have a green tinge to their basic silver color, while others with downy leaves are so bright that they seem to reflect the sun. Dusty millers have long been used as edging plants or plugged into sandy or rocky slopes. They are an essential part of container garden combinations, quelling disagreements between conflicting colors with their cool, calm demeanor.

When, Where, and How to Plant

Set out hardened-off plants a week before your area's spring frost-free date. Most plantings are started from plants in cell-packs or pots in a full-sun location. Since all species prefer dry soil, consider mixing a 2-inch layer of play sand and a 3-inch layer of ground pine bark into heavy clay soils. A raised bed perhaps 3 inches above the surrounding soil should result. Alternatively, work up the soil and spread 2 to 3 inches of cracked gravel atop it. Scrape the gravel aside, set the dusty miller plants in place, and pull the gravel up around the rootballs. *A. stellarana* responds particularly well to growing in gravel-topped beds that simulate its native habitat.

Growing Tips

Thorough but infrequent watering will help young plants strike new roots. Once the transplants perk up, water only when plants begin to look wilted. One or two feedings with water-soluble 1-2-2 ratio flower fertilizer should suffice for the season. Wait two weeks after transplanting before feeding. When planting in potting soils, go easy on watering. Mix controlled-release fertilizer into the potting soil used for container gardens, unless the potting soil label says it's included.

Regional Advice and Care

Dusty millers have no plant pests. Their only serious problem is root rot that can come from soil that stays wet. You may have to pinch plants in containers to keep them compact. Thin volunteer seedlings to stand 24 inches apart. This plant flaunts silver foliage from the time you set it out until winter. Gold flowers may appear in late summer but foliage is what dusty miller does best. In warm regions, prune back in late winter to remove windburned leaves before going into spring

Companion Planting and Design

What a perfect plant for container gardening! Container garden design often begins with dusty miller. Stick with other drought-resistant plants when designing plant combinations for flowerbeds. Moss rose, purslane, creeping zinnia (*Sanvitalia*), lantana, blanket flower, any of the fleshy-leaved sedums, Mexican bush sage, dahlberg daisy, and diascia would qualify.

Try These

Choose 'Cirrus' for its silver, wavy-edged leaves, and 'Colchester White' for height.

Fan Flower

Scaevola aemula

Botanical Pronunciation
skay-VOL-ah am-U-lah

Bloom Period and Seasonal Color
Summer to fall, continuous blooms of bluish purple, pink, and white

Mature Height × Spread
8 to 12 inches × 24 inches

If you are looking for a rock-solid annual for a container garden or waterwise landscape, look no further. Fan flower is a prostrate, spreading sun-lover that hails from Down Under. This Australian native immigrated to the States at a time when gardeners were looking for low-maintenance flowers and to reduce their time watering. Its long season of bloom and colorful flowers make fan flower a great foil for border plantings. The flowers, indeed, resemble tiny fans with gold eyes. Give this Aussie lots of sun and you will be happy with its performance. Garden designers are quick to choose this tender annual with its trailing stems for a "spiller" in mixed hanging baskets and window boxes. Expect continuous blooms from summer until frost as it performs best when the days get hotter.

When, Where, and How to Plant
Plant in spring after danger of frost has passed. Like petunias, it sits quietly until the soil warms, so there is no big hurry to beat the Joneses. Find a sunny spot with southern exposure to get full bloom potential. Prepare the soil to get perfect drainage, which means adding a coarse amendment, such as bark soil conditioner, to clay. Adding several inches of soil from surrounding beds to set the plants higher will help. Avoid shade! Plant at the depth of the container; loosen roots that are potbound and water well to remove air pockets. Space plants at least 1 foot apart.

Growing Tips
Fan flower requires minimal care to perform well. Fertilize monthly using a liquid fertilizer for outdoor blooming annuals. Water during periods of drought, or to keep plants from wilting in container plantings. But too much water and heavy shade are big "no-nos" for this plant. Fan flower does not like wet feet.

Regional Advice and Care
Most Tar Heel gardeners will buy plants at a garden shop, but gardeners in Zone 9 report fan flower overwintering during gentler seasons. What a blessing; cuttings taken in fall can be rooted and stored in a coldframe to increase spring plantings! During summer, fan flower can get leggy and may need cutting back to keep it looking full. It responds to light pruning in summer by producing more flowers and vigorous stems shortly thereafter. Mulch during midsummer. An autumn freeze will end the growing season; plants can be removed quite easily from a flower bed. Consult your County Extension agent if pests appear.

Companion Planting and Design
Fan flower's growing habit lends itself to cascading in window boxes. Weave it among other annuals and perennials in sunny beds. Locate it as an edging in a sunny entranceway. Combine it with colorful annuals of magenta, gray, yellow, and blues. Africa daisy, lantana, Mexican heather, geranium, and petunia are good companions.

Try These
Try 'Blue Wonder' and 'New Wonder'®. Its color choice is limited, but it serves as a great companion for a plethora of seasonal plants.

Geranium

Pelargonium × hortorum

Botanical Pronunciation
pel-er-GON-ee-um ho-TORE-um

Other Name
Zonal geranium

Bloom Period and Seasonal Color
Summer blooms in red, salmon, pink, white, orange, coral, magenta, and bicolors

Mature Height × Spread
10 to 20 inches × 12 to 20 inches

"If a window or a garden could have but one plant, that plant would likely be a Geranium," wrote the great American horticulturist Liberty Hyde Bailey. Gardeners can buy blooming plants or sow seeds of hybrid geraniums indoors in winter to grow dazzling new seedlings in myriad colors and leaf variations. In the Carolinas, geraniums are grown as annuals unless a thrifty gardener digs the plants and takes them inside before frost. Bright blooms are arranged in ball-like clusters above the foliage. Round leaves have wavy edges and, when bruised, emit a characteristic odor. True geraniums are woodland edge perennials. The plants we call "geraniums" in North America are actually from a different genus, *Pelargonium*. Breeders have been busy developing new selections with both dense bloom clusters and colorful foliage.

When, Where, and How to Plant

Set plants in garden beds after the last spring frost. Afternoon shade is preferred, but if given water when needed, geraniums can thrive in full sun. Potted plants can be set out anytime during the growing season, but peak bloom time is from late spring through midsummer. To improve soil drainage, plant in slightly raised beds amended with bark soil conditioner. Do not use fresh manure! Information on page 19 will detail how to improve your soil. Geraniums need good air circulation; space accordingly.

Growing Tips

Geraniums establish quickly with very little care. In fact, too much water in spring rots the roots. Keep foliage dry during watering by using a water wand to wet only the soil. Drip irrigation also moistens the soil without wetting the leaves. Geraniums respond well to fertilization, particularly if they are grown in soils lacking a ready source of nitrogen. Small yellow leaves indicate that additional fertilizer is needed. Water-soluble fertilizer (the "blue stuff") is suitable for bimonthly feedings.

Regional Advice and Care

During the dog days of summer, geraniums may stop blooming. If so, cut the plants back slightly and feed and water them; cooler weather should bring them around. Don't hesitate to prune leggy geraniums; they will respond with more flowers. Wet summers can lead to geranium leaf diseases. Always remove diseased or yellowing foliage when deadheading. When wet summer weather arrives, apply a fungicide twice, at an interval of one week, to prevent leaf spot and flower diseases. Good air circulation helps prevent leaf spot fungi. Be sure to leave sneak paths among your geranium plants to access them for deadheading. Geraniums can look awful when loaded with spent flowers.

Companion Planting and Design

Geraniums make stunning container or patio plants. Use them to create color beds with tall annuals such as salvias or sun coleus used in the background or in containers combined with bacopa, million bells, and variegated ivy.

Try These

The Oglevee and Orbit series have intensely patterned foliage and large flower clusters on compact plants.

Gerbera Daisy

Gerbera jamesonii

Botanical Pronunciation
ger-ber-RAH james-ZONE-eye

Other Name
Transvaal daisy

Bloom Period and Seasonal Color
Intermittently through summer in all colors except blue and purple

Mature Height × Spread
12 to 18 inches × 12 inches

Long before gerberas became a major bedding plant, thousands of long-stemmed blossoms were air-shipped yearly from California to florists. In home gardens, gerberas were mostly seen in mild winter areas. The development of shorter-stemmed, earlier-blooming varieties pushed them into the bedding plant arena and into more northerly states. Breeders are working for greater uniformity in height and larger-diameter blossoms. They are also developing many fanciful blossom forms. Gerbera plants in bloom are still rather expensive, and one seldom sees them massed in sizable beds. Instead, they are often planted near the front door of a home, in ground beds, or in containers. In these intimate settings, uniformity isn't important. Near the coast and occasionally farther inland, gerberas act as perennials if they're grown in well-drained soil or containers.

When, Where, and How to Plant

Plant from late spring through midsummer. Once hardened off, gerbera plants can withstand a few degrees of frost. Gerbera daisies are technically half-hardy perennials, but it is prudent to delay setting out plants until frost danger is past. Select a site in afternoon shade near the coast, full sun elsewhere. Prepare well-drained beds and scatter dolomitic limestone per soil test directions. Set potted plants in prepared beds or containers so that the tops of the rootballs are level with the surface. If you want the old-fashioned, long-stemmed kinds for cutting, you will need to order seeds, start them in fall, and grow them under lights through winter.

Growing Tips

Gerberas like a moderate, sustained level of soil fertility. They respond well to controlled-release fertilizer (CRF) worked *into* the soil. Topdressing CRF is not recommended, as the beads of fertilizer need to be surrounded by soil for optimum release of nutrients. Water gerbera daisy every seven to ten days between rains. Water the soil, but keep the foliage as dry as possible. Gerbera daisy resents wet feet.

Regional Advice and Care

The blossoms of gerberas are so large that they sap a plant's energy. Cutting them for arrangements encourages more blooms to form. Slugs are the worst problem; gerbera's large-leaved rosettes provide shelter and nourishment if you allow it. Scatter the type of snail bait that is harmless to pets and wildlife. It will also kill earwigs and pillbugs (roly-polys).

Companion Planting and Design

You won't often see gerbera daisy growing among other flowers. They are so special that few gardeners wish to divert attention from them. Use in clusters for an accent by a garden gate or patio. Dress up a container garden with their elegant blooms. Combining them with aggressive vines like ornamental sweet potatoes and verbenas should be avoided. The slow-growing gerberas should be matched with docile annuals.

Try These

Curiously, gerbera plants on sale at garden centers are rarely identified by variety. You can choose between large-flowered types with a single layer of ray petals or somewhat smaller blossoms with long, thin, twisted petals.

Impatiens

Impatiens walleriana

Botanical Pronunciation
em-PAY-shens wall-eer-e-ANA

Other Name
Busy Lizzie

Bloom Period and Seasonal Color
Spring through fall in all colors

Mature Height × Spread
10 to 24 inches × 15 to 30 inches

Incredibly versatile impatiens, including the sun-tolerant New Guinea species, are the top-selling bedding plant. When established in a moist bed, they will frequently self-sow, returning the next summer for a floral display. Grow them in part sun or moderate shade and watch that area glow! Impatiens come in a wide range of colors, most of which can be mixed effectively. They are among the most shade-tolerant of annual flowers, and the color they provide to the garden does not stop until the first killing frost. The recent introduction of a hybrid series called SunPatiens® has created a lot of buzz. They have larger flowers on plants that are bushel-basket sized. Time will tell if these become the exclusive impatiens of Carolina gardeners.

When, Where, and How to Plant
Set out transplants in spring after the danger of frost has passed. Plant in moist, well-drained soil. Keep the soil moist and the SunPatiens® type can take the sun. Even sturdy New Guinea impatiens, if planted in full sun, will look wilted by midafternoon but will recover by nightfall. Impatiens loves humus-laden soils. See page 150 and follow instructions for planting azaleas. After setting out transplants, water with a liquid starter solution to ensure quick establishment, then mulch lightly to conserve moisture and control weeds. In large beds, mulch before planting.

Growing Tips
Newly planted impatiens are quite succulent and wilt readily if soil dries out. To get bushier plants, cut new seedlings back by one-third two weeks after planting. Keep the bed moist for the first month, then maintain a moderate level of soil moisture throughout the growing season. Some impatiens varieties are bred to grow low. A midsummer supplemental feeding with dry granular flower food will provide nutrition for extra growth and color.

Regional Advice and Care
North Carolina gardeners have lost plantings to downy mildew fungus (though SunPatiens® are resistant). Seeded impatiens are susceptible and will shed leaves if infected. Remove these promptly. Proper spacing and air circulation may provide the remedy. In fall, cover beds with a floating row cover to protect from frost. Slugs may be a problem in the damp, shady environment that suits impatiens. Reduce slug infestation by avoiding watering at night or using a slug bait that is safe for pets and wildlife.

Companion Planting and Design
Plant white-flowered, as a foil for brilliant varieties of impatiens. Impatiens make a fine edging when used with foundation shrubs planted on the north or east side of a house. Mass in drifts by color or in mixed borders. Tuck into corners by entranceways or grow in windowboxes. Certain New Guinea cultivars have wildly variegated foliage.

Try These
'Victorian Rose' hybrid is a great semidouble selection for beds and containers. The 'Accent' and 'Bruno' hybrids are well tested for performance. SunPatiens® are vigorous and sun tolerant.

Marigold

Tagetes spp. and hybrids

Botanical Pronunciation TAH-get-eez

Other Names
African, American, French marigolds

Bloom Period and Seasonal Color
Spring through fall, from yellow and orange to maroon, white, nearly red, and bicolors

Mature Height × Spread
African (and American): 14 to 36 inches × 20 inches French: 8 to 12 inches × equal spread Signet: 24 inches × 24 inches

Marigolds are one of the most popular annuals in the Carolinas. Although they are native to Mexico, some are incorrectly called "African" or "French." Marigolds come in any height needed for gardens and in various flower forms. With carnation-like or domed blooms up to 4 inches in diameter, African hybrids make fine cut flowers and can be planted at the back of a border. French types are low growing and make superb edging and container garden flowers. Signet types have small flowers but loads of them. Marigolds grow well in poor soil even during the hot summer months but may sulk during August in Zone 8. The single-flowered French marigold such as 'Dainty Marietta' draws more butterflies than types with convoluted double flowers.

When, Where, and How to Plant

Sow seed outdoors or set out transplants in spring after all danger of frost has passed. Plant in full sun in ordinary garden soil. Marigolds will grow with afternoon shade but will tend to stretch. Do not plant in rich, high-nitrogen soil; this will produce foliage at the expense of flowers. Marigolds grow quickly and easily from seeds. Before planting seeds, read the instructions on the seed packet. The seeds should be planted at a depth of ⅓ inch. Covered with play sand, they will germinate in seven to ten days at soil temperatures of 65 degrees Fahrenheit and higher. For early flowers, use transplants. Space African (*Tagetes erecta*) types 18 to 24 inches apart—French (*T. patula*) varieties 9 to 14 inches apart. Keep seedbeds moist until the seedlings are well established.

Growing Tips

Water weekly, more often during droughts. Some water should drain from containers with each watering to avoid a buildup of salts. Avoid the overstimulation produced by high-nitrogen fertilizers. After setting out plants, drench the soil with a water-soluble flower fertilizer (bloom-starter type) or scatter a 1-2-2 ratio fertilizer. Keep it 3 inches from the stem to avoid injury. Always water well before feeding plants.

Regional Advice and Care

Remove spent blooms to promote continuous flowering. Stake taller varieties for support. When using marigolds as cut flowers, clip off the leaves. Leafhoppers may attack marigolds, and watch for spider mites in dry weather. Systemic insecticides or soap sprays will take care of most pests. No serious diseases occur except where the soil drains poorly.

Companion Planting and Design

Marigolds are awe-inspiring when grouped in large mass plantings and are an excellent choice for edging hot, dry beds. Welcome visitors by planting bright marigolds in an entrance bed or by a mailbox. Blue summer flowers such as blue daze and ageratum look good with marigolds.

Try These

The 'Inca' hybrids have it all—big 4-inch blooms, compact erect plants, and heat resistance.

Million Bells

Calibrachoa sp.

Botanical Pronunciation
cal-ee-bro-Co-ah

Other Name
Calibrachoa

Bloom Period and Seasonal Color
All summer in shades of blue, pink, red, lavender, yellow, and coral

Mature Height × Spread
4 to 8 inches × 12 to 24 inches

At first glance, you might think that million bells are small-flowered, little-leaf petunias. Not so—million bells are a different species and a relative newcomer to American gardens. It quickly made a good name for itself in container gardens and window boxes where it spreads and trails. In garden beds, it hugs the ground. In a container filled with good potting soil, million bells will continue blooming without letup until fall frost. It prefers the good drainage and aeration of sandy garden soils because on heavy soils its dense mat of foliage tends to trap water. Consistently moist foliage tends to mold. The blooms on million bells are flared like the "bells" of trumpets and are positioned on the stems where you can look right into them.

When, Where, and How to Plant
Million bells are almost always grown from in 3- to 4-inch potted transplants, with first blooms showing to validate the color. Heads up—calibrachoa plants go on display as much as a month before it's safe to set them into your garden or containers. Wait until frost danger is past to avoid losing your baby plants. Grow in full sun or morning shade. Two types are available, mounding and trailing. The tiny flowers of million bells are best enjoyed close up in containers or, if in garden beds, on raised berms or planter boxes to maximize visibility. On heavy soils, mulch around your million bells with 1 inch of play sand to keep the surface dry.

Growing Tips
Go easy on feeding million bells. Heavy feeding with nitrogen-rich plant foods can overstimulate the plants and result in sparse blooming. In good quality potting soils, there is no need to worry about overwatering. They are designed to drain off surplus water and attain a good level of aeration within minutes of watering. So water container plantings every other day or as needed in summer. Irrigate in-ground beds weekly during drought. Avoid mulching too closely to stems on these low spreaders.

Regional Advice and Care
Million bells are nearly care-free. The mounding types planted in landscapes are subject to stem and root rot in poorly drained, clay soils. Remove diseased plants promptly or remove dying twigs. Control leaf-eating caterpillars using a spray of *B.t.* or handpicking. Keep the foliage dry to avoid fungal molds like *Botrytis*. This puppy is self-cleaning and branches freely.

Companion Planting and Design
In large containers where combinations of tall, mounded, and trailing plants are used, consider combining million bells with bacopa (*Sutera*), wax-leaved begonias, and blue salvia or dracaena. For continuous color, interplant million bells among perennials, which go in and out of bloom rather quickly.

Try These
Use 'Terra Cotta' for the coral color that deepens to bronze with age. The Superbells® series has a good performance record.

Moss Rose

Portulaca grandiflora

Botanical Pronunciation
port-you-LACK-ah grand-eh-FLOR-ah

Other Name
Purslane

Bloom Period and Seasonal Color
Early to midsummer (plus an encore if sheared
and fed), in red, pink, yellow, peach, and white

Mature Height × Spread
3 to 6 inches × 12 to 20 inches

Few flowers can match moss rose (also called rose moss) for brilliance, partly because its petals are so thin that they are backlighted by sun for part of the day. At one time, moss rose was notorious for closing its flowers, reacting to changes in cloud coverage and time of day. Now, plant breeders have selected for flowers that remain open during most of the day and during sunny or partly cloudy weather. Few flowers are more drought resistant, although drought-stricken moss rose can look pretty shriveled until its leaves plump up with renewed soil moisture. Modern varieties have been purged of virtually all "single" blossoms, leading to fancy, fully double, many-petaled blooms in a delicious range of colors. Modern varieties also have considerably larger blossoms than "your grandma's moss rose."

When, Where, and How to Plant

Moss rose flourishes in heat, drought, and full sun but will languish in wet clay soil. Set out plants soon after spring frost danger is past and the soil feels warm to the touch. Plant seeds to get lots of seedlings at low cost. Work up a bed about 2 feet × 2 feet and cover it with a 2-inch layer of play sand. Wait until early May and make shallow furrows across the sand. Trickle seeds down the furrows and cover with the barest sprinkling of sand. Water with a fine mist, twice daily. When they put on six to eight leaves, pry out seedlings with a knife and transplant them on 12-inch centers into prepared soil or into 2-inch pots to grow on before transplanting.

Growing Tips

Give only light applications of plant food when preparing the soil and another when you cut back the plants. *No wet feet, please!* Let plants get by on nature's bounty. Leave sneak paths in beds; portulaca and purslane are brittle and easily damaged.

Regional Advice and Care

Don't be afraid to pinch them when they look leggy. Moss rose blooms so prodigiously that it wears itself out by the dog days of August. Shear plants to half-height, and feed and water them lightly to stimulate a late show of color. Portulaca is usually free of plant diseases and damage from insects. Performance is always improved by growing it in raised beds covered with 2 inches of play sand or in sandy, dry soil.

Companion Planting and Design

Combine moss rose with other drought-resistant plants such as Indian blanket, *Nierembergia* 'Mont Blanc', sedum, hen and chicks, creeping zinnia (*Sanvitalia*), and dusty miller. The related purslanes, which have plump leaves larger than moss rose, trail better and can be combined with rose moss in containers. Rock gardens are enhanced with mixed color plantings.

Try These

'Sundial Hybrids' are good portulacas, as are the 'Yubi' and 'Hotshot' color series in the purslanes.

Pansy

Viola × wittrockiana

Botanical Pronunciation
veye-OH-lah witt-rock-ee-AY-na

Other Name
Viola

Bloom Period and Seasonal Color
Fall through June in blue, rose, purple, maroon, red, yellow, orange, white, and tricolor.

Mature Height × Spread
5 to 9 inches × 10 inches

What would we plant for color in our winter landscapes if we didn't have pansies? No other flower can deliver consistent color during fall, winter, and spring from fall plantings. Come out on an icy morning and see pansies face down, apparently in distress. Return later when the sun has warmed the plants and they will be perked up, no worse for the wear. A spring-planted crop is also possible except in the cool mountains, but only a few weeks of color will be realized before summer heat and humidity takes the starch out of your plants. Pansies are loved for their bright velvety faces and their numerous colors. Landscapers value them for their relatively low cost and versatility. In the horticultural industry, pansies with slightly smaller flowers and often with solid colors are usually labeled "violas."

When, Where, and How to Plant

Begin setting out started plants in late August and continue through late fall. Group them in large containers or in ground beds. Plant in spring when the soil is dry enough to work. Grow in full sun during the winter, afternoon shade if spring planted. Amend poor soils with several inches of compost, cow manure, or bark conditioner. Where soil drainage is suspect, build up beds 4 inches or more above the surrounding soil. Pansies are easy to work with and will "catch" if you settle them in with a thorough soaking.

Growing Tips

Water new plantings every two or three days and weekly after new growth starts. When daffodils are in full bloom, scatter a granular slow-release fertilizer made for flowers or a general fertilizer that is high in phosphorus (some shops sell a product formulated just for pansies) Wash off foliage within a few minutes following application.

Regional Advice and Care

If plants grow leggy and floppy, prune them back halfway to encourage branching and flowering. Mulch with 1 inch or more of fine pine bark scattered between plants in spring. Deadhead and cut back leggy plants in mid-spring. Leaf spot and stem rot diseases can occur in poorly drained or crowded beds; remove blighted leaves promptly. Sprinkle pine straw over pansy beds if temperatures are forecast to fall into the teens. In the western Carolinas, mulch beds heavily and plant through the mulch to delay freezing of soil. Deer love pansies, so be prepared to use a repellent.

Companion Planting and Design

Use pansies in rock gardens, containers, and mass groupings. Many public gardens interplant pansies with Darwin tulips so that the pansies serve as a groundcover. It is hard to beat the sight of red tulips poking out of a bed of blue 'Crystal Bowl' pansies—wow! Try pansies or violas with cold-tolerant ornamental kale and cabbage.

Try These

The old-fashioned 'Maxim Blue' with the "clown face" is my preference. All-America Selections winner 'Ultima Morpho' is a free-flowering bicolor.

Pentas

Pentas lanceolata

Botanical Pronunciation
PENT-tahs lan-see-o-LAY-tuh

Other Name
Star cluster flower

Bloom Period and Seasonal Color
All summer in red, pink, lavender, and white

Mature Height × Spread
Ultra-dwarf: 10 inches × 8 inches
Standard: 20 inches × 15 inches

Pentas had to wait for widespread popularity until breeders developed shorter, earlier-blooming varieties. When the new varieties appeared in bedding plant displays, they were an instant hit, and when they showed southern gardeners their durability under heat and humidity, they pushed ahead of more delicate annuals. Now they rank among the top twenty annuals in the Carolinas. One common name given pentas, star cluster flower, certainly fits them. The plants support tight 2- to 3-inch wide clusters of small, star-shaped flowers in a great range of pastel and dark colors. Butterflies, especially swallowtails, like the secure footing and nectar provided by the clusters. The clusters look up at you, which is a visual plus in a flower with a short frame.

When, Where, and How to Plant
Buy plants of pentas and set them into flowerbeds or containers after frost danger is past. Grow them in full sun or, near the coast or in the hot sandhills, in afternoon shade. Read the labels to be sure you are getting the right height plants for your particular landscape situation. Improving your soil can prolong the span of bloom and help pentas maintain good condition through periods of dry weather. Information on page 19 will tell you how.

Growing Tips
Pentas respond to controlled-release fertilizer (CRF) mixed into the soil. Apply according to directions. Read the package label on potting soils carefully. Premium grades contain enough controlled-release fertilizer to feed plants until August. At planting time, swirl a supplementary amount of CRF into the surface of the potting soil to maintain robust growth and flowering until frost kills the plants. Alternatively, feed every two weeks with water-soluble fertilizer diluted per directions. Water pentas deeply and weekly during periods of drought and just before fertilizer feedings.

Regional Advice and Care
Pentas send up so many flower clusters that they place a drain on the vigor of plants, especially the dwarf varieties. When you see spent clusters begin to turn brown, deadhead the plants. Use pruning shears; the stems are tough. Rabbits will nibble pentas; deer repellent usually works for rabbits as well. Pentas are seldom bothered by insects or diseases. Leafhoppers occasionally appear, but pentas recover on their own.

Companion Planting and Design
Pentas are such fun to work with because you can pick and choose just the right colors from bedding plant displays. They combine beautifully with blue salvia, kangaroo paw, nicotiana, and petunias. You might wish to avoid the fast-spreading varieties of petunias or ornamental sweet potatoes as they tend to overgrow pentas.

Try These
The New Look series has small plants and colors ranging from deep red through the pastels and white. No blue, but you can bring blue in from some other species.

Petunia

Petunia × hybrida

Botanical Pronunciation
pe-TOON-e-ah hi-BRI-dah

Bloom Period and Seasonal Color
All summer from white and palest pink to brilliant red, yellow, mid-blue, and dark purple

Mature Height × Spread
6 inches to 1 feet × 1 to 3 feet

Some gardeners cooled on petunias when they became garden clichés, but new colors and plant habits are winning back the disenchanted. Petunias are summer garden workhorses, sturdy annuals that come in myriad colors as either spreading or compact plants. They produce masses of trumpet-shaped blooms on drooping branches. An edging of 'Fantasy Pink Morn', a pale pink milliflora type, will stay low and compact. What a contrast with the 'Wave' series, which has groundhugging branches up to 2 feet in length! They can be planted in a window box or can serve as a groundcover on a slope. Millifloras have especially dense plants with quarter-sized flowers. Petunias grow beautifully in containers—the cascading types in hanging baskets, and the compact types as filler plants in container gardens.

When, Where, and How to Plant
Hold off planting until the soil is warm and the chance of frost has passed. Petunias need lots of sun to thrive and show off their brilliant color. Good soil drainage and air circulation is paramount for disease prevention. Amend beds with compost or bark soil conditioner. Add limestone to soil with a pH level below 6.0. Page 19 will help you prepare soil to grow this easy-care, mounding annual. Space seedlings or rooted cuttings 10 to 24 inches apart, depending on the cultivar. Thoroughly water after planting and mulch lightly.

Growing Tips
Petunias need frequent watering their first few weeks. Once they begin to grow, taper off to occasional irrigation, watering weekly and as needed to prevent wilting. Slow-release flower fertilizer or traditional fertilizer at planting gives nutrients balanced for flower production. If you use a water-soluble product, fertilize every three or four weeks, using a 1-2-2 ratio product. Petunias are moderately drought tolerant though they may flop daily in hot afternoon sun.

Regional Advice and Care
Water in the morning to reduce the incidence of leaf diseases and blossom blight. Mulch plantings early in the season for weed control and to prevent soil-splash; a 1- to 2-inch layer will do. Pinch or shear back petunias anytime they ramble too far. Root and stem rots are common in poorly drained clays; rotate with other annuals periodically. 'Purple Wave' petunias are exceptional but are not immune to problems from overwatering. Wilted and yellowing foliage spell trouble; consult your Extension agent.

Companion Planting and Design
Petunias are great plants to follow pansies; plant them when the pansies fade out in late May. Group petunias in drifts for a color impact, or interplant with perennials to provide color when other annuals are taking a time-out. The cascading habit of 'Wave' or 'Cascade' hybrid petunias makes them ideal for planters or as groundcovers.

Try These
'Wave' hybrids continue to score high marks and can act like tender perennials in Zones 8 to 9. 'Misty Lilac Wave' is just one of eight amazing available colors.

Polka-dot Plant

Hypoestes phyllostachya

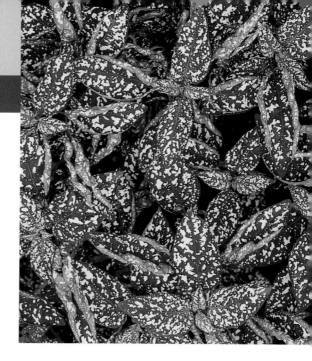

Botanical Pronunciation
hy-po-S-dees phy-low-STACK-key-ah

Other Name
Freckle face

Bloom Period and Seasonal Color
Season-long colorful speckled foliage in greens, pinks, and dark reds

Mature Height × Spread
1 to 1 ½ feet × 1 feet

The leaves of polka-dot plant are covered with white- or cream-colored spots over a green, pink, or dark red base color. Its flowers are inconspicuous. Why, then, would *anyone* bother to plant it? Polka-dot plant is one of the few richly colored ornamentals that will grow well in moist soil in light shade while standing up to hot, humid weather. Also, it shows its characteristic colors from seedling stage through maturity. Southern gardeners have found many uses for polka-dot plant, as a mound-shaped ornamental for container gardens, as a colorful bedding plant for lightly shaded areas, and as an edging for medium-height shade plants. Using brightly colored foliage plants to light up shaded areas is nothing new, but polka-dot plant expands the narrow range of choices for such difficult sites.

When, Where, and How to Plant
Polka-dot plants are usually sold in six-packs or 2- to 3-inch pots. Wait until frost danger is past before transplanting them to container gardens or to flower beds. Site in beds that will receive afternoon shade or light shade all day. Ideal soil is moist and well drained. Mix in a 2-inch layer of organic soil conditioner and granular 1-2-2 ratio fertilizer, and spread a 1- to 2-inch layer of aged pine bark or hardwood bark mulch. Scrape the mulch aside and dig individual planting holes 12 inches apart. Set the plants in place, pull amended soil around the rootball, and spread a shallow layer of mulch over the rootball.

Growing Tips
Be faithful in watering. Spritz new plantings mornings and afternoons until you see signs of new growth, usually within seven to ten days. Later, reduce watering frequency to twice weekly during dry weather. If you allow the plants to dry out enough for leaves to parch or discolor, they will need two or three weeks of intensive liquid feeding and watering to produce enough new growth to hide the results of neglect.

Regional Advice and Care
Polka-dot plants are forgiving of pinching. They tend to shoot out the occasional ungainly branch, but a hard pinch on branch tips will result in reserve buds breaking into new foliage. Near the coast, polka-dot plants may live through mild winters. No serious plant diseases or pests have been noted, though snails or slugs like shady environs too.

Companion Planting and Design
Use mondo grass or clump liriope as edgings for beds of polka-dot plants, and a backdrop of Persian shield or caladiums. In container gardens for shaded sites, choose a foliage color that agrees with other plants in your design. Pink is the liveliest color. The white on green combination has a formal look and the red on green is a bit heavy. The effect can be lightened by adding white impatiens to the design.

Try These
The Splash Select series of three-color combinations (pinkish red, pink, and white), is outstanding.

Snapdragon

Antirrhinum majus

Botanical Pronunciation
ann-ther-RYE-num MAY-jus

Other Name Snaps

Bloom Period and Seasonal Color
Early summer through midsummer, shades of red, pink, yellow, purple, and white

Mature Height × Spread
Tall: 24 to 30 inches × 12 inches
Ultra dwarf: 8 to 10 inches × 8 inches

At one time, most varieties of snapdragon produced tall plants with stately spikes that needed staking. During the past several decades, plant heights have steadily decreased as have the days from planting seeds to "first color." The individual blossoms have been bred to be larger and more ornate. Recently introduced varieties with lax branches take on a semi-trailing form to give snapdragons more utility in hanging baskets and container gardens. More experienced gardeners still start tall varieties of snaps from seeds indoors to produce inexpensive plants for their cutting gardens. Regardless of the décor of one's home, an arrangement of tall snaps, perhaps mixed with late-spring-blooming spikes of larkspur, attests to the skill of the grower. Yet the modern trend is toward beds of the shorter varieties of snaps.

When, Where, and How to Plant

Many gardeners like snaps so much that they start seeds indoors in late fall to have seedlings ready to set out in early spring. Once hardened off by gradual exposure to cold winds, the seedlings will weather light frosts. In coastal areas, seeds can be started in pots or flats out of doors in late summer and set into the garden in October. Other gardeners opt for seedlings in packs or pots, just showing color. Plant snaps in well-drained soil, in a sunny site. Afternoon shade won't hurt them. Be sure to leave room between plants for air passage when they mature. Space tall varieties 24 inches apart, intermediate varieties 12 inches apart, and the ultra dwarfs 8 to 10 inches apart for good air circulation.

Growing Tips

Weekly, flow water on the soil between plants or use drip irrigation to avoid wetting the foliage. Mix controlled-release flower fertilizer into the soil prior to planting to feed all season.

Regional Advice and Care

Watch for aphids (you can see them clustering on spikes) and thrips (they are hard to see; you know they may be there if blossoms are distorted). Aphids are relatively easy to control with sprays of insecticidal soap, but thrips are difficult and may call for a combination fertilizer/systemic insecticide. Snaps are vulnerable to foliage diseases. Keep an appropriate fungicide handy for spraying on plants when a hot spot breaks out. On heavy clay soils, try spreading a mulch of play sand between your snapdragon seedlings to keep down the soil splash that spreads some foliage diseases. Slow-draining soil can encourage root rot. Deadhead spent spikes.

Companion Planting and Design

Snaps come in myriad colors. They make excellent cut flowers. Gardeners often mix colors in beds edged with other cool-weather flowering plants such as dianthus, calendula, pansies or violas, or ornamental kale or cabbage.

Try These

Plant 'Butterfly' snaps for their fancy flowers. The tall Rocket mix provides vertical accent.

Spreading Zinnia

Zinnia haageana and hybrids

Botanical Pronunciation
ZIN-nee-ah hay-GEE-ann-ah

Other Name
Narrow-leaved zinnia

Bloom Period and Seasonal Color
Late spring to fall blooms in various colors

Mature Height × Spread
10 to 20 inches × 10 to 20 inches

This zinnia species is for gardeners who dislike the care required by many annuals. For years, only orange or yellow colors were available. They were used for dry, hot sites that received little attention. Now you can enjoy 'Crystal White', an All-America Selections introduction, which is a compact plant that grows to 10 inches in height and has a somewhat wider spread. Its single pure-white flowers are over an inch in size. The hybrid 'Profusion' series also garnered AAS Gold Medal awards, adding cherry and apricot to the color range. Their narrow, medium green leaves are resistant to powdery mildew disease, unlike the standard garden variety (*Zinnia elegans*). Spreading zinnias are tolerant of heat and humidity in the Carolinas, and attract butterflies.

When, Where, and How to Plant

Set out plants or sow seeds well after the danger of frost has passed. Zinnias prefer full sun and well-drained soil in garden beds or containers. If you start with plants it is best to select stocky transplants that have few blooms. Sow seeds in lightly fertilized soil, tilled to a depth of 4 to 6 inches and raked smooth. Cover seeds with ⅓ inch of soil and firm them into the soil with the back of an iron rake. Water the bed thoroughly, using a watering wand or a nozzle designed for misting seedbeds. Keep the bed or row moist until the seeds germinate. Space plants or thin seedlings 18 inches apart so the plants can develop their natural shape.

Growing Tips

For container gardens, read the potting soil label. If it is not fortified with controlled-release fertilizer, mix in 1 tablespoon of fertilizer per gallon of pot capacity. In ground beds, fertilize the plants monthly by broadcasting 1-2-2 ratio fertilizer (for example, 10-20-20) between the plants to keep them healthy and blooming. Irrigate established plants for the first month with about an inch of water per week. Avoid wetting the foliage late in the day.

Regional Advice and Care

In late summer, spreading zinnias can be sheared to rejuvenate the planting. If the seedlings were not thinned properly, plants may become crowded, which can contribute to mildew susceptibility during wet summers. They have no pests and are low-maintenance annuals. It is not uncommon for seedlings to reappear magically the next summer.

Companion Planting and Design

Spreading zinnia is often used to fill large beds and in containers. In areas that can't be watered frequently, this is the zinnia of choice. For highest visibility at dusk, plant the yellow or white-blooming varieties. Spreading zinnias can be used in mass groupings with blue ageratum and 'Wave' petunias.

Try These

'Profusion Cherry' and 'Profusion Apricot' get rave reviews from veteran gardeners. Weather-tough 'Crystal White' or 'Crystal Orange' zinnias are deer resistant too! 'Persian Carpet' offers a mix of colors for seeding sunny beds.

Sun Coleus

Solenostemon scutellarioides

Botanical Pronunciation
so-leh-ne-STEM-un scoo-te-lar-e-OID-ez

Bloom Period and Seasonal Color
Spring to fall, richly variegated foliage in many color combinations

Mature Height × Spread
2 to 4 feet × 2 to 3 feet

Coleus has been the backbone of annual shade gardens for generations, but it is has broken out into the sun. The new vegetatively propagated sun coleus selections offer brilliant garden color that never stops, and if you water them frequently, they will thrive in full sun. In the Carolinas, this tropical is grown as an annual. In moist or irrigated beds, its vibrant, nonstop color will attract favorable attention from spring to fall. Sun coleus is ideal for container gardens or borders to create significant color accents. There has never been an annual easier to grow in our Piedmont clay soil. Some garden centers offer two dozen or more choices in bicolors, solid colors, and different leaf sizes and shapes. Compared to old-fashioned, seed-grown, shade garden coleus, the sun-tolerant types are slow to produce flowers and need less deadheading.

When, Where, and How to Plant
Set out plants in spring when the soil temperature warms to 55 degrees Fahrenheit and after fear of spring frosts passes, or anytime through late summer. Moisture-retentive soils are advised for full-sun locations and result in less maintenance in partial sun or dappled-shade locations. (See page 19 for soil preparation and planting instructions.) Space large cultivars 30 inches apart and small-leaved types 18 inches apart. Vigorous, large-leaved cultivars grow so large that they are usually planted alone in containers and grown as eye-catching specimens. Leave sneak paths among plants in ground beds. Coleus plants are quite brittle and can be damaged by foot traffic during watering or weeding.

Growing Tips
Sun coleus demands moist soil to perform. Use soaker hoses or water by hand to irrigate roots weekly and deeply during hot weather. A 1- to 2-inch layer of mulch helps to retain water and suppress weeds. Use controlled-release fertilizer in container plantings. Apply water-soluble fertilizer to ground beds monthly, more often in sandy soils.

Regional Advice and Care
Pinch or cut leaders to make coleus dense and bushy, with a mounded habit. To keep foliage vigorous, remove flower spikes before they elongate. Sun coleus is pest-free, except for slugs and snails that decimate small plants. Control slugs with baits or saucers of beer. Root tip cuttings in potting soil to propagate more plants. Take tip cuttings in September to pot up for next year's plants and to enjoy indoors during winter.

Companion Planting and Design
Use sun coleus as a background for lower-growing annuals, such as wax begonias, angelonias, 'Blackie' sweet potato vines, or lavender-blue fan flowers to hide their ankles and knees. Mass plants for best effect. In shade gardens, combine with evergreen ferns and caladiums. The light-colored cultivars show up better in shaded sites; there's a plethora of colors.

Try These
For a fall show with mums, 'Alabama Sunset' has burgundy-tipped leaves with gold centers. The unusual leaf shapes of the Duckfoot series of colors are novel and amusing.

Torenia

Torenia fournieri

Botanical Pronunciation
toe-REN-ne-ah four-nee-ERR-ee

Other Name
Wishbone flower

Bloom Period and Seasonal Color
Late spring to fall blooms in pink, rose, lavender-blue, and burgundy

Mature Height × Spread
6 to 12 inches × 8 to 18 inches

Some annuals are introduced with the Southern gardener in mind. Torenia was made for a Carolina summer as it relishes moisture normally coming in the form of rainstorms in July. This shade-loving plant covers the ground in a blanket of small, two-lipped tubular blossoms. It will tolerate a half-day of direct sun except in the coastal and sandhill regions. Multiple flushes of blooms keep on rolling through the heat. Individual flowers have a touch of yellow in the throat and their crossing stamens, which, with some imagination, resemble a "wishbone." Sprawling torenia can be used in planter boxes, hanging baskets, and for edging in color beds in the ground. The word is out: this one is a keeper!

When, Where, and How to Plant
You can start planting ground beds after the last frost. Plant in warm soil; there's no need to hurry in spring. Make multiple plantings even into summer provided you can give them supplemental water. Give torenia morning sun in the Piedmont and afternoon shade along the coast. Ordinary garden soil is adequate for growing this annual, provided it is well drained and fortified with controlled-release fertilizer and raked smooth. Gritty soils should be improved with plenty of compost or soil conditioner to retain moisture. In heavy clay soil, create a 4-inch-high berm to ensure adequate drainage and to warm the soil. Space potted plants 1 foot apart. Thoroughly water in new plantings.

Growing Tips
Water new plants thoroughly twice weekly and monitor until they begin strong growth. Once established, torenia tolerates heat, but not dryness. Mulch ground beds and water when the soil feels dry to touch. Container plantings should flourish if a moisture-holding material was used at potting time. A second application of flower fertilizer in summer may keep it blooming. A hand spade is a good tool for checking soil moisture in late summer.

Regional Advice and Care
Annuals often "play out" after the first flush of flowers. Pay attention to moisture and lightly shear them to get them over the doldrums. Keep a close eye on plantings for missing leaves, a sign of slugs or caterpillars. Gardeners can apply B.t. products or follow recommendations of County Extension agents for other natural pesticide treatments.

Companion Planting and Design
Plant in containers and hanging baskets to complement other heat-tolerant annuals. Use as an edging with marigolds, SunPatiens®, periwinkles, Dragon Wing® begonias, and pentas.

Try These
The 'Clown' hybrids have plenty of vigor. If you are into seed propagation, 'Suzie Wong' is a torenia species with golden yellow blooms that may be worth trying.

Verbena

Verbena × hybrida

Botanical Pronunciation
ver-BEAN-ah HI-bri-dah

Bloom Period and Seasonal Color
Season-long blooms in violet-blue, red, pink,
lavender, and white

Mature Height × Spread
6 to 18 inches × 12 to 48 inches

This family includes both annual and tender perennial selections. Verbena has risen to stardom in an incredibly short period of time since the introduction of 'Homestead Purple', a garden-hardy cultivar. Dozens of new hybrid verbenas sporting a range of colors find their niche in container plantings. Gardeners love the dependability of hybrid verbena to cover difficult areas with a flowering carpet of dark green foliage that always looks healthy. In Zones 8b to 9, many are winter hardy and come back year after year, but in colder zones they are handled as annuals. Verbena is incredibly resistant to heat and humidity during the growing season. Planted in flower beds and mixed containers, their richly colored blooms appear from spring to fall at the tips of 1- to 2-foot stems.

When, Where, and How to Plant

Plant verbenas from early spring through early fall. Clumps of the hardy hybrids can be separated as new growth begins. Average garden soil is fine with little in the way of soil amending. Verbena likes a warm, sunny location, especially in the western Carolinas. Spade the soil to loosen it and frill out the roots after removing transplants from their containers. Loose, well-drained soil is ideal. Space according to variety; annual verbenas need less space while hardy ones can use several feet. Water thoroughly and mulch.

Growing Tips

After planting, water every third day for two weeks. Water once weekly during the dry periods of summer. Containers will need special attention to a watering regime. Apply a granular garden fertilizer in spring, and again in summer if growth is slow. Do not overfertilize, or the plant will grow leggy with fewer blooms. Shear it lightly after the first flush of blooms for more flowers.

Regional Advice and Care

In Zone 7 or colder, treat verbena as an annual or container plant and you will not be disappointed. Garden plantings in the lower Piedmont should be left unpruned at season's end; winter foliage may add protection. Mulch beds of hardy verbena with pine needles in December. Many coastal plantings are lost when early cold sets in and the plants haven't hardened off properly; back off on late summer feeding. Mites and leafminers can appear; handpick affected leaves or use plant oil sprays.

Companion Planting and Design

Verbena combines perfectly with other annuals in the sunny to partially shaded garden. Add to containers with calibrachoa, petunia, bacopa, and diascia, as well as foliage plants from plectranthus to dichondra. Interplant with daylily and in perennial borders. Team hardy 'Homestead Purple' verbena with the gold foliage of the mops cypress and lemon spirea. It's great for container gardens.

Try These

'Homestead Purple' is hard to beat, though the new 'Taylortown Red' is quite cold hardy. For containers, use the Estrella® Voodoo and Imagination series for countless blooms.

Wax Begonia

Begonia semperflorens-cultorum

Botancial Pronunciation
bee-GOHN-e-ah sem-per-FLOOR-ens cul-TOR-um

Other Name
Fibrous-rooted begonia

Bloom Period and Seasonal Color
All summer foliage in pink, coral, white, red, or bicolored blossoms against green, red, or bronze

Mature Height × Spread
6 to 12 inches × 12 inches, taller on large-leaf varieties

If you need a colorful, durable annual to dress up an entrance bed, wax begonias may be the right choice for you. Plants show their colors at small sizes and are often sold in cell-packs, which translate to a relatively low price per plant. Do not confuse this plant with the wimpy tuberous begonias used in states north of the Carolinas or with the fine pink perennial *Begonia grandis* that is often seen in shade gardens. Wax begonia varieties with colorful, bronzy foliage are wonderfully tolerant of sun and heat, and they like afternoon shade. Varieties with green foliage tend to scorch in full sun unless watered faithfully. Planting can take place anytime during spring or summer for an instant show of flowers and foliage.

When, Where, and How to Plant
Begonias can be injured by late frosts, but planting is safe across the Carolinas by mid-May. Mix organic soil conditioner into your flowerbed both for water-holding capacity and good drainage, and wax leaf begonias will thrive. They will do even better if mulched. Set plants 12 to 18 inches apart. Choose your sites carefully; bronzeleaf varieties can withstand full sun except in highland areas. Lustrous greenleaf varieties prefer afternoon shade. Begonia seeds are like dust and can be a challenge to handle; use started plants (transplants) for faster, more predictable results.

Growing Tips
Water twice weekly if no rain falls; begonias are shallow rooted and can drop leaves if neglected. Liquid-feed begonias monthly; always soak the soil before feeding. Leave a few open, mulched patches in beds so you can step into spread granular flower fertilizer in midsummer.

Regional Advice and Care
If begonias grow leggy by midsummer, prune them back halfway. Shape plants into mounds rather than giving them "flattops." Small caterpillars may try to wrap leaves into tubular hideaways; spray them with nontoxic *B.t.* Crowded beds may lead to leaf diseases, so leave room between plants for wind to pass through and for easy weed removal without mangling the brittle plants. Tip cuttings of 2-inch lengths will root in moist potting soil, an inexpensive way to expand plantings.

Companion Planting and Design
Wax-leaved begonias make choice plants for containers because of their relatively small, free-flowering plants. They are effective in mass plantings, grouped with other summer annuals, or around mailboxes. Grow begonias as an edging with taller salvias or perennials or in drifts of separate colors to fill beds. Companions include ageratum, torenia, zinnia, and fan flower.

Try These
'Cocktail' hybrids are dwarf and sun-resistant. 'Pizzazz' hybrids are superior in flower power.

BULBS, CORMS, RHIZOMES & TUBERS

FOR THE CAROLINAS

A passion for flowers often begins with a handful of bulbs. Many a beginning gardener has gotten a start in horticulture with a plump amaryllis bulb or a few paperwhite narcissus. It's rare when a garden shop fails to offer these special plants in season, as they have become a symbol of winter gardening for sun-lovers of all ages. Bulbs, unlike seeds, contain reproductive parts—flowers—as well as undeveloped plants. When given proper growing conditions, bulbs will spring to life, with the guarantee of lovely flowers in a short period of time. Bulb culture opens up a whole new realm of possibilities for skilled gardeners as well as beginners.

When we gardeners think of bulbs, what usually comes to mind is Holland, not the Carolinas! There is no doubt that Holland is world-renowned for its tulip tradition and its famous Keukenhof Gardens with ten million flowering bulbs on display. In the Netherlands, bulbs have been grown as an economic staple since the sixteenth century. But with some planning, we in the Carolinas can create a Dutch delight in our yards. You will get the greatest enjoyment from bulbs by planting varieties of both species and hybrid tulips.

Not Just for Spring Anymore

Bulb flowers are not just spring flowers. In the Carolinas, bulbs can bloom twelve months of the year, depending on the species. While the familiar anemones, crocuses, and daffodils are valuable garden bulbs and require little care, they finish their showy performance before spring is over. By Mother's Day, bearded iris and peonies are ablaze on the heels of the early bloomers, and there is plenty of activity to come in the months that follow.

Indulge yourself with the wonderful woodland varieties like magic lilies and autumn crocus. For vertical accents, scatter a few gladiolus and liatris bulbs in a sunny perennial border. The "Oriental" lilies produce large, exquisite, picture-perfect blooms for cutting, while their smaller "Asiatic" cousins are made for color beds. Read the descriptions of the named cultivars; some are deliciously fragrant.

What Is a Bulb?

To set the record straight, not all bulbs arise from the smooth-skinned true bulbs like tulips and daffodils. True bulbs contain fleshy leaf scales, flower buds, and stored food surrounded by a papery skin for protection. Many of our summer-flowering bulblike plants—such as crocus, iris, and gladiolus—grow from stems called corms or rhizomes; others develop from thick root tissues called tuberous roots or tubers. All of these storage organs are capable of holding food reserves from season to season for the survival of the species. This gives bulbs the ability to "naturalize" (come back year after year) in the garden. Though some bulbs produce seeds after flowering, the seeds are difficult to germinate and may compete for the plant's energy. It is probably best for a gardener to remove the seedpods before they develop, unless of course you are a hybridizer introducing new varieties.

Tuberous roots

Rhizomes

True bulbs

Corms

Tubers

Many of the summer-flowering bulbs bloom when gardens are short on color. On balance, they are better landscape plants than their spring-blooming counterparts. Their foliage as well as their flowers can make a statement in the garden. The bold, variegated foliage of cannas and caladiums provide an exclamation point in a border or in the shadow of a majestic shade tree. If big leaves suit your fancy, gigantic elephant ears can be used judiciously as bold foliage accents in color beds and water gardens. The dainty rain lilies, one of our native bulbs, spring to life when a shower breaks a summer dry spell. Cyclamen steal the show in the shade garden as summer comes to an end. Dahlias crank up again and again and produce even better blossoms as State Fair-time rolls around each year.

Canna planted in a container add height.

Preparing the Bed

Successful gardeners prepare bulb beds for the long haul. Unless your planting is for one-season color, as with caladiums, you will want to amend the soil deeply. Studies at North Carolina State University (NCSU) revealed that many bulbs fail to naturalize due to soil acidity and poor fertility. Testing the soil should be a standard practice with new bed installations. Contact your County Extension agent for directions on taking and submitting soil samples. Bulbs will perform well in soils that have been limed to raise the pH to 6.0. Amend poorly drained clay soils with organic matter such as finely ground bark soil conditioner, or create a raised bed for your bulbs using a quality loam soil.

After NCSU discovered bulbs need controlled-release nitrogen more than other major nutrients, they developed a specialty bulb fertilizer. Bulb-booster products supply balanced nutrition and encourage repeat flowering in our gardens. People have commonly used bonemeal at planting time, but this is no longer recommended since bonemeal attracts vermin to the garden and may be a health hazard. The appropriate times for fertilizing spring-flowering bulb beds are in late summer and again in winter when the new shoots are popping out of the ground. These application times correlate to the periods of highest absorption of nutrients. Summer-flowering bulbs can be fertilized with the specialty products in spring as they emerge from their winter rest. But in the warm months, use a liquid flower fertilizer every six weeks to keep the plants vigorous.

Gardeners complain most about the wildlife they encounter when attempting to grow bulbs. Though squirrels will leave your poisonous daffodil bulbs alone, browsing deer will consume entire beds of tulips. Even the family dog running through a fragile bulb bed at peak bloom can certainly cause distress. The real menace for lily growers is the presence of pine mice (voles). Fortunately, there are legal ways to control voles, including snaptraps and rodenticides. For the average homeowner in suburbia, a good cat or amending the soil with gravel or PermaTill™ goes a long way.

Specialty bulb catalogs and garden centers offer many bulb options for gardening year-round. For every sunny garden or shady nook, you can find just the right bulb. Some bulbs may be left in the ground for years, producing flowers for your enjoyment. Others will need to be lifted following the first frosts of autumn. Many of them are capable of surviving harsh storage conditions because they naturally go dormant until they receive an environment conducive to a normal growth cycle. You won't be disappointed with your bulb choices when you find the perfect places for them in your garden.

The Weekend-Wonder Bulb Bed

If you are in a hurry and have hundreds of daffodils or similar bulbs to plant, you may find it helpful to set the bulbs on leaf compost. This quick bed method works in lieu of double-digging a large area that may be heavy clay soil. Most cities offer leaf compost at nominal fees or have seasonal Saturday giveaways. You can always stockpile compost for fall bulb planting. Pick a well-drained site that is sunny, of course. Spread a layer of newspaper (three sheets thick) and use a pitchfork to put 3 to 6 inches of compost over the newspaper. Scatter controlled-release bulb fertilizer at the label rate. Using a small piece of concrete reinforcing wire laid on top of the bed; the wire provides a 6-inch grid/template for staging the planting design. Set the bulbs to the grid pattern and orient them with the nose up, broad end down. Press them into the compost layer; remove the re-wire for use in another area. Cover the bulb planting with another 5 to 6 inches of leaf compost or bark soil conditioner. Irrigate the planting thoroughly. You have now created a raised bed without digging holes or hurting your back attempting to turn clay soil by hand. This technique has been employed successfully by landscape professionals. Try this method on a small scale first with daffodils, before you attempt to grow other bulbous perennials. Some soils amending with limestone, so consider a soil test when planting new garden spaces.

Lilies line a stone pathway.

Amaryllis

Hippeastrum × *hybrida*

Botanical Pronunciation
hip-ee-AS-strum × HI-brid-ah

Bloom Period and Seasonal Color
Late spring blooms in white, pink, red, salmon, orange, or pinstripes

Mature Height × Spread
12 to 30 inches × 24 inches

Most Dutch amaryllis are sold to force indoors for the Christmas season. But in hardiness Zone 8, this bulb can be added to the perennial border *en masse* for a striking display when the spring garden has passed its peak. After its leaves emerge from the ground, 18-inch green stalks bear a cluster of four to six extraordinary trumpet-shaped flowers. Once they establish their permanent root systems, they provide the brilliant color and bold forms that are sorely needed until perennials kick in. In cooler parts of the Carolinas, forced amaryllis bulbs can be kept in pots indoors until frost danger is past and then transplanted to the garden. They can be dug before hard frost comes, allowed to dry, then repotted for winter bloom. Amaryllis make superb cut flowers!

When, Where, and How to Plant

Plant hardy amaryllis in late spring. North of Zone 7b, plant in spring in a protected location and handle as you would dahlias. In Zone 8, plant outdoors in fall. Amaryllis divisions *can* be planted, but it's best to stick with bulbs! Give it sun in rich soil where the plants will not be disturbed for several years. Their deep, foraging roots should not have to compete with tree roots. Prepare the bed by digging deep to break up compacted soil. Good drainage is the key in naturalizing. By adding a soil amendment such as PermaTill™, winter moisture will not be a problem. Mix compost or shredded leaves to enrich and loosen it; this will help your bulbs sink deep roots and increase their chances of survival. If needed, lime the soil. Use a bulb-booster fertilizer in the backfill. Dig a hole 4 to 6 inches deep and cover with the prepared soil, leaving necks at ground level.

Growing Tips

When flower stalks emerge in late spring, water during blooming period only if rainfall is short. Well-established amaryllis requires little attention. Fertilize beds with a CRF flower product, organic fertilizer, or apply compost annually after the bloom cycle.

Regional Advice and Care

Do not remove foliage when you groom mature plants. Deadhead flowers while the flower stalks can be pruned to just above the foliage. When cutting amaryllis blooms for flower arrangements, leave a few inches of stem aboveground. It is best to cut the flower stalks when the first buds show color. Remove aphids by gently hosing off. Divide established and crowded beds when foliage turns yellow as the plants go dormant. Maintain a thick winter mulch after frost.

Companion Planting and Design

Plant in a prominent place like an entrance garden, by an ornate garden gate, or in a decorative container. The bulbs naturalize in the warmer regions of the Carolinas, growing larger each year until each plant has as many as three stalks of blooms.

Try These

'Apple Blossom' is great for forcing indoors. *Hippeastrum* × *johnsonii* and dark red lady 'Voodoo' are reliable outdoors.

Anemone

Anemone coronaria

Botanical Pronunciation
a-nim-O-nee cor-a-NAR-ee-us

Other Name
Windflower

Bloom Period and Seasonal Color
Spring or fall in red, white, blue, pink, and purple

Mature Height × Spread
3 to 12 inches × 6 to 10 inches

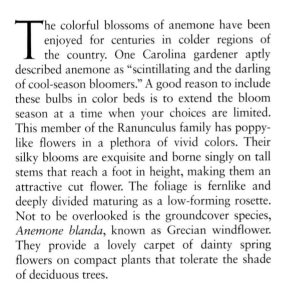

The colorful blossoms of anemone have been enjoyed for centuries in colder regions of the country. One Carolina gardener aptly described anemone as "scintillating and the darling of cool-season bloomers." A good reason to include these bulbs in color beds is to extend the bloom season at a time when your choices are limited. This member of the Ranunculus family has poppy-like flowers in a plethora of vivid colors. Their silky blooms are exquisite and borne singly on tall stems that reach a foot in height, making them an attractive cut flower. The foliage is fernlike and deeply divided maturing as a low-forming rosette. Not to be overlooked is the groundcover species, *Anemone blanda*, known as Grecian windflower. They provide a lovely carpet of dainty spring flowers on compact plants that tolerate the shade of deciduous trees.

When, Where, and How to Plant
Plant corms in late fall and throughout the dormant season. In fall plantings, select 6-inch potted plants for color beds. Until recently, the most common method to grow this gem was to purchase rock-hard corms from mail-order catalogs. Garden centers now conveniently potted anemones that flourish where planted. Sunny to partially shaded spaces are ideal. Avoid poorly drained soils as they will rot during their resting stage. Prepare fertile, well-prepared beds by spading in bark soil conditioner; beds should be raised to facilitate drainage. Use a bulb fertilizer at planting. Soak the corms overnight; plant 3 inches deep orienting vertically on their sides.

Growing Tips
Anemone performs best on north exposures and during the cooler gardening months. Don't be surprised when the foliage yellows as hot weather approaches. They benefit from an application of composted manure or mulch layer. Irrigate in fall to keep soil evenly moist. The corms rest in summer and aren't fussy about dry soils during that stage.

Regional Advice and Care
They hold their own with other late-season flowering bulbs. With proper care, they can produce multiple flower flushes. To encourage repeat blooming, groom plants after petals drop by cutting back bloom stalks to the leaves. Deer find the foliage tasty. They are often treated as annuals in coastal gardens.

Companion Planting and Design
Comingle anemone with cool-season favorites such as pansy, snapdragon, calendula, viola, and ornamental kale. Consider 'White Nancy' lamium and white sweet alyssum (*Lobularia*) for edging. Use masses of plants or corms in groupings. In containers, mix with caladiums. Select the cheery, white-flowering *Anemone blanda* for woodland gardens in Zone 7.

Try These
Anemone flowers are both single (poppy) and double with some resembling dahlias. Choose a color palette that is most appealing. 'De Caen Hybrids' and 'Mr. Fokker' are quite popular. Tall anemone, *A. virginiana*, is a native species.

Bearded Iris

Iris germanica

Botanical Prononciation
EYE-ris jur-MAN-ee-ka

Other Name
German iris

Bloom Period and Seasonal Color
Late spring blooms in wide range of colors; some cultivars rebloom in fall

Mature Height × Spread
1 ½ to 2 ½ feet × 1 to 2 feet

These sensational showy plants, named after the Greek goddess of the rainbow, are among the most useful, colorful, and widely grown bulbs. The bearded iris flower is made of two sections, an inner section consisting of three upstanding petals called "standards" and three outer drooping or horizontal petals called "falls." The common name comes from the dense, hairy line seen along the midrib of the outer petal falls. The leaves of bearded iris are sword-shaped, and their stiff foliage and upright form contrast well with the rounded form of many border perennials. Bearded iris is available in standard and dwarf forms. These lovely late-spring bloomers are easily grown under ordinary garden conditions provided the soil does not stay wet. There are hundreds of named varieties of this marvelous Mother's Day flower.

When, Where, and How to Plant
Plant potted iris in early spring. Plant dormant divisions in July to August. Plants can be transplanted while in bloom to ensure the correct flower color is selected. Give them strong morning sun. If bearded iris doesn't receive enough sun, it produces smaller flowers. Average garden soil is fine. Prepare beds by spading or tilling in bulb-booster fertilizer and lime to a pH of 6.5. Form mounds of soil at 1 to 2 feet spacing. Place so the rhizome can be seen above the ground; cover roots. Water thoroughly to settle.

Growing Tips
Bearded irises require moist soil only during the blooming season; they endure long periods of drought at other times. Water weekly during the flowering period if less than 1 inch of rain falls. Do not mulch iris beds. Fertilize lightly with 10-20-20 in spring before bloom time. A second application one month after blooming is needed to stimulate foliage and rhizome growth. Stake flower stalks in part-sun location to prevent lodging.

Regional Advice and Care
In Zone 8b, site them with afternoon shade. Overcrowded clumps bloom poorly; divide them immediately after flowering every three to four years. To divide, remove old flower stems and cut the leaves back to 6 inches. Cut clumps with a sharp knife so there is a rhizome and a fan of leaves in each division. Discard rhizomes showing signs of decay. The most serious pest is iris borer. Rake out the pinkish 2-inch larvae from rhizomes at replanting, using a pencil point. Where borers are a problem, apply an insecticide spray to foliage in spring as a preventative. Hand weeding and grass preventer products help control weeds in large iris beds.

Companion Planting and Design
Interplant with earlier- and later-blooming perennials for a striking textural contrast. Plant an entire bed of bearded iris in a border. Use loropetalum and cherry laurel as a backdrop foil. Add roof iris, *Iris tectorum*, and KNOCK OUT® roses to share the bloom season.

Try These
In my collection are 'Art Deco' (violet-on-white flowers), 'Aunt Mary', 'Pure Sapphire' (blue), and tall yellow 'Melted Butter'. Miniature 'Think Spring' is fragrant.

Caladium

Caladium bicolor

Botanical Pronunciation
ka-LAY-dee-um bi-co-lor

Bloom Period and Seasonal Color
Summer blooms are non-showy; late spring to fall bold colorful leaves in red, pink, white

Mature Height × Spread
1 to 2 ½ feet × 1 to 2 feet

With their large flamboyant leaves, caladiums put most other bulbous plants to shame. These beautiful plants prove that foliage can be just as important as flowers in landscapes. These tropical plants come in many shapes, sizes, and color combinations and are generally grown from tubers. They come in two types: fancy-leaved caladiums, which have heart-shaped leaves, and strap-leaved varieties, which have narrow arrow-shaped leaves. Both types are available in a range of color combinations and in sun-loving and shade-loving cultivars. The shade-loving types are more common and are the perfect plants for partial- to full-shade gardens and containers. Forty to 60 percent shade is ideal for most varieties. Though they are not winter hardy, caladiums are a great asset in the summer shade garden. Their brilliant foliage can brighten dark corners.

When, Where, and How to Plant

Plant potted caladiums or tubers outdoors after all danger of frost has passed. Soil must be porous and well drained. Pot up large tubers in early spring to force in a warm room. Use three per 6-inch pot in sterile, soilless, seed-starting mix in a well-lighted room. Apply a water-soluble fertilizer twice monthly until the caladiums are ready to transplant in spring. In landscape beds, caladiums do best in morning sun or dappled shade. Spade in organic matter where soils are sandy or contain clay. Use bulb fertilizer per label rate before planting. Place the bulbs 1 to 3 inches deep, and water the beds to encourage sprouting.

Growing Tips

Caladiums *love* water. Water landscape beds monthly or as needed in summer. Water plants in containers two to three times a week in summer and fall. Bedded plants need irrigation once weekly, more often during drought and heat in late summer. Fertilize plants in containers or color bowls with water-soluble 14-14-14 analysis every other week. If dry fertilizer is broadcast on top of the soil, water promptly and thoroughly to avoid foliage burn. Sunny beds need more fertilizer than plants in shade gardens.

Regional Advice and Care

Sunburn can spot the leaves; sun cultivars are best. Remove the insignificant bloom pods during the growing season. Slugs or snails can spoil new foliage; use a snail bait that is labeled "safe for children and pets." After frost, cut back leaves; lift tubers, and dust with sulfur or a similar fungicide before storing tubers in dry peat moss in a dry, cool place for winter.

Companion Planting and Design

Caladiums make great backdrops for shady borders of impatiens and forget-me-nots. Use them with bacopa in containers, with cascading ivies, or in window boxes. The white varieties make a strong visual statement in a shady nook or dull green area of the garden.

Try These

'Florida Sweetheart' and 'Hearts Delight' are lance-leaf types and sun tolerant. 'Fire Chief' and 'White Cap' are fancy-leaf types.

Canna

Canna × generalis

Botanical Pronunciation
CAN-uh gen-err-AL-less

Bloom Period and Seasonal Color
Summer to fall in red, white, pink, yellow,
orange, or bicolored; black to blue-green leaves

Mature Height × Spread
3 to 8 feet × 1 to 3 feet

Cannas have become garden favorites because of their big bold leaves and brightly colored flowers. In mid-spring, leaves emerge quickly, growing to 3 to 8 feet tall depending on variety. Showy blooms open atop upright plants that resemble miniature banana trees. Their flowering frenzy lasts until a hard frost in fall. Gardeners have discovered that cannas are not finicky plants and are resilient despite weather-related stresses. They offer a great backdrop to the perennial border or tropical garden. Cannas reached stardom when massive plantings appeared along Piedmont interstates many years ago. Thousands have been planted since then to complement the crapemyrtles beautifying our roadsides. New cultivars are spectacular with dazzling variegated or striped leaves, as well as bicolored flowers. Cannas are enjoying a revival and are here to stay!

When, Where, and How to Plant

Plant potted canna and its rhizomes when soil warms in spring. Seeds of 'Tropical Red' can be sown indoors in late winter. Provide a lot of space in full sun and well-drained soil. Cold-damaged rhizomes can recover and send up sprouts later in the season. Plant cannas in well-tilled, amended garden soil. Add bulb-booster plant food during soil preparation. Heavily amend soils using compost or aged manure. Cover the rhizomes with 3 inches of backfill and 2 inches of compost. Firm-in rhizomes (hand or foot), then water beds thoroughly.

Growing Tips

Keep the soil moist until the stalks are 1 foot tall. Irrigate cannas generously once the leaves are full grown. Use a deep mulch of leaf compost for maintaining large beds. If the plants will be irrigated, fertilize with a liquid flower product every six weeks until early September. Too much nitrogen will result in great foliage but few blossoms.

Regional Advice and Care

The biggest canna concern in the western half of the Carolinas is winter hardiness. Spring-planted rhizomes will tolerate early frosts. Some varieties are irresistible to Japanese beetles. Shake the foliage routinely in June and catch the beetles in a pail of soapy water. Canna leaf roller caterpillars can distort leaves. Cut off the affected leaf or apply an insecticide. North of Zone 7b, dig up rhizomes in November and store inside at 45 degrees Fahrenheit. In December, mulch clumps with 6 inches of pine needles or cover with a bushel basket stuffed with straw. Prune off old foliage and mulch in spring.

Companion Planting and Design

Few herbaceous perennials will catch your eye like cannas. Plant in clusters or mass in single colors. Their coarse foliage is a good backdrop for fine-textured perennials and ornamental grasses. Grow as a seasonal screen in a border. Variegated cannas are fabulous accent plants in landscapes and containers. Their bloom period overlaps crapemyrtles.

Try These

'Thai One On' is a favorite pink and resists leaf rollers. The foliage of 'Bengal Tiger' is extraordinary.

Crinum

Crinum spp.

Botanical Pronunciation
KRY-num

Other Name
Milk and wine lily

Bloom Period and Seasonal Color
Summer blooms in pink, white, red, and bicolors

Mature Height × Spread
2 to 4 feet × 2 to 5 feet

Crinum is a great pest-proof heirloom plant. It has been grown for generations and survivors are still found on old homesteads across the South. This summer-flowering bulb is a member of the Amaryllis family and is one of the more cold-hardy bulbs. It is safely planted in the eastern mountain regions. The fragrant flowers of crinum resemble those of the common Easter lily but are smaller. Each tubular pink bloom is about 4 inches long and has a characteristic rose-red stripe on each petal. Up to fifteen flowers are clustered atop each rigid stalk. The South African crinum, *Crinum moorei* 'Schmidtii', a white-flowering variety, is especially adapted to the heat and summer rainfall of Zone 8b. You will be delighted with numerous late-summer surprises when you plant crinums in a moist garden spot.

When, Where, and How to Plant
Plant potted crinum spring to fall. Remove offsets (suckers or pups) from established mother bulbs for planting in summer. Crinums thrive in sun to partial shade, provided the soil is rich and well drained. They tolerate wet or dry conditions. When planted facing the south sun, the foliage will look rather shabby. Add large quantities of organic matter to sandy or gravelly soils. Bulbs are quite large, requiring a deeply spaded planting hole. Spade up an area at least 1 square foot per bulb and mix in bulb-booster fertilizer as the label directs. Space bulbs 2 feet apart, planting each with its long neck deep in the soil. Once planted, they should be left undisturbed for many years. If they're planted in a sunny bed, mulch thinly.

Growing Tips
Water weekly during the bloom period if there is no rain. Newly planted crinums need a season or two before they begin blooming freely. Apply 10-20-20 fertilizer or compost in mid-May each year after the first flowering season. In fall, topdress with organic mulch or rotted manure to keep them vigorous.

Regional Advice and Care
Sparse blooming is a symptom of too much shade or planting too deeply. Crinums are tough as nails and stalwarts because they tolerate ordinary soils. There are no serious pests. Manage weeds by hand; mulch is sufficient for small beds. After four to five years, remove the bulb offsets and replant them to enlarge your collection. Old bulbs can weigh in at 30 pounds! In Zones 6 to 7a, grow crinums in containers.

Companion Planting and Design
Arching swordlike foliage provides a pleasing contrast to fine-textured ornamentals such as plum yew and deutzia. The species *C. moorei* grows well in a woodland shade garden along with perennial companions such as hosta, ferns, and Japanese aster. Swamp lily, *C. americanum*, is native to southern wetlands.

Try These
'Sangria' has burgundy leaves. Deep sea lily ('Milk and Wine') and 'Ellen Bosanquet' are suitable for most gardens. Hybrids abound via mail-order.

Daffodil

Narcissus hybrids

Botanical Pronunciation
nar-SIS-us

Other Names
Buttercup, Jonquil

Bloom Period and Seasonal Color
Late winter to early spring in yellow, white, and bicolors

Mature Height × Spread
6 to 20 inches × 4 to 8 inches

These hardy spring-flowering bulbs are quick to naturalize along the margins of woodland gardens. Technically, all are *Narcissi*, but the name "jonquil" is reserved for the species with tubular leaves like chives. *Narcissus* flowers symbolize spring, and the bulbs adapt to a wide range of climates in the Carolinas. The bulbs grow larger each season and will grow in tight clay soils much better than most other bulbous plants. To have daffodils flowering from late winter until early summer, choose varieties that bloom during different months from among thirteen different divisions. If you're looking for fragrance, try the paperwhites, *N. tazetta*. They are intensely aromatic and are terrific for potting or for planting in borders. Purchase daffodils by the bushel to make inexpensive, magnificent spring floral displays. A Carolina spring is not complete without daffodils.

When, Where, and How to Plant

Plant after the first frost in October or November in full sun to partial shade. While rich, loose soil is preferred, these workhorses grow amazingly well in nearly any condition and location. Purchase high-quality bulbs—only the largest and firmest—for success. Bulbs that have 2 or 3 "noses" (segments) produce more blooms their first year. Shop early at the garden centers in fall or buy from mail-order nurseries. Plant as you would tulips, adding lime to the soil if needed, and bulb fertilizer. Incorporate large quantities of ground pine bark into poorly drained beds. Cover bulbs with 3 to 6 inches of amended topsoil or leaf compost.

Growing Tips

Water newly planted bulb beds weekly during dry fall weather. Mulch beds in winter and fertilize in January as the new shoots appear, and again in early fall. When planting, apply 2 pounds of 10-10-10 fertilizer for a 100-square-foot bed or use bulb-booster fertilizer.

Regional Advice and Care

Remove stems after blooming but *do not* prune the foliage back until it begins to turn yellow. For cosmetic reasons, some gardeners fold the leaves and secure them with a rubber band, but this is not recommended by experts. Crowded plantings can be divided when leaves yellow. When dividing, dry bulbs in the sun and store them until fall in a cool, dry location. Poorly drained soils can result in rot diseases. Daffodils are toxic and are generally avoided by deer, voles, and other furry pests.

Companion Planting and Design

Miniatures such as 'Tête-à-Tête' make stunning rock garden plants. Combine mass groupings of daffodils with pansies, thrift, and candytuft. Use *N. tazetta* and 'Hawera' in container gardens. Comingle with vining groundcovers; grape hyacinths combine well.

Try These

'Ice Follies' has been a great performer both in the landscape and for forcing. 'Double Smiles' has cheery double blooms; 'Baby Boomer' is a fine miniature.

Dahlia

Dahlia × hybrida

Botanical Pronunciation
DAL-yuh HI-bred-dah

Bloom Period and Seasonal Color
Summer to fall in every imaginable color
and bicolors

Mature Height × Spread
1 to 7 feet × 8 to 24 inches

You can choose from more than 1,500 dahlia cultivars. Though the iridescent blossoms of dahlia can be as small as a nickel, some grow larger than the biggest dinner plate. This tuberous-rooted ornamental varies tremendously in color, form, and size. Some dahlia flowers are perfectly ball-shaped; others have daisylike or cactus-shaped blossoms. Their jewel-toned brilliance is unmatched among tender perennials. The stunning blended or bicolor blooms are the result of decades of hybridization. The fast-growing succulent dahlia stems can mature at 1 foot or top out at over 6 feet in height, depending on the variety. Dahlias are native to Mexico so they do well in the warm weather and intense sunshine of the Carolinas.

When, Where, and How to Plant
Most tall, large-flowered dahlias are grown from tubers. Quick-growing dwarf varieties are often started from seeds. Start seeds indoors in late winter. Start tubers indoors a month before the last frost date. Place tubers in large nursery pots containing soilless mix. Keep soil semi-dry until the tender shoots emerge. Move pots outdoors to a protected area and keep moist until time to transplant. Tubers can be planted directly in a sunny spot in the garden after danger of frost is past. Dahlias prefer rich, well-drained soil but will grow in ordinary loam. Amend tight soils with compost or pine-bark soil conditioner to a depth of 10 inches, then spade in cow manure or slow-release flower fertilizer. Place tubers sideways about 3 inches below the soil line. Do not water before shoots appear!

Growing Tips
To ensure flowers later in the season, water consistently during dry periods. Mulch to conserve moisture. Dahlias are greedy; feed with a 10-20-20 or similar fertilizer every four to six weeks during the growing season. (Always water the day before fertilizing!) Periodically apply foliar applications of a water-soluble fertilizer containing micronutrients.

Regional Advice and Care
Pinch shoots soon after they first emerge; pinch often for more blooms. Tall varieties require support. Combining a wire cage and a stake (like those used for growing tomatoes) is effective. Few pests other than thrips and Japanese beetles bother with this plant; consult your County Cooperative Extension service for any necessary pest identification and control. Cut the canes back to 3 inches from the ground after frost. Lift the tubers, hose off the clinging soil, and dip in a fungicide. When thoroughly dry, store indoors for the winter in dry peat moss at 50 degrees Fahrenheit. Separate tubers in spring. Plants can over winter in Zone 8 and warmer.

Companion Planting and Design
Tall dahlias look best as background plants in plantings with cannas and fall-blooming perennials. The shorter annual varieties are excellent in borders, windowboxes, and containers.

Try These
My favorites are the dark red bicolor 'Duet' and 'Snowstorm'.

Elephant Ears

Colocasia esculenta

Botanical Pronunciation
call-o-KAY-sha es-QUE-lent-ah

Bloom Period and Seasonal Color
Late spring to fall leaves in green, golden,
reddish purple, and black

Mature Height × Spread
3 to 6 feet × 3 to 8 feet

Nothing says tropical more than growing elephant ears in your summer garden. They are the new "hip" plant because of their giant foliage and bold statement. They make great specimen plants and provide an accent when placed in a large decorative container. The bulb is a compressed stem as big as a softball, requiring a large planting hole. In late spring, pointed leaf shoots emerge quickly from the warm earth. The colorful foliage and petioles can range from golden to almost black. Most plants grow to an average size of 4 by 5 feet, some bigger, some much smaller. With sufficient sunlight and plenty of moisture, elephant ears become an outstanding tropical performer. Whether you have a small patio garden or acres on which to play, elephant ears will suit your perfect location.

When, Where, and How to Plant
Set potted elephant ears plants and bulbs after danger of frost has passed in spring through midsummer. Give them a large space to fill. Plant in a location where the soil is rich and moist, and within a hose length of a water faucet. For container plantings, select a bagged, peat-lite soil mix. Use a shovel or mattock to excavate a 1-foot-diameter hole and amend the backfill with copious amounts of peat moss or compost; add bulb fertilizer. Bulbs are planted in holes and covered completely and topped with 4 inches of soil. Water thoroughly to settle the backfill; add a layer of mulch.

Growing Tips
Keep the soil moist until the plants establish or the bulbs produce a mature leaf. Maintain a deep mulch layer to help reduce the need for watering. Water during the driest months. Apply 20-20-20 liquid fertilizer monthly to encourage fast growth.

Regional Advice and Care
Given warm weather, elephant ears are carefree. In regions north of Zones 8 to 9, this herbaceous bulbous perennial is treated like an annual and must be planted each spring. To grow elephant ears year-round outdoors in Zone 7b, simply provide a blanket of shredded leaves and pine straw during the winter months. Allow frost to dessicate the stems and leaves naturally. If you cut the stems, the cuts will absorb water, causing them to rot. Make a circle of chicken wire to surround the central stem and fill the 16-inch diameter circle with leaves or straw.

Companion Planting and Design
Elephant ears makes a great conversation piece and focal point when planted as a single specimen. Use clusters in large perennial borders as a backdrop for tall summer flowers.

It's an interesting thriller for large containers. Experiment with the showy nursery types. Note: both *Alocasia* and *Colocasia* genera are referred to as "elephant ears." *Alocasia* 'Nancy's Revenge' thrives in ponds and water gardens.

Try These
All elephant ears give a tropical feel. Colorful cultivars 'Mojito' and 'Midnight' are fabulous garden accents. 'Thailand Giant' produces monster plants with leaves to 6 feet!

Lily

Lilium spp.

Botanical Pronunciation
LIL-ee-um

Bloom Period and Seasonal Color
Late spring and summer blooms in white, yellow, orange, gold, pink, and red

Mature Height × Spread
3 to 7 feet × 8 to 15 inches

"Consider the lilies of the field . . ." The appeal of lilies is timeless. As far back as 1550 B.C., lilies have been revered for their exquisite flowers and heavenly fragrance. Lilies are fast-growing tender bulbs that produce erect stems and narrow lustrous leaves. During the summer months, Oriental lilies produce up to ten spectacular, often powerfully fragrant, open-faced blooms on each stalk. Oriental hybrids are considered simple to grow. The Asiatic lily is well adapted to the perennial border. Before the 1930s, only skilled plantsmen could revive the desiccated planting stock that was imported from the Far East. Today, with our modern storage capabilities and new hybrid lily varieties, these delightful bulbs are available to all gardeners, all throughout the planting season.

When, Where, and How to Plant

Plant in late fall or spring as soon as the ground thaws. Plant promptly; do not let them sit. Container-grown lilies can be planted even while in bloom. Oriental lilies tolerate full sun in the western Carolinas, but give them afternoon shade in Zone 8. Heat causes Oriental lily flowers to be short-lived. Remember, "head in sun and feet in shade." Provide white or pastel-colored lilies with dappled shade (preferably away from trees). Grow in well-drained, moist, organically rich, acidic soil. Large amounts of sphagnum peat moss or a little sulfur will acidify marginally alkaline soils. In areas where sticky clay soils predominate, lilies do well in raised beds or berms. To ensure good planting conditions, especially in clay soils, incorporate a 2- to 3-inch layer of bark soil conditioner with bulb fertilizer.

Plant bulbs 2 to 4 inches deep. Cover them with soil, water well, and mulch.

Growing Tips

Mulch well to conserve moisture. Water 1 inch weekly during the flowering period. Keep the soil moist but avoid overwatering, which can rot bulbs. Provided you enriched the soil with compost, lilies won't need much in the way of nutrients. Too much nitrogen is harmful; use a bulb fertilizer.

Regional Advice and Care

Cut plants back after they bloom, leaving at least half the stem and leaves to nourish the bulb for next year. Remove anthers from cut flowers, since pollen stains fabric. Divide and transplant old established lily beds in fall. Diseases are bigger threats than insects. Lily roots and stems can rot if planted in poorly drained soil. Voles will eat bulbs; deer browse the tops. In fall, cut stalks to ground level.

Companion Planting and Design

Plant lilies in clusters for the best effect, and use them in containers. For color, interplant lilies with annuals like sun coleus and impatiens. Use the shorter, more vivid Asiatic lilies in masses for perennial borders. Interplant garden phlox and coneflowers for color echo.

Try These

'Star Gazer' and 'Muscadet' are magnificent Oriental types—the queen of bulbs. Asiatic lily is exceptional in sunny Zone 8 gardens; try 'Rosella's Dream' and 'Pieton'.

Magic Lily

Lycoris squamigera

Botanical Pronunciations
LAHY-ker-is squa-my-GER-ah

Other Name
Naked lady

Bloom Period and Seasonal Color
July and August, pink blooms

Mature Height × Spread
24 inches × 15 inches

One of the first signs of new life following a mid-July rainstorm is the sudden appearance of the long, green, leafless stems of magic lilies. The flower stems each bear up to seven 3-inch, trumpet-shaped, lavender-pink flowers. They are not only visually spectacular but also mildly fragrant as well. Magic lilies are cold-hardy and can survive 20-below-zero winters in states to the north. They may be left in the ground for eight years or more without dividing. Unlike the common red spider lily (*Lycoris radiata*) that produces fall foliage after blooming, magic lilies sport their leaves in spring. The 2-foot-long, dull green leaves wither and die as the warm days arrive. Plant magic lilies where they can be observed frequently as the blooming drama unfolds.

When, Where, and How to Plant
Plant bulbs in summer. Magic lilies prefer a deep, humus-conditioned soil, but any quick-draining soil should do fine. Morning-sun locations are perfect. Spade an area 1 foot deep by 15 inches wide for each trio of bulbs. Mix in soil amendments and bulb-booster fertilizer. Place three bulbs in the planting hole, spacing them 5 inches apart. Cover the bulbs with 4 inches of easily crumbled soil. Water well after planting to settle the soil. Before planting in difficult, shallow soils, build the soil by stockpiling layers of leaves and topsoil on the beds. The decomposing leaves will raise the soil level and increase the life expectancy of your bed.

Growing Tips
Magic lilies don't need a great deal of water. Water only during the bloom period and when there is a dry period in spring. Fertilize when the foliage appears, using a complete fertilizer such as 10-10-10, scattering it over the bed at a rate of 1 pound per 100 square feet. If using bulb-booster fertilizer, apply at a rate of ½ cup per 10 square feet.

Regional Advice and Care
In Zone 8 counties, red spider lily is a more dependable bloomer. In Zone 6 mulch heavily in winter. Mark planting locations to avoid accidentally digging up or damaging bulbs. Prune back foliage after leaves yellow in late spring, and divide. Bulbs can be lifted and air-dried, and replanted in June. *Lycoris* doesn't like to be moved and can take a couple of years to bloom again. Remove flower stalks after blooms fade. There are no serious insect pests.

Companion Planting and Design
Pink magic lilies are elegant! Their straplike leaves complement hostas, autumn ferns, and hellebores; bloom stems popping out of low perennials beds are truly magical! Plant clusters in an entrance bed or by a patio where they can be appreciated. The bright red spider lilies are perfect for naturalizing in groundcovers and along a woodland walk.

Try These
All *Lycoris* are so special. The 'Peppermint' cultivar is exquisite. Experiment with the Chinese introductions.

Rain Lily

Zephyranthes spp.

Botanical Pronunciation
zef-uh-RAN-theez

Other Name
Fairy lily

Bloom Period and Seasonal Color
Late spring through early fall blooms in white, rose, pink, yellow, red, and striped

Mature Height × Spread
6 to 8 inches × 6 to 12 inches

Rain lilies are small, unobtrusive bulbs that respond to spring and summer rainfall by blooming within a week. Give them a sunny location in a bed or border and you will appreciate the occasional surprise when flowers pop up during a time that gardens are starved for color. Narrow, grasslike leaves grow to 8 inches tall, forming clumps that give rise to numerous star-shaped flowers. The flowers could be mistaken for that of crocus if it were not for the late season of bloom. There are numerous colors in rain lilies, but it is more common to find selections in varying shades of pink and white. When planted in clusters among perennials they will naturalize and create interest in flower beds. Some varieties multiply rapidly and offsets can be divided to share with friends or enlarge plantings.

When, Where, and How to Plant
Plant rain lily bulbs from fall to spring, and potted plants anytime they are available. This native perennial grows best in full sun with moist, well-drained soils. Given a few seasons, large clumps will form, providing a ready source of bulbs for fall planting. Amend dry sites or areas where soils are sandy using liberal amounts of peat moss or compost. Plant the onion-like bulbs 1 to 2 inches deep and space them 4 inches apart. Cover the bulbs with backfill and water thoroughly. Top with a 1-inch layer of mulch to prevent soil erosion.

Growing Tips
Rain lily plantings are carefree after establishment. Watering twice monthly in late summer will be beneficial the first year. They will respond to moist soil and light watering when planted in fall or warm weather. Rain lilies will tolerate drought but they appreciate moist soils in hottest months. Maintain a thin mulch layer of crushed pine bark or similar material. Apply a bulb fertilizer or organic fertilizer in spring to beds to encourage offsets (baby bulb) growth.

Regional Advice and Care
While *Zephyranthes atamasco* is a native of the southeastern United States, there are other species available to gardeners. *Habranthus* is another rain lily genera found in garden centers. Central American *Z. citrina* can tolerate the worst conditions and keep flowering. There are few pests other than an occasional caterpillar or grasshopper; hand removal is the best remedy.

Companion Planting and Design
Plant rain lilies in mass groupings along a walkway, or by a patio where they can be appreciated when in bloom. Add to a container for close observation as some possess a colorful throat and have a double appearance. Rain lilies fit into virtually any landscape, rock garden, or border. They will often bloom multiple times in a year.

Try These
Zephyranthes 'Yolkster' is a fast multiplier with bright yellow blooms on bright green stems. Native plant enthusiast will go for *Z. atamasco*. *Z. grandiflora* bears large blooms.

Spanish Bluebell

Hyacinthoides hispanica

Botanical Pronunciation
HI-uh-sinth-OID-eez his-PAN-ee-kah

Other Name
Wood hyacinth

Bloom Period and Seasonal Color
Late spring blooms in pink, blue, and white

Mature Height × Spread
8 to 12 inches × 6 to 10 inches

I magine a shade-tolerant "hyacinth" that becomes a good naturalizer in the woodland garden but performs beautifully in a sunny border of early blooming perennials. Spanish bluebell is a little-known heirloom bulb that has actually been around for years. They ask for so little yet give so much in return. By April, the rosette of straplike, medium green leaves begins to send up an 8- to 10-inch flower spike. Shortly thereafter, the first of what will become a loose cluster of pastel-colored bells begins to opens. Typically blooming in blue, pink, and white, Spanish bluebell is an excellent choice for the front of borders and creates a nice contrast when planted in groundcovers of ajuga or vinca. *Hyacinthoides non-scripta*, the English bluebell, has smaller pendent flowers that are very fragrant.

When, Where, and How to Plant
Plant bluebell bulbs in late fall. Established beds can be divided in late summer and replanted elsewhere. Give them full sun to part filtered shade. Too much shade can cause the flower stalks to stretch and lean over in a rainy spring. They are easy to grow in average garden soil especially where it's well drained. Turn the soil 5 inches deep and rake out large clods. Add a bulb fertilizer according to package directions and bed size. Space 6 to 8 inches apart with planting depth equal to twice the height of the bulb, about 3 to 4 inches deep. Cover the bulbs with 2 inches of compost or bark soil conditioner. Water thoroughly after planting.

Growing Tips
Water beds weekly in spring during the flowering period only if soil conditions are dry. Do not water bluebell plantings in summer, as the foliage will turn yellow naturally as summer dormancy occurs in hot weather. Apply a 10-20-20 analysis fertilizer every other year in March.

Regional Advice and Care
English bluebell is better for cooler climes, Zones 6 to 7. This perennial bulb is basically carefree when established. Over a period of three- to five-years the bed may be divided to prevent overcrowding and encourage flower production. Loss of bulbs is normally due to inadequate soil drainage or pine mice nibbling at the bulbs. PermaTill is used to amend compacted soils and deter moles or voles. Multiplies into clumps for sharing among your gardening friends.

Companion Planting and Design
Select one color to create a formal garden look; a mixture of Spanish bluebells is ideal for the relaxed ones. A mixture is a blend of pink, blue, and white plants. Blooming begins in early May with azaleas and rhododendrons. Normally, the bloom time lasts for several weeks. Use individual cultivars as a color echo, such as 'Queen of Pinks' planted under soft pink azaleas. Naturalize in woodland settings.

Try These
Spanish bluebell mixture is great *en masse*. 'White City' is excellent for contrast.

Tulip

Tulipa spp.

Botanical Pronunciation
TOO-lip-pah

Bloom Period and Seasonal Color
Early to late spring blooms in all colors

Mature Height × Spread
6 to 24 inches × 4 to 8 inches

In fifteenth-century Netherlands, when elitist Europeans lusted after exotic flowers, three tulip bulbs could be sold to pay for a house. Now sensational tulip bulbs are three-for-a-dollar. With hundreds of tulip varieties to choose from, the color opportunities are boundless. Varieties include peony-flowered, singles, fringed, parrot, and the diminutive species tulips that grow to only 6 inches tall. The biggest and showiest of all the tulips are the Darwin hybrids. It was long felt that it was just "too hot" in the South for tulips, but studies conducted at North Carolina State University led to the formulation of a special bulb fertilizer and a list of tulip cultivars that are dependable when planted in the Carolinas. They effectively complement spring-flowering shrubs like few other plants. No other bulb says spring like tulips!

When, Where, and How to Plant

Plant bulbs between the first frost and Thanksgiving. Adequate root systems must develop before the ground freezes. Given sun and fertile, well-drained soil, tulips are generally very easy to grow. A completely new bulb must form for the plant to bloom again or perennialize. Plant tulips in raised beds. Spade soil to a depth of 12 inches and add generous quantities of pine bark soil conditioner. Use bulb-booster fertilizer at the recommended rate. Tulips can be planted in a trench in the border or in groups. Plant large bulbs 4 to 6 inches deep and 5 inches apart. Water the bed and mulch well.

Growing Tips

Water beds during drought. Fertilize tulip beds twice each year, first in mid-September then again when the plants emerge in late winter. Use a bulb fertilizer such as 9-9-6 at a rate of 2 ½ pounds per 100 square feet of bed. For large bulb plantings, one application of bulb-booster in early fall will suffice. Remove weeds before they set seeds and multiply.

Regional Advice and Care

Mild winters can produce freaky-looking tulips with blooms at ground level. They need significant cold when making roots in winter. After the bloom season do not cut back foliage until it turns yellow, though flower stems can be removed. Bulbs can be divided at that time. Discard the weak ones and dry the rest in the sun for a week or so. Store bulbs in a cool basement until replanting. Gardeners lose tulip bulbs to voles. Use snap traps, legal baits, or sharp gravel in beds to control them.

Companion Planting and Design

Tulips show best when planted *en masse* using a single color and interplanted with miniature narcissus, pansies, or violas. Fancy double-flowered hybrids are gorgeous in planters and when grown for cut flowers. Plant along a path or at the edge of a water garden.

Try These

'Apeldoorn' returns well. The double-flowered 'Angelique' is a showstopper. *Tulipa clusiana* var. *chrysantha* is a vigorous lady tulip.

GROUNDCOVERS

FOR THE CAROLINAS

At one time, only turfgrasses were used to prevent soil erosion and to provide green in the home landscape. Often referred to as "living mulch," groundcovers are now what landscape designers use to carpet our outdoor rooms. Groundcovers can be defined as any dense, spreading plant that covers the ground when planted *en masse*. They can transform a barren area into a blanket of lush foliage and, if you wish, flowers as well.

Advantages of Groundcovers

What gardener wouldn't be happy to find a low-maintenance solution to a problem area? Once established, groundcovers choke out most unwanted weeds, reducing maintenance. Planted in sun or shade, they will hide the ugly knees of some taller-growing plants. Some are especially handsome when placed under small specimen trees or edging a garden border. Flowering groundcovers are spectacular grouped for seasonal color. Groundcovers are excellent plants to naturalize over bulb plantings, especially surprise or spider lilies. Carolina gardeners find it irresistible to plant flowerbeds without first edging the beds with monkey grass (clumping liriope). Some, like Asiatic jasmine, are aggressive growers, while others, like cast iron plant, stay put.

Many gardeners love groundcovers because of the savings in "sweat equity." Groundcovers can reduce the time spent mowing and solve landscape design problems. The right groundcover can grow better in shaded areas than lawn grass. Creeping juniper and creeping raspberry are ideal for steep slopes and rocky sites that make mowing hazardous and for open areas where exposed tree roots make mowing or gardening difficult. They can help define shrub beds and add variety to woodland gardens. As a supplement to turf areas, groundcovers blend and unite the yard into a harmonious picture.

A blossoming cherry tree is underplanted with flowering groundcovers, uniting the lawn with the landscape.

Problems

In areas that receive less than one-half day of direct sun, turfgrasses will ultimately fail, often due to fungus diseases. While several soil diseases can injure groundcovers in shaded environs, most are chronic and temporary setbacks. In rainy springs, stem fungi, for example, may cause occasional circular, dead patches in ajuga. Prune out wilted or browning foliage of vinca early in the season to allow the spots to fill in with new growth. These problems generally disappear as the season progresses and the groundcover continues to spread. Edging beds and weed control are important elements of grooming. In the early years, hand weeding and mulches will be required for best establishment. In sunny plantings, a crabgrass pre-emergence product may prove useful.

A major advantage of groundcovers is their increasing spread and thickness that becomes more attractive each year. Your task is to prepare the soil properly for a long-lived planting. Test the soil a couple of months prior to the project and amend it appropriately. Some soil types will not need the addition of limestone and phosphorus, but don't make the mistake of guessing.

A Few Tips for Planting

A month or two prior to planting, begin killing perennial grasses with a non-selective herbicide. Two or three applications may be needed to provide a clean area for planting. Covering an area with black plastic eliminates only annual weeds.

Purchase vigorous plants and prepare the soil thoroughly. Choose the varieties that will flourish in your particular garden. New cultivars show up at garden shops often, especially colorful selections with variegated foliage that add seasonal interest. Many can be added to mixed container plantings as spillers. Keep yard maintenance in mind when selecting a groundcover. For example, a heavy growth of crisscrossed vines complicates raking.

Except beneath the canopy of trees, work the planting area with a tiller or turn the soil by hand to a depth of 6 to 8 inches. Incorporate lime and fertilizer if needed, and on heavy clay or light sandy soils, a couple of inches of organic matter as well. If lacking a soil test, use 1 pound flower fertilizer per one 100 square feet and 3 pounds pelletized dolomitic limestone. Rake out clods and rocks, then plant at the correct spacing.

Beneath trees, spread three layers of newsprint. Lay down 2 to 3 inches of bark mulch from the trunk to the drip line. Mulching prior to planting makes things go better.

Dig planting holes the same depth as the container and two times as wide. Use a garden fork/cultivator to loosen the roots, snip off long roots, set the plant in place, pull the soil around it, and firm it lightly. Irrigate deeply and routinely during the first season and dig out opportunistic weeds.

Groundcovers are said to sleep the first year, creep the second, and leap the third. This adage is not true for the half-hardy perennials and annual varieties. As with any landscape installation, expect to provide some care to these low-maintenance plants. In some cases it may be a little grooming as spring arrives to remove cold-damaged leaves, or a summer shearing to maintain a dense mat of foliage. Once established, groundcovers are durable are integral part of a functional landscape design.

Asiatic Jasmine

Trachelospermum asiaticum

Botanical Pronunciation
TRAY-key-loh-SPER-mum A-ze-ATIC-come

Other Name
Small leaf Confederate jasmine

Bloom Period and Seasonal Color
Year-round, white flowers rarely seen

Mature Height × Spread 1 feet × trailing

Zones 7b to 8

Gardeners are always looking for an evergreen substitute for invasive English ivy. Asiatic jasmine is a dark green, running vine that is not a strong vertical grower and will not engulf a tree like ivy. This groundcover is catching the eye of landscape designers for Zone 8 and warmer regions because of its versatility in myriad garden applications. Few groundcovers grow equally well in sun or shade, but the small leaf Confederate jasmine is uniquely adaptable extending its range during the summer months. It grows fast and works best in large areas where you need a dense, vegetative mat, such as on slopes and under shade trees. With shiny, pointed 1-inch leaves it is an elegant vining plant. Unlike fragrant Confederate jasmine, *Trachelospermum jasminoides*, this family member rarely blooms in the Carolinas.

When, Where, and How to Plant

Plant Asiatic jasmine anytime a shovel can be pushed into the ground. The most stress-free time is spring to summer. Root divisions can be planted in early spring when there is plenty of moisture. Plantings need well-drained soils to prevent root rot problems. Plant in sun to partial shade. Most any soil will grow this groundcover, just loosen it and incorporate 2 inches of organic matter. Plant 4-inch potted plants on 1-foot spacings and 1-gallon pots 18 to 24 inches apart. Water-in and lay down a thin layer of mulch. Water twice weekly until the planting is established.

Growing Tips

Keep plantings moist by irrigating weekly or as needed during its first summer and into fall. Asiatic jasmine is drought tolerant but appreciates a thorough soaking during prolonged dry spells. Six weeks after planting feed using a slow-release fertilizer; another application may be warranted, but stop feeding by September to slow its growth before winter.

Regional Advice and Care

This vining groundcover is easy to grow, but can get rangy without an occasional grooming. It looks best when sheared back to 5 inches or lower. To keep it in-bounds, trimming will be required. Large areas can be sheared using a lawn mower or string trimmer. Asiatic jasmine is not recommended for the upper Piedmont and Mountain regions where winter temperatures dip into the low teens. If cold injury occurs, the roots of established plantings recover in spring. A purple tinge to foliage is normal winter color. Cooperative Extension staff can diagnose problems.

Companion Planting and Design

Asiatic jasmine is a designer's dream to use as a lawn substitute, short wall covering, or difficult space subject to erosion. Plant where it cascades over a bank or retaining wall. In tight spaces it can overrun small shrubs if planted in foundations and mixed borders. Variegated selections are versatile for accent.

Try These

The species is the best for groundcover use. The wonderful 'Snow 'N Summer'™ has pink and white variegation; 'Tricolor' shows promise. Unfortunately, most are not reliably hardy in the Mountains and upper Piedmont.

Creeping Juniper

Juniperus horizontalis

Botanical Pronunciation
jew-NEP-er-us hor-ee-zone-TALH-is

Bloom Period and Seasonal Color
Evergreen blue-green foliage (best in summer)

Mature Height × Spread
4 to 6 inches × 5 to 8 feet

From southern California to the coast of North Carolina, gardeners love 'Blue Rug' juniper, one of the woody evergreens we call "creeping junipers." This cultivar is arguably the finest prostrate juniper in its class. 'Blue Rug' juniper hugs the ground with intense blue-green foliage. It is a moderate grower, and it sporadically forms blue berries. When planted in full sun, it takes on a plum color during the winter months. When you plant it in the proper location, you can enjoy a soft-textured living carpet that is nearly weed free. Junipers can withstand hot, dry weather. If you plant creeping junipers in poorly drained soils, you can expect big problems. They can actually take a little shade better than they can tolerate wet feet.

When, Where, and How to Plant
Plant from late spring to early fall. Creeping junipers adapt to a variety of soils, from light sands to heavier clay soil. In their native habitats, creeping junipers grow best where exposed to full sun, so plant them in areas that receive at least eight hours of sunlight. 'Blue Rug' and other creeping junipers look best when planted in large beds rather than singly. Water well, scatter a granular weed-preventer, then mulch. On steep banks of poor soil, plant Sargents juniper instead of 'Blue Rug'.

Growing Tips
Water your newly planted junipers for fifteen minutes twice each week for the first month, using a hose adjusted to a low flow. Water only during dry periods in summer for its first growing season;

it is drought tolerant. For better color and faster growth, fertilize with a slow-release product (for example, 12-6-6) in spring and early fall.

Regional Advice and Care
Prune creeping junipers only to contour the shape in early spring. Selectively remove individual shoots. You must not allow runner-forming grasses to get started among your creeping junipers. Remove grassy weeds with herbicides; otherwise, hand weed. (One way to safely remove runner-forming grasses is to slip on a cotton glove over a rubber glove. Dip your gloved hand in an herbicide solution, grip the runner and slide it through your hand.) Common diseases and insects include juniper blight, branch dieback, and spider mites, each of which may become serious at times. Declining foliage color is a symptom. Creeping junipers tend to be most resistant to these problems when planted in full sun where there is good air circulation and excellent soil drainage.

Companion Planting and Design
The trailing habit of 'Blue Rug' makes it especially suitable for use on berms or just for its unique color when interspersed among broad-leaved evergreen shrubs. For edging and themed gardens, the dwarf Japanese garden juniper, *Juniperus procumbens*, is a likely choice. 'Prince of Wales' has a similar growth habit but remains green year-round.

Try These
'Blue Rug' is a personal favorite for slopes and as a facing plant in mixed shrub borders.

Creeping Phlox

Phlox spp. and hybrids

Botanical Pronunciation
FLOKS

Other Name
Thrift

Bloom Period and Seasonal Color
Spring in pink, magenta, white, blue, and lavender

Mature Height × Spread
4 to 12 inches by 10 to 24 inches

Throughout the Carolinas in springtime, brilliant sheets of color can be observed on hillsides and in bulb beds. The most common species, *Phlox subulata*, is referred to as thrift. It makes a grand entrance for a few weeks then lives in near obscurity until the next year. What a bold shot of color from a sun-loving groundcover! It is hard not to be impressed with this evergreen denizen of harsh environments. If your landscape has more shade and may be better described as a woodland garden, there are creeping phloxes that equally adapt. Two species, *P. divaricata* and *P. stolonifera*, are attractive native, woodland plants. These carefree jewels form a mat of loosely entwined stems with tender oblong leaves. Softly fragrant flowers are borne on clusters on erect stems.

When, Where, and How to Plant

Purchase and plant creeping phlox in spring for color preference reasons. The woodland phlox requires rich soil and part-sun to shade. Thrift (*P. subulata*) is not fussy about soil type, provided it gets ample sunlight. The planting season for thrift extends throughout the year as its foliage is wiry and equipped for dry sites and extended drought. Plant this species by digging a hole that is twice as wide as the rootball and of equal depth. The soil could benefit from a limestone application. Plant the woodland creeping phlox in soil that is enriched with compost or peat moss. Thoroughly irrigate new plantings. The best soil is well-drained but stays moist during the blooming season.

Growing Tips

In hot summers, when weekly rainfall is less than an inch, irrigate woodland phlox until it is well established. Thrift will not need special attention after the first summer and can be damaged by overwatering. Mulch plantings in natural settings, and use a monthly application of a water-soluble flower fertilizer to help thin stands fill in. Apply slow-release fertilizer, as needed, after the bloom period to this sun-lover.

Regional Advice and Care

Shade-loving woodland species need no pruning other than normal grooming. Dense masses can be thinned and divided in fall or winter. Gardeners in Zone 8 with sandy soils will appreciate the durability of thrift and its drought-tolerance. Shear back by one-half after flowering is completed to keep plantings compact. Few pests bother creeping phlox. Loss of plantings can be attributed to too much water and planting where soils do not drain well.

Companion Planting and Design

Combine with trillium, Spanish bluebell, columbine, foamflower, and hellebore in part sun locales. Work thrift into sunny perennial borders of heuchera, tulip, daffodil, and evergreen azalea. It can serve as an edging plant and spring accent.

Try These

Phlox subulata 'Candy Stripe' is glowing pink with a white stripe. *P. divaricata* 'Blue Moon' or 'Clouds of Perfume' are distinctive. *P. stolonifera* 'Home Fires' is hot pink.

Hardy Iceplant

Delosperma cooperi

Botancal Pronunciation
DELL-oh-spur-mah coup-per-EYE

Bloom Period and Seasonal Color
Summer blooms in yellow, purple, and hot pink;
year-round light green foliage

Mature Height × Spread
3 inches × 10 to 18 inches

With a name like hardy iceplant, you would think this groundcover would melt in our summer heat and flourish in the harsh winter weather of our mountains. The opposite is true. This wonderful plant is a member of a family of low-growing succulents native to the deserts of South Africa. Hardy iceplant is a semi-evergreen groundcover introduced to the Carolinas two decades ago. The fleshy leaves of hardy iceplant, shaped like tiny sausages, approach 2 inches long. The dense foliage grows quickly in a hot, sunny garden spot. The long creeping chains of its succulent stems lie flat on the ground and are clothed with daisylike, cerise-pink flowers. No doubt the thickened leaves conserve the plant's moisture, allowing it to survive dry desert-like conditions and winter cold.

When, Where, and How to Plant
Plant potted hardy iceplant during the warmer months. Divide plants for enlarging beds throughout the summer; even non-rooted 4-inch stem segments transplant with virtually 100 percent success. Plant in a sunny spot in well-drained soil. The plants survive in poor soils, and they are pH-adaptable. Hardy iceplant grows best in heavy clay Piedmont soil when 3 inches of play sand is spread to make a perfectly drained seedbed. Space 1 foot apart for spreading room. Water to settle the planting, and forget it for a week. Lightly water new plantings weekly for three weeks.

Growing Tips
Keep in mind that this is a desert plant and too much water is harmful. They are extremely drought tolerant when established and very low maintenance. After new growth appears in spring, feed hardy iceplant with an organic fertilizer. New plants are somewhat fragile, so handle carefully. However, damaged plantings are resilient and always spring back.

Regional Advice and Care
Pruning is not needed, except following winter cold when the fleshy foliage "melts down." Hand shears and a rake will take care of minor cleanup. Remember, iceplant is cold-sensitive in the Mountain region and may need replanting periodically. It can look shabby from December to March. No pests attack it. Avoid low spots where rainwater collects and puddles; root rot can be its nemesis. It's not one of the "steppables;" where there is foot traffic use another groundcover, such as ajuga, 'Georgia Blue' veronica, or leadwort.

Companion Planting and Design
Use hardy iceplant as a low edging in front of perennial borders. It offers a colorful cover on sloping ground and berms. It can be tucked into crevices in stone walls or into open spots in rock gardens where a touch of color is desired. It's versatile and deer resistant.

Try These
The hot pink species performs well in all gardens, including coastal gardens where it takes salt spray. 'Starburst' and 'Lavender Ice' are striking new selections.

Liriope

Liriope muscari

Botanical Pronunciation
luh-RYE-oh-pee muss-CARE-ee

Other Name
Monkey grass

Bloom Period and Seasonal Color
Summer blooms in blue, white, or violet blooms;
solid green or variegated green-and-white foliage

Mature Height × Spread
1 foot × 12 to 18 inches

Liriope, also known affectionately as monkey grass, is extensively planted throughout the Tar Heel and Palmetto states. It is an evergreen, grasslike member of the lily family and is popular for its ease in growing. In midsummer, spikes of violet blooms rise from dark green clumps of foliage, followed by small berries that ripen to black. Liriope is suited to shade or full sun where it can be used to tidy up beds or create a smooth transition from lawn to shrub border. In marginal areas with the worst of conditions, it helps prevent soil from eroding away, serving as a turfgrass substitute. You don't need a "green thumb" to grow liriope, just a hatchet to divide their dense clumps when a neighbor shares this pass-a-long sweetheart.

When, Where, and How to Plant
Potted plants can be added anytime the ground is not frozen. Liriope is slow-growing and thrives in most soils, but if it's planted in loam, the results are dramatic. Plant in sun or dappled shade; in dense shade mondo grass is best for a lawn lookalike. Score potbound rootballs with a knife or roughhouse the rootball to free up roots. Space 1 foot apart. Backfill and water thoroughly to settle the soil. Soluble fertilizer can be used at planting time.

Growing Tips
Water new plants generously the first month and during prolonged dry spells their first season. Liriope resists drought once established. Fertilization is optional; any general garden fertilizer will do. Since lirope is often used along walk- and driveways, please sweep fertilizer particles off hard surfaces to prevent it from washing into water systems. Keep crabgrass seeds from germinating in large, sunny beds by applying a granular weed preventer in early March before mulching. Mulch to a depth of 2 inches.

Regional Advice Care
No pruning is required during the growing season. In late winter, before spring growth emerges, trim to within 3 inches of the ground to remove cold-damaged foliage. In shade gardens, there is no need to shear back. Sometimes rabbits or deer will chew liriope; apply an animal repellent. Remove grassy weeds by hand or select an approved selective herbicidal "grass killer." Constantly wet soils can kill plants. If you notice scale insects or vole damage, consult your Extension agent for advice.

Companion Planting and Design
'Big Blue' is fabulous when underplanted *en masse* with groups of river birch or tree form crapemyrtles. Add where space is limited and in containers. Variegated liriope complements plantings of loropetalum and numerous broadleaf evergreens. Use on hard-to-mow slopes and rough settings. The one to avoid is creeping liriope, *L. spicata*, as it becomes invasive. However, it tolerates deplorable conditions when installed on a steep bank.

Try These
'Variegata' and 'Silvery Sunproof' take sun and are quite spectacular when in flower. 'Peedee Gold Ingot' sports chartreuse foliage to light up dark areas. 'Majestic' is for part shade.

Mondo Grass

Ophiopogon japonicus

Botanical Pronunciation
O-fee-O-poe-gon juh-PON-i-cuss

Other Name
Dwarf lilyturf

Bloom Period and Seasonal Color
Year-round dark green foliage; pale lilac flowers in season

Mature Height × Spread
3 to 10 inches × spreading

Carolina gardeners reply upon mondo grass to link shady areas to the sunnier landscape elements. It is similar to the ever-popular liriope, but is more refined and grasslike in texture with leaves ⅛ inch wide. Comparing growth rates, mondo grass is slower and takes time to establish. A mature stand of dwarf lilyturf is a magnificent sight and a well-groomed planting is a gardener's pride and joy. Standard mondo grass can mound to 10 inches high and is a good choice for a power mower-free lawn under tall shade trees. The groundhugging 'Nana' forms little green buns and is frequently selected to use among stepping stones and in specialty applications, such as Asian garden design. Few groundcovers are so versatile and docile.

When, Where, and How to Plant
Plant mondo grass in spring or summer to allow time for establishment. It prefers moist, fertile soil and a little shade during the day. Full shade is acceptable; just accommodate its water needs during the first couple of years where tree roots compete. Unless pots are planted singly, till up the area where this long-lived groundcover will be installed. Incorporate a large volume of organic amendment to enhance the soil. When the soil is prepared properly, hand planting is a snap. Spread your mulch first, then plants. Position a sprinkler to keep the installation moist for a month. Space 6 to 10 inches apart.

Growing Tips
Pay attention to irrigation in the first season or two. Late spring applications of compost or organic fertilizer will increase its growth rate. Use a leaf rake to disperse the material through the fine foliage. Like spreading liriope, you will need an edging installed to check the spread of stolons or suckering into adjacent lawns. Use a string trimmer or hedge clipper to remove cold-damaged foliage in spring on the species variety.

Regional Advice and Care
Mountain counties at high elevations may have difficulty growing this groundcover as hardiness is questionable in Zone 6. However, in warmer zones it should be grown extensively. Once a planting has settled in, dwarf mondo grass is carefree and durable. It is reported that mondo grass is host to scale insects in the Deep South though the author has not seen this problem in the Piedmont. Remove fall leaves to prevent them from smothering plantings.

Companion Planting and Design
The shining star is dwarf mondo grass; it is stylish in small, formal gardens. Use it for edging an entrance, walkway, or border. Plant between stepping stones in woodland settings. Mondo grass is adapted for replacing grass under dense shade; just think, no more mowing!

Try These
Dwarf forms 'Nana' and 'Gyoku Ryu' are tops for urban gardens. The black foliage of *Ophiopogon planiscapus* cultivars adds interest in part-shade areas and containers.

Pachysandra

Pachysandra terminalis

Botanical Pronunciation
pak-uh-SAN-druh tur-muh-NAL-is

Other Name
Japanese spurge

Bloom Period and Seasonal Color
Nonshowy, white spring flowers and year-round dark green or variegated foliage

Mature Height × Spread
8 to 10 inches × 12 to 18 inches

Pachysandra is an evergreen groundcover grown in shade gardens throughout the world. It has veined, toothed leaves, 2 to 4 inches long, that grow in clusters at the top of upright stems. This plant may not be as exciting as many other groundcovers since it doesn't produce showy blooms, but its redeeming quality is its dense growth in full-shade conditions. It grows by means of stolons (aboveground stems) and flourishes in moist leaf litter. This gem flourishes in the shade of dogwoods and towering oaks where the lawn gives up the ghost. The key is mulching, then letting pachysandra do the rest. Wildflower gardeners are fans of our underrated mountain native *Pachysandra procumbens*. It grows slower than the Japanese type but has mottled leaves and small, fragrant pink flowers.

When, Where, and How to Plant

Set out potted pachysandra in early spring or late fall when soils are reasonably moist. New plants can be started from divisions in spring; divide by cleaving clumps with two spades and prying them apart. Japanese spurge prefers full or part shade and moist, acidic soils. Allegheny spurge, *P. procumbens*, is more tolerant of limey soils. Groundcovers are as close to being permanent plantings as anything, so a well-prepared bed makes sense for large plantings. For the best growth, pachysandra needs moist soil with plenty of organic mulch. A mulch layer will encourage faster growth since the stolons don't have to fight their way into tight or compacted soils. Planting under trees may be a challenge, so put on your kneepads and dig wide, shallow planting holes. Keep the soil moist by watering twice weekly for the first month and then as needed.

Growing Tips

Irrigate to maintain health in the drier years. Pachysandra should not need fertilizer the first year. If the color looks good in summer, don't fertilize at all. Every few years a spring application of slow-release fertilizer can be made; too much fertilizer can kill sections of the bed, so go easy! Scatter aged leaf compost over old beds to invigorate.

Regional Advice and Care

Pachysandra never needs pruning, though beds may be edged. Your Extension agent can advise you if dead circular patches (Volutella fungus or tip blight) occur, especially in poorly drained areas, or if you see scorched foliage. Sunburn is common in sunny beds under deciduous cover, resulting in yellow leaves in winter. The biggest challenge is removing leaves from plantings in fall. A leaf blower does wonders if you start early in autumn before rain packs down the leaves.

Companion Planting and Design

Pachysandra is suitable for large-scale planting projects or in small gardens for a lush look. Add to plantings of moisture-loving clethra, hydrangea, and Japanese maple. Place Allegheny spurge on the forest's edge to naturalize.

Try These

'Green Sheen' has attractive lustrous leaves. For shade, try variegated 'Silver Edge'. Search native plant suppliers online to find starts of Allegheny spurge, *P. procumbens*.

Vinca

Vinca minor

Botanical Pronunciation
VING-kuh MY-nor

Other Name
Common periwinkle

Bloom Period and Seasonal Color
Early spring flowers in violet blue, white, or plum red

Mature Height × Spread
6 inches × 36 inches

Whether you call it vinca or periwinkle, this evergreen groundcover is popular anywhere there is a shaded garden. It sends out vinelike shoots that root readily, making the plant quite attractive to gardeners. Once established, this durable perennial will resist drought like a champ. The narrow-leaved, dark green species has slender, 1- to 2-inch leaves that hold their outstanding color despite the cold of winter. In the spring, it delights the gardener with a wonderful show of nickel-sized blue flowers. What could be more peaceful than large shade trees surrounded by a forest green groundcover dotted with soft blue flowers? The broad-leaf vinca species, *Vinca major*, is not recommended because it tends to escape and run wild in forest lands. Add it to container plantings.

When, Where, and How to Plant

Set out potted plants in spring or fall, or divide clumps in late winter and spring. Vinca prefers light shade and moist soil but is adaptable. In woodland gardens where the humus layer is deep with decaying leaves, this groundcover gallops across the forest and steep banks. Plant vinca with the top of its rootball slightly above grade. Water plants well and cover the surface roots with loamy topsoil or bark mulch. A water-soluble starter fertilizer can be applied when planting. You will need 100 clumps to cover a 10-foot by 10-foot area. It helps to mulch before planting in large areas; crabgrass preventer can be used in part-sun locations only until the plantings fill in.

Growing Tips

Water as needed during the first two summers. Once established, vinca tolerates drought, but responds to late summer irrigation to keep it looking lustrous. Fertilize every other year using a slow-release product. In older beds, maintain growth by mulching periodically with a fine layer of compost or bagged cow manure in lieu of fertilizer. Irrigate after fertilizing if dry products are used.

Regional Advice and Care

Vinca is virtually maintenance free. Tip prune only if your personal taste dictates. If a stem blight disease strikes, prune out the plate-sized dead patches. Consult an expert about using a preventative fungicide in early spring, and repeat if necessary. To avoid fierce competition for water, don't plant vinca in an azalea bed or among newly planted trees unless those areas are irrigated. Groom beds after fall leaf drop.

Companion Planting and Design

Plant vinca for its spring flowers that complement daffodil beds. Use it as an edging for shrubs or borders. Many of us have large, shaded areas where it is difficult to grow anything; vinca will naturalize in these areas. Vinca partners well with dense evergreen shrubs like boxwood and holly, but be sure you keep plantings from running amok.

Try These

'Bowles' is the standard in the trade. 'Illumination' and 'Wojo's Gem' have stunning gold variegation for containers. 'Moonlit' has double blue blooms, 'Atropurpurea' sports plum-purple flowers, and 'Alba' has white blooms.

LAWNS

FOR THE CAROLINAS

Treat your lawn like a garden and you'll have great-looking turfgrass. Our temperate climate in the Carolinas is suitable for growing either cool-season or warm-season grasses. In the western region, we can have success with bluegrass, perennial ryegrass, and tall fescue. On the coast and south, St. Augustinegrass and carpetgrass are fine choices, depending on the location of your lawn. The Piedmont is the transition zone where you will find a plethora of turfgrass varieties and cool-season blends. The cardinal rule is don't mix cool-season and warm-season turfgrasses together, or your lawn will have the appearance of a checkerboard in spring!

Choose the Right Grass for Your Location

Often the most important contributions to a high-quality lawn is the number of hours of direct sunlight your property receives in the summer. The warm-season turfgrasses win hands-down in the warmer Zone 8, and some Zone 7 gardens have bermudagrass or zoysia lawns. Unfortunately, there's no way to have a green lawn twelve months of the year with this class of grasses unless you overseed with perennial ryegrass in the fall—or dye the grass green! For this reason, most residents prefer to sow their lawns in tall fescue mixtures. These cool-season varieties tolerate partial shade and provide a lush green lawn during the time that our dogwoods and azaleas are at their peak of bloom. Again, turfgrass requires direct sunlight to survive more than a year or two.

Best Management Practices Ensure Success

North Carolina State University and Clemson University agronomists have developed an establishment-and-maintenance program for every grass variety grown in the Carolinas.

To have a beautiful lawn, it is important to follow the program. This means maintaining the proper mowing height for the variety, fertilizing on schedule, and irrigating during the growth cycle. As for the new lawn establishment, the key to a high-quality lawn is soil preparation. (This is a critical step whether you are seeding, sprigging, or laying sod.) Test the soil; acidic soil is a lawn's nemesis. Incorporate the recommended amount of limestone by tilling it into the top 5 to 8 inches of soil before seeding. Poorly drained soils benefit greatly from the addition of bark

Before seeding your lawn, spread amendments across the top of the soil and use a shovel or rototiller to mix them in.

soil conditioner (25 percent by soil depth) during soil prep. Apply a starter fertilizer and rake well to ready for seeding.

Choose the right grass for your area to have the greenest lawn.

Good Seed Is the First Step

Always buy good grass seed—one with high seed purity and low weed-seed content. Check the label and choose one with low "crop seed"; otherwise, you will find it difficult to eliminate the stray grassy weeds that sprout with your new turfgrass. Extensive turfgrass research conducted annually at NCSU yields numerous top performing cultivars for the Carolinas. Visit a garden center and write down the cultivars offered. Then, visit three websites: www.ntep.org, virtual.clemson.edu/groups/turfornamental, and www.turffiles.ncsu.edu to research.

In lieu of seeding, consider quality sod for a new lawn. Consult a lawn care professional for a quote on sod installation; the cost may be comparable to seeding. When laying sod, always use good quality turfgrass that is fresh at the time of installation.

Turfgrasses Are Plants, too!

A lawn has more plants per square foot than any garden space on your property. For a high-quality lawn, you must make a commitment to provide the basic needs of the millions of individual grass plants in your yard. Every grass plant will need room to grow, air for its root system, water during its active growth stage, fertilization, and proper maintenance.

When your new grass is tall enough to mow, go ahead and mow but never remove more than one-third of the top growth with each mowing. This prevents starving the root system and giving weeds the upper hand. Once the lawn is established, follow a regimen of recommended practices that will ensure high-quality, dense turfgrass. This doesn't mean indiscriminate pesticide dumping on your property. You must be consistent with your mowing practices, weed control, and fertilization; on clay soils, core aeration pays big dividends.

When selecting fertilizers, use a turf-starter product with new lawn establishment. Slow-release turf fertilizers are economical for their benefits and are less apt to pollute groundwater. For most grass varieties, apply the equivalent of 1 pound of nitrogen per 1,000 square feet of lawn. The amount of product to use can be determined by dividing the first number on the fertilizer bag into 100. For example, 4.3 pounds of 23-7-7 fertilizer is needed for 1,000 square feet.

Minimize the Competition

Thick turf provides the best defense against weeds. Neglect and poor maintenance guarantee bare spots that quickly fill in with weeds. Until you have a dense turf, you may consider using lawn herbicides. Some will prevent summer crabgrass if applied in March, or winter chickweed with a September treatment. Some selectively control broadleaf or grassy weeds. In the case of common bermudagrass encroachment on tall fescue lawns, homeowners frequently eradicate the infested lawn in summer and seed again in fall. However, applying a selective grass killer containing fluazifop may be an option worth considering. Interest in organic lawn control continues to grow. This is a healthy trend, but it requires patience and above-average knowledge in the field of Integrated Pest Management (IPM). For most people, using organic fertilizers, removing thatch, and properly identifying turf problems are steps in the right direction.

A Beautiful Tall Fescue Lawn

To reap the rewards of a handsome tall fescue or tall fescue/bluegrass lawn, take great care in the selection, maintenance, and renovation of your turfgrass. The key to a successful lawn is getting the grass well established at the beginning of its growth cycle. Gardeners in the Piedmont and west are best served by the cool-season turf types, primarily tall fescue blends or mixtures, seeded in late summer and fall.

Many people try to duplicate golf course perfection and are often disappointed with their attempts at lawn care. One extreme on the lawn care scale is a perfectly green carpet of turfgrass on which no one is allowed to walk, versus the other extreme in which fertilizing is considered bad because it equates to more mowing. Most people probably fall somewhere between these two extremes. Fortunately, a beautiful lawn is attainable for those who are willing to spend reasonable amounts of time and money on their yards. Keep in mind that a beautiful tall fescue lawn next spring begins this fall. Use this lawn care guide to get started!

Getting Started with a New Lawn

- When planting a new lawn, make soil preparation a priority. Eliminate perennial weeds either mechanically or with glyphosate products starting three weeks out. Have the soil tested. Based on the results, apply the needed lime and fertilizer, and mix these materials thoroughly into the top 5 to 8 inches of the soil. Note: the soil must drain well.
- For seeding a fescue lawn, the rule of thumb is to apply 6 to 8 pounds per 1,000 square feet of lawn. Use a turf-type tall fescue mixture, such as a shade mix, if your yard has lots of trees.
- Mulch the newly seeded lawn lightly with straw to reduce erosion and to maintain soil moisture. Don't overdo it; one or two bales will cover 1,000 square feet.
- Keep the seed moist with frequent light waterings, twice or more daily.
- As the seed begins to germinate, water for longer periods and less frequently.
- Begin mowing when the grass is about 4 inches high and continue routine mowing.

How to Renovate an Existing Lawn

- Early fall is the best time to renovate tall fescue lawns. Renovation is defined as overseeding an existing stand of grass.
- Remove weeds prior to overseeding. If using an herbicide, follow instructions. Remember to use post-emergence herbicides 4 to 6 weeks before overseeding. If you use a non-selective herbicide, such as Roundup™, do so seven to ten days prior to renovation.
- Mow grass at the lowest setting and collect the clippings. If needed, use a dethatcher at this time to collect thatch in the grass. Then core aerate (also called aerification or plugging) to provide good seed-to-soil contact.
- Apply a starter fertilizer over the prepared lawn area, according to directions.
- Apply the grass seed at the rate of about 3 pounds per 1,000 square feet of area.
- Keep the renovated area moist with light sprinklings of water several times daily. As the seed germinates, reduce the frequency of watering.
- Mow the renovated lawn at a height of 2½ to 3½ inches. Do not bag clippings.
- In November, make your second fertilizer application. Also apply pelletized lime in November if the soil test indicates a need.
- Use proper lawn management to prevent having to renovate annually.

Lawn Care Maintenance

- If you have not had a soil test within the last two to three years, do it now. Test results will indicate how much lime, nitrogen, phosphorus, and potassium your lawn needs. You can use a complete fertilizer with a ratio of 4-1-2 or 3-1-3 (N-P-K) in lieu of a soil test, but it is not a good substitute for a soil test. Fertilize the fescue lawn in September, November, and February using 1 pound of nitrogen per 1,000 square feet of lawn.
- Continue to water the lawn in the fall, applying about 1 inch of water per week slowly to allow for soil absorption. Irrigate in the early morning hours.
- For weed problems, apply a broadleaf herbicide in early fall. Be sure to follow label directions. Contact spray treatments are best, but weed-and-feed products are convenient.
- Core-aerate compacted lawns to move air and water down to the roots. This can be followed by seeding. If your lawn is well established, do not overseed.
- Continue to mow tall fescue grass during the fall months at a height of 2½ to 3½ inches.

A high-quality lawn is an asset to your neighborhood and to the environment as a whole. Turfgrasses prevent soil erosion, provide oxygen, filter contaminants, and beautify our landscapes. Your lawn deserves a little attention . . . after all, it is a garden too!

Bermudagrass

Cynodon dactylon

Botanical Pronunciation
SIGN-o-don dak-TILL-on

Color and Texture
Medium green color; medium to fine texture

Best Mowing Height
¾ to 1 inch

Zones
7 to 8

Bermudagrass is a warm-season, sod-forming turfgrass that is dormant in winter and greens up quickly in spring. As temperatures rise, the growth rate of bermudagrass increases. It tolerates drought and loves hot, sunny growing conditions. It is available from commercial sources as seeds, sprigs, and sod. If the soil in your yard is less than perfect (shallow or rocky), bermudagrass is a good choice. Hybrid bermudagrass, which has to be sprigged or sodded, is premier. The most cold-hardy of these hybrids, 'Vamont', covers athletic fields across the Carolinas. Seeded varieties such as 'Princess', 'Shangri la', 'Sultan', and 'Mohawk' consistently perform well, producing dense, high-quality turf. Overseeding established bermudagrass in the fall with ryegrass provides a green lawn during the dormant season.

When, Where, and How to Plant
Seed bermudagrass about the time dogwoods bloom. Sprigging and sodding can be done two weeks after trees green up in spring through June. Bermudagrass prefers full sun; sprigging in shady lawns gives poor results. It often creeps into partially shaded areas by means of its prolific rhizomes. Take a soil test; strive for 6.0 pH. Rototill the soil, mixing in lime and fertilizer. Rake all the clods for the finished grade. Broadcast seed with a cyclone seeder at the rate of 1 pound per 1,000 feet (or 3 pounds unhulled seed). Lightly rake in seed and apply wheat straw mulch at forty bales per acre. Roll the lawn to firm-in the seed; water daily until the grass seed germinates. The sprigging rate for hybrid bermudagrass is ¾ bushel of sprigs per 1,000 feet. Press sprigs into the top inch of soil by hand or using a disk plow.

Water 1 inch, slowly, to new lawns, preferably in 30-minute increments.

Growing Tips
Keep soil continuously moist until seed germinates or the sprigs begin growing vigorously. Reduce watering to twice weekly until the grass establishes. Water throughout the first growing season. This may mean more watering in dry weather. Fertilize every four weeks until mid-August with 3 pounds of 34-0-0 or equivalent per 1,000 square feet.

Regional Advice and Care
Reel-type mowers are preferred. After establishment, bermudagrass requires minimal care. The biggest objection to using "wiregrass" is its invasive nature—it will thrive in your flower and shrub beds. This was a major issue before the advent of selective grass herbicides. These products can be sprayed into ornamental plantings. Mow, thatch, and edge frequently. Consider using a winterizer fertilizer in August. Raise the mowing height in fall. There are no serious pest problems.

Landscape Use
Bermudagrass withstands wear and foot traffic, especially for recreational purposes. It recovers rapidly from injury, and takes drought, salt, and heat. It can also be seeded.

Try These
Tifway 419 is a sterile hybrid available as sod. TifSport tolerates foot traffic. New seeded bermudagrass hybrids are looking good. Shade varieties may be in our future!

Carpetgrass

Axonopus fissifolius

Botanical Pronunciation
ak-on-NO-puss fiss-ee-FOL-ee-us

Other Name
Louisianagrass

Color and Texture
Light green color; coarse texture

Best Mowing Height
1½ to 2¼ inches

Zone 8

I n coastal regions of the Carolinas where infertile, wet soils are not uncommon, carpetgrass offers uncompromising utility. This low-growing grass naturalizes where planted and eventually spreads like a groundcover into marginalized areas. Though not as popular as other warm-season types, it is a viable option in this hot, humid region. Carpetgrass has a creeping habit like Kentucky bluegrass, producing persistent stolons in acidic soils that are poorly drained. A carpetgrass lawn could be mistaken for one of centipedegrass was it not for its lighter green color and proliferation of rangy seedheads in summer. This coarse-textured grass has wavy leaf margins. Its ragged, unmown look may not appeal to everyone, but this turfgrass gets the job done in the Southeast.

When, Where, and How to Plant
Carpetgrass can be seeded, sprigged, or plugged in spring. Wait until the soil warms and growth starts before beginning planting. It grows in wetter soils where few grasses thrive and performs best in moist soil. Take a soil test before applying limestone for soil preparation; pH 5.0 to 6.0 is ideal. Incorporate a seed-starter fertilizer after tilling the ground for seeding. Rake to create a smooth seeding surface. Use a rotary spreader to apply seed at 2 pounds per 1,000 square feet. Hint: mix fine sand with seed. Though it's not frequently planted as sprigs, complete this task as you would other warm-season grasses using 1½ bushels of sprigs on a similar area. Be prepared to control weeds until sprigged lawns establish. Keep soil moist during its first six weeks.

Growing Tips
This grass will need occasional watering during late summer to avoid shallow root development in dry soils. Fertilize lightly with a 10-0-10 or similar general garden fertilizer in early June at the rate of ½ pound of nitrogen per 1,000 square feet. Too much fertilizer and the seedhead production increases, not a desirable trait. Apply a second fertilizer application in mid-August using a slow-release product. Mow frequently to keep a tidy appearance and remove unsightly, crab-grass-like seedheads. Keep the mower blades sharp. Carpetgrass is sensitive to herbicides; manage weeds by hand and mowing.

Regional Advice and Care
Choose this turfgrass for the warmest locations in the Carolinas where it can be found flourishing in low-lying yards of Zones 8b to 9. It has poor drought tolerance. Though its quality is not what you may get in St. Augustinegrass, it is a trade-off in questionable sites that have shade issues. It should not be bothered by chinch bugs, but nematodes may be problematic. Do not interplant with other warm-season grasses to avoid competition and stand loss. A lawn maintenance calendar is available at www.turffiles.ncsu.edu.

Landscape Use
Carpetgrass does not produce a high-quality turf, but it is a true problem-solver where sustainability carries a high priority. Sow seed in wet, shady, acidic soils.

Try These
There are no improved cultivars.

Centipedegrass

Eremochloa ophiuroides

Botanical Pronunciation
era-mow-CLOW-ah off-ee-ure-OY-dees

Color and Texture
Apple green color; fine-textured

Best Mowing Height
1 inch

Zone 8

Centipedegrass is one of the most popular lawn grasses in the warm Southeast. Its major strengths are low growth habit, tolerance of acidic soil and shade, and low fertilizer requirements. One major disadvantage is its susceptibility to winter injury when planted in the Piedmont region and west. It is relatively easy to establish, and its seed, though expensive, is readily available in garden centers. Compared to hybrid bermudagrass, it grows slowly and has a gray color. It propagates by means of horizontal spreading stems. Allow three years for full establishment. Centipedegrass does not produce a dense sod, but it makes a beautiful low-maintenance lawn where it can be planted. You could call it "an ideal grass for the couch potato."

When, Where, and How to Plant

March through early July is the planting season for centipedegrass in the Piedmont and Coastal regions. Centipedegrass won't grow in the cold mountains. It will take two or three years to establish from seed; a quicker method is to plant sod or plugs. Centipedegrass is a sun-loving turfgrass, but it will thrive in partially shaded lawns. Have the soil tested before establishing a centipedegrass lawn. Plant in soil with a pH of 5.0 to 5.5; a higher pH will cause it to be perpetually yellow due to an iron deficiency. Incorporate recommended amounts of fertilizer and limestone into the soil. You will have better establishment if you irrigate the lawn a few days before seeding to allow the soil to settle. Use a hand-cranked rotary seeder to sow. The seeding rate is ¼ to ½ pound of seed per 1,000 square feet of lawn. Apply clean straw mulch at a rate of thirty to forty bales per acre. If plugging centipedegrass, for

every 1,000 square feet use 3 square yards of sod cut into 2-inch squares set on 12-inch centers. *Water!*

Growing Tips

Centipedegrass is slow to establish unless sod is used. Irrigate twice a week, more often for seedlings. Mowing is less often with this turfgrass. Fertilize with ½ pound of nitrogen per 1,000 square feet in June (and again in August on the Coast). Avoid using any phosphorus after establishment. Overfertilized lawns, though dark green, are short-lived and might succumb to disease and winterkill. Save your money for other gardening activities.

Regional Advice and Care

Winter temperatures, even in Zone 7b, can be too extreme for centipedegrass. Use a reel-type mower at a mowing height of 1 inch to cut this lawn. It can tolerate drought by going semi-dormant. If thatch buildup becomes a problem, consider power raking or core aerification, but do not burn lawns. Apply iron sulfate if the grass is yellowing. Ground pearls and nematodes are serious pests; consult your Cooperative Extension for help.

Landscape Use

Primarily associated with the Coastal Plain region. It does not tolerate foot-traffic and should not be used for recreational purposes.

Try These

TifBlair® has the best cold hardiness offered by commercial sod farms. Generic seed is commonly used in coastal plantings.

St. Augustinegrass

Stenotaphrum secundatum

Botanical Pronunciation
sten-o-TAF-rum second-DATE-um

Color and Texture
Pale to medium to dark green color; very coarse texture

Best Mowing Height
2 to 3 inches

Zone 8

While zoysia grows at a snail's pace, St. Augustinegrass gallops like a thoroughbred when it is planted. This fast-growing, coarse-textured turfgrass is in the same class as bermudagrass; both flourish in the warm months and go dormant after the first frosts. Residents in the southeastern counties of the Carolinas like this drought-resistant and shade-tolerant grass. St. Augustinegrass has tropical origins and broad, rigid leaf blades. It spreads aggressively by means of stolons, making a dense, spongy sod and beautiful lawn. Anyone growing this grass knows that it will require periodic edging. It is best adapted to warm, humid areas without periods of cold weather. Beachfront property owners will appreciate its salt- tolerance and affinity for sandy soil.

When, Where, and How to Plant

Plant St. Augustinegrass when average daytime temperatures are above 60 degrees Fahrenheit. Small areas can be sodded until early July. This warm-season grass thrives in fertile, well-drained soil and part to full shade. It is not tolerant of heavy playground traffic, nor will it survive in the cold western regions. Begin with a soil test. Apply amendments as recommended. Using a rototiller, incorporate amendments into the top 6 to 8 inches of soil. After leveling the yard with a rake or harrow, plug or sprig the lawn using plugs planted on 12-inch centers. Space and plant sprigs at the rate of 1½ square yards of sod per 1,000 square feet. Water thoroughly the first week after planting, applying ½ inch of water every three days.

Growing Tips

Keep the soil slightly moist during the first summer to prevent drought stress. Proper irrigation will also prevent pest attacks. Fertilize in May, June, and August with ½ pound of nitrogen per 1,000 square feet using a 3-1-2 analysis turf-grade fertilizer.

Regional Advice and Care

This grass is sensitive to low winter temperatures in Zones 7 to 8a; it likes to stay warm. Maintain the mowing height at 2 to 3 inches. Dethatch when the thatch layer gets ¾ inch thick (check in late spring). St. Augustinegrass is sensitive to some post-emergence herbicides. Control summer weeds while they are small and when the grass is not drought stressed. Chinch bugs can kill this turfgrass. Check for these pests in sunny locations by pushing a coffee can into the ground and pouring a quart of soapy water on the turf. Treat if you see twenty chinch bugs per square foot. St. Augustinegrass encroaches on ornamental plantings, so be prepared to edge beds and do a little grunt work. Fortunately, this grass yields more easily than bermudagrass.

Landscape Use

St. Augustinegrass is best adapted to warm, humid coastal lawns. It does not take cold.

Try These

The Raleigh variety has the best cold tolerance. Floratam is resistant to chinch bugs.

Tall Fescue

Festuca arundinacea

Botanical Pronunciation
fes-TUKE-ca a-RUN-dee-nace-ee-ah

Color and Texture
Deep green color; medium to coarse texture

Best Mowing Height
2 to 3½ inches

Zones 6 to 7

Tall fescue is one of the Carolinas' most widely used turfgrasses. When compared with other bunch-type grasses, this cool-season grass has excellent heat and drought tolerance. It is often preferred over the warm-season grasses since it remains evergreen practically year-round. Though the old standard is 'Kentucky 31', plant breeders have introduced new cultivars that are lower growing and darker green with narrower blades. They are referred to as "turf-type" tall fescues; all produce a dense, high-quality turf at lower mowing heights. Studies support claims of improved brown patch disease resistance when a blend of several cultivars is used. No wonder that more lawns are seeded with tall fescue than any other grass variety.

When, Where, and How to Plant
The first step to a healthy tall fescue lawn is a soil test. Till and rake the soil, adding leaf compost or soil conditioner. Cool-season lawns seeded in September have better summer survivability. Buy quality seed that has few weeds. Till and rake the ground; broadcast seed at the rate of 6 to 8 pounds per 1,000 square feet. Spread fertilizer and cover with clean straw. 'K-31', a less desirable pasture grass, requires full sun and high mowing for survival as yard grass. Turf-type cultivars, however, tolerate partial shade though they prefer open sunlight. Until germination occurs, you must irrigate—use a sprinkler daily.

Growing Tips
Once you begin mowing, water weekly or as needed; an irrigation system is preferable. Fescues survive dry summers by browning out; if you cannot irrigate, water every two or three weeks to keep the roots alive. Fertilize twice in the fall (1 pound of nitrogen per 1,000 square feet in September and November) and at half that rate in early March.

Regional Advice and Care
Mow when grass is 4 inches high, removing only 1 inch at each mowing. A thick turf properly mowed and fertilized is the best weed control. Don't scalp your lawn, and leave clippings if you mow regularly. Core aerify (known as "plugging") in fall for long-term maintenance and for reseeding. The reseeding rate is 3 to 4 pounds per 1,000 square feet. Tall fescue is subject to brown patch in summer. In irrigated turf, consider using a fungicide at its onset. Otherwise, spend your hard-earned money on fall reseeding. Thatch only if you are preparing to reseed the lawn. Test your soil every three years in case the pH falls below 6. Pelletized lime is wonderful for maintaining high-quality lawns.

Landscape Use
The finer texture and color of turf-type tall fescue cultivars make an attractive lawn. You can have a lush, green lawn in sunny or filtered shade almost year-round with minimal fertilization.

Try These
A blend provides a high-quality lawn. Mixtures containing fine fescue are best in shade. Good performers include Rebel III, Wolfpack, Jaguar 3, Endeavor, and Dynasty. The National Turfgrass Evaluation Program offers more cultivars.

Zoysia

Zoysia japonica

Botanical Pronunciation
ZOY-see-ah juh-PON-i-ca

Color and Texture
Medium green; fine-textured

Best Mowing Height
¾ to 1 inch

Zones 7 to 8

Zoysia is so thick that weeds don't stand a chance! It becomes a lush green carpet under your feet in the hotter months. Once established it tolerates drought like bermudagrass, but grows slower. However, zoysia is brown for as many months as it is green. Consequently, if you plant this grass in the Piedmont or western region of the Carolinas, you will probably get some disapproving looks each winter from neighbors who have lush, green, tall fescue lawns. This dormant period can also detract from the early-spring garden display unless it is dyed green. Zoysia grasses are cold hardy throughout the state and they are being used as a substitute for tall fescue. Plant the fast-spreading 'El Toro' on a slope that is too steep to mow.

When, Where, and How to Plant

Plant zoysia in spring and early summer—at least two weeks following spring "greenup." Don't fall prey to the slick zoysia ads. Professionals use sod, purchased by the pallet. Zoysia can be seeded, but that practice is best left to sod growers. It likes hot sites and full sun. It will tolerate partial shade, but grows slowly. Optimum soil pH is 6.0. Broadcast lawn-starter fertilizer and limestone; rototill the nutrients to a depth of 5 to 6 inches. This step is crucial for establishing a permanent lawn. Rake or harrow to leave the soil surface as smooth as possible. Sprig in May or June, using ¼ square yard of sprigs (1 to 2 bushels of stolons) for every 1,000 square feet. Press the sprigs into the top ½ of soil or cover with a ½ of topsoil. When plugging, cut the sod into 2-by-2-inch or larger squares; plant on 1-foot spacing. Water daily for two weeks after planting.

Growing Tips

Irrigate weekly, applying 1 inch of water during the first growing season. In succeeding years taper off; prevent summer brownout by irrigating during drought. Fertilize zoysia twice a year with 10-10-10 or 34-0-0 fertilizer, in May and July at the ½ pound of nitrogen rate per 1,000 square feet. Yards established using zoysia plugs can take up to two years to fill in.

Regional Advice and Care

In early spring mow off its winter foliage to groom. Mow before the grass gets 2 inches high, cutting to ¾ to 1 inch high. A reel-type mower is preferable since push-mowing a zoysia lawn is strenuous. Zoysia occasionally needs dethatching in summer to prevent dieback. Established zoysia can be overseeded with perennial ryegrass in fall. There are no serious pest problems. Edge shrub beds to prevent encroachment.

Landscape Use

Low-maintenance zoysia can also be used as a groundcover on sloping land. Zoysia feels pleasing on bare feet, but it creeps into beds. It survives drought by going semi-dormant.

Try These

Fine-bladed Emerald is best on level yards. El Toro covers a new lawn in one season. Zenith comes in both seed and sod. Meyer is the most cold-hardy.

ORNAMENTAL GRASSES

FOR THE CAROLINAS

Three decades ago pampas grass was, without exception, the most widely planted ornamental grass by gardeners in the Carolinas. Then, plant explorers and landscape architects began to introduce and promote ornamental grasses for large commercial landscape installations. Adventurous gardeners saw them and asked garden centers to stock them. Now you see at least one plant of ornamental grass in almost every home landscape.

Not everyone appreciates ornamental grasses, perhaps because they have spent hours pulling or digging unwanted grasses out of flowerbeds. And others prefer to populate landscapes with shrubs and perennial flowers rather than ornamental grasses. Yet ornamental grasses continue to gain popularity as more gardeners see their advantages in summer and winter landscapes and as they reach beyond the species that have become so popular as to be in danger of becoming landscape clichés.

Virtually all ornamental grasses are native to other countries. Ecologists call them "exotic" species. Along the way, a few bad visitors were brought in. They have bullied their way into wildlands and are pushing out native species that are ill-equipped to compete with these robust imports. For the most part, however, the ornamental grasses are not aggressive spreaders and represent little or no threat to the environment.

Red fountain grass

Landscape Advantages

Ornamental grasses come in many sizes, from small mounds of sweet flag to mighty clumps of pampas grass. All prefer full sun or afternoon shade. The size, texture, colors, and flower heads of a given cultivar determine its best use in the landscape. For instance, many landscapes have sizable sunny areas

Ornamental grasses serve many purposes in the landscape.

where mowing is difficult, too expensive, or too time consuming. A gardener just wants to fill up the space with something that looks good, isn't expensive, and requires little maintenance. Among the many ornamental grasses, they can find species that will meet those requirements. Like any other landscape plant, these beautiful grasses require upkeep, and it is often in proportion to the size of the plant.

Cultivar Versatility

The variegated cultivars of ornamental grasses may carry cream or white stripes the length of their leaves (like hakone grass *Hakonechloa macra* 'Aureola'), or in the example of at least one cultivar—porcupine grass—across its leaves. All of these look especially good against dark green backgrounds such as those provided by coniferous or broad-leaved evergreen shrubs. And all look good as tall backgrounds against which to display flowers or flowering shrubs of significant size, such as butterfly bush and rose-of-Sharon. All are awesome when backlighted by morning or evening sun slanting low across the garden.

Certain ornamental grasses are an intense silvery blue color like lyme grass, or reddish purple like annual purple fountain grass. Some, like muhly grass, offer spectacular pink clouds to fall gardens providing a single-plant show. Others, like inland sea oats and rattlesnake grass, are grown more for their novel seeds than for their form or foliage.

Ornamental grasses change in size and appearance as they cycle through the seasons. Their presentation varies from flowers and seedheads to blanched foliage caused by frost and winter rains. Many gardeners refuse to cut them back until early spring, preferring to let them stand to deliver strong architectural effect and movement during the winter.

The Other Side of the Story

Leaving large clumps of ornamental grass to fend for themselves leads to their eventual failure. Even near the coast, clumps freeze back part-way, and all the way to the ground farther west. Emerging new blades are partially obscured by the old, and the visual effect is messy. So cutting old clumps to the ground each spring can be approached ritually or with trepidation, depending on your age and energy level. Even with electric-powered hedge shears the job isn't easy, and you are left with large piles of hay. Fortunately, ornamental grasses make good raw material for composting.

Certain ornamental grasses will reward you with far more seedlings than you desire. Common maiden grass, *Miscanthus sinensis*, for example is spreading from its original planting sites along interstate highways and invading adjacent farmlands. Inland sea oats drops so many seeds that the phrase, "like hair on a dog's back," accurately describes the crop of volunteer seedlings. Near the coast, Japanese blood grass, which spreads slowly by underground runners, can get out of control in moist, fertile soil. In city or suburban gardens these problems are manageable, but potentially troublesome grasses should not be planted in country gardens where they can jump the fence into wild lands or roadsides. Though introduced to America with the best of intentions, some have escaped to become pesky weeds. The more responsible garden centers and mail-order suppliers of ornamental grasses are sensitive to environmental issues and present the advantages and disadvantages of ornamental grasses in their descriptions.

Grass Lookalikes

Virtually all ornamental grasses prefer sun and well-drained soil. When it comes to shaded or wet sites, the sedges in the genus *Carex* really shine. Some of the forest understory types grow into perfect mounds of rather wide, grasslike foliage. Others that adapt to stream banks or the shallows of ponds grow knee to waist high. Out in the sun, the sweet flags, *Acorus*, are proving indispensable in moist soil areas. Mondograss, despite its name, is not a grass but is in the Lily family, but no matter. It is found in almost every Carolina shade garden in either dwarf or standard height cultivars.

Soil Preparation

Most ornamental grasses will grow in unimproved soil. However, they will establish sooner and produce better-looking plants in improved soil. If you are among the fortunate few with clay

Pine bark mulch worked into the ground is a good soil amendment.

Cut plants back to about 2 inches in the spring.

loam soil, adding amendments will result in only marginal increases in performance. However, on Piedmont red clay soils, incorporating limestone and a 2-inch layer of organic soil conditioner or aged pine bark will improve drainage, water intake, and microbiological activity in the soil. On sandy soil near the coast and on the old sand dunes running southwest from Pinehurst to Columbia and Aiken, generous amounts of limestone and moistened peat moss or leaf compost worked into the soil will greatly improve its moisture retention. Aged pine bark generally works best on clay soils, peat moss on sand. Initially and thereafter, yearly applications of organic mulch will help maintain a healthy organic content in your soil.

Managing Ornamental Grass

Be prepared for a tedious job when it comes to dividing big, old clumps of ornamental grasses. You'll need a sharp hatchet or machete. When just getting a start, purchase vigorous plants and prepare the soil thoroughly as suggested above. It will take up to a year for these plants to get firmly established and two years for them to grow to significant size. Once they have settled in, your patience will be rewarded. Weeds and weedy grass will try to grow among clumps of ornamental grasses. Save yourself labor by applying an approved granular pre-emergence herbicide that keeps weed and grass seeds from germinating.

The Tip of the Iceberg

Descriptions of a few of the most popular ornamental grasses follow. Entire books are written on the subject. If you need to see the actual plants to visualize how they would look in your garden, visit your nearest botanical or estate garden. A visit to a well-stocked garden center will help, but their plants are young and can't give you more than a hint of how they will look when full grown.

Feather Reed Grass

Calamagrostis × acutiflora 'Karl Foerster'

Botanical Pronunciation
KAL-ah-my-GROS-tis ah-CUE-ti-flor-ah

Bloom Period and Seasonal Color
Summer; light pink plumes that turn tan by winter

Mature Height × Spread
4 to 6 feet × 1 ½ feet

The first Perennial Plant of the Year award of the twenty-first century went to this ornamental grass. It is a shoulder-high, erect grass with highly ornamental flowering plumes. Feather reed grass is one of the most versatile, attractive, low maintenance plants in its class. Its deep green, shiny, narrow blades appear in early spring and hold their color until early winter. Loose feathery plumes called "inflorescences" pop out in hot weather, changing from a pinkish color to a golden tan at maturity. The variety 'Karl Foerster' forms a tidy, attractive clump. The growth habit is vertical with a tuft of foliage 2 to 3 feet tall and flower stems to 5 feet in height. Feather reed grass is called the "perpetual motion grass." It's clear why; the slightest breeze sets it in motion.

When, Where, and How to Plant
Feather reed grass, a cool-season grass, allows planting in early spring or fall. In the western Carolinas, this grass will remain green into early winter because of its tolerance for cold. Plant in sunny locations with good air movement, especially in hot eastern regions. 'Karl Foerster' grows best in well-drained soil with sufficient moisture but adapts to heavier clay soils on drier sites. Set potted plants in beds fortified with organic matter. Prepare new beds by spading or rototilling clay soils and incorporating fine pine bark or compost. Firm-in the plants and water immediately.

Growing Tips
Irrigate every three days for three weeks. Feather reed grass needs watering during the coolest months of spring and fall. It may go into a semi-dormant (but still attractive) state in midsummer due to the heat. Don't fertilize in summer. Apply a turf-grade fertilizer like 16-8-8 in March after green leaves appear; ¼ cup per plant suffices for the spring season. Fertilize again after Labor Day.

Regional Advice and Care
Feather reed grass is sterile and will not reseed itself. Heavy rain or wind causes stems to droop, but they return to vertical after the storm. It is free of serious diseases and insects and overwinters well, even in containers. It's care-free in Zones 6 to 7, but in Zones 8 to 9, high humidity and poor air circulation can aggravate fungal diseases. Korean feather reed grass, *Calamagrostis brachytricha*, can tolerate hot summers in the eastern Carolinas.

Companion Planting and Design
Group in masses for a striking vertical accent in the perennial garden. Use this ornamental grass as a specimen plant by a gate or water garden. For companions, select perennials with large leaves or coarse texture and use feather reed grass as a backdrop. Some designers use it for a fast-growing screen and in large containers with trailing tricolor sweet potato vines.

Try These
'Karl Foerster' and 'Eldorado' are dynamic ornamental grasses. Variegated feather reed grass cultivars 'Overdam' and 'Avalanche' are striking for cooler Zones 6 to 7.

Fountain Grass

Pennisetum setaceum

Botanical Pronunciation
pen-NEH-see-tum set-A-see-um

Bloom Period and Seasonal Color
Summer foxtail-like flower plumes; golden foliage in autumn

Mature Height × Spread
1 to 6 feet × 1 to 4 feet

Zone 8

Fountain grass, a semi-hardy perennial, is immediately recognizable in landscapes or containers. It is by far the most popular and easiest ornamental grass to grow. The fountain grasses are well named, as their narrow leaves form graceful, arching fountains of foliage. Modern landscape designs use this fabulous grass in sweeping, undulating curves. Large containers show the fountain shape and tessellated plumes to good advantage. The purple variety with blond plumes, *Pennisetum setaceum* 'Rubrum', became an instant hit in the South following the Atlanta Olympic Games. *P. orientale* 'Karley Rose' bears beautiful rose-tan plumes on dark green foliage. The dwarf selection 'Little Bunny' looks great as a groundcover. The various species of fountain grass will overwinter in Zone 8 but farther west are treated as annuals.

When, Where, and How to Plant
Fountain grass can be planted anytime from spring through fall as long as the soil is not frozen or too wet. It prefers full sun for optimum growth, and average to good soil is suitable. Dig a hole as deep as the container and twice as wide for individual plantings. Rototill entire beds 8 to 10 inches deep for solid plantings. Space the fuller-figured varieties at least 5 feet apart, while the dwarfs can fill in with 1-foot spacings. Mix a starter fertilizer into the soil and backfill with the loosened soil. Water well at planting and a few weeks following.

Growing Tips
For vigorous growth, water fountain grasses occasionally; they flower more fully and for a longer period with adequate moisture. In spring, provide a CRF product, or 10-10-10 fertilizer at ½ cup per plant. To maintain plant health on sandy soils, summer feeding is recommended. Mulch to a depth of at least 2 inches.

Regional Advice and Care
Fountain grass is relatively trouble free. Apply a granular weed-preventer in group plantings for the season or be prepared to hand weed later. It requires no regular pruning during the growing season and is drought tolerant once established. In early spring or late fall, cut it back to 6 inches high if cold damage occurs. A couple of varieties, like *P. alopecuroides* 'Moudry', self-sow freely in the warmer zones; the black-seeded annual variety can become a weed problem even in Zone 7. Divide large clumps every five years to prevent centers from dying out in crowns. 'Hameln' does not survive wet feet.

Companion Planting and Design
Mass plantings can have a breathtakingly beautiful effect when the wind swirls the foliage. Clusters of fountain grass work quite well as an anchor for the ends of planting beds. Single plants of annual purple fountain grass can serve as focal points in beds of low-growing annuals, and adds a thrill to large containers.

Try These
'Cassian', a 2-foot dwarf, is attractive for edging shrub beds. Colorful introductions like dwarf 'Burgundy Bunny' and tender annual 'Cherry Sparkler' brighten containers.

Maiden Grass

Miscanthus sinensis

Botanical Pronunciation
miss-CAN-thus sigh-NEN-sis

Other Name
Silver grass

Bloom Period and Seasonal Color
Fall; silver-white blooms

Mature Height × Spread
3 to 7 feet × 3 to 5 feet

Maiden grass, once a plain green, has seen a transformation thanks to the breeding efforts of keen plantsmen. New introductions deliver improved forms, colors, and dramatic plumes. The upright, arching leaves of this species have a white midvein that is distinctly visible close up. It is completely hardy all across the Carolinas where it forms large clumps of finely textured silver-green blades. Maiden grass is most useful as a naturalizing grass where it can be used in groups for vertical accent and texture but also kept under control. Its substantial plants can substitute for shrubs. In autumn, the leaves are topped with large, fan-shaped, delicate silver-white blooms. These flower heads are at first reddish, then silver. The autumn foliage turns vivid golden and looks good until beaten down by ice storms.

When, Where, and How to Plant
Maiden grass can be planted spring through fall as long as the soil is workable. Grow in sun, in any type of soil from wetlands to dry, rocky slopes. (Overly rich soil may cause stems to stretch and topple over.) Dig a planting hole twice as wide as the rootball and of equal depth. Space plants 6 to 8 feet to allow for mature spread. Loosen the roots of potbound plants; make several vertical slits in the rootball and shake off soil into the planting hole. Water well to settle the soil. With group plantings, till the entire area instead of digging individual holes. Mulch to a depth of 2 inches.

Growing Tips
Water weekly until it's established. Afterward, water bimonthly if there is no rain. A little water during dry summers will win you a garden friend for life. In May, or one month after planting, feed with a garden fertilizer to help establish a new plant. Fertilize in late spring with a slow-release turfgrass fertilizer for the first two growing seasons. Once established, clumps won't need fertilizing every year; they'll thrive on neglect.

Regional Advice and Care
Remove suckers or daughter-shoots from the base of the grass in late spring for transplanting into new beds. Prune vigorous grasses using power hedge shears or handheld lopping shears. Cut back only during early spring before new growth emerges. You may cut the grass as close as 6 to 8 inches to the ground. Thinning rejuvenates old plantings. Maiden grass resists diseases and insects.

Companion Planting and Design
The feathery plumes make photo ops when reflected in water gardens and pools. Group plantings of tall *Miscanthus* 'Gracillimus' can double as a summer privacy screen and a delightful foil for perennial borders of Mexican bush salvia, 'Red Shield' hibiscus, and lantana. Use dwarf maiden grass cultivars as a backdrop for annuals like pentas, marigold, and sun coleus.

Try These
Dwarf maiden grasses 'Adagio' and 'Little Kitten' are great for smaller yards. Variegated 'Cabaret' and 'Morning Light' are considered the best for color and texture.

Pampas Grass

Cortaderia selloana

Botanical Pronunciation
coor-tah-DARE-e-ah sell-low-A-nah

Bloom Period and Seasonal Color
Summer to winter plumes of silvery white or pink

Mature Height × Spread
5 to 10 feet × 5 to 10 feet

Pampas grass is the matriarch of ornamental grasses. Summer foliage is a light gray-green, turning beige-tan in winter. In September, pampas grass develops its signature feature: 2-feet-long, 8-inch-wide, feather duster flower plumes. They remain throughout winter, providing visual relief to drab landscapes. The plumes display especially well in windy sites or coastal gardens where the tall fluffy heads are continuously on the move. In addition to its dominant presence in the landscape, this giant, clump-forming grass offers low maintenance and high tolerance of drought. *Cortaderia selloana* 'Rosea' has impressive pink blooms and may spread to 10 feet at maturity. Not every landscape is suitable for pampas grass because of its potential size and razor-sharp, arching leaf blades, but where it can be used it is a conversation piece both in fall and winter.

When, Where, and How to Plant
Container-grown pampas grass may be planted during the spring through fall seasons. Plant in full sun in well-drained soil. Set the plant in a hole as deep and twice as wide as the rootball. Backfill with the original soil if it is loamy; mix bark soil conditioner or compost into heavy clay soil before backfilling. Space plants 6 to 9 feet apart for future growth. Water well to settle the soil around the roots. Mulch to a depth of 2 inches. Dig and divide clumps in mid-spring after leaf growth appears.

Growing Tips
Water thoroughly weekly for the first month. Apply a slow-release 2-1-1 ratio lawn fertilizer or similar organic fertilizer around plants when your pampas grass has greened up in mid-spring. Established plants require watering only during extended droughts. In large-group plantings with wide spacings, a weed-preventer may be practical. Consult your Extension agent for herbicide recommendations around newly planted grasses.

Regional Advice and Care
In the Piedmont and western regions of the Carolinas, delay pruning the spent foliage until the worst of the cold has passed, possibly late March. Old leaves add winter protection. Cut back the entire plant (wear gloves and goggles!) to a 9-inch height before any new growth begins. Note: pampas grass seeds produce both male and female plants. The female plants (unlike birds) have the large showy plumes. Purchase plants in fall to get plants with the gaudy plumage. This grass has no pests and is disease-free.

Companion Planting and Design
Use pampas grass as a windscreen on the coast or as a background for a border of fall-blooming perennials. The fluffy plumage is wonderful against the red foliage of Japanese maples or alongside cannas and hardy hibiscus. A pink-flowered variety would make a fine companion for large-frame perennials. If you see pampas grass with red plumes, suspect a Gamecock or Wolfpack fan with spray paint cans.

Try These
The foliage of dwarf *C. selloana* 'Pumila' may remain evergreen in Zones 8b and south; it fits small residential landscapes.

Pink Muhly Grass

Muhlenbergia capillaris

Botanical Pronunciation
MOO-len-BER-gee-ah cap-ILL-air-is

Other Name
Muhly grass

Bloom Period and Seasonal Color
Early fall seedheads in pink or white

Mature Height × Spread
3 to 4 feet × 3 feet

A native American species, pink muhly grass looks best in sizable drifts. Individual plants are green and rather ordinary and insubstantial looking for much of the year. But near the end of August, your drift of muhly grass will look as if a pink fog had settled on it. The flower heads are large and delicate, with the texture of spider webs, and spangled with dew each morning. Its autumn display is spectacular with fall-blooming perennials. You won't find a more drought-tolerant ornamental grass as evidenced by the massive beds popping up on interstate highway medians across the Carolinas. If you think you've seen it somewhere else, wild stands of coarse muhly grass grow in a few undisturbed fields. Given a choice location, your neighbors will marvel at your bed of cotton candy.

When, Where, and How to Plant
To enjoy the pink fog the following summer, set out plants in early fall while the soil is still warm. Plant your potted grass in full sun, in well-drained soil to mimic their native habitat. Muhly grass is particular about where it will settle. It likes well-aerated, rather dry soil. Start with at least twelve plants set on 1-foot centers to create a significant drift in a landscape. Locate the bed so you won't have to see the plain green plants during much of the year but where they'll get attention at bloom stage. Score or cut the root system and shake the rootball before planting. Set them at grade level or slightly higher. Water thoroughly!

Growing Tips
Water the planting twice weekly for two weeks especially if you set the muhly grass in fall or warm weather. Decrease watering to bimonthly between rains or until new growth is observed. Fertilize with 10-10-10 or liquid feed in early summer. Be faithful in keeping your patch of muhly grass weed-free by hand removal or using a scuffle hoe that doesn't dig deep into the soil.

Regional Advice and Care
Let the seedheads stand until at least midwinter to drop seeds and thicken the stand. Muhly doesn't have to be mowed or cut with a string trimmer. If you don't mind a little natural messiness, the new shoots will come up through the old and hide them. Transplant volunteer seedlings to the perimeter of the patch to increase its size.

Companion Planting and Design
Muhly grass is best for naturalizing and is out of place when prettied up with garden flowers or used as an edging. However, in drifts among other ornamental grasses, it's perfectly in place. Burgundy foliage and flowers blooming in September are fine companions in autumn. In scree or rock gardens, plant with sedums and perennial salvia.

Try These
Be sure you specify pink muhly grass. Some species are native to Southwest ecosystems. 'White Cloud' produces billowy white seedheads and is more upright.

Porcupine Grass

Miscanthus sinensis 'Strictus'

Botanical Pronunciation
miss-CAN-thus sigh-NEN-sis

Bloom Period and Seasonal Color
Late summer seedheads in pinkish tan

Mature Height × Spread
4 to 8 feet × 3 to 6 feet

Porcupine grass is a handsome, upright clump-forming *Miscanthus* cultivar. Its unusual horizontal stripes on ½-inch leaves are unique in the plant world. In hot weather *Miscanthus sinensis* 'Strictus' grows quickly to 8 feet including the fan-shaped seedheads held high above the foliage. It makes a terrific landscape accent when used as a specimen plant and viewed in close range to appreciate its signature creamy bands. Place this ornamental grass in a sunny spot where a more structural form is needed. Blonde coarse plumes wave in the wind creating motion in the fall garden, and in winter a rustle is heard as breezes blow over parched dried leaves. A similar variety yet shorter, M. 'Zebrinus' bears striped leaves on arching foliage. No border is complete without a *Miscanthus* sited for color and contrast.

When, Where, and How to Plant
Plant potted porcupine grass anytime from late winter to fall. Divide established plants in late spring. The best location for this ornamental grass is where it gets direct sun. It's not finicky about soil type, as average clay soil supports successful plantings. Dig a planting hole twice as wide as the pot and of equal depth. Loosen potbound roots and backfill the rootball using loosened native soil. No amendments help with the exception of amending sandy soils that dry out quickly. Apply a 2-inch mulch layer and water well to get your plantings established. Continue watering twice weekly, for two weeks then taper off to an as-needed basis.

Growing Tips
Water monthly when rainfall is limited in late summer. It tolerates moderate drought, but in coastal regions pay attention to watering new plantings. Leaf tips that fade or dry out signals water stress, so increase irrigation. This grass will grow tall without much attention when rooted-in well. Overwatering may cause some grasses to get top-heavy. Fertilize in late spring with a CRF product to get it established during the first growing season; thereafter, no feeding is necessary.

Regional Advice and Care
Porcupine grass tolerates neglect in the landscape and is cold hardy across the Carolinas. It is considered care-free, with no serious insects or diseases. Over time, mature plantings can swell in width; groom by removing outer sprouts if space is limited. Cut back in spring as new growth is seen coming through the dormant basal shoots. The entire plant can be pruned back to one-half in late winter. Wear eye protective while grooming.

Companion Planting and Design
Plant porcupine grass in small clusters for a screen or border. Use single plants as an accent. Companions are tall flowering perennials, loropetalum, pygmy barberry shrub, and smaller muhly grass to hide its feet. The variegated foliage is more yellow than white in sunny locations.

Try These
Porcupine grass is special and durable. 'Little Zebra' has a compact, mounding habit; a good size for small gardens and planters.

Switchgrass

Panicum virgatum

Botanical Pronunciation
PAN-eh-cum vihr-GAIT-um

Bloom Period and Seasonal Color
Late summer beige to pink panicles

Mature Height × Spread
3 to 5 feet × 2 to 3 feet

When gardeners consider their options in selecting the perfect low-maintenance ornamental grass, durability is usually at the top of the list. One of America's most versatile grasses is native to our prairies in the Midwest. Switchgrass grows in an upright habit with a cloud of airy seed heads. It thrives in wet or dry conditions and is a champion in hot, sunny locations. Plant this grass in a garden setting of poor soil and its roots run deep. Among garden center selections, *Panicum virgatum* 'Northwind' is special and was awarded the honor of Perennial Plant of the Year for its narrow open heads atop blue green foliage. Where grouped in masses one gets the feel they are back on the Plains, minus the buffalo. Switchgrass is great for naturalizing and prevents soil erosion on a slope.

When, Where, and How to Plant

Plant potted switchgrass from late winter to fall. It tolerates the deep sands in coastal gardens and thrives in dry clay soils of the western Carolina. Plant in large masses, such as meadows, to eliminate mowing. No soil amendments are needed. Prepare planting holes that are 2 to 2½ feet apart for dense clusters; give specimen cultivars double that space. Loosen the native soil and plant at equal depth of the rootball. Water thoroughly to settle the backfill. Apply a mulch layer and water again in two days.

Growing Tips

Grasses need minimal care once established. Water weekly for the first month to help move along the root system initially. Water sparingly again in the dry months of the first growing season. Fertilize with a CRF or 10-20-20 analysis in spring within a month after planting. Afterwards all nutrients come from rainfall and decaying mulch or leaf litter.

Regional Advice and Care

Switchgrass thrives on neglect after established. It is extremely drought tolerant, and soils that are occasionally boggy do not bother it. Spring fertilizing will cause it to lodge down in a wet season. Other than cutting back in late winter or early spring, it's virtually maintenance free. No serious disease problems in most seasons of the year, and deer find it unpalatable. An outbreak of caterpillars is only a temporary setback; employ organic pest control methods with grasses. No patent on 'Northwind', divide in spring.

Companion Planting and Design

Switch grass is a smart alternative to exotic grasses for borders and abandoned areas. Taller varieties form beautiful, refined-looking screens and backgrounds; shorter cultivars create sweeps of color and texture. Carefree switchgrass is a natural for sustainable landscapes and meadow gardens. It provides shelter for birds and wildlife. Red leaf cultivars are especially garden-worthy as a focal point for beds of sun-tolerant perennials.

Try These

'Northwind' is a *Panicum* of distinction. Gardeners like the wide, blue leaves of 'Dallas Blues' and fall red foliage of 'Shenandoah'. 'Heavy Metal' is one of the oldest cultivars.

Variegated Sweet Flag

Acorus gramineus

Botanical Pronunciation
ah-CORE-us gra-me-NEE-us

Other Name Golden sweet flag

Bloom Period and Seasonal Color
Summer blooms are nonshowy; year-round variegated foliage

Mature Height × Spread
4 to 15 inches × 6 to 15 inches

Dense variegated sweet flag is one of the more diminutive ornamental grasses; it can also be considered an evergreen groundcover. It has broad blades up to 15 inches tall that retain their intense color through the heat of summer. Most members of the ancient *Acorus* family thrive in cool, wet environments; this species is heat-tolerant. The creeping rhizomes of sweet flag form compact clumps up to a foot in diameter, making it ideal for use in a container or as an edging plant. With close spacing, the deep yellow blades will grow together, forming a brilliant low mass. Golden sweet flag 'Ogon' at 1-foot height would be an interesting choice for a turfgrass-like edging alongside hardy perennials or as an accent by a water garden. Place it like a writer uses a punctuation mark!

When, Where, and How to Plant

Since sweet flag is sold in pots, it can be planted anytime from late winter throughout fall. When planting in full sun, avoid late summer planting. The best location for this ornamental grass is where it gets part shade or dappled shade if in hot, sandy soil. Heavy, clay soil that is often poorly drained can support successful plantings. Dig a planting hole that is twice as wide as the pot and of equal depth. Loosen potbound roots. Compost or other organic amendments would be of benefit in sandy soil types that dry out quickly. Apply a 2-inch mulch layer. Water several times weekly for a month, then taper off.

Growing Tips

Water routinely when rainfall is limited in late summer. Leaf tips that fade or dry out signals water stress; increase irrigation. Use a hand spade to check soil moisture at the 3-inch depth for landscape plantings. Once established, this grass tolerates moderate drought. Fertilize the second spring as needed to maintain plantings.

Regional Advice and Care

Two species are found in the horticultural trade: *A. gramineus*, a dwarf Japanese species, and *A. calamus*, a tall grasslike variety. The colorful cultivars are considered care-free plants. In coastal regions, pay attention to watering new planting. The grassleaf sweet flag species can become bushy over time; groom by pruning back winter-damaged foliage as new growth begins. In established beds, thin for new plantings. Control weeds with mulch and hand weeding.

Companion Planting and Design

Plant showy sweet flag in small groupings as a landscape accent with garden statuary and water feature. Use it as an edging along a walk. Plant alongside a threadleaf Japanese maple, coralbells, or paperbush. Its variegated foliage is more intense during the cool weather and in sites with some shade. A wonderful choice for mixed container plantings.

Try These

'Ogon' has gotten the most media exposure for its fancy foliage. 'Oborozuki' and 'Variegatus' are equally cheerful. Tiny 'Minimus Aureus' is under 5 inches.

PERENNIALS

FOR THE CAROLINAS

A perennial, in the broadest horticultural definition, is any plant that lives three or more years. Although trees, shrubs, and vines are perennial, gardeners usually use the term to refer to herbaceous perennial flowers. In autumn, the soft tops of most perennials die to the ground, while their root system persists through winter. In spring, the cycle begins anew, with growth from a crown or modified roots. Among the most rewarding traits of perennials is that they come up unprompted each year to offer masses of color in ever-changing patterns from April to November. They flower abundantly and multiply without being coaxed. Some tolerate considerable neglect, and a few, like artemisia, prefer it that way.

Perennials are classified based on their hardiness. Hardy perennials normally survive Carolina winters with little or no protection. Tender or half-hardy perennials survive a mild winter in Zone 8 gardens but need mulching in Mountain counties.

A variety of perennials can help add color to your garden.

Some, such as verbena and lantana, are usually grown as annuals in cold zones. Hardiness does not refer to the ability to withstand heat and drought. Microclimates and soil drainage are factors in determining how long-lived a perennial will be at any particular site.

How to Be Successful

Unlike annuals, which bloom continuously for many months and die in one year, many perennials bloom for a few weeks each season but need not be replanted. For this reason, consider what a plant will look like throughout the year. One of the basic goals of gardeners should be to obtain continuity of color by planting different varieties for bloom at different times. Perennials with colorful foliage may be more valuable in the garden's design than those that only bloom and have foliage of marginal interest.

Site selection is very important to perennial gardens since these plants will be left in place for several years. Most thrive in full-sun conditions where the soil drains well. The showiest floral display is in the sunniest beds. Soil pH requirements vary, but most prefer a pH between 5.5 to 6.5. Consistent, moderate levels of soil moisture are important because most perennials are succulent and non-woody. While many tolerate wet locations for a short period, most will be killed by extended periods of wet soil, especially during winter. A 2- to 4-inch layer of fine pine-bark soil conditioner can be tilled into beds before planting to improve soil drainage and aeration. Sedum, salvia, and other semi-woody perennials will benefit greatly from quick-draining soils where coarse soil amendments are incorporated.

Place your plants where you want them, and move them around until you have the look you want.

When planting, the hole should be just as deep as the plant's rootball, but no deeper.

Rake some mulch around the newly added perennials, but be careful not to mound mulch around the plant stems.

Opportunities and Challenges

When growing perennial flowers, you are not limited to sunny borders, since many flourish in the shade. Plants such as lungwort, wild ginger, ferns, and hosta can create a showstopper garden where a majestic oak shadows the bed. Shaded sites *can* be problematic in that tree roots forage into well prepared sites; you'll find it challenging to meet the water requirements of some perennials in shade gardens. Most woodland perennials thrive in moist, dappled shade conditions, but the list of flowering plants that survive in the dry soils found in some shady locations is quite a bit shorter. A few to consider include toad lily and epimedium.

The survival of many ephemeral wildflowers has to do with their ability to bloom in early spring when light and moisture are plentiful, after which they phase into dormancy during less favorable environmental periods. Many native woodland orchid species and trilliums flourish because of their resilience.

Another challenge with perennials is to keep some of them from overgrowing others in the same bed, becoming an unsightly jungle. Two aggressive plants are obedient plant and pink showy primrose. (Ironically, the name of the former has nothing to with its land-grabbing proclivity.) Both native perennials waste no time dominating a border. Your success with perennials, as it is with many landscape ornamentals, has much to do with selecting the right plant for a particular site. Iris, for example, grows in a variety of soil types. Siberian iris is content in extraordinarily dry soil, while Japanese and Louisiana iris thrive in bog gardens. Planting in the right spot ensures that minimal care will be required to get the best results.

Perennial Maintenance

Whoever said that perennials were low-maintenance plants was either an exceptional garden designer or one who moved across town before the garden matured. Maintenance is an inescapable part of gardening, and will be required for any perennial species.

Spacing so plants produce a solid canopy and mulching are the best ways to minimize weeds. In sunny beds, using crabgrass preventer may be helpful until a new bed establishes. Some plants require staking, others deadheading, to encourage repeat flowering. Gardens need water during dry periods and occasional fertilization for healthy foliage. While you can overdo fertilizer, you should not have problems if you amend beds based on a soil test report. Some gardeners fertilize every four to six weeks with a

Place cages around large plants when the plants are just sprouting.

water-soluble bloom-booster fertilizer. An alternative is to use a continuous feed, slow-release product applied early at planting and again by midseason. Other gardeners mulch perennial gardens with aged cow manure or leaves.

There has been much concern about the volume of water required to maintain plantings in the Carolinas. Many counties are experiencing water shortages and have set mandatory water restrictions to conserve this resource. In order to be good

Deadhead (remove faded flowers from the plant) on a regular basis to keep more blooms growing.

stewards, many gardeners in urban areas elect to use perennials that are less dependent on irrigation. Since many perennials are water hogs, pay special attention to the ones that are drought tolerant. Cooperative Extension agents provide lists of these durable species in most counties. Many of these are found in the following pages.

While there is specific information about pests in "Regional Advice and Care" sections, consider these general comments. First, don't apply excess fertilizers as it is an open invitation to sucking insects, such as aphids or whiteflies. Insects feast on luscious new growth produced in abundance as a response to excess nitrogen. While beneficial insects found in flower gardens can usually manage most pests, they need your help. Use a garden hose to dislodge insect pests with a stream of water. To eliminate infestations, reach for nontoxic insecticides containing soaps and horticultural oils. To thwart diseases, irrigate early in the day to keep foliage dry at night, and mulch beds. Consult a horticulturist when diseases appear and especially before purchasing a curative fungicide.

The Benefits of Planning

Plan a perennial garden much as you would a room addition. Traditionally, perennials are planted in large beds 6 to 12 feet wide and are best displayed against backgrounds such as evergreens, a stone wall, or a fence. Consider using a walk or edging material in the foreground to reduce maintenance. Place tall varieties in the back, graduating to smaller plants toward the front. Use color in bold groups, not spotted here and there. Vertical interest can be achieved by incorporating ornamental grasses, accessories, and structures. While perennials are not generally associated with formal design, they are versatile and provide enjoyment in myriad locations.

Creating Well-Drained Soil

Gardeners use this term to define drainage within the soil, not just water that runs off. Most perennials demand well-drained soil, but most upland Carolina soils emphatically aren't. You can make them so. To prepare ground beds, use the procedure outlined on page 19. (However, you'll find that perennials are more often planted individually or in small groups, perhaps among established perennials or shrubs. This becomes a routine way to distribute the bounty that comes from dividing crowns of perennials, receiving plants from gardening, or moving plants for a better display.)

"Spot" soil improvement, involving limited areas, is a good way to ensure that new perennials will grow well and endure for years. Dig the soil to spade depth, break up clods, and add soil conditioners to loosen and aerate it. On Carolina clays, delay digging until the soil has dried enough to crumble. Spread 2 inches of organic soil conditioner or PermaTill®, a heat-expanded slate product that looks like gray gravel. Add 1-2-2 ratio garden fertilizer at the rate of 2 pounds per 100 square feet and pelletized dolomitic limestone at the rate of 5 pounds per 100 square feet. If you have had your soil tested, use those recommendations instead. Thoroughly mix the additives into the soil.

On coastal sands and the rare sandy land that occurs elsewhere, add only organic soil conditioner and cut fertilizer and lime applications by half. Sandy soil has little capacity to store surplus amounts of mineral additives. It may sound implausible, but certain sandy soils drain slowly. If that's so, suspect a layer of compacted fine particles (called hardpan) some distance below the surface. Break it up by spading.

Berms

In clay soils, perennials grow better, live longer, and display beautifully when planted on berms. Picture irregularly shaped mounds of sandy loam topsoil in your yard, rising to a height of 15 to 20 inches at the center, and sloping down to ground level around the perimeter. Now, surround that image with metal edging that protrudes high enough to trap mulch and keep it from washing into the lawn. Berms are expensive to install but are well worth their cost. However, if you practice pay-as-you-go gardening, you can expect as good results from less expensive raised beds created by adding pine bark soil conditioner and play sand or organic conditioners, such as leaves and compost.

Planting Perennials

Perennials are almost always sold in larger containers than annuals because they are customarily grown from cuttings, divisions of crowns, tubers, or explants from micropropagation rather than from seeds. Read and save plant labels in a garden journal or record into a database. They will tell you which cultivars demand well-drained soil and those that will thrive in wet, poorly aerated areas. (The latter includes obedient plant, Joe-pye weed, ironweed, turtlehead, cardinal flower, hardy hibiscus, and many others.)

Prepare soil as directed. Container-grown perennials can be planted anytime, but fall through early spring is by far the best. In mountain areas, spring is the best planting time, after the soil has thawed. Cool soil, frequent showers, and decreased transpiration encourage root development that prepares the plant to bloom the following year. Transplanting perennials from late spring through summer steadily decreases survivability due to increased water needs. You must water every two or three days between rains to keep up with the demands of a developing root system and burgeoning top growth and the loss of soil moisture taken up by roots and transpired through the foliage.

Dig planting holes the recommended distance apart, and be prepared to water when you're ready to plant. Tap the plant out of the container. If only a few roots surround the rootball or mat at the bottom, set the rootball in the planting hole with as little disturbance to it as possible. More often than not, perennial plants are potbound, with substantial root development "girdling" the sides of the rootball and matting at the bottom. Using hand shears, snip off the mat and cut major girdling roots. Then, bang the plant on a solid surface to knock off some of the rooting medium and to expose root tips. This seemingly rough treatment prepares the plant to send new roots into surrounding soil.

Set the plant in the hole so that the top of the rootball is level with the surface of the surrounding soil or as much as ½ inch above it. Pull the conditioned backfill around the rootball and firm it lightly. Complete planting the other selections chosen for that spot and soak the area with water without delay.

Use only water at planting to settle the backfill and remove air pockets. Drench the soil with soluble plant fertilizer two to three weeks later when the plants have begun to send out new feeder roots. Fertile garden soil rich in organic matter may not require fertilizer. Overdoing it will result in open, leggy plants with few flowers. After observing your garden for a while, you'll develop techniques that work for you and keep your plants flourishing. Gardening is more art than science in some locales. How to handle home-divided perennials is a different matter. When you dig clumps of perennials during fall or winter, wash the soil off the roots before surgery and cut, saw, or break the clumps into smaller, well-rooted parts. You can set out the divisions at the same time. Or if they are from choice, expensive plants or ones with sentimental value, you can pot the plants in potting soil, grow them for a few weeks, and set them in place with a well-developed root system. The former approach requires more frequent watering to guarantee that your new plants will "take." Having a small "nursery" at home where divisions are pampered while they develop roots is helpful. Locate holding areas near water faucets and circle them with hardware cloth to protect from foraging wildlife.

Watering

The difficulty of watering increases exponentially in proportion to the distance between plants and a water faucet. Most gardeners prefer to coil water hoses when they're not in use. But leaving them out, with a sprinkler attached, will simplify frequent watering of new plantings. Turn the pressure on just enough to water the planted area, set a timer for an hour, and turn it off. Do this every two or three days until you see new plant growth, then reduce watering to weekly during dry spells. Thereafter, watering frequency depends to some extent on the species you plant. Most perennials grow well within a wide range of frequency and duration of watering. A few kinds languish if not watered frequently and deeply, but others will die with the same treatment. Research will help keep the species sorted by water requirements, but over the long haul, only experience will reduce your failures closer to zero.

Mulching

Don't mulch perennials as deeply as you do shrubs and trees. One to 2 inches is sufficient; if you apply it any deeper, mulch tends to drift into the crowns of perennials, which can lead to stem rotting. In addition to the benefits common to mulching—suppression of weeds, conservation of moisture, and gradual conversion into humus—mulching around perennials creates a seedbed where seeds dropped by perennials can sprout and grow into additional plants. (This can be a blessing or a curse, depending on the amount of the seed crop and the difficulty of removing excessive seedlings.) Any organic mulch, such as aged ground pine bark, shredded hardwood bark, cottonboll compost, or peanut or rice hulls, works well. But across the Carolinas pine straw is preferred. It can be pulled in around perennials to a depth of four inches without causing stems to rot. It will soon pack down to an inch or 2 in depth and will begin slowly to decompose. Removal of pine straw is rarely necessary but easy to do.

Maintaining Fertile Soil

Most fertilizers mentioned in this book are not acceptable to organic gardeners. While I subscribe to organic gardening methods in my vegetable garden, using mineral fertilizers is easier, faster, and more predictable than strictly organic sources. If applied wisely, mineral fertilizers need not damage the environment and are acceptable for flower gardening. City gardeners may opt out of producing homemade compost to maintain soil fertility. Most urban waste management departments now stockpile free or low-cost leaf compost, a splendid resource. Whether you purchase bagged commercial compost or prefer a pickup truck load from the city yard, a layer of compost at planting increases the biological activity of your garden soil and supports growth and development. Feed the soil, not the plant. Applying compost annually during autumn isn't a bad routine to adopt, since organic matter rapidly decomposes in our hot, rainy weather of the Southeast. Most of us are working with problematic, disturbed urban soils, hence the importance of amendments.

Successful perennial gardeners use plenty of organic soil conditioners and mulches plus modest amounts of mineral fertilizers. Neither works at peak performance alone; they need each other to "feed the soil," which in turn feeds plants. I also believe in soil testing, in large part to regulate soil pH. Neither organic nor mineral fertilizers will release nutrients at optimum rates in the Carolinas' acidic soils. The optimal pH range for perennials is 5.5 to 6.5. Liming per soil tests every three years helps regulate nutrient release, dissolve rock minerals, and enhance soil structure. Limestone could be the "secret" to sustainable gardens. Soil test kits are reliable for gardening purposes, though I prefer the results from a state laboratory.

Included in the several categories of fertilizer are granular, "complete" garden or flower fertilizers, water-soluble crystalline fertilizers for liquid feeding, and controlled-release fertilizers. The most efficient is controlled- or extended-release fertilizer. It is also the most expensive. Next in efficiency is liquid feeding, but it can be expensive if soils are drastically short on major nutrients. A number of organic products include seaweed, kelp, and fish emulsion concentrates that are diluted before applying. Fish byproducts are customarily juiced up with mineral additives to raise the nutrient content on the package label. They are smelly, but gentle on seedlings and new plantings. Some specialty garden shops now brew compost teas and biodynamic nutrient solutions for organic clientele.

The least efficient but cheapest is granular garden fertilizer. You can improve its effect by "drilling" or "banding" it into furrows and covering the furrows with soil. Drilling decreases the amount of nitrogen lost to volatilization and traps the phosphate and potash so they don't wash away during heavy rains. Drilling the fertilizer into bands concentrates the fertilizer into a small area rather than mixing it with the soil. Raking fertilizer into the soil is better than scattering it over the surface, to insure that fertilizer particles become soluble and release their nutrients.

But enough science—let's talk about some of the perennial flowers known to grow well in the Carolinas!

Hostas are a shade-loving perennial in endless variations.

Artemisia

Artemisia spp.

Botanical Pronunciation
ART-ee-me-sha

Other Name
Wormwood

Bloom Period and Seasonal Color
Late summer; nonshowy flowers on feathery gray foliage

Mature Height × Spread
½ feet to 4 feet × 1 to 2½ feet

Dozens of artemisias, including some annuals, are available, but it is the robust ornamental perennial ones that are most garden worthy. While the flowers are not particularly attractive, the silver-gray foliage of artemisia is quite distinctive and delivers great value as an accent in the garden. The variation in texture among the artemisias is as vast as their variation in height. Plant this perennial herb in dry sites where many flowers shrivel. Gardeners in rural or suburban parts of the Carolinas often have problems with deer browsing their gardens. Artemisia is one perennial that deer seem to ignore while they forage through landscapes. The day or night luminescence of artemisia, its season-long foliage color, and its drought tolerance make this plant an irresistible choice for the garden.

When, Where, and How to Plant

Plant artemisia after the soil has warmed in May and through early November. Plants are usually sold in 1-gallon pots. Do not plant in moist soils but in sunny, low-fertility, dry sites. When planting in clay soils, incorporate a shovelful of granite screenings, aged pine bark, or Perma-Till® per plant for drainage purposes. All major cultivars are adapted to container gardening as well as ground beds. Spacing varies from 1 to 4 feet. Read plant labels carefully; some cultivars grow to impressive bushes while others lie flat on the ground and grow to only 2 feet across.

Growing Tips

Artemisia will grow in poor soils but develops better color with light fertilization. Feed when you cut plants back in the spring following bud-break. Water established plants only when tip growth flags a bit but before plants begin to lose color.

Regional Advice and Care

It can be sheared by one-third in July to shape. Flowering causes the plant decline, so remove flower stems early. Some artemisias spread like wildfire, especially 'Silver King', and 'Oriental Limelight'. You may wish to grow them in containers. Others, such as the popular 'Powis Castle', spread slowly by roots but billow out to cover large areas. You will need to cut them back severely, preferably in early spring. Few pests bother strongly scented artemisia. Divide crowns in late summer and fall, or locate where branches have touched the ground and rooted. Cut fore and aft of the rooted area, dig up and pot the plant, and set it out when a full root system has formed. Flower arrangers who grow artemisias for drying often confine them in raised, framed-in beds.

Companion Planting and Design

The silver artemisias look great interspersed among other perennials and shrubs. The tiny 'Silver Mound,' while beautiful, may be too delicate for the coast and hot sandhills but flourishes in the mountains. Try pairing artemisias with plumbago, perennial salvias, and blue mist shrub.

Try These

'Powis Castle' is a winner, followed by 'Silverado'. Southernwood, a shrubby, green artemisia, makes an attractive (if smelly) waist-high bush.

Aster

Aster spp.

Botanical Pronunciation AS-ter

Other Name
Perennial aster

Bloom Period and Seasonal Color
Late summer to fall in crimson, pink, lavender, violet-blue, and white

Mature Height × Spread
Dwarf cultivars: 1 to 1½ feet × 1½ feet
Taller cultivars: 2 to 4 feet × 2 to 3 feet

Experienced gardeners usually grow several aster species or hybrids among their spring- or summer-blooming perennials. For much of the growing season, perennial asters put their energy into developing rounded clumps of foliage. Late in the season, when days begin to grow short, flower buds form and break into bloom. Unimproved species of asters tend to grow waist-high, but dwarf varieties are available for smaller gardens. *Aster frikartii*, a hybrid, is perhaps the most popular, beloved for its 2½-inch blossoms in blue or violet shades. A tougher native, aromatic aster (*A. oblongifolius*) blooms later and has smaller but more numerous blooms in violet-blue shades. One that always attracts admiration is the pink 'Alma Potshke', a hybrid between two native species, New England aster and New York aster.

When, Where, and How to Plant

Plant in full sun or light afternoon shade anytime through early summer. Plants are usually offered in 6- to 8-inch pots during spring. A few garden centers grow them to first color stage and sell the plants for instant color in fall. Set plants 2 to 3 feet apart. Most asters aren't well suited to container growing; they grow too large. Native species will grow in unimproved soil, but all will perform better with a little help.

Growing Tips

Two drenches with water-soluble flower fertilizer thirty and sixty days after spring planting should prevent nutrient deficiencies. Fall-planted asters shouldn't be fed until the following spring, in order to avoid making the plants too tender going into winter.

Regional Advice and Care

In late winter, cut perennial asters back to 4 inches in height. Cut back tall varieties halfway in late spring to improve habit, which may delay flowering slightly. In rich soil, when blooms begin to open, you may need to circle clumps with twine and pull the stems into a loose column to keep them from flopping. Asters are care-free with no pests.

Companion Planting and Design

Asters bloom so late that they have the show pretty much to themselves. For this reason, buy three of each cultivar and set them in groups. Single plants can be lost in the jumble of late summer foliage. In large gardens try Tatarian aster, *A. tataricus*, which can grow taller than head high. Its huge trusses of small, light blue flowers sustain Monarch butterflies on their way to Mexico for the winter. Consider planting a meadow garden.

Try These

Aromatic aster performs well all over the South. 'Purple Dome' is the first true dwarf form of New England aster; it never needs pinching or support. 'Fanny's Aster' is a real "looker," with spectacular powder blue flowers on a compact 18-inch plant. Our natives, *A. concolor*, Eastern silvery-aster, and *A. ericodes* var. 'Pink Star' are important nectar sources for beneficial insects.

Baptisia

Baptisia alba

Botanical Pronunciation
BAP-tiz-ee-ah AL-bah

Other Name
White wild indigo

Bloom Period and Seasonal Color
Early summer in white, yellow, purple, or blue

Mature Height × Spread
3 to 4 feet × 1½ to 3 feet

You may find it hard to believe that the beautiful and showy baptisia is a wildflower. It grows along many rural Carolina roadsides where it is spared the ministrations of the DOT mowing teams. In early summer, tall, curving spikes of white pea-like flowers are in bloom for two to three weeks. The flowers are followed by bladder-like seedpods. Its three-part leaves usually keep their blue-green color long after the flowers have faded. Less common but equally beautiful is the violet-blue-flowered species, *Baptisia australis*. No, it isn't native to Australia; the botanical name simply indicates it is from the South. Plant breeders have intensified the color of blue baptisia to such a degree that even the stems of these selections take on a deep purple tinge.

When, Where, and How to Plant
Set out plants in spring so they can establish before blooming. Handle carefully; new growth is brittle. Plant seeds in pots filled with potting soil and leave them outside to "stratify" the seeds with colder temperatures to hasten germination. Baptisia develops a deep root system to support heavy crops of spikes that are notoriously sensitive to being moved. Although baptisia tolerates afternoon shade, it grows best in full sun. Baptisia does not demand good soil, but it does seek out well-drained sites in the wild. You might have to wait two or three years for baptisia to bloom.

Growing Tips
Baptisias aren't accustomed to being fussed over. Being a deep-rooted legume, they don't need regular watering and benefit from being planted away from wimpy annuals that need an inch of water a week from rain or sprinklers. To feed, water the plants thoroughly, drenching the soil around each plant with 1 gallon of soluble flower fertilizer dissolved per directions. During a very dry year, give them a good soaking when flower spikes begin to lengthen. They are permanent once established in the garden and are low maintenance.

Regional Advice and Care
After blooming is over, use hedge shears to prune back by one-third to prevent flopping over. The blue-green or purple-green foliage is handsome all summer. To maintain plant vigor, snip off spent spikes before they form seeds. If you wish to save seeds, harvest them early and let them dry in a paper bag. Mix and store the seeds with a tablespoon of ground hot peppers to keep seed-eating insects away.

Companion Planting and Design
The commanding spikes of baptisia combine well with the vigorous plants of 'Becky' Shasta daisy, artemisia 'Powis Castle', and salvia 'May Night'. The blues bloom later than the white species that gives a succession of color. Baptisia blooms from persistent crowns and develops very rapidly.

Try These
'Purple Smoke' and 'Blueberry Sundae' are lavender-blue baptisias. The vigorous 'Carolina Moonlight' and hybrid 'Blonde Bombshell' glow with soft yellow spikes. 'Screaming Yellow' and 'Solar Flare' promise more color options.

Black-Eyed Susan

Rudbeckia fulgida var. *sullivantii* 'Goldsturm'

Botanical Pronunciation
ruhd-BEK-ee-uh ful-GIL-dah sull-eh-VANT-ee

Bloom Period and Seasonal Color
Summer blooms of distinctive black disks and golden yellow petals

Mature Height × Spread
1 ½ ft to 2 feet × 1 ½ feet to 2 feet

Our native black-eyed Susan, *Rudbeckia hirta*, is perfectly happy adorning the Carolina countryside—but its quasi-refined cousin 'Goldsturm' is more at home nestled in a bed of summer-blooming perennials. Gardeners everywhere love this hybrid because it is durable and easy to grow. Its unmistakable, rich yellow flowers sporting protruding black cones or "eyes" are a welcome sight when they appear in July. 'Goldsturm' provides a fabulous display and continues to bloom throughout our miserably hot summer months and into fall. It makes quite a show in a bed flanked by variegated miscanthus. Goldfinches will zero in on bed plantings and finish off the fine black seeds as the blooms fade. Annual *Rudbeckia* varieties such as 'Cherokee Sunset' and 'Indian Summer' are popular across the Carolinas.

When, Where, and How to Plant
Plant black-eyed Susans anytime the ground can be worked, though the preferred season is spring. Purchase vigorous plants in quart-sized or larger pots to ensure blooms the first season. For maximum flowering, grow this robust perennial in full sunlight. It adapts to most conditions and soil types, although it prefers well-drained, moisture-retentive soils. Set plants directly into the garden after loosening the soil thoroughly. Space plants 2 feet apart; mulch after watering-in the newly set plants.

Growing Tips
Irrigate your planting every five days for the first month if there's no rain. An application of a slow-release or flower fertilizer in spring will keep the plants going. Its strong rhizomatous roots will spread to form a colony in moist, but not saturated sites.

Regional Advice and Care
Black-eyed Susans are durable once established and are virtually maintenance free. Remove flower stalks in winter. These stalks can be used in dried flower arrangements. Mulch beds annually after raking. After many years in the garden, black-eyed Susans may need replacing, or just rework the soil and reset vigorous plants. The plants can be divided for transplanting in spring and fall. Seeds are viable and can be planted in the fall in flats; they will germinate in late spring. The progeny may not look like their parents. An occasional caterpillar will nip a flower, and *B.t.* spray can be used if an infestation occurs.

Companion Planting and Design
Black-eyed Susans add a bit of nostalgia to the cutting garden. They are great for naturalizing, using in containers, and ideal in beds of spring-blooming annuals. They make excellent border plants to pair with ornamental grasses. *R. triloba* blooms after 'Goldsturm' and grows taller. *R. maxima* has silver-blue foliage and produces very tall stems.

Try These
'Goldsturm' has been at home in my garden for decades. Use compact 'Little Goldstar' for small beds. The All-America Selections winner 'Prairie Sun', an annual, has green centers and large, yellow flowers.

Bleeding Heart

Dicentra spectabilis

Botanical Pronunciation
Die-CENT-rah spec-TAB-eh-lis

Bloom Period and Seasonal Color
Spring blooms in pink or brilliant red hearts and white inner petals

Mature Height × Spread
12 to 24 inches × 12 to 24 inches

Bleeding heart is an old-fashioned beauty that is commonplace in Zone 7 gardens and the cooler mountain region. Carolina gardeners can enjoy the delicate, heart-shaped flowers of bleeding heart for many springs to come when care is given to finding an ideal site for this perennial. This is a "must-have" selection for a cottage garden, available in traditional pink and white. Foliage color is a grey-green and has dainty, deeply divided leaves. The plants are care-free in the cooler months, but will die back with onset of the summertime temperatures. In warmer zones, *Dicentra formosa* 'Luxuriant' is a good substitute in woodland gardens where it can serve as groundcover in filtered light. This species has a longer bloom period and more heat tolerance.

When, Where, and How to Plant

Most perennials, purchased as bare-root plants, should be planted in fall. They will develop root systems over winter for spring. Potted bleeding hearts can be planted anytime except during summer. Place in partial shade with some protection from drying winds. While this perennial enjoys moisture it is subject to root rot in poorly drained sites. Bleeding heart loves humusy soil; work liberal amounts of compost or peat moss into the planting hole. Position the plant so it sits high in the bed. Space 18 inches apart.

Growing Tips

Keep container-grown plants watered until planted, especially if they are in bloom. After planting, pay close attention to watering their first month. Keep soil moist; irrigate twice weekly for several weeks and then as needed to keep the foliage full. A liquid fertilizer solution can be used during the spring.

Regional Advice and Care

After the blooms fade the flower stalks can be removed (deadheading). The foliage will begin to fade with hot weather and can be removed when it fades. Mulch with a 1-inch layer of compost. The *Dicentra* genera can have establishment problems, most likely related to soil conditions. They are known to thrive in rich soils that are quick draining. For this reason, both the site and planting technique are critically important.

Companion Planting and Design

Because of their ephemeral nature this perennial is frequently interplanted with summer-hardy perennial and annual flowers. Plant shade-loving favorites in beds and borders with bleeding heart. Good companions include: wild blue phlox, Lenten rose, foam flower, hosta, hardy begonia, astilbe and ferns. A climbing species, *D. scandens* 'Athens Yellow', requires a trellis.

Try These

The common species is adored, with its pendant, two-spurred, pink flowers. Brighten up a shady spot with the white blooms of 'Alba' and 'Pantaloons'. 'Gold Heart' has gold foliage. Our American species, *D. eximia,* is a popular native. *D. formosa* 'Zestful' and 'Luxuriant,' fringed bleeding heart, are reliable groundcover choices for part sun. New is 'Valentine,' with stunning brilliant red hearts.

Blue Salvia

Salvia farinacea

Botanical Pronunciation
SAL-vee-ah FAIR-in-A-see

Other Name
Mealy-cup sage

Bloom Period and Seasonal Color
Early summer to fall spikes of deep violet
blue blooms

Mature Height × Spread
16 to 20 inches × 14 inches

Depending on your cold hardiness zone, blue salvia may be a perennial or an annual. In most Carolina counties in Zone 8, it performs as a perennial. However, in my Zone 7b garden I grow it as an annual and am pleasantly surprised when it returns for another round following a mild winter. *Salvia* 'Victoria' tolerates heat, drought, and virtually any soil. Violet-blue flower spikes stand well above the gray-green foliage and are continuous throughout the summer. Planted in masses, blue salvia provides much-appreciated blue tones that gardeners seek. The dwarf hybrid, *S.* × *superba* 'Blue Queen', is better adapted to Zone 6. Blue salvia is one of many perennials caught in the conundrum of climate change. Don't let that stop you from adding it to your garden. Butterflies love this plant!

When, Where, and How to Plant

Plant potted blue salvia anytime from spring to early summer. Most gardeners prefer to purchase cell-packs to install after the last frost. Enterprising gardeners looking to plant a large area and save a buck can buy mail-order seeds for sowing. Give it lots of sun and well-drained loam. Dappled shade is fine but the flower show will be sparse (yet plants will be robust). No special soil prep is necessary other than loosening and enriching the soil with a flower fertilizer. Frill out roots for planting, plant on high ground, and space on 10-inch centers for a full color bed. Water thoroughly and mulch thinly.

Growing Tips

Water beds twice weekly for the first few weeks to promote root growth. Irrigate when the soil is dry to the touch or rainfall is lacking in summer. Apply a fertilizer of your choice after pruning with hedge shears, be light-handed to favor blooms over foliage. Blue salvia is tolerant of drought and can perform on its own with minimal maintenance. Don't pamper, just enjoy!

Regional Advice and Care

Shear plants after their first bloom to remove spent flower spikes. In the warmest regions, hardy blue salvia can be planted in late summer, provided it can be watered, to establish before winter. Treat it like hardy lantana a similar perennial familiar to coastal gardeners. Established plantings can be divided in fall or spring and transplanted to other beds. It is wise to plan for permanence and avoid the hassle of division, since they don't form rhizomes that demand handling in this fashion. It is virtually pest-free. Avoid root rots by keeping mulch off the basal stems.

Companion Planting and Design

Blue salvia is impressive in a color bed comprised of pink geraniums, or intermingled with white marigolds, Wave™ petunias, spreading zinnias, and periwinkle. In the Mountains, sow 'Blue Queen' seeds in summer for mass groupings as the main feature. Like scarlet sage, blue salvia gets lots of hummingbird visits.

Try These

'Victoria' is easiest to locate at garden shops. A bicolor, 'Strata ', can be dried for floral arrangements.

Chrysanthemum

Dendranthema × *morifolium*

Botanical Pronunciation
den-DRAN-the-mah × grand-ey-FLORA-ah

Other Name
Garden mum

Bloom Period and Seasonal Color
Midsummer to fall (even after frost) in a huge range of colors except blue

Mature Height × Spread
1 to 2 ½ feet × 1 to 3 feet

The chrysanthemum is now, botanically speaking, *Dendranthema*. For most gardeners, it is sufficient to know that there are basically three kinds of chrysanthemums, the tender kind sold at full bloom stage for gift giving year-round, and the hardy garden mum bred for planting outdoors. Nurseries and garden centers load up on colorful pots of garden mums in late summer timed for fall festivals and Halloween. The third kind involves fewer gardeners who force cutting chrysanthemums, a special commodity for flower show competitions and florists. They are produced by manipulating the hours of light, which fools the mums into blooming on a set schedule instead of Nature's long nights of autumn. Many garden mum varieties will survive Zone 7 and 8 winters to regrow the following spring and bloom again the following fall.

When, Where, and How to Plant
Plant garden mums spring to fall in prepared soil in full sun, or where they receive afternoon shade in Zone 8b. Loosen the roots or "butterfly" them to alleviate potbound conditions. Well-drained soil is a must; see page 19 for soil preparation recommendations. Space 2 feet apart, and mulch well. Water thoroughly to settle them, and, three times weekly for a few weeks in hot weather plantings.

Growing Tips
Water weekly between rains until plants show signs of new growth, then back off to an as-needed basis. Mums are fairly heavy feeders and benefit from monthly applications of granular fertilizer when bloom buds begin to form. Spread mulch to increase the percentage of survival and continuing performance.

Regional Advice and Care
Potted plants bought in spring can be pruned back for height control, which delays blooming. In established beds, shear off spent blooms and dead shoots in winter. Divide hardy mums in spring as new shoots appear and apply a ¼ cup of controlled-release fertilizer per division. In established beds, shear plants in spring by one-third and at least twice to induce more flowers. Watch for aphids on tender shoots and leaf miners. Insecticidal soap applied weekly will wipe out aphids, but leaf miners or thrips may require a systemic insecticide that is absorbed through the foliage and roots. Bacterial leaf spot can cause black, greasy-looking blotches on leaves. Overhead watering with sprinklers can create the moist foliage that spores need to germinate and invade tissues. For prevention of leaf diseases, try a potassium bicarbonate fungicides laced with spreader-sticker or a copper-based fungicide.

Companion Planting and Design
Few garden flowers are in bloom late in the season. Mexican bush salvia, *Salvia leucantha*, is one of the best tall companions for fall-blooming mums as is spreading zinnia and Wave™ petunias. Near the Coast, try candelebra cassia. It has massive plants with spectacular yellow "candles."

Try These
New colors continue to be added to the Prophet™ series. Two new hardy introductions to watch are 'Gethsemane Moonlight' and 'Matchsticks'. Japanese mums are popular too.

Columbine

Aquilegia spp.

Botanical Pronunciation
aqua-LEE-gee-ah

Bloom Period and Seasonal Color
Late spring to early summer in a range of colors and bicolors

Mature Height × Spread
1 to 4 feet × 1 foot

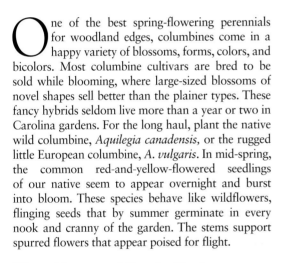

One of the best spring-flowering perennials for woodland edges, columbines come in a happy variety of blossoms, forms, colors, and bicolors. Most columbine cultivars are bred to be sold while blooming, where large-sized blossoms of novel shapes sell better than the plainer types. These fancy hybrids seldom live more than a year or two in Carolina gardens. For the long haul, plant the native wild columbine, *Aquilegia canadensis,* or the rugged little European columbine, *A. vulgaris.* In mid-spring, the common red-and-yellow-flowered seedlings of our native seem to appear overnight and burst into bloom. These species behave like wildflowers, flinging seeds that by summer germinate in every nook and cranny of the garden. The stems support spurred flowers that appear poised for flight.

When, Where, and How to Plant

Blooming plants are sold in spring. Choose a site that gets afternoon shade or full sun. More than anything, columbine appreciates a well-drained, moist bed. Adding soil conditioners or compost will raise the soil into a hill about 3 inches high. Set your new plants in the prepared soil and trickle water around them. If you want to start seeds in early spring, fill a tray with 3-inch pots of potting soil, scatter seeds on top, and barely cover them with play sand. Native columbines will also grow well in dry, poor soil without coaxing. They drop seeds and naturalize, making themselves at home anywhere. Keep new plantings watering weekly in until hot weather.

Growing Tips

Water new plantings in sunny beds every two weeks between rains. Shaded beds are sustainable with little care. In established beds apply a flower fertilizer before spring growth starts. Seeds are dispersed widely by being flung as the pods spring open. To contain native columbine promptly remove flower stems after blooming. The airy, blue-green compound foliage is a sweet filler.

Regional Advice and Care

Columbine won't ask much from you. Tall cultivars require staking with thin bamboo stakes and loops of green-dyed twine to keep them neat and upright. If you see serpentine patterns on leaves, suspect leafminers, which are maggots of flies that tunnel between the surface layers. Once damage appears snip off damaged leaves. Certain plants show resistance to leafminers. Pull out the infected plants after they bloom to allow the resistant plants more room to self-sow. Generally, plants live only three years.

Companion Planting and Design

The lobed, blue-green leaves are distinctive and the unique flowers are appreciated in close range. Woodland phlox, *P. divaricata*, comes in blues and blooms in season with columbine, lungwort, and silver-variegated brunnera. Avoid groundcovers that might overtake gentle columbine. Size varies; some hybrids stretch to 5 feet.

Try These

It's hard to beat 'McKana's Giant' for elaborate, long-spurred blossoms. Brighten woodland gardens with the golden foliage of English hybrid 'Mello Yellow'. Blue alpine columbine, *A. alpina*, self-sows and needs no staking.

Coneflower

Echinacea purpurea and hybrids

Botanical Pronunciation
ECH-ah-NAH-she-ah pur-PUR-ee-ah

Bloom Period and Seasonal Color
Summer blooms in purplish pink, white, or yellow ray petals with dark central cones

Mature Height × Spread
2 to 5 feet × 1 to 2 feet

This wonderful perennial has daisylike flowers, each with a prominent center cone or disc surrounded by a skirt of ray petals. An easy-to-grow native of North American prairies, purple coneflower has been accepted as a garden plant around the world. It produces long-lasting flowers from early summer through late fall; the strong-stemmed blooms make excellent cut flowers. A sturdy, rather coarse plant, purple coneflower has showy purplish pink to almost-white flowers. Seed-bearing cones last for months until discovered by songbirds. *Echinacea laevigata*, the smooth coneflower, is an endangered sister species native to the Piedmont. Plant breeders using tissue culture have turned out wonderful new hybrids in myriad colors and flower forms. Many of these are very site- and zone-specific requiring sage advice from seasoned plantsmen for sustainable hybrid recommendations.

When, Where, and How to Plant

Plant potted coneflower in spring or early summer. Full sun or dappled shade works well. If buying native coneflowers, make sure they were seed-grown, not dug from wild populations. Start seeds in early spring or summer in nursery flats and transplant when plants have four to six leaves. Expect flowers their second year. Rich, sandy soils provide the best growth, but well-drained clay soils also produce fine plants. Dig planting holes twice as wide and of equal depth to the container. Plant in clusters with individuals 12 to 18 inches apart or as the label states per variety. Water in.

Growing Tips

During extreme drought, deeply water every two or three weeks to sustain blooming. Remove spent flower heads for the first few weeks on new plantings. Once established, coneflowers are very drought-tolerant and do not demand fertilization, but keep an eye on plants, and if they develop poor foliage color, feed them. Thin layers of bark or leaf mulch aid in weed control and stabilization of soil moisture.

Regional Advice and Care

Once established, purple coneflowers produce abundant volunteers. Transplant seedlings after rain soaks the soil, but do not do transplant after late summer in Zones 6 to 7. Disease- and pest-resistant purple coneflower reblooms if deadheaded. In winter remove dead stalks and thin beds. Once established, it requires no extra care for survival. Handpick Japanese beetles that attack tender flower petals.

Companion Planting and Design

Dependable purple coneflower is the backbone of a wildflower garden or more formal border. Because of its height, place plants toward the back of your perennial border, unless compact hybrids are chosen. Plant in sizable drifts for best effect. Good companions are artemisia, bluebeard, aster, and dwarf butterfly bush. Butterflies are attracted to the large flowers all summer and expect goldfinches when seeds mature.

Try These

'Red Knee-High' and 'Pixie Meadowbrite' fit in among shorter flowers. To confound your "expert" gardening friends, plant *E. paradoxa* (yellow flowers!) or golden 'Sunbird'. 'Razzmatazz' and 'Secret Affair' are doubly wow! Other worthwhile hardy perennial coneflowers include yellow coneflower, *Ratibida pinnata*, and Mexican hat, *R. columnifera*.

Coralbells

Heuchera sanguinea

Botanical Pronunciation
WHO-curr-ah san-QUIN-nee-ah

Other Name
Alumroot

Bloom Period and Seasonal Color
Summer flowers in white, pink, and crimson

Mature Height × Spread
1 to 2 feet × 1½ to 2 feet

Today's coralbells boast long-stemmed flowers, foliage in many colors, and tolerance of hot weather. A parent of many improved hybrids is Carolina native *Heuchera americana*. Coralbells is a low-growing perennial with maple-like, lustrous foliage that radiates from a rosette. Its beautiful foliage alone would be reason enough to grow this semi-evergreen perennial. Showy coralbells vary from peach- to yellow-colored leaves and plum glistening with a metallic sheen. Others display foliage patterns like stained glass windows. The airy flower spikes range in color from cherry to coral and can be as lovely as the distinctive foliage. In early summer, the sway of the 18-inch spikes creates movement in the garden as the delicate bell-shaped blooms toss about in the breeze. Surprisingly, hummingbirds are attracted to its tiny individual blossoms.

When, Where, and How to Plant
Plant potted specimens in spring or fall. Coralbells prefer dappled light and are happiest in partial shade. To prevent problems, plant coralbells only in moist, fertile soil. Good drainage is essential. Plants grow well in acidic soils, so there is no need to add lime. When setting out potted plants, dig a hole three times the size of the rootball. In heavy clay soils, work bark soil conditioner or granite screenings into the soil before you transplant. In wet sites, plant on slightly elevated berms. Water well to settle the soil. Mulching with compost will enrich poor sites.

Growing Tips
Water deeply, twice weekly until plants establish. When flowering begins, water weekly, particularly during dry periods. Mulching in summer is important for plant survival, but keep mulches away from the fleshy crowns. Apply slow-release fertilizer in spring if needed for vigor.

Regional Advice and Care
Rake beds clean in spring to remove old debris. A heavy layer foliage of leaves can suffocate plants. In autumn following a hard freeze, remove frozen plants. Clumps of coralbells can get quite large over time. Divide every four or five years to invigorate the bed and increase your holdings. Slugs and snails can damage or destroy young plants; use a slug bait or saucers of beer for control. Sow coralbells seed in early fall for spring seedlings. Seedlings can be divided in early summer and set 1 foot apart in beds.

Companion Planting and Design
This perennial is suitable for using along a walk or by a water garden. Collections of several varieties of coralbells plus related foamflowers and hybrid "heucherellas" look great when interspersed with *Lamium* 'White Nancy', ferns, and astilbes in shade gardens. The low-growing, variegated yellow-and-green vincas make exotic foils for coralbells. 'Palace Purple' has stood the test of time—durability and lush burgundy foliage.

Try These
New cultivars 'Venus', 'Caramel', 'Citronelle', 'Georgia Peach', 'Tiramiso', 'Stoplight', and 'Crème Brulee' provide colorful leaf selections for the *Heuchera* connoisseur.

Coreopsis

Coreopsis lanceolata

Botanical Pronunciation
cor-ee-OP-sis LANCE-oh-lat-ah

Other Name
Lanceleaf coreopsis

Bloom Period and Seasonal Color
Late spring and summer with golden yellow flowers

Mature Height × Spread
1 to 2 feet × 1 to 2 feet

You have probably seen them on the roadside and remarked about the pretty yellow wildflowers. Coreopsis is a member of the Aster family and a durable perennial for gardens that must fend for themselves. Two-inch, lance-shaped leaves form a rosette of foliage that gives rise to slender flower stems topped with golden daisies. When blooming commences with hot weather, a constant supply of blooms continues for weeks on end. As some have observed, lanceleaf coreopsis can flower into exhaustion if not lopped back in summer to revitalize it. Although not a long-lived perennial like its cousin threadleaf coreopsis, it makes up for this deficiency by unpacking a lot of color over a period of several years. It relishes a warm spot in the sun, which reminds me of my lounge chair at the beach!

When, Where, and How to Plant
Plant potted lanceleaf coreopsis in spring. Wet months of winter can weaken roots. Give it full sun and soil with good drainage. When planting in groups, spade up the ground to create a bed and add limestone to counter soil acidity. Space plantings to allow for sprawl during the flowering period. If prepared well, the soil should be easy for hand planting. This perennial can fill a pot with its roots; frill out roots at planting time using a knife or hand cultivator. Use loose backfill to set the rootball at soil level or higher. Water thoroughly and twice weekly for two weeks.

Growing Tips
Several weeks after planting feed with a soluble flower fertilizer and monthly to keep flowers coming. Too much fertilizer can cause the plants to flop. Coreopsis is tolerant of normal summer dry weather. During the first season, irrigate only to avoid wilted leaves during blooming. It's best to let it live and survive on its own determination. Remove faded flowers weekly by deadheading. This encourages continuous bloom and regrowth of basal foliage.

Regional Advice and Care
Treat coreopsis like a wildflower. Plant it and leave it alone once established. In formal garden settings, remove declining flowers and plant parts as necessary for plant health. When bloom period ends prune it back in hot weather for a shot of more flowers in fall. Mulch plantings lightly, keeping the mulch back from the lower stems to prevent leaf disease. It has few pests, but goldfinches will monitor plants for snacks.

Companion Planting and Design
Use coreopsis in perennial beds for bursts of color heading into summer. Plant in clusters for care-free gardens intermingled with drought-tolerant annuals geranium, Diamond Frost® euphorbia, angel flower, and red verbena. This is a good choice for a flower meadow.

Try These
'Early Sunrise' has the longest bloom period. For tight spaces, try the compact cultivar 'Goldfink'.

Daylily

Hemerocallis spp.

Botanical Pronunciation
hem-erh-oh-CALL-lis

Bloom Period and Seasonal Color
Late spring to September in a plethora of colors

Mature Height × Spread
1 to 4 feet × 1 to 2½ feet

M ost Southerners don't appreciate *Hemerocallis* fully unless they've visited a daylily nursery in late spring. Impressive introductions include colorful miniatures, sturdy tetraploids, spider-shaped blooms, and repeat-bloomers. Pink, plum, or scarlet colors? Sure, there's no need to settle for just yellow or orange. Most daylily cultivars have one primary bloom period. Enthusiasts plant cultivars that bloom one after the other. Some new introductions, however, break ranks. One continuous bloomer is 'Stella de Oro', an 18-inch beauty with yellow or yellow-orange flowers and a Perennial Plant of the Year status. It is a star performer in Carolina gardens with the longest bloom season of any daylily. If it slows down, shear off the top third of plants, feed and water, and the plants will rebloom in the fall.

When, Where, and How to Plant
Plant in early spring or late fall. Daylilies prefer full sun. They tolerate part-shade conditions, but require six hours of direct sun for explosive blooming. Any good soil is appropriate if it is well drained. In heavy clay, loosen the soil with an organic soil conditioner. In good soil, plant with very little preparation other than a wide planting hole, 10 inches deep. Soak the crowns of bare-root plants for several hours. Make a cone of loose soil in the middle of the hole and spread the roots out as you do for roses. Work the soil in and around and between the roots. Firm the soil and water well. Space at least 1 foot apart or farther if you will not be dividing them.

Growing Tips
Water during the flowering period. Fertilize in spring with a general flower fertilizer and again in late summer for fall blooms. A thick mulch layer will do wonders for weed control and moisture conservation; however, leave air space at the crown.

Regional Advice and Care
Remove spent blooms daily; they last for only a day. Daylilies are virtually insect free, tough, and resilient, with daylily rust being their only disease problem. Be prepared to apply a deer repellent! They divide easily, though it is best to retain two to three fan sections per clump when transplanting in late summer. Aphids may be a problem on the unopened flowers; blast them off with a spray from a garden hose. Remove stalks completely once the blooms have wilted. Rake out frozen foliage in late winter.

Companion Planting and Design
Daylilies perform admirably near tall pine trees. They are best used *en masse* for a color accent, preferably with an evergreen background. Plant near the entrance to the home or in perennial borders. Enjoy the blossoms of 'Stella de Oro' alongside sun coleus, purple heart, or 'Homestead Purple' verbena. Cut daylily stems for arrangements.

Try These
'Stella de Oro' and 'Happy Returns' are durable repeat-bloomers. In large-flowered types, look for a high bud count that will guarantee a long succession of blooms.

English Lavender

Lavandula angustifolia

Botanical Pronunciation
lav-an-DO-lah an-GUST-ee-FOL-ee-ah

Bloom Period and Seasonal Color
Summer flowers in lavender, pink, or white; gray-green to blue-gray foliage

Mature Height × Spread
12 to 24 inches × 15 to 30 inches

Lavender has been called the "Queen of the Scented Garden" and has been a major player in the perfume and soap industry for decades. Horticulturists recognize this wonderful herb as a durable landscape ornamental. It has fine-textured foliage that can be a dull green or a pleasant silver-gray color and spikes of (what else?) lavender-colored flowers. As with many herbs, it is pest-free and ideal for a low-maintenance border. One of the better varieties, 'Lady', has attractive, long-lasting, lilac-colored flowers borne on 10-inch stalks that are great for drying. Lavender is a tough evergreen herb with a remarkable ability to withstand harsh winter exposure. Though rarely used in cooking, lavender is often dried for arrangements and potpourris. The silver-gray foliage spices up many a perennial border.

When, Where, and How to Plant

Take full advantage of the first growing season and buy quart-sized pots. Plant anytime spring to fall. Lavender thrives in full sun and likes alkaline soil. To succeed with lavender, select a well-drained site or make it so. Incorporate limestone into beds at the rate of 1 pound per 10 square feet. Spread the roots horizontally to ensure that the plant is set high— or plant lavender in a raised bed or berm. Improve poorly drained soil by mixing granite screenings or ground pine bark into it. English lavender can be grown from seed; 'Lady' will bloom ninety days after sowing. Cuttings can be taken in late spring, rooted, and set out in early fall.

Growing Tips

Water weekly for the first month then only during a drought. Overwatering can kill even the most robust lavender plants. Don't be afraid to move lavender if you discover a better location. It is incredibly resilient. Use a water-soluble flower fertilizer monthly.

Regional Advice and Care

Shear lavender in early spring to clean up the plant. Trim off foliage burned from winter exposure by pruning the tips of stems by 2 inches. Prune back after flowering to groom. Research indicates that on clay soils the best mulch for lavender is a 1-inch layer of white sand that reflects light and heat. There are no special problems that require routine care. If you want to cut the spikes for drying, harvest when the flower buds are just beginning to open. Its aromatic foliage is considered a natural repellent for deer and a few household pests.

Companion Planting and Design

Plant in drifts or edgings for the best floral impact. Compact 'Hidcote' can line a walk or driveway. The handsome blue-gray foliage works well with wax begonia, perennial salvia, coreopsis, and geranium. With variegated foliage, Platinum Blonde™ 'Momparler' is neat and tidy for sunny mixed containers.

Try These

Try the taller, free-flowering 'du Provence', *L. × intermedia*, or 'Grosso'. 'Lady' won an All-America Selections medal. Use Spanish lavender 'Kew Red' for showy blooms.

Ferns

Many genera

Botanical Pronunciation
Varies

Bloom Period and Seasonal Color
Most with year-round foliage and spring fronds

Mature Height × Spread
2 to 2½ feet × 2 ½ feet

For care-free shade gardening, investigate our native Carolina ferns. Christmas fern goes virtually unnoticed until fall leaf drop, then its deep green fronds show up against the tan of fallen leaves. It can frequently be found along streams and in damp woodlands. Ferns are easy to transplant and will brighten up dark corners where almost nothing else will grow. Even less demanding is the small native ebony spleenwort fern often seen in dry sites. Evergreen holly ferns grow best near the coast. There, their leathery leaves are often seen in woodland landscapes. Japanese painted fern has broad, silvery fronds that can light up moderately shaded beds. The *Dryopteris* genus gives us great garden ferns, such as the care-free autumn fern.

When, Where, and How to Plant
Hardy species of ferns can be planted practically all year but "take" best in late winter or early spring. Once established, some ferns can tolerate up to four hours of direct sunlight. Plant them in rich, moist sites, such as by a stream or leaking air-conditioner or next to a water garden. Prepare the soil by tilling in large volumes of sphagnum peat moss or aged leaf compost. The soil mix should be a minimum of 50 percent organic matter. Good soil drainage ensures that the fibrous roots have oxygen. Ferns adapt well in acidic or alkaline soils. Don't add fertilizer to the planting hole. When planting, be careful not to break the tender fronds. Plant shallowly, water well, and apply mulch.

Growing Tips
Ferns are truly low-maintenance plants, amazingly resilient after they are established. Watering is essential during the first season but only in dry spells in the years that follow. Water three times per week after planting, especially during growth spurts. Spread compost annually as a nutrient source. Organic mulch provides some nutrients for ferns as it decays, but applying an organic fertilizer or compost every few years will keep them in tip-top condition.

Regional Advice and Care
Evergreen ferns require only an occasional light pruning to remove sunburned foliage or injury from weather, pets, and slugs. Wait until late winter or spring for heavy pruning to clean beds and nip off discolored fronds from tender species. Hardy ferns, like autumn fern, are long-lived and moderately drought-resistant when mature. Consult with a native plant society for care-free species for naturalizing.

Companion Planting and Design
Ferns provide summer and fall interest after the ephemeral spring wildflowers have finished their song and dance. They are ideal for shady, high humidity areas. Certain species like cinnamon fern and royal fern grow tall and command attention at quite a distance. Companions are hellebores, lungwort, hosta, ground orchid, and wild ginger.

Try These
An outstanding evergreen fern for landscapes is autumn fern, *Dryopteris erythrosora*. The deciduous Japanese silver-painted fern, *Athyrium nipponicum* 'Pictum' is elegant. Gold Mist wood fern, *D. labordei,* has striking golden foliage.

Foxglove

Digitalis purpurea

Botanical Pronunciation
dij-i-TAL-is pur-PUR-ee-ah

Other Name
Digitalis

Bloom Period and Seasonal Color
Early summer blooms in mostly purple, pink, and white

Mature Height × Spread
2 to 5 feet × 2 feet

Foxglove provides a substitute for tall delphiniums, which are forbiddingly difficult for gardeners in the Carolinas to grow, including in cool mountain cottage gardens. When given plenty of organic matter in their root zones and grown in afternoon shade with abundant soil moisture, foxgloves can produce spikes that top 48 inches in height. The spikes are clothed with pendent bells that stay in color for nearly a month. Foxglove is often grown as a biennial. Set into a deep organic mulch in late summer, the seedlings will grow through mild winters as hardy rosettes and shoot up flowering stalks early the following summer. They provide a wonderful backdrop for hosta. A yellow-flowering species, *Digitalis grandiflora*, is long-lived and often self-sows in garden beds.

When, Where, and How to Plant
Potted foxgloves can be planted in spring or fall. Small, non-blooming plants have a better chance of developing the expansive root system needed to carry the tall spikes. If the planting site is beneath towering oak trees, don't dig the soil. Mow the grass short, lay down three to five layers of newsprint, and spread pine or hardwood bark mulch 4 to 5 inches deep over the area to be planted. Scrape the mulch aside to make planting holes and create an equal mixture of mulch and potting soil. Set the plants in place, 2 feet apart, and backfill around them with the mixture. Water daily for the first seven to ten days.

Growing Tips
Foxglove performs best in moist, acidic soil enhanced with organic matter. Water beds with a soaker hose serpentized among your plants to give abundant moisture, especially near shade trees. Trees can suck up the soil moisture and nutrients needed by understory plants. Feed foxgloves every two weeks with water-soluble flower food dissolved per directions.

Regional Advice and Care
Groom and deadhead this perennial. When spikes begin to form, secure 3-foot bamboo stakes to the spikes loosely with twine or florist's tape. If you fail to stake them, the first wind or rainstorm will flatten them. After flowering is complete, cut bloom spikes back to the basal rosettes; this keeps plant tidy and ensures plant vigor by reducing excessive seed production. A few pods can be retained for propagation purposes. Foxglove is treated as an annual by many gardeners since flower spikes may be less showy the second season.

Companion Planting and Design
Ferns are natural companions for foxgloves. Both love partial shade and thrive on humus-rich soil and abundant moisture. However, use a different nutrient source and schedule for ferns; they resent overfertilization. Beware that leaves and seed of foxglove are toxic if ingested, so it's not a good choice for a school garden.

Try These
'Foxy', an All-America Award winner, will bloom in summer from spring-planted seeds. 'Camelot Lavender' and 'Rose' take to sunny beds.

Garden Phlox

Phlox paniculata

Botanical Pronunciation
FLOX pan-NIC-you-la-tah

Other Name
Summer phlox

Bloom Period and Seasonal Color
Summer blooms in purple, magenta, pink, and white

Mature Height × Spread
2 to 3 feet × 1 to 2 feet

This old-fashioned, easy-to-grow perennial remains a garden standby. Wild stands of garden phlox along rocky roadsides in the Carolina mountains are especially picturesque. The wildlings provided genes to develop garden phlox, which is valued for its erect plants topped by spectacular sprays of flowers, its long bloom period in summer and fall, and the butterflies it attracts. Because of our humid climate, volunteer seedlings and certain phlox cultivars can be disfigured by powdery mildew disease. Buy only the cultivars that are listed as resistant to mildew. Be merciless; pull out any mildew-infested artifacts from earlier gardens. Several other species of phlox are often found in Carolina gardens, most commonly the early-blooming creeping phlox and, in dappled shade in woodland glens, blue phlox or wild sweet William.

When, Where, and How to Plant
Plant or divide for transplanting in spring or fall. Phlox blooms best in full to partial sun. In shade, mildew problems are more numerous. Phlox grows quickly in hot weather and reaches full potential in moist, fertile soil. Spade a little compost or soil conditioner into the planting hole of a garden bed and set your plants at grade. Well-drained, fertile soils require no special soil preparation. Superphosphate works much better than bonemeal; organic gardeners may prefer to use unprocessed rock phosphate.

Growing Tips
Water weekly during the flowering season and when drought prevails. Water early in the morning to avoid wetting the foliage, which leads to chronic leaf diseases. Phlox is not a heavy feeder. Apply slow-release flower fertilizer early during the growing season in poor soil. Apply a 2-inch layer of mulch in early summer. Prune back one-half in May for height control; this increases bloom display later.

Regional Advice and Care
Plant mildew-resistant varieties, or seek advice on organic fungicides. Many gardeners use horticultural oil as a preventative, especially during hot, humid weather. Thin new shoots in spring to five strong stems per crown. This allows air to circulate. Thinning discourages powdery mildew disease and favors stronger stems to withstand storms. Deadhead garden phlox after peak bloom to enjoy a second flush of flowers and to prevent a rash of unwanted seedlings. Divide summer phlox every two or three years to maintain vigor. Perennials, including phlox, are vulnerable to voles when planted in a woodland garden. Cats and mousetraps reduce vole populations.

Companion Planting and Design
For the ambiance of an English cottage garden, try garden phlox as a background plant behind coralbells and coneflowers. Plant phlox against a picket fence or in front of an evergreen hedge to show off the brilliance of the flowers. A plethora of new cultivars have been released that offer fragrance and disease-resistant foliage in colors from bubblegum pink to coral crème. It's perfect for the butterfly garden!

Try These
'David' (white) and 'Laura' (purple) are mildew-resistant, while 'Nora Leigh' has striking variegated foliage. Look for new introductions coming soon.

Gaura

Gaura lindheimeri

Botanical Pronunciation
GOW-rah lind-HY-mer-eye

Bloom Period and Seasonal Color
Early summer to fall blooms in white or pink

Mature Height × Spread
2 to 4 feet × 2 to 2 to 3 feet

In the 1980s, Jim Wilson, the renowned horticulturist, spotted this wildflower blooming along dry, sandy fencerows in East Texas wildlands and wondered why the green industry hadn't offered it to gardeners. Well, it happened, and gaura moved into the mainstream of Southern perennials. Designers like its wispy, see-through plants and the way the individual blossoms perch on thin, flexible stems that flutter in the slightest breeze. The original species with pinky white blossoms has morphed into shorter, more manageable selections with larger, deeper colored blossoms and foliage. You can grow gaura easily in well-drained garden soil, but keep the sprinklers away when it's established. In Texas, it gets by with scattered showers and no pampering. Think of "benign neglect" as an appropriate program for growing gaura.

When, Where, and How to Plant
Plant gaura anytime in the growing season. Hardened-off plants can be set out quite early and adjust quickly. In clay soil, build up beds by mixing 3-inch layers of bark soil conditioner and play sand with the surface 6 inches of soil to create a fast-draining environment. Plants that like dry soil will grow like never before. In sandy soils, mix in 2 to 3 inches of moistened sphagnum peat moss. Set out gaura plants in full sun, 1½ to 2 feet apart. Stir a tablespoon of CRF into the backfill soil. Water plants weekly until new growth shows.

Growing Tips
A layer of mulch is okay on sandy soil but tends to keep clay too moist. Despite guara's drought resistance, an occasional deep watering won't harm your plants. But you can kill gaura with kindness by overfeeding and overwatering. Apply controlled-release fertilizer around established guara plants in late spring after new growth begins, or as needed.

Regional Advice and Care
Gaura can get leggy in our Carolina heat and humidity. A heavy shearing of established plants in early summer prior to bloom will produce fuller clumps and more flowering branches. When flowering spikes begin to look shabby, deadhead them to encourage new spikes if you wish to reduce the number of seedlings that will sprout from dropped seeds. Don't eliminate all seedlings because this short-lived perennial needs to renew itself. At season's end, if you want lots of seedlings for gifts to friends, scatter seed on flats or pots of starter mix.

Companion Planting and Design
Plants that also like dry soil include spreading zinnia, sedum, agave, variegated yucca, lavender, verbascum, and portulaca. Use in a scree or meadow garden. It's perfect as a thriller plant for large containers.

Try These
'Siskiyou Pink' has darker flowers than the wildling and matures at a shorter height. Its terminal growth is dark pink. White 'Whirling Butterflies,' and Stratosphere™ White produces no seeds and blends well in borders. 'Corrie's Gold' is variegated.

Ground Orchid

Bletilla striata

Botanical Pronunciation
blah-TILL-ah STRY-ah-tah

Other Name
Chinese ground orchid

Bloom Period and Seasonal Color
Summer flowers of lavender and white; medium green foliage

Mature Height × Spread
12 inches × 20 inches

The orchid family is a large group with thousands of species growing on trees in rainy tropical regions. Two terrestrial orchids, cranefly and pink ladyslipper, are widespread in Carolina woodlands. Ground orchid is an exotic, herbaceous perennial with clump-forming habit. From a short distance a full bed of ground orchids could be mistaken for stout gladiolus. Given moist ground and partial shade, five to ten beautiful flowers resembling cymbidium corsage orchids appear on 1-foot stems on its narrow, upright leaves. Foliage turns a lovely yellow to brown in fall as the rhizomateous roots prepare for a rest. Ground orchids flourish in gardens where they receive some cold weather during dormancy. Most blooms are shades of lavender but white and yellow varieties are available from mail-order suppliers.

When, Where and How to Plant

Add potted plants spring to fall; plant dormant root sections in spring. A dappled sun to part-shade area where the soil stays evenly moist is ideal in Zone 8. It's often found thriving in the shadows of a building on east and north exposures. Prepare the garden space by incorporating a generous amount of peat moss or soil conditioner for drainage and moisture-holding capacity. Gently slip the plant from the pot and space at 6 inches. Dormant roots are spaced five per square foot and set at a 2- to 3-inch depth. Mulch thinly and water thoroughly to settle plantings.

Growing Tips

Tropical orchids make their home on tree bark, but ground orchids need terra firma. Clay soil holds moisture but can get bone dry in late summer. Irrigate beds during dry spells. Flowers will be long lasting in moist soil. After bloom, remove flower stems to tidy up the bed. Leaving the spent flowers to develop seedpods is an option. Most perennials respond to aged manure or compost at the onset of new growth in spring. Allow it to grow undisturbed, since crowded clumps bloom best.

Regional Advice and Care

This hardy perennial is limited only by a lack of winter cold for the roots. It has few pests except aphids. Take a garden hose and remove with a quick spraying, or wait for ladybugs to feast on them. Plants that fail to bloom may need more sunlight. I have seen them growing in direct sun in Zone 7. Clay soils that are poorly drained can be fatal to perennials, particularly in winter. Divide and transplant clumps during the fall season. Store roots dry overwinter in vermiculite.

Companion Planting and Design

Ground orchid is stunning in thick masses of single or mixed colors for accent and enjoyment. Interplanting with Dragon Wing™ begonia, sun coleus, and impatiens in dappled shade can be glorious. It's a great spike for planters and mixed container gardens.

Try These

For larger flowers select 'Big Bob'. Mail-order nurseries offer 'Murasaki Shikibu' and 'Kate'. A yellow bicolor is 'Fukurin'; 'Albostriata' blooms white.

Hardy Banana

Musa basjoo

Botanical Pronunciation
MEW-sa BAS-you

Other Name
Japanese fiber banana

Bloom Period and Seasonal Color
Late summer flowers emerge as a yellow-orange scape

Mature Height × Spread
10 to 18 feet × 10 feet

Gardeners plant tropicals in the Carolinas, but a banana tree in the Midsouth instinctively gets a second glance from passersby. What bold texture and structure! Hardy banana adds a little of the tropics to your yard. Hailing from China, this species is the world's hardiest banana. Don't expect edible fruit from this tall, herbaceous species since it is mainly ornamental, but relish the light green leaves that expand to a whopping 6 feet. Broad, arching leaves form near the top of a thick, green trunk producing a heavy canopy reminiscent of an island paradise. The red-leaved variety has gained in popularity as gardeners seek out foliage color in lieu of flowers to create interest or punctuation for bed design. Hardy bananas often flower, and produce 2-inch bananas and great conversation!

When, Where, and How to Plant
Plant in spring after the last freeze date, and throughout summer. Choose a location that is sunny and offers some protection from winds. Bananas love water, so plant within close proximity to a water source. Avoid poorly drained soils that can rot the underground stem. Dig a hole twice the diameter of the rootball and 18 inches deep. Enrich the soil with leaf compost or bark soil conditioner to ensure that the planting hole is friable (loose) and well amended. Place the root stem (corm) to a depth of 8 inches, then cover with the backfill soil. Water thoroughly to remove air pockets.

Growing Tips
As new leaves appear, water daily. Continue irrigating every other day for three weeks and weekly if rainfall is limited. Hardy banana is a heavy feeder and will respond to liquid plant fertilizer applications applied weekly during the rapid growth stage. Once established, this perennial will form a dense colony of plants. Some companies offer banana seeds, if you are up for the challenge.

Regional Advice and Care
In cold regions of Zone 7 or lower, mulch 3 feet deep its first winter until your planting is established. Hardy banana tolerates winter temperatures to minus 20 degrees Fahrenheit. It appreciates constant soil moisture during the driest months of summer. Winter care in the mountains requires a wire cage full of leaves, or a PVC pipe teepee covered with a tarp. A 4-inch mulch is maintained during the early years for sucker and root protection. After an autumn freeze cut back trunks to 2 feet using a pruning saw. No pests bother hardy banana.

Companion Planting and Design
Hardy banana makes a big design statement, so a planting can easily stand alone. It can be planted in perennial borders of large-statured plants with seasonal interest, such as elephant-ears, Joe-Pye weed, perennial salvia, and hibiscus.

Try These
Musa velutina, pink velvet banana, is fine. Darjeeling banana, *M. sikkimensis*, takes cold. Other selections are best handled as tender annuals, including rojo or blood banana, *M. acuminata*, and 15-foot variegated 'Ae-Ae'. One online source is www.tytyga.com.

Hardy Hibiscus

Hibiscus moscheutos

Botanical Pronunciation
hi-BIS-kus mos-SHOOT-toes

Other Name
Rose mallow

Bloom Period and Seasonal Color
Summer blooms in pink, red, maroon, white, and bicolors

Mature Height × Spread
3 to 8 feet × 3 to 5 feet

These are not the tropical hibiscus that grace landscapes along the Gulf Coast, nor the woody shrub found in your grandmother's garden. Hardy hibiscus has its roots in the southeastern United States—literally. The native *Hibiscus coccineus*, a marsh plant called Texas star, is cherished for its large iridescent crimson blooms and vigorous cut-leaf foliage. The sturdy perennial hibiscus, *H. moscheutos*, is also fond of water and a more adaptable hibiscus for perennial borders. While both species are workhorses, the latter has blooms up to 10 inches across and is available in an assortment of colors. Our native hibiscus species grow quite tall in moist soil. Accordingly, plant breeders developed the waist-high 'Disco Belle' for small yards. Its flowers are larger than salad plates.

When, Where, and How to Plant
Plant in spring when the soil is moist but not wet. A sunny garden and average soil encourages rapid growth. Finally, a plant that flourishes in clay! In dry or rocky soil amend backfill with several shovels of leaf compost or rotted manure. Set clumps at the depth they were originally growing, 4 to 5 feet apart. Spade a little 5-10-10 fertilizer or similar flower food into the planting area at the rate of 1 pound per 100 square feet. Water deeply for two weeks. Hardy hibiscus appreciates mulch.

Growing Tips
In dry sites, keep the plant irrigated during the bloom season. A light fertilization of water-soluble plant food when flowering begins should get it up and running. Established plants are moderately drought tolerant for short durations.

Regional Advice and Care
Hardy hibiscus is a low-maintenance plant with few pests. Japanese beetles and weevils nibble on the leaves or flowers, but they can be removed by hand or with insecticides applied in the evening hours. Spent flowers drop off neatly. Hot afternoon sun can scorch leaf tips if the soil is too dry. Cut the plants to the ground after a hard freeze. In Zone 7a and west, delay this pruning until late winter, and follow with a deep mulching to protect the crowns. When clumps grow too large, dig them, wash off the soil, and divide them with a hatchet. Divide in early spring or in early fall. Remove faded flowers to encourage more bud development, but beware of bees trapped in closed blooms. To control the height, lop back one-half in June.

Companion Planting and Design
Grow it in the background of perennial borders where its height is an advantage. Rose mallow is native to wetlands, and a site by a seep, water garden, or exuberant fountain would be perfect. Hibiscus is right at home in a sunny corner near a faucet for frequent watering. Use with colorful annuals such as sun coleus and sweet potato vine.

Try These
The immense flowers of 'Southern Belle' mix are traffic stoppers. Its little sister, 'Dixie Belle', is often grown as a hedge plant. Hybrid Summerific® hibiscus include floriferous 'Cranberry Crush' and 'Plum Fantasy'.

Hellebore

Helleborus spp. and hybrids

Botanical Pronunciation
hell-la-BORE-us

Other Name
Lenten rose

Bloom Period and Seasonal Color
Winter and early spring blooms in white, pink, green, and deep purple

Mature Height × Spread
1 to 1 ½ feet × 2 to 2 ½ feet

The glossy, evergreen foliage of Lenten rose, *Helleborus orientalis*, stands out when everything else is drab and winter-weary. The 2-inch nodding flowers with showy bracts and yellow stamens decorate gardens in the colder months of the year. Christmas rose, *H. niger*, bears large white flowers during winter. Many photos have been taken of Christmas rose blooming when virtually buried in snow. Lenten rose has elegant palm-like leaves up to a foot wide, with most plants blooming in late winter. This lovely species is recognized for its white- to maroon-colored blooms that are often speckled. Breakthough breeding programs have yielded new hybrids with double flowers, striking foliage, and new color combinations. The magnificent foliage alone makes this a worthwhile addition to any garden.

When, Where, and How to Plant

Fall is the best time to plant. Hellebores make new roots then and establish easily. However, hybrids are sold for planting in spring too. They grow in most well-drained soils. Although hellebores grow in alkaline soil in their native habitat, they don't demand it. Plants grow well in light shade but bloom better with morning sun. Prepare the area by spading plenty of compost or organic matter into the planting hole. Set plants 18 inches apart with the crown of the plant level with the surrounding soil or slightly higher. Mulch well and water promptly.

Growing Tips

Hellebores seldom require additional water after an initial soaking, provided they are growing in a moist, woodland location. In other sites, water

routinely their first summer. Slow-release fertilizer applied very early in spring will please most species of hellebores. *H. niger* may respond to additional magnesium; dissolve 1 tablespoon Epsom salts in 1 gallon of water and apply to stimulate flowering.

Regional Advice and Care

Hellebores are low maintenance and pest-free. Some gardeners cut off weatherbeaten leaves in late winter for cosmetic reasons and to reveal emerging flowering shoots. During a severe winter, flower buds may be damaged, but leaves escape unscathed. When established, hellebores self-sow freely, particularly *H. foetidus*, stinking hellebore. Mulch old plantings with leaf compost annually. This perennial is shunned by both deer and voles. To encourage volunteers, spread a 1-inch layer of sand around plants to act as a seedbed. Established plants may be divided in early fall, but they recover slowly.

Companion Planting and Design

Plant hellebores where they can be viewed from an indoor room during winter, or in an entrance flower bed. They are to woodland gardens what sedums are to rock gardens. With the magnificent habit of 'Anna's Red' and unique foliage of 'Ivory Prince', designers get to rethink where to place new releases. The 'Royal Heritage' hellebores offer a sumptuous range of colors.

Try These

Oriental Lenten rose, *H. × hybridus*, has outstanding qualities for a shade garden. Take a look at 'Royal Heritage' hellebores and the stunning Pine Knot Strain.

Hosta

Hosta spp.

Botanical Pronunciation
HOS-tah

Other Name
Plantain lily

Bloom Period and Seasonal Color
Summer blooms in white to pale lilac; plethora of leaf sizes and colors

Mature Height × Spread
3 inches to 4 feet × 4 inches to 7 feet

Hosta, the ultimate shade plant, is on a roll. Ease of culture, colorful foliage, resilience, and low maintenance make hosta the perfect perennial for contemporary gardens. More than 2,000 different varieties are in the trade. Hostas are grown primarily for their foliage, and there are four basic color groups: blue, green, gold, and variegated. The white-flowered species is fragrant. Hostas are versatile, ranging from miniatures to huge 7-foot spreading specimen plants. If weather conditions become too extreme, hosta will simply go dormant early. Here in the South, plant this beauty in afternoon shade or mottled all-day shade and you'll be rewarded with a marvelous, long-lasting ornamental. When choosing cultivars, opt for ones that emerge late; their new shoots escape frost damage. Hostas are easy to grow!

When, Where, and How to Plant
Plant anytime the ground is not frozen. Hosta prefers shade from the afternoon sun; filtered light suits them best. Too much sun turns variegated cultivars green and parches the leaves of those with white or cream markings. Blue-green or green cultivars are more sun-tolerant. Hosta prefers moist, well-drained soils that are rich in organic matter. Soil prep is the key! Spade up a wide area for a plant; make it three times the diameter of the rootball. Spread the roots when planting. It is better to plant too shallow than too deep. Water every two to three days for the first two weeks.

Growing Tips
During dry seasons, be diligent in watering hostas weekly, and mulch them annually. Fertile, organic soils are preferred; they are heavy feeders. Broadcast a slow-release fertilizer each spring. Keep it off the plants; it can burn holes in foliage.

Regional Advice and Care
After blooms fade, cut flower stalks back to near the soil line. Groom beds after the autumn freeze by trimming away melted leaves; reapply mulch. Dry leaf tips and margins indicate drought stress. Yellowing foliage is a sign of waterlogged soils, which can result in bacterial diseases and root rot. Major pests are slugs, voles, deer, and blister beetles. Voles can present the biggest threat to plantings in woodland gardens. Mousetraps give some relief, or add Stalite rock (Vole Block™) or gravel to beds prior to planting. Baits control slugs; apply early. Divide as new shoots peek out of the ground in early spring or early fall while the plants are inactive.

Companion Planting and Design
Hostas are traditionally used as border plants and planted in large clusters with ferns, hellebores, ground orchid, rhododendrons, and azaleas. The ultra-dwarf cultivars can be lined up as edgings and larger kinds as groundcovers in a woodland garden. A single plant can make a nice specimen for a shady nook or container; versatile and adored.

Try These
There are hundreds of cultivars to explore; consult the American Hosta Society website. Hostas have great names: 'Seducer', 'So Sweet', 'Goodness Gracious', 'Hanky Panky', and 'Empress Wu'.

Iris

Iris spp. and hybrids

Botanical Pronunciation
EYE-ris

Bloom Period and Seasonal Color
Seasonal blooms in blue, white, lavender, red,
and many color combinations

Mature Height × Spread
8 to 42 inches × 1 foot to 3 feet clumps

Southern gardeners are familiar with bearded iris as the standard for the Carolinas. Sadly, many exciting species of the *Iris* genera are overlooked. As a group, iris ranges from alpine dryland perennials to bog dwellers and range of light exposure from sun to shade. Broad straplike foliage adds vertical interest and texture to gardens. I have grown Japanese, Siberian, and Chinese roof iris in average clay loam soil and always look forward to spectacular blue flowers in late spring to complement my daylilies. This diverse group of hardy plants includes two American natives, *Iris cristata* and *I. × louisiana*, which are equally at home in woodland or wetland settings. You'll enjoy their exquisite flowers for cutting, as well as the easy-to-grow culture of iris.

When, Where, and How to Plant

Set potted plants out in spring or fall, weeks ahead of the bloom period. Mature plantings produce clumps and rhizomes that can be divided for transplanting before or after the active growth period. Locate most iris species in full sun or give afternoon shade to preserve their flowers. Woodland species are the exception. Add peat moss or compost to beds of Japanese and Louisiana iris, to retain moisture, plus a handful of controlled-release fertilizer. Japanese iris (*I. ensata*) and wetlands species appreciate acidic soils; no limestone is added at planting. However, most iris grow in pH 6.0. Space by variety; check plant labels. Water every two or three days for a week to get them off to a good start, then back off.

Growing Tips

Iris benefit from occasional watering during the growth and flowering cycle. If rainfall is not sufficient, irrigate weekly to maintain moist soil while blooming. Most iris fare well in summer and are not high maintenance plants. Fertilize it with water-soluble flower food to jump-start new growth in spring. Landscape plantings do well with minimal fertilization; feed on an as-needed basis. Mulch to manage weeds.

Regional Advice and Care

Iris needs little attention except for a severe trimming in fall to remove weatherbeaten foliage. Old flower spikes form unsightly seedheads; remove pods and stems to tidy plants. Wetland species or flag iris can be grown in containers; plant in potting soil and sink these into the edge of a koi pond or rain garden. Make it a practice to remove yellowing leaves from perennials as they develop. Few pests bother iris, including deer.

Companion Planting and Design

Iris companions include daylily, coral bells, and cottage pinks. Woodland species serve as groundcovers and accents when interplanted with wildflowers. Wetland species unabashedly steal the show in bog gardens and water features. Plant Siberian iris with Mexican bush salvia, butterfly weed, or Japanese anemone for great late-season color.

Try These

Got to have those plate-sized blooms of Japanese iris! It is nearly impossible to have just one species. Experiment with the new colors of Louisiana iris and shade-loving crested iris.

Japanese Anemone

Anemone × hybrida

Botanical Pronunciation
AH-nem-o-nee HI-bred-da

Bloom Period and Seasonal Color
Fall blooms in white, rose, and pink

Mature Height × Spread
1 to 4 feet × 1 to 1½ feet

Late fall flowers are rare. While most herbaceous perennials reach their zenith during the summer months, Japanese anemones make their debut around Labor Day. Their clump-forming plants are wonderful for partially shaded gardens where they will bloom continuously until frost. Japanese anemones produce 2- to 3-foot, nearly leafless flower stalks from wide, low-growing foliage rosettes with maple-shaped leaves. The tall stalks support small clusters of single- or double-flowered daisylike blooms that make long-lasting cut flowers for fresh bouquets. The pure white cultivar lights up the garden during evening hours. Under moonlit skies, it is even more romantic. Do not confuse the colorful anemones (windflowers), spring-planted from tubers, with this sturdy, long-lived Japanese species. This perennial beauty is slow to establish but certainly worth the wait.

When, Where, and How to Plant

Plant potted Japanese anemones in spring or fall. Mail-order nurseries sell bare-root plants for spring planting. Filtered shade or morning sun is ideal, as is rich, organic soil with excellent drainage. Japanese anemones require a neutral pH soil and that has been amended by adding compost and a dusting of limestone. Remove plants from their containers and set them in soil that has been tilled to a depth of 6 inches. If planting individual clumps, dig a hole about twice the size of the rootball and firm-in the roots with amended soil. Water thoroughly every three days for the first two weeks. Apply 2 inches of mulch. Plant in a semi-permanent location; it resents being moved once established.

Growing Tips

Water Japanese anemones once a week during summer and more often during drought. This is very important while plants are blooming and for beds that receive intense sun and heat. They become quite drought tolerant after a few years. Apply a flower fertilizer in May. For height control on established plants shear back by one-third as plants grow to 1 foot.

Regional Advice and Care

Remove dead flower stalks by snipping off their stems near the base of the plant. Groom beds by removing all dead foliage during early spring. Overirrigating your plants in heavy clay soils will encourage root rot disease. Monitor for blister beetles, mites, and aphids; eliminate with a water blast or labeled bug spray. Mulch beds of mature plantings annually. Virtually no pruning or maintenance is required other than for cosmetic reasons. Clumps expand rapidly in fertile soil; cut runners back in spring and pot up rooted sections to give to friends. Divide large clumps every ten years to renew.

Companion Planting and Design

Ferns, hosta, coralbells, coleus, and impatiens are good companions for Japanese anemone; all are "easy" flowers ideal for cottage gardens. Mass groups are wonderful.

Try These

No variety is as popular in the Carolinas as white 'Honorine Jobert'. The pink varieties *A. hupehensis* 'September Charm' and 'Hadspen Abundance' are appealing.

Lantana

Lantana camara

Botanical Pronunciation
lan-TAN-ah ka-MARR-ah

Bloom Period and Seasonal Color
Summer to fall blooms in yellow, orange, and red to peach

Mature Height × Spread
2 to 4 feet × 3 to 5 feet

This showy member of the verbena family is valued for its profusion of blooms over a long season. Southern gardeners have found lantana drought-resistant, easy to grow in average soils, and a magnet for flocks of butterflies. It's grown as a tender summer annual in most Carolinas climate zones. Flattened bloom clusters are borne on coarse, upright to arching woody stems covered with rich green, 3-inch, leathery leaves. Each flower cluster may contain thirty or more tiny blossoms that may change colors as they mature. Some varieties are naturally shrublike while others are low-growing and spreading. The latter growth habit is valued for containers. All lantanas release a pungent odor when handled. Spring-planted hardy lantana cultivars become perennial in Zone 7b and in southerly reaches of the Carolinas.

When, Where, and How to Plant

Plant in spring or early summer. Starting from potted plants is preferred to growing from seeds, particularly in Zones 6 to 7. Plants begin blooming when quite small and never let up until killed by frost. Lantana likes hot, sunny locations. It is fabulous in planters and container gardens but will need consistent watering since it is a rampant grower. Use it as a bedding plant in ordinary soil without amendments, but avoid soils that are poorly drained, or incorporate bark soil conditioner to improve drainage. Water twice weekly for several weeks until established.

Growing Tips

Lantana is care-free as long as it gets a little water in hot, dry periods. Mulch flower beds to encourage sustainability. Feeding a continuous flower fertilizer in late spring keeps lantana happy in ground beds. Use a liquid fertilizer monthly in mixed containers. Some varieties are best grown as annuals; in borders, choose winter-hardy cultivars.

Regional Advice and Care

There are no pests or diseases. Prune occasionally to keep lantana dense and loaded with flowers. It is not important to deadhead blooms, but heading back rangy shoots will help maintain symmetry. Lantana will perennialize if it's not cut back at the end of the season. Wait to prune old stalks until new growth appears in spring. A pine needle mulch will give added winter protection in Zone 8 gardens; remove mulch and prune back in early spring. This plant comes with a warning for children: The porcelain black berries are poisonous when eaten! Use in the background so children won't notice the fruit. Wear gloves when handling lantana plants; the leaves have hairs that can irritate skin.

Companion Planting and Design

Lantana is as content in a landscape bed with annuals as it is in a hanging basket or container. Grow in a sunny perennial garden or with companions like globe amaranth, butter daisy, spreading zinnia, blue salvia, and ornamental grasses.

Try These

The profuse blooming of 'New Gold' is special in containers. 'Miss Huff' and 'Mozelle' hardy lantanas are sterile and bloom nonstop to frost. Many new selections on the way!

Perennial Salvia

Salvia spp. and hybrids

Botanical Pronunciation
SAL-vee-ah

Other Name
Hardy sage

Bloom Period and Seasonal Color
Late spring to fall (depending on species),
in red, blue, lavender, pink, and yellow

Mature Height × Spread
1 ½ to 5 feet × 2 to 7 feet

Carolina gardeners are all too familiar with scarlet sage, *Salvia splendens*, the showy bedding plant. Discovering a whole world of salvias that are true perennials has changed the way color beds are now designed. Perennial salvia is a diverse group of species and hybrids supplying the bones for a sustainable garden. They come in all sizes and flower colors. Most are native to the southwestern United States and to Mexico and will not languish in a sunny border in August. Two popular choices are *S. guaranitica*, a tall, spreading sage, and *S. greggii*, the autumn sage. The waist-high Mexican bush salvia, *S. leucantha*, is beloved by all providing late-season accent. Collectively, the salvias offer great promise, being easy to grow and undemanding.

When, Where, and How to Plant

Set out potted plants in full sun in spring and early summer. Space plants according to the cultivar chosen; those with stoloniferous habit need much wider spacing. Not a lot of soil preparation is required. Incorporate a handful of limestone and a 2-inch layer of soil conditioner into a square yard of bed. Spread out the roots and place the plants with the top of the rootball level with the soil surface. Backfill around the rootball, mulch lightly, keeping it from contact with the stems. Soak the bed thoroughly.

Growing Tips

Perennial salvia can get by with occasional, deep watering during dry weather. A spring and late-summer application of 1-2-2 ratio flower fertilizer will build strong roots and send the plants into winter with a good outlook for survival. The more aggressive varieties may need dividing as they mature. If you're transplanting, wait until fall.

Regional Advice and Care

Established plantings of perennial salvia should overwinter well with little concern in most zones. However, in the northwest and mountain regions, pine needle mulch applied in December will provide added winter protection. Groom the tall perennial salvia by snipping back spent flower stems and give a light haircut in midsummer. Delay bed cleanup until spring. Leaf-eating caterpillars may attack salvias. Grow a few plants of garlic chives or mountain mints in your garden to attract beneficial wasps and let them help take care of the worms. Or, spray with *B.t.* and remove by hand.

Companion Planting and Design

The medium-height salvias are used for filling beds, but the tall, robust types are often employed like temporary shrubs and interspersed with pink or yellow annuals to bring out their splendid colors. Few quick-growing plants are taller than Mexican bush salvia. Hibiscus 'Red Shield' is one, and it looks elegant when grown in banks behind *S. leucantha*.

Try These

Well worth trying are Brazilian blue sage (*S. guaranitica*); Mexican bush sage 'Santa Barbara' (*S. leucantha*); forsythia sage (*S. madrensis*); pineapple sage (*S. elegans*); and the shrubby autumn sage (*S. greggii*).

Purple Heart

Setcreasea pallida

Botanical Pronunciation
set-CREASE-ee-ah pa-LID-da

Other Name
Purple wandering Jew

Bloom Period and Seasonal Color
Summer blooms in dark pink on purple foliage

Mature Height × Spread
8 to 10 inches × 16 to 22 inches

Zones 7b to 8

Southern gardeners love this endearing foliage plant. Its long, lax, brittle stems and fleshy leaves, which may remind you of dugout canoes, flourish through extremes of heat and humidity yet can live through winter in Zone 8. Its small, dark pink flowers in the leaf axils redeem its plainness. Purple heart is an amusing plant, yet it is to be marveled at because of its courage and durability despite long periods of neglect. Purple heart is perfect for clothing steep slopes exposed to afternoon sun and where water has to come from rainfall. It's terrific for window boxes facing west or south, or for oft-neglected container gardens. What a great facing plant to use as edging and companion to many.

When, Where, and How to Plant
Wait until frost danger is past before planting. Give purple heart the most challenging, hottest, driest, most sun-drenched spot in your garden and it will be happy. It can withstand afternoon shade but doesn't require respite from the sun. Mix in 2 inches of organic soil conditioner before planting, not that purple heart needs it, but because organic matter makes it easier for water to soak into the soil. Potted plants or rooted segments from last year's plantings should be set 18 inches apart. On slopes, set plants where they can trail down to cover exposed soil.

Growing Tips
Even with its desert-like endurance, purple heart appreciates a slow drink of water from a sprinker after a week of bone-dry August weather. When drought-stricken, the leaves tend to fold up lengthwise to reduce their surface area. With a good watering, they will plump up and unfold. Two drenchings with water-soluble flower fertilizer during the growing season will maximize foliage color and new growth.

Regional Advice and Care
When you forget to water for weeks, purple heart can develop leaf scorch. Snip off and compost disfigured leaves. Spray a repellent if deer browse your purple heart. Insect problems are few; disease problems mostly come from summer root rot due to too much water from sprinkler systems set for the needs of lawn grass. Turn sprinklers away from your planting of purple heart. Top growth will die back during winter. Come spring, twist it off to allow new growth to emerge. Save the branches you shear off. Cut them into short segments, each including at least two joints, and stick them in potting soil to root. A really severe winter will eliminate plantings in Zones 6 to 7.

Companion Planting and Design
Tall salvias such as Brazilian sage, coreopsis, and 'Stella de Oro' daylily look good planted behind a bed of purple heart. Ornamental sweet potatoes, pink 'Wave' petunias, and purple fountain grass combine well in containers. It's great in rock gardens and low-maintenance mixed borders.

Try These
There is only one variety in the species. You can't go wrong. It may be listed as *Tradescantia pallida*.

Rosemary

Rosmarinus officinalis

Botanical Pronunciation
rose-mare-RINE-nus oh-FISH-ee-NAL-is

Bloom Period and Seasonal Color
Early to midsummer (sporadically in winter) pale blue or pink flowers

Mature Height × Spread
2 to 6 feet × 1 to 4 feet

Zones 7b to 8

In the Carolinas, we are able to grow rosemary to a great size. (Well, not in the mountains where it can be killed by severe winters, but elsewhere.) What a treat to have big, evergreen rosemary shrubs ready year-round to contribute sprigs for seasoning meats, especially chicken, stews, and soups. And what a joy to be able to create rosemary topiaries such as Christmas trees and Valentine hearts. This ever-popular herb is at home in the perennial border or in a container garden. It is easy to grow, and its gray-green foliage gives it a carefree look. Its 1-inch, needlelike leaves are intensely aromatic. The flavor of dried rosemary in meat or poultry dishes is distinctive and delectable, but wait until you have tried it fresh. Wow!

When, Where, and How to Plant

Plant potted rosemary from spring through fall. In the mountains, grow it in a container and overwinter it indoors; a sunny window is adequate. Rosemary is a true sun-lover, though a semi-shaded location will suffice. It thrives in fast-draining alkaline soil. Rosemary is the plant to grow in hot sites, as it stands up well in heat and drought. In containers, use a coarse soilless mix. In poor soils, amend beds before planting; pH of 7.0 is best. See page 99 for advice on soil preparation. Plant rosemary shallowly, with its uppermost roots showing after planting. Use compost to cover the top inch of roots. Water thoroughly after planting.

Growing Tips

Water rosemary in containers as needed, and weekly in raised beds until established, normally in eight weeks. Don't overwater plants in clay soils. (Err on the dry side with most herbs.) Dry weather is not a threat, but rosemary will use a lot of water in gravelly soils. Fertilize at least once, in April or September. Do not mulch deeply; mulch can hold too much moisture during winter.

Regional Advice and Care

Many established rosemary plantings survive harsh winters. Close attention should be given to cold-hardy varieties for Zones 6 to 7. Good soil drainage should help preserve this perennial. Prune in early spring and snip sprigs routinely. Train into a topiary using wire forms. It is not bothered by deer, drought, or pests. Harvest rosemary leaves anytime, although its fragrant oil peaks before the flowers open. Dry sprigs in a paper bag indoors.

Companion Planting and Design

Prostrate forms such as 'Renzels' are suitable for a groundcover. Rosemary is fantastic in rock gardens, cascading over walls, and in planters. Interplant with colorful perennials for an informal garden. Use with groundcover oregano 'Kent Bounty' and English lavender for an aromatic treat. Rosemary topiaries add interest to any space.

Try These

In large gardens, use 'Arp' for its wide spreading, shrubby form. 'Irene' and 'Huntington Carpet' have a pendulous habit. 'Tuscan Blue' is a beautiful, upright plant with leaves twice the width of standard cultivars.

Sedum 'Autumn Joy'

Sedum × hylotelephium and cultivars

Botanical Pronunciation
SEA-dum hi-lo-TELL-ee-FY-ee-um

Other Name Stonecrop

Bloom Period and Seasonal Color
Summer blooms in reddish to brilliant carmine

Mature Height × Spread
1½ to 2 feet × 1 to 1½ feet

A garden favorite, 'Autumn Joy' sedum may be one of the first cultivars that gardeners think of when selecting perennials. Members of the genus *Sedum* are referred to as stonecrops because many of the cultivars are rock garden plants. Sedums like hot, sunny weather and don't mind thunderstorms. In early spring, established plants push fleshy, gray-green buds out of the soil. As temperatures rise, the powdery blue leaves expand. By summer, the erect stems and leaves are topped by greenish flower buds. In mid- to late summer, the buds expand into 3-inch flower heads that slowly transition to a reddish to brilliant carmine color. The blooms fade to a coppery color then finally to rust by cooler weather. Butterflies flock to its broad, nectar-filled flower heads.

When, Where, and How to Plant
Set plants in 6- to 8-inch pots in the garden after danger of hard frost is past. The sunnier the site, the better. One of the "musts" for growing stonecrops is perfect drainage. Mix coarse gravel or rock screenings into the soil before planting to raise the soil level, or plant in containers. Sandy loam soils need no amendments. Avoid wet or shady sites. Dig a hole the same depth as the rootball and twice as wide. Work loosened soil in and around sedum's fleshy roots. Trim the longest roots back by one-third. Water to settle the soil around the rootball. Don't water again for two weeks unless you are planting sedums in dry midsummer weather.

Growing Tips
These plants are drought tolerant and rugged. Water every two weeks in dry weather, but don't overwater. When 'Autumn Joy' begins to push up in spring, scatter 10-10-10 fertilizer between the plants at the rate of 1 pound per 100 square feet. This should take care of its nutritional needs for the growing season. Too much nitrogen can cause flower heads to flop over in wet summers. If you mulch, do it sparingly, keeping it a couple of inches away from the base of plants.

Regional Advice and Care
In January, prune the woody stalks to the ground. Do not mulch for winter. The only serious pests are termites in dry weather. Control them with a soil drench of insecticide. An occasional rabbit, slug, or deer may nibble the tender spring buds or shoots. Repeated sprays of animal repellent should convince them to feed elsewhere. Divide clumps in fall or late spring.

Companion Planting and Design
Use in clusters to edge large beds containing perennials and ornamental grasses. Plant with the finer-textured spreading sedums, such as 'Vera Jameson' and 'Angelina'. Plant groundcovers creeping phlox, hardy iceplant, and verbena at its base. Stonecrop sedum works well with gray-colored plants like dusty miller and Russian sage.

Try These
'Autumn Joy' is the standard. 'Brilliant' has icy pink flower heads. The burgundy foliage of Garnet Brocade™ and 'Matrona' is stunning *en masse*.

Yarrow

Achillea millefolium

Botanical Pronunciation
Ah-KILL-lee-ah mill-ee-FOL-ee-um

Bloom Period and Seasonal Color
Spring to summer in dark reds, pinks, and white

Mature Height × Spread
2 feet × 2 to 3 feet

This showy native plant is tough and reliable, growing in poor ground where many perennials refuse to shine. Yarrow has basal leaves forming a see-through mound of dark green, aromatic fernlike foliage. This easy-to-grow perennial produces tall stems bearing flat heads of dark red, white, or pink blooms. The 3-inch flattened flower heads called corymbs are delightful, fresh or dried. Adaptable, resilient yarrow can rescue a barren area and cover it with bloom. It has been proven from the dry Southwest to the hard-baked clay soils of the Carolinas. Grandmother's garden would have included this perennial and called it milfoil in her day. Common yarrow is lower-growing than the popular fernleaf hybrid 'Coronation Gold', which is found in the cutting garden of every floral design since its dried flowers are truly "everlasting."

When, Where, and How to Plant

Plant yarrow in spring or early fall from divisions and container-grown stock. Yarrow grows easily in average to poor, dry soil. Given a full-sun location, yarrow will bloom in late spring throughout summer. Shade causes it to grow lanky and open. Give yarrow plenty of space (3 feet apart) to minimize mildew. If you have trouble, it's most likely due to "wet-feet." Prepare the soil so it is loose. Gravel or bark amendments can be added along with a ½ cup of superphosphate per plant. Break up the soil to a 1-foot depth, and set plants shallowly. In heavy soils, plant on berms to ensure excellent drainage. Yarrow does fine without mulch.

Growing Tips

Water weekly the first month only. Supplemental watering can be beneficial, but keep the foliage dry. Yarrow survives drought and our hot summers better than most perennials. Feed with any liquid general garden fertilizer occasionally if you wish to increase flower production. Too much moisture and it will become leggy. Cut back young plants by one-third to prevent flopping. Deadhead after blooming to prevent seeds and to encourage repeat-blooming.

Regional Advice and Care

Once established, yarrow thrives on neglect. To produce dried flowers, wrap bunches of long-stemmed flowers in paper and hang them upside down in a dry, dark area. Deadhead by cutting back to lateral buds. Divide the heavy clumps by digging them, washing the soil away with a water jet, and cutting them apart with a hatchet or sharp spade. Remove wind-burned foliage in later winter. Mildew disease can spoil the leaves of cutting cultivars like 'Moonshine.' Baking soda-and-oil spray may help with prevention.

Companion Planting and Design

Interplant yarrow to set off the colors of perennial salvias. Good companions are santolina, lavender, lantana, and ornamental grasses. Consider growing various species of *Achillea* to get the full range of colors for your garden. Cut flower gardeners yearn for 'Anthea' and 'Coronation Gold'.

Try These

'Summer Berries' is a cheery mix of colors and given the highest accolades for shunning heat and attracting butterflies.

ROSES
FOR THE CAROLINAS

Perhaps no flower in the world is more popular than America's national flower, the rose. Its beautiful form, rich pleasing colors, delightful fragrances, and incredible versatility have made it a favorite of gardeners and flower lovers for generations. No wonder it is called the Queen of Flowers. The rose is a testament to human creativity. Once a wildflower, it has been cultivated and engineered to suit all types of gardens. There is a rose for every region of the Carolinas and a form for every location. Varieties are available for borders, for growing on arbors and trellises, and even miniatures for color beds. The unique tree roses grown as standards are ideal for container gardening, while the newer groundcover roses adapt well to small spaces. Of course, the hybrid teas are superb for cutting and are the rose of choice for millions of Americans.

Why Grow Roses?

Is there anyone who doesn't like roses? People have grown them for centuries and for many reasons. In times past, the rose was revered for its value as food and medicine. Its quaint herbal concoctions were believed to cure many ailments. Their flavor is coveted in Middle Eastern and Indian cuisine. Not until recently have we known that rose hips have as much Vitamin C as citrus fruits. Rugosa rose provides both lovely flowers and large, red hips. Of course, rose petals are associated with wooing a lover.

Today we grow roses mostly for their beauty in the garden. Another magical allure is the color combinations available. There is a rose that complements any color bed or accessory. Flowers like *Rosa mutabilis* frequently open with one color and fade to another hue; then there are the bicolors such as 'Gemini'

Rosa mutabalis

and 'Moonstone' with blooms that are bordered or marbled with contrasting colors. In the past, people hesitated to grow roses because of widespread fungal diseases. However, with the latest hybrids, such as KNOCK OUT®, these problems are not as daunting. New shrub rose introductions allow success without heavy pesticide use. Gardeners are revisiting the heritage roses because of their hardiness, fragrance, and tolerance of neglect.

Blackspot is a serious rose disease.

First Things First

When researching roses, begin with the All-America Rose Selections (AARS) organization. Winners of its awards will perform best and are most resistant to blackspot and mildew disease. Several websites carry the AARS list and a handbook that rates varieties. The greatest challenge will be settling on a few plants to avoid crowding your garden bed—a big no-no in rose culture.

Not too long ago we thought roses for cutting, like hybrid teas, were the only choice for gardeners. Nowadays, there are varieties from a number of rose classes for color and easy maintenance. This is evidenced with the introduction of Earth-Kind® roses from the Texas AgriLife Extension Service. American gardeners are being directed to a select group of cultivars that have been extensively researched in field trials. Included on the roster are small shrub roses, such as 'Carefree Beauty'™, and a few climber selections. These roses perform well throughout the South and demonstrate superior pest tolerance, combined with outstanding landscape performance. Earth-Kind® roses have a long blooming season and their no-nonsense pruning needs appeal to every homeowner. There are numerous roses entering the marketplace today with similar care-free characteristics. It is exciting to think that these will grow anywhere in the Carolinas—but for some gardeners, old garden roses and English roses will always take first prize.

What Do Roses Want?

A traditional garden of roses for cutting is like a marriage. The first heady rush of blooms in spring is wonderful. The flowers are perfect, the leaves deep green, and the fragrance divine. By June, the Japanese beetles arrive, and blackspot sets in. By August, the reality of growing cut roses in the South confronts you. It's like facing a sink full of dirty dishes after a romantic candlelit dinner. Like a good marriage, navigating through rough waters together brings with it satisfaction and optimism for the seasons ahead.

Choose a site with good air circulation and six hours or more of daily sunshine. Morning sun is best for disease prevention. You had better do your homework in bed preparation too. Follow the rule of "a 50-cent plant in a 5-dollar hole." Roses love water yet need perfect drainage to flush surplus water away from their roots. Dig a deep bed in clay soils and consider installing a drainage system. Have the soil tested and amend as needed. Organic amendments such as leaf compost or aged manure will improve soil condition. Most rosarians emphasize the importance of air circulation in growing roses. (In less-than-ideal circumstances, plant landscape shrub roses.)

Care for roses is equally important. They benefit from monthly fertilizing using either 10-10-10 or special rose fertilizers. Water-soluble fertilizers can supplement dry feeding, as can organic products ranging from alfalfa and cottonseed meal to Epsom salts and fish emulsion. You can overdo it with fertilizers. Be sure the bed is moist before feeding, and don't fertilize after mid-August so plants can harden-off (prepare for the coming season) before winter.

Successful gardeners recognize rose pests and diseases and develop an integrated pest management (IPM) plan to combat them using least toxic methods. Cutting roses will require routine applications of garden fungicides to prevent chronic diseases such as canker, mildew, and blackspot. Your Cooperative Extension's county offices provide current pesticide recommendations; these change occasionally. Some old pest-control recipes still circulate; they may or may not be effective in specific locales.

Pruning is an enigma for many people. How can you butcher a plant and expect more flowers and vigorous growth? You had better know upfront that you prune climbing roses after they bloom and shrub-type roses (summer flowering) in early spring. To gain confidence, think about attending a rose-pruning clinic sponsored by a local rose society or Master Gardener program. Here are some general pruning tips that are worth noting.

- Use bypass-type hand shears. They cut cleanly. Anvil-type shears tend to crush stems.
- Pruning stimulates new growth, and pruning too early is risky. Begin spring pruning when buds swell and new growth is pushing. This varies widely in the Carolinas, but normally is in March. If in doubt, prune on the date of your area's last frost.
- Pruning and training are different. Pruning is a seasonal chore which increases the number and size of blooms. Training is the removal or shortening of errant shoots or sprouts originating from the rootstock. Landscape roses can be sheared back in summer.

Bypass loppers are best for rose pruning and maintenance.

- Prune to an "outside" bud, meaning cut ½ inch beyond a bud on the outside of the branch or cane. If you cut above an inside bud, the shoot that grows from it will congest the interior of the bush.
- In order to avoid transferring disease from one plant to another, hand shears (secateurs) should be cleaned in rubbing alcohol after pruning a diseased plant infected with gall.
- At times, you will need to use a pruning saw or loppers to remove woody old canes so that new canes can sprout from the crown. Prune flush with the crown to avoid leaving a stub. Be careful not to damage surrounding canes. Rejuvenating old rose plantings is prudent and should be completed by late spring.

Buying Roses

Increasingly, garden centers are selling containerized rose bushes in full bloom, which allows you to preview the color,

'New Dawn' rose

blossom form, and fragrance of the various cultivars. Numbers are assigned to the bushes based on the number of canes. Substantial, well-branched plants with higher number of canes are No. 1; No. 2 roses have a lower number of canes.

Mail-order specialists supply most of the newest roses by mail. Breeders announce them in their catalogs and, when demand has built up, sell to garden centers for resale to home gardeners. Traditionally, garden centers sell the bushes with tops waxed to decrease water loss and with the root system pruned and wrapped in a bag filled with peat moss or shavings to keep the roots from drying out. Buy No. 1 packaged rose bushes soon after they arrive at the garden center. Take them out of the package and soak them in tepid water overnight. Plant them in prepared soil after frost danger is past; their performance is similar to containerized bushes.

Jackson & Perkins' latest series of hedge roses and miniatures hails the advantages of "own-root" roses. Grafted (budded) roses have been the mainstay of the industry for decades, but there is now a rapid movement toward own-root rose production. Gardeners may appreciate the easy care of own-root roses since no graft union means no suckers to remove. Survival rates for roses go up when gardeners know how deeply a grafted plant should be planted.

Smart Choices to Avoid Diseases

Search for roses that have genetic resistance to blackspot and powdery mildew diseases. These plagues disfigure bushes and can weaken them to the point that they will gradually decline and die. The humid climate of the Carolinas, the rose grower's worst enemy, fosters serious foliar diseases. We must underscore the importance of good air circulation to ensure success with your roses. Plant pathologists periodically evaluate the cultivars for disease tolerance, and each class has something to offer. Experiment with these if your garden has less-than-ideal conditions for roses. And if your garden has filtered shade, there are even some shady ladies for the choosing. Good choices include 'Sea Foam', Carefree Wonder™, Mary Rose®, 'New Dawn', Ice Meidiland®, and 'Zephirine Drouhin' (just to name a few).

A new trend, started in the 1960s from an environmental awakening of sorts, gave rise to the first modern shrub roses, such as Carefree Beauty™. Years later, the immensely popular disease-tolerant Bonica™ rose followed from the successful breeding efforts of the Star Roses® project. These roses were an instant hit because they provided all-season color yet required little or no spraying. However, experienced Carolina rosarians have learned the reality that disease pressure varies from year to year in our climate. In some seasons even resistant varieties will show signs of disease, and a regular spray treatment will be needed. A battery of chemicals is available to reduce damage from foliar diseases in susceptible cultivars. Not everyone is willing to take on the work, expense, and environmental risk posed by pesticides. Properly identifying the pest problem is the first step in an IPM approach to sustainable rose gardening; manage accordingly.

Finally, when buying rose bushes you need to understand what is meant by "miniature." Most miniature roses have considerably smaller frames and smaller blossoms than their standard prototypes. However, some have fairly large plants with miniature blossoms. So, check out the ultimate height listed on the label. Be aware, too, that most miniature roses are own-rooted, which means that they are grown from cuttings taken from stock plants of the cultivar. As such they can withstand colder weather than can grafted cultivars.

Rose Planting Tips

- Soil preparation for roses is similar to that of shrubs (as directed in the Shrubs chapter on page 148). Locate a site away from tree roots, which will rob water and nutrients.
- First and foremost, have your soil tested; amend as directed for a pH range of 6.0 to 6.5.
- Dig planting holes to the depth of the rootball or root system and twice as wide.
- For containerized roses, since extreme cold is rarely a consideration in the Carolinas, set the rootball so that its top is 1 inch above the surface of the surrounding soil.
- For bare-root roses, shake off the packing material, soak the roots overnight, and dig a planting hole to the depth of the root system. Amend soil with limestone, superphosphate, gypsum, and soil conditioner as recommended by soil tests.

Rose varieties offer gardeners both form and color.

- Make a cone of amended soil in the bottom of the hole, and drape the rose roots over the cone.
- Pull in amended soil around the roots, and firm it down with your hands; don't tamp it down.
- Spread 2 inches of mulch in a circle 2 feet in diameter.
- Settle the roses in place by trickling water over the dug area. For the next month, water twice weekly between rains.
- Wait two weeks, use a liquid fertilizer application the first year to protect tender new roots. In the following years, scatter granular rose fertilizer around the plant at the rate recommended on the package, and water it in. Fertilize monthly, but not past Labor Day, which encourages winter hardening.

Note: The slight difference in planting depths evens out as the plants settle. Having the graft union at or slightly below the soil level reduces the incidence of suckers growing up from the rootstock.

A Delightful Ornamental

With proper feeding and maintenance, many roses will bloom continuously for up to seven months in your Carolina garden. It is not unusual to find a rose bloom right up to Thanksgiving and beyond in coastal gardens. Most of them are spoiled by frosts in the foothills region by early November. They have served the gardener well by the time Old Man Winter arrives and have earned their rest. It would be difficult to find a more delightful ornamental than the rose.

Climbing Rose

Rosa species and hybrids

Botanical Pronunciation
ROW-sah

Bloom Period and Seasonal Color
Late spring to early summer blooms; white, yellow, pinks, and reds

Mature Height × Spread
6 to 8 feet × 6 to 20 feet

Nothing is more picturesque than a gorgeous climbing rose. Traditionally, the large-flowered climbers are the most popular roses because of their longer flowering time. While no rose is a true climber (having no tendrils for attaching to a support), these plants do produce long canes that can be trained and tied to a fence or trellis. The climbing rose consists of a single group known as "ramblers." They bloom only once, in late spring to early summer, but their full-bloom display is well worth the wait. Climbers have mixed parentage and therefore vary in aroma, height, and color. Some can be pruned into cascading bushes or permitted to crawl on the ground. The fragrance is wonderful as it wafts across the landscape.

When, Where, and How to Plant
Plant bare-root climbing roses February through April. Potted roses can be planted anytime if proper watering practices are followed. Early fall planting is acceptable, though they must establish well before the ground freezes. Planting where the rose receives six hours of intense sun and air circulation is good. Support with fences, arbors, or trellises. Spade in plenty of compost, aged cow manure, or bark soil conditioner. Remove a container rose from its pot carefully. Keep the rootball intact and place gently into a hole large enough to accommodate the roots. Plant a grafted rose with the bud union (the swollen bulge at the plant's base) just *above* the soil. Roses benefit from facilitated drainage with one-fourth of their planted rootballs above the soil. Backfill and firm the soil around the roots. Water thoroughly and mulch.

Growing Tips
Drip irrigation, rose food, and mulching keep roses looking good. These plants prefer at least 5 to 10 gallons of water per week with the moisture penetrating deep into the soil.

Regional Advice and Care
Prune climbers in spring only to remove errant shoots. Prune the hardest immediately after blooming to control growth or to invigorate older plants. Use carefully placed structures to support climbers' stiff canes. Spray dormant oil at least once during a winter warm spell and consult your local County Extension office for a spray schedule for the growing season. Well-established climbers depend less on water and pesticides than other rose types. Apply fungicide if blackspot appears.

Companion Planting and Design
Use climbing roses to create a privacy screen or trellis on a bare wall (plant 2 feet from wall) or grow them for the shade they will cast on an arbor swing or gazebo. Opt for the fragrant varieties. 'New Dawn', an everblooming hybrid, grows rapidly and requires plenty of space.

Try These
'Altissimo'® will brighten any landscape with medium red blooms. 'Eden Climber'® offers pastel blooms and is ideal for small gardens. Medium pink 'Clair Matin'® and orange-pink 'America'® receive high marks from the American Rose Society (ARS).

Floribunda Rose

Rosa hybrids

Botanical Pronunciation
ROW-sah

Bloom Period and Seasonal Color
Late spring to summer; white to deep crimson

Mature Height × Spread
2 to 5 feet × 2 to 4 feet

During the early twentieth century, the floribunda class of roses originated from a cross between the hybrid tea and polyantha types. Floribunda roses have smaller flowers than do the hybrid teas, but they produce more flowers on each stem. In fact, the word "floribunda" means "abundantly flowering." Floribundas are low-growing, densely branched bushes adapt to many landscape uses. Their buds and blossoms lack the grace of hybrid teas, but this is a consideration in rose shows, not in landscapes. They have fewer disease problems than hybrid teas, in my experience. Floribundas bloom and rest, and by planting more than one cultivar, you can enjoy color through the season. They provide cut flowers for bouquets and can be planted among small shrubs.

When, Where, and How to Plant

Plant when they're dormant; this is particularly true of the mail-order plants shipped bare root. Container-grown roses can be planted successfully throughout the growing season and can grow in large containers. Roses need at least six hours of intense sunshine to thrive, preferring full sun all day. They require organically enriched soil with *excellent* drainage. Dig a hole 12 inches deep and 18 inches wide. Blend plenty of organic matter into the backfill soil and adjust the pH to 6.0 by liming (if needed). Spread the roots of bare-root roses over a soil mound in the bottom of the hole. When planting container roses, keep the rootball intact and place gently into the hole. Plant grafted roses with the bud union just above the soil. Backfill, firmly pack the soil until it's level with the ground, water-in, and mulch.

Growing Tips

The more often you water, the better your roses will perform. Give them 1 to 2 inches of water per week, giving a good soaking rather than light sprinklings. Roses need moisture to penetrate the soil 18 inches deep. Keep foliage dry when you're watering and try to water in the morning. Roses love to be fed monthly. Use organic amendments such as composted manure or compost, or fertilize using commercial rose food.

Regional Advice and Care

Thin in midsummer to encourage more blooming. Prune lightly in late fall after a killing frost. A final pruning is done as the buds swell going into spring. Regularly spraying to control mildew and blackspot is a *must* for floribundas; combining two different fungicides gives better results. You can root many roses by taking cuttings from new growth in summer.

Companion Planting and Design

Plant clusters in borders or as an edging along the front property lines. Monochromatic plantings create quite a show. Enjoy the newer floribundas by a patio for their fragrance; some like 'Hannah Gordon' are appreciated close up for blended or bicolor blooms.

Try These

'Europeana' and 'Showbiz' have lustrous foliage and rich red blooms. The nearly thornless 'Iceberg' lights up any garden. 'Playboy' is a single, red blend.

Hybrid Tea Rose

Rosa hybrids

Botanical Pronunciation
ROW-sah

Bloom Period and Seasonal Color
May to November; a rainbow of colors

Mature Height × Spread
6 feet × 4 feet

The aristocratic hybrid tea roses are known for their elegant buds and heavenly scents. Their long stems and beautiful blooms make this the queen of flowers, perfect for cutting single buds or collecting for a bouquet. The number of colors and variegations is truly endless, and the fragrances can range from sweet and fruity to bold and spicy. Most flowers are double with long, pointed buds. Hybrid teas are grown more widely in Southern rose gardens than all other roses combined. They are called "everblooming" roses by some rosarians. Hybrid teas are winter hardy in the Carolinas. The American Rose Society's *Handbook for Selecting Roses* is helpful for choosing the best varieties. Local rose societies offer recommendations and invaluable assistance to beginners.

When, Where, and How to Plant

Plant bare-root roses while they are dormant. Container-grown roses in full bloom can be planted successfully through June if watered regularly. To thrive, roses require at least six hours of intense sunshine, good air circulation, organically enriched soil, and excellent drainage. Work the soil to a depth of 16 inches, incorporating plenty of bark soil conditioner. Dig a hole large enough to accommodate roots, allowing at least 3 feet between bushes. Keep the rootball of container roses intact. Plant grafted roses with the bud union 1 inch above the soil. Backfill the hole, firm-in the soil, water-in well, and layer 2 inches of pine bark (or similar) mulch.

Growing Tips

As a rule, roses need water regularly. Hybrid roses require 5 to 10 gallons of water per week. Water in the morning and keep the foliage dry. Rosarians prefer drip irrigation or soaker hoses for rose growing. Roses are heavy feeders, so fertilize monthly using organic products such as composted manures or rose food.

Regional Advice and Care

Hybrid teas need the most maintenance of all. Cut them to waist high after the first hard frost in autumn. In early spring, prune to 15 to 18 inches. Remove the oldest and weakest canes, leaving three to five strong ones. For arrangement cutting, remove flower stems at the leaf node containing five to seven leaflets. The remaining bud will produce another strong flower stalk. To harden off for winter in the western Carolinas, stop fertilizing and quit cutting the flowers by late August. Follow a strict spray schedule to manage diseases, Japanese beetles, spider mites, and thrips.

Companion Planting and Design

A cutting garden of mixed cultivars will bring fragrance and beauty indoors. The flowers are exquisite. Or use hybrid tea roses to accent a gazebo, patio, or barren lamp post.

Try These

Try 'Double Delight' and 'Mr. Lincoln' for fragrance. Elle® is shell pink with glossy, disease-tolerant foliage. 'Touch of Class'™ and 'Louise Estes' get high judges' scores at rose shows. 'St. Patrick'™—you guessed it—is a green blend.

Shrub Rose

Rosa hybrids

Botanical Pronunciation
ROW-sah

Other Name
David Austin rose

Bloom Period and Seasonal Color
Spring or summer blooms; white, pink, and red

Mature Height × Spread
8 feet × 4 feet

Shrub roses often fulfill a gardener's desire to enjoy the beauty and fragrance of roses without employing a crew of landscape horticulturists. Easy-care shrub roses like rugosas, Meidiland, Knock Out®, and Earth-Kind® are a sure bet for superb hedges and informal plantings. They make great barrier plantings or no-shear shrub borders. *Rugosa* is the name of a species of rose as well as a rose classification. Rugosas, commonly called Japanese roses, are large plants with stiff, spiny canes. They are well suited for coastal planting since they are salt-tolerant and can hold down sandy slopes, preventing soil erosion. Two other likely candidates for hedge plantings are 'Carefree Beauty'™ and 'Simplicity' roses. These grow to 4 feet high, are very disease-resistant, and yield rather large, open pink flowers.

When, Where, and How to Plant

Plant during their dormant stage, although you can successfully plant them throughout the growing season. Shrub roses are vigorous and need space in a wide open, sunny location. Dig a 15-inch hole or large enough to accommodate the roots, and blend in plenty of pine-bark conditioner. When planting a container rose, keep the rootball intact but free up circling roots if potbound. Plant grafted roses with the bud union just above the soil level. Backfill the hole and firm-in the soil until level with the ground. Water-in well and mulch with pine needle or bark mulch.

Growing Tips

Shrub roses will survive with once-a-week watering when they are established, but water more often their first month following planting. When watering, keep the foliage dry. Try to water in the morning. Shrub roses are not immune to pests but can recover lost foliage after being fertilized.

Regional Advice and Care

Prune in late winter, leaving enough cane so you can prune off cold damage later in spring. These roses require the least amount of care in the "family," but watch out for powdery mildew and blackspot disease. If these occur, spray with a fungicide and remove all infected foliage. Fertilize in spring after the final pruning and feed only enough thereafter to keep the foliage healthy.

Companion Planting and Design

Plant in groups or use for mass plantings. They will "stop traffic" when placed in front of a picket fence or gate. Shrub roses are suitable for forming dense barriers and great hedges. The stiff branches and spines on *Rosa rugosa* will keep passersby from snitching blossoms. Look for newer color introductions, such as mauve 'Outta the Blue'.

Try These

R. KNOCK OUT® range in color and flower type on robust plants. Pink 'Bonica' is compact and free-flowering. 'Graham Thomas'®, a David Austin Rose®, has fragrance and old garden charm. 'Heritage' is perfect for small gardens or perennial borders. Apricot 'Prairie Sunrise' is a Griffith Buck rose. Light pink 'Quietness' is a favorite.

Miniature Rose

Rosa hybrids

Botanical Pronunciation
ROW-sah

Bloom Period and Seasonal Color
Spring to fall; myriad colors

Mature Height × Spread
15 to 30 inches × 12 to 25 inches

Miniature roses are true dwarf members of the rose family and can easily be grown with a minimum of care and space. More of these little jewels deserve to be planted in the Carolinas. Since they are not grafted and grow on their own rootstock, they handle our unpredictable winters like troopers, peeking their small heads out as spring arrives. They are available in a vast selection of colors and cultivars. A new class of miniatures is the miniflora. Individual flowers of minifloras are 1 inch in diameter or slightly larger but the compact plants are similar in size to the miniature. Like an intricate tapestry, these roses lend a captivating element to any garden area. They are generally much hardier than other roses and usually do not require winter protection in our area.

When, Where, and How to Plant

Plant when they're dormant, though they can be planted in spring and early fall. They require at least six hours of intense sunlight and organically enriched soil with excellent drainage. Blend plenty of organic matter and soil conditioner into the existing soil. Dig a hole large enough to accommodate the roots. Keep the rootballs of container roses intact and place gently into the hole. Backfill and firm the soil until level with the ground. Water-in well and mulch. When planting in a container, be sure it has good drainage and rich but porous potting soil. Move the container to shelter during severe winters. Miniatures can be grown indoors on a sunny windowsill or under fluorescent lights, but they need more light than the average houseplant.

Growing Tips

Water weekly using a drip watering system to keep the foliage dry. Rosarians agree that all roses need regular feeding. Use a specialty rose fertilizer or various organic products; some of these contain systemic insecticides. Maintain a 2-inch mulch layer.

Regional Advice and Care

Prune miniatures after the last frost date. Cut canes back to active new growth and remove any winter-damaged canes to maintain an appealing and healthy appearance. Miniatures are propagated on their root systems, so they can endure difficult weather. Light mulching gives some winter protection as well as helps conserve moisture during summer. These roses are prone to blackspot and spider mites. Use a preventative pest control program. Protect greenhouse-grown roses purchased in early spring from frost by placing them in a sheltered location or holding them in a sunroom.

Companion Planting and Design

Miniatures, especially minifloras, are great in a perennial border or shrub bed. Though the flowers are small, arrangements of miniatures are attractive. This rose class is suitable for container gardening when combined with million bells.

Try These

The full white 'Irresistable' makes a bold statement. 'Crazy Dottie' is a single in cheery red. 'Miss Flippins', medium red double, raises eyebrows. Fine minifloras include 'Sunglow', 'Abby's Angel', 'Buttercream', and 'Foolish Pleasure'.

Old Garden Rose

Rosa species and hybrids

Botanical Pronunciation
ROW-sah

Bloom Period and Seasonal Color
May through September; pink and white
to crimson

Mature Height × Spread
3 to 14 feet × 3 to 12 feet

This group of roses is making a comeback all over the country. In Carolina gardens, old garden roses are appreciated for their repeat flowering and disease resistance. The old garden rose category consists of roses that were introduced to America before 1867. These varieties evolved hundreds of years ago from Asiatic species, consisting of both shrub and climbing forms. Old garden roses are often planted because their old-fashioned, informal look is reminiscent of grandmother's garden, and they offer gorgeous, fragrant blooms. They are quite rugged during our hot, dry summers and have few problems with pests. Old garden roses should not be limited to the formal rose garden. Many of the old garden roses can be seen at the National Herb Garden in Washington, D.C.

When, Where, and How to Plant
Plant in late winter or early spring. Full sun, *at least* six hours daily, ensures compact plants and better flowers. Roses require organically enriched soil with excellent drainage. Dig a 16-inch-deep hole large enough to accommodate the roots, and blend in plenty of organic matter and soil conditioner. When planting a container rose, gently place the intact root-ball into the hole. Plant grafted roses with the bud union just above the soil level. Spread the roots of bare-root plants atop a small mound. Backfill the hole and firmly pack the soil until level with the ground. Water-in well and mulch. In mountain regions, deep mulch is necessary for winter protection.

Growing Tips
Water lots during its growing season; once-a-week watering or even less will suffice after the first year. Try to water in the morning. Note that roses prefer one good soaking rather than three to four sprinklings a week. A drip irrigation system is ideal. There are many rose fertilizers designed to create beautiful blooms and lush, green foliage. Though you have many choices, all rosarians agree that roses love plant food.

Regional Advice and Care
Remove flower clusters of old, spent (dead) roses routinely. Prune in midwinter or when bud eyes begin to swell in spring. Spray dormant oil during the winter and repeat in spring. A spray or two of fungicide in May is beneficial. Let Extension agents advise on rose pest management and new biological products. Thin top growth of old garden roses if they become a mass of dense twigs. Seal pruning cuts using an aerosol spray of tree pruning paint to prevent borer infestation.

Companion Planting and Design
Old garden roses are ideal perennial backdrops in formal rose gardens. 'Nastarana' and other climbing Noisette variety, *Rosa* 'Crepuscule', will be appreciated on a pergola or trellis. Catmint and colorful canna varieties are good companions.

Try These
R. × centifolia is the typical pink cabbage rose portrayed by Dutch Masters. 'Old Blush' is one of the South's oldest roses with "roots" in Charleston. 'Mrs. B.R. Cant' and 'Belle Poitevine' bear pink blooms continuously.

SHRUBS

FOR THE CAROLINAS

Shrubs help us shape and delineate space in the landscape. They can be colorful entities, or when placed in masses, collectively add beauty to a stark, unattractive yard. A landscape would not be complete without the seasonal interest of some varieties. They are frequently placed just out from the walls of our homes to fill bare foundations, soften architectural features, and enhance entrances. We use shrubs in so many ways that it is hard to list all their wonderful qualities and distinctive habits.

What Are Shrubs?

By definition, shrubs are woody plants, usually with multiple stems, that mature at less than 15 feet in height. They come in every imaginable size and form—weeping, columnar, round, pyramidal, open, or compact. Some, like azaleas, burst into vivid color in springtime; others, like sasanqua camellias, bloom for weeks in autumn. Large shrubs can be "limbed up" to produce small specimen trees. Many are planted close together—and sometimes stair-stepped in ranks to create privacy hedges and to screen views. The most popular use of shrubs is to skirt foundations and emphasize corners, giving new homes a finished look. Best of all, shrubs provide winter interest and color during the gray, often rainy days leading up to spring.

Types of Shrubs

Evergreen shrubs are the ones most sought after for screening purposes. Evergreens keep their leaves year-round. They are either conifers (narrowleaf with scale or needlelike leaves) or broadleaf evergreens (with flattened leaves). Some broadleaf plants are deciduous; that is, they lose their leaves in winter. For example, spirea is a deciduous broadleaf shrub. Narrowleaf evergreens include junipers, spruce, false cypress, and plum yew. Some dwarf forms are available among all species. ("Dwarf" implies more compact but not always physically small.) The Carolinas are blessed with many native woody ornamentals, both broadleaf and conifer. They thrive in our gardens and lift our spirits. Flowering shrubs will always endure in the nursery trade, as they are loved by gardeners and non-gardeners alike. Today there is renewed interest in old-fashioned deciduous shrubs such as viburnum and rose-of-Sharon. Many of these shrubs from the past are pest-free and bloom consistently in mixed borders. One can have sasanquas flowering until Christmas and winter jasmine blooming on the first warm days of January. And when the paperbush begin flowering in February, the excitement for gardening is always rekindled.

Going Native

There is a debate brewing across the country about the use of native plants versus the use of introduced ornamentals. Carolinians garden in three hardiness zones, and there is no doubt that many "exotic" landscape shrubs are superior to our natives. According to one landscape architect, "Clients want low maintenance, year-round beauty, and 'toughness' in their landscape plants." Many shrubs native to the mountain region will not thrive in the coastal region. Compacted red Piedmont clay, hot and humid summers, and wildly fluctuating winters put a lot of stress on plants. Conversely, native species with a coastal provenance have trouble surviving northwest Piedmont winters and are hopeless at high elevations. Yet if you plant a native species in an environment that simulates its native habitat, it can surpass most exotics in beauty and performance.

More Than Green Foliage

Shrubs offer a variety of individual traits. Without shrubs such as Koreanspice viburnum, gardenia, osmanthus, and lilacs, you would be deprived of wonderful fragrance in the garden. Many shrubs, such as variegated abelia, aucuba, and dwarf nandina, boast interesting color from variegated foliage. Deciduous holly is perfect for the winter garden since its red berries sparkle in sunlight, and the marvelous dwarf conifers offer myriad forms and foliage colors. Dwarf conifers, looking like tiny bonsai, are popular for rock gardens and toy railroad gardens. Another desirable feature of many shrubs is the attraction they hold for butterflies. What butterfly garden is complete without a butterfly bush?

Carefree Landscapes?

Before purchasing your shrubs, keep in mind that few are maintenance-free. Almost all shrubs need light pruning during early summer to open up dense growth and to remove weak or damaged twigs. Hedges require the most maintenance; they can be pruned with power shears as needed. Handpruning with loppers or bypass pruners maintains the natural form of individual shrubs. Some plants, such as azaleas and loropetalums, will produce long vigorous shoots that extend well beyond the canopy. Prune back the shoots to a lateral branch within the plant canopy; this hides unsightly stubs. Conifers can be sheared in late spring by removing one-third of current season's growth. Timing is critical to pruning success. If you don't know when to prune a flowering shrub, always prune it immediately after bloom time. If your shrub produces berries, wait until after birds have gotten their fill before pruning them off. Prune summer-flowering shrubs, such as butterfly bushes, in early spring. Pruning in late winter will

Garden bench between clipped boxwood shrubs.

invigorate a shrub, as strong new wood arises from a well-nourished root system. Older shrubs that have outgrown their location may need more-severe pruning to reduce their size. Cut these back to within 15 inches, or thin heavily by removing half their mature canes at the base. Late-summer pruning slows growth and prevents rangy watersprouts. Pruning paint or tar are worthless; what's more important is keeping pruning shears sharp and avoiding leaving unsightly stubs. More detailed pruning information is available at all Clemson and NCSU Cooperative Extension offices and online.

Be careful when siting plants in the landscape. It is better to use several of the same variety of shrub in clusters than it is to use a pastiche of plant types, especially in foundation plantings. Invest in a plan drawn by a professional and you may actually save money by not overplanting. Instead of planting shrubs in single-file formations, add depth by planting taller ones to the back and spreading forms to the front. Install edging to give the project a finished look and to keep mulch in place.

New Plants On-Board

New woody ornamental introductions continue appearing in record numbers at public arboreta. In North Carolina the Evaluation Network tests new plants in the different hardiness zones and microclimates and includes the J. C. Raulston Arboretum at NCSU, North Carolina Arboretum in Asheville, and the N. C. Botanical Garden at Chapel Hill. The South Carolina State Botanical Garden at Clemson tests new species and introductions brought into the United States, mostly from the Orient. Of course, large domestic wholesale growers have a continuing program for developing and introducing improved shrubs. Prime examples of the new faces on well-known garden shrubs are 'Kaleidoscope' abelia, 'Goshiki' osmanthus, and the hybrid Chinese 'Venus' sweetshrub. Take the time to experience the offerings in the marketplace, but stay focused on the ones that are not demanding or temperamental in your landscape. You visit furniture showrooms before decorating your home; why not visit public gardens to pick up ideas and inspiration for your home landscape?

Planting Directions for All Shrubs
(Except Rhododendrons, Azaleas, and Pieris)

- With the shrub still in its container or wrapping, position it where you plan to plant it. Look at it from several directions. Review the plant label for mature size to make sure the shrub won't crowd your house or block the view from a window when it grows to full size.
- Dig a planting hole to the depth of the rootball and three times its diameter.
- Pile the excavated soil to the side and mix it with one-quarter organic soil conditioner by volume in sandy or heavy clay soils. Crumble large clods into small pieces. Rototill planting beds for dwarf shrubs spaced closely together.
- Mix in ¼ cup of controlled-release fertilizer and ½ cup of pelletized limestone. (Prepare beds using limestone and fertilizer as recommended by soil tests.)
- Shovel a cone of crumbled, conditioned soil 4 inches high into the hole.

- If planting a container-grown shrub, slide it out and loosen the roots. Prune off long or girdling roots or, using hand shears or a sharp knife, cut any roots that are circling the rootball. If balled and burlapped (B&B), set the rootball in the hole and loosen the twine around the top. Remove synthetic ties and twine.

- On small container-grown shrubs you can "butterfly" the rootball by using both hands to split open the bottom half of the rootball. This will encourage new roots to form.

- Bang the rootball on the ground a couple of times to dislodge some of the soil around the roots. This will also encourage feeder roots to penetrate the backfill.

- Turn the shrub so that the best side is out and not facing the house.

- Shovel the conditioned soil or non-amended good topsoil into the hole in layers. Tamp or lightly firm-in each layer using your foot or the shovel handle, but don't overdo it—roots need air.

- The top of the rootball should stand at least 1 to 2 inches above the surrounding soil. Form a basin or low berm with the remaining backfill on the hole's rim to catch water.

- Water each shrub with a 5-gallon bucketful. If the water runs off, let the shrub soak for a while then continue watering around the rootball. Water trickled from a hose works best.

- Support tall, slender shrubs by tying them loosely between two stakes using degradable twine or flexible plastic tape. Loose tying allows the shrub to flex but not break in the wind, which strengthens the central stem.

- Spread mulch 2 to 3 inches deep to the outermost branches. Spreading three layers of newspaper before you mulch will diminish later problems with weeds and grass sprouting through the mulch. (Wet the newspaper immediately after setting in place.)

Special Planting Instructions for Rhododendrons and Azaleas

More ericaceous (acid-loving) shrubs are killed by too much water than by drought. In the wild, these plants grow in deep, well-drained organic "duff" in high shade. They send roots down into mineral soil to sustain them during dry weather.

Plant these special shrubs with half of the rootball above ground. Here's how:

Rhododendrons are gorgeous in garden settings.

- Spade or till the soil in the planting area. Don't walk on it prior to planting.
- Regardless of what you have learned previously, scatter ½ cup pelletized limestone over the area where the shrub will be planted. (Most Carolina soils have been depleted of calcium and magnesium by farming, and the rise in pH won't be significant.)
- Slide the shrub out of the container and loosen the roots. Bang the rootball on the ground a couple of times to shake off some soil particles.
- Pull circling roots loose from the rootball. If a pad of rootlets has formed on the bottom of the rootball, slice it off. Cut off long, stringy roots.
- Borrow 5 gallons of soil from elsewhere in your garden and dump it to the side of the planting site, or buy a bag of topsoil. Crumble the borrowed soil and mix it with an equal volume of organic soil conditioner, aged leaves, peat moss, or mushroom compost. Avoid dried cow manure as it is alkaline in reaction.
- Turn the plant best side forward and set it in the shallow hole where it is to grow.
- Pull the conditioned soil around the rootball and taper it down to the original soil level. The plant may seem "high and dry," but it will love the good drainage and aeration.
- Shovel any remaining conditioned soil into a shallow basin to catch water.
- Mulch as directed for other shrubs. Do not use peat moss as a mulch; it repels water. Keep bark mulch away from the crown of plants. It is okay to tuck pine needles (pine straw) beneath branches to conserve water and keep down weeds.
- Give each plant at least 4 gallons of water trickled from a hose.

Irrigation Protocol

Watering plants is a "seat of the pants" operation. There are no set rules. Amount and frequency depend on the soil and the weather. Drip irrigation allows you to conserve water while watering deeply for better root development. Without exception, fall is the best time for planting in coastal areas and the Piedmont . . . spring in the mountains. Fall planting, when the weather is usually cooler at night, will let you get by with minimal watering after the plant has settled in. But when planting during warm months, new plants shocked by transplanting will need frequent watering for their first month in the ground. Clay soils will actually extract moisture from the rootball. If there is no rain, give each plant about 4 gallons of water every three days, preferably by trickling a hose. Carolina sands are notorious for not retaining enough moisture to keep plants alive. However, if you condition your soil with organic matter and mulch around your shrubs, water will soak into clay soils and stay with sandy soils. After the first month, you can decrease to weekly watering during dry spells or when rainfall is deficient. At the beginning of the second season, your shrubs will have "established" by sending many feeder roots into the soil surrounding the rootball.

Shrub Health

Controlled-release fertilizers (CRF) simplify feeding new or established shrubs. When you mix them into the backfill or apply on top of the ground, they will feed plants for three to eight months, depending on the thickness of the plastic coating on the beads of fertilizer. When you fertilize established shrubs with them, you should rake back thick mulch layers, scatter the recommended amount, and replace the mulch. Examples of shrub products include 12-6-6 or 14-14-14 similar analysis. (Note: skip the CRF at planting time for azaleas and rhodies and use compost.)

Soluble crystalline fertilizers are yet another matter. When you drench the soil around plants with them or apply them to the foliage, it is called "liquid feeding." They work well, but they don't stay in the soil as long as granular fertilizers or CRF. The usual dilution rate for soluble fertilizers is 2 teaspoons per gallon of water; liquid feed at least every two weeks.

Last but not least are the organic fertilizers made from grain, seed, or fish byproducts. Cottonseed meal is an old-fashioned but still very effective fertilizer. It is especially desirable on coastal sands where nutrients are leached out by rain and irrigation. Fish emulsion, humates, and kelp products are used for liquid feeding and will produce good results where mineral fertilizers are doing only a passable job.

Liming

Virtually all soils in the Carolinas are acidic due to many years of depletion of calcium and magnesium to leaching by our abundant rainfall. Soil tests by laboratories are the most accurate method for determining limestone requirements needed to neutralize soil acidity. Clay soils need comparatively large amounts of lime to bring their pH into the 5.5 to 6.0 range preferred by most plants and to restore calcium and magnesium to desired levels. Sandy soils respond to smaller amounts of limestone but lose it faster to leaching. Limestone always works better when mixed with the soil.

Pelletized dolomitic limestone is the preferred instrument for pH change. It is easier and neater to spread than powdered lime and contains both calcium and magnesium.

Generally, 10 pounds of pelletized dolomitic limestone per 100 square feet is sufficient for clay soils, and 5 pounds per 100 square feet for sandy soils. You need to reapply lime every two to three years on clay soils and every one to two years on sandy soils. Soluble liming products are also available.

Abelia

Abelia × grandiflora and hybrids

Botanical Pronunciation
ah-BEE-lee-uh grand-dee-FLOR-ah

Other Name
Glossy abelia

Bloom Period and Seasonal Color
Spring to fall blooms in white, pink, rose, and purple

Mature Height × Spread
2½ to 7 feet × 3 to 6 feet

This tough ol' garden shrub has had a complete makeover since its introduction to America from Italy more than a century ago! Plant breeders have done more with *Abelia* genetics than dermatologists have done with Botox. New selections boast cheery leaf variegation, compact form, and different flower colors. 'Kaleidoscope', 'Sunrise', and 'Radiance' are a few examples of stunning cultivars that get a second glance at the nursery and often a trip to the checkout counter. Clusters of tubular flowers open from spring to frost on new growth. The twigs of this deciduous shrub are arching and tend to form layers, some spread widely. Abelia can handle drought and is care-free. Hybrids 'John Creech' and 'Edward Goucher' are standards in the trade. What other Southern favorite is both durable and a butterfly attractant?

When, Where, and How to Plant
Plant potted abelia anytime the soil can be worked and plants watered. Though it performs best in full sun, it is resilient in a wide range of exposures. Give abelia acidic, well-drained soil and room to grow. Loosen potbound roots, and shake off some of the soil mix. Plant in a wide hole and don't bother with amendments. Water thoroughly and mulch with ground hardwood mulch or pine straw.

Growing Tips
Water newly planted abelia for thirty minutes every third day for two weeks using a trickle from a garden hose. Taper off to once weekly for another month. Fertilize with a CRF product in late spring if more rapid growth is needed. Maintain a mulch layer in non-irrigated gardens.

Regional Advice and Care
After establishment this shrub requires only occasional grooming. In warm Zone 8 and south, abelia may be semi-evergreen depending on the cultivar. However, in zones to the north, glossy abelia in grandmother's garden was normally leafless by January. It can be pruned in late winter to maintain desired size. Spreading forms make decent groundcovers and can be sheared to keep them dense. Some cultivars, though variegated and beautiful, may not be as vigorous as the standard glossy abelia. 'Sunrise' may revert to the species; remove wild green shoots. Do not spray insecticides.

Companion Planting and Design
It's most effective used in mass or as border plants. Upright hybrids conform to shearing as hedges. The long blooming season is unusual among shrubs and serves as a great feeding station for beneficial insects. Chinese abelia, *A. chinensis*, is a virtual butterfly magnet in hot, summer gardens; there's no better shrub for sustainable landscapes.

Try These
Colorful, low-spreading 'Kaleidoscope' is Carolina born. Seasoned gardeners can look at new *Abelia* cultivars, including 'Sunny Anniversary'™, 'Sunshine Daydream', and 'Mardi Gras'.

Azalea

Azalea spp. and hybrids

Botanical Pronunciation
ah-ZAY-le-uh

Bloom Period and Seasonal Color
Early spring blooms in white, red, and pink

Mature Height × Spread
3 to 6 feet × 3 to 6 feet

Admired the world over, azaleas epitomize spring in the Carolinas. Home landscapes in April are stunning with a riot of color from Kurume azaleas, dogwoods, and spring-flowering bulbs. Carolina gardeners are hooked on these dwarf evergreen azaleas. Azalea is a member of the heath family and appreciates moist, well-drained soil. Popular varieties include pink 'Coral Bells', 'Hershey's Red', and the white cultivar 'Delaware Valley'. They are floriferous and durable in spite of the poor planting sites they are frequently destined to endure. Encore® azalea has taken the Carolinas by storm, migrating from Deep South nurseries. It is twice-blooming with spring flowers commencing after the Kurumes fully peak. Another group of hybrid azaleas, the Gumpo or Satsuki, is a good choice for sunny locations in entrance gardens.

When, Where, and How to Plant

Plant azaleas in spring, preferably before they bloom, and in late October when the weather moderates. Site in dappled shade in Zone 8, protected from the afternoon sun. Gumpos do fine in full sun in irrigated, mulched beds. Azaleas are a species of rhododendron with similar cultural requirements including moist, rich, well-drained soil. They thrive when "planted high" in a bed of loose organic soil. Prepare planting beds by mixing in 4 inches of leaf compost or peat moss. Loosen the rootball by cutting from the bottom about halfway. Butterfly the rootball and place the plant on the prepared soil. Position the roots higher than the surrounding ground. Cover the roots, water thoroughly, then mulch well.

Growing Tips

Water azaleas well during their early years. Irrigate new plantings three times the first week, twice the second, and taper to weekly; irrigate in summer as needed thereafter. Specialty fertilizers may be used the second spring after blooming, though compost and mulch supply adequate nutrition. Established beds may need a little limestone even though these are acid-loving shrubs.

Regional Advice and Care

Encore® azaleas are better suited to the warmer Zones 7b to 9. Reblooming Bloom-A-Thon® azaleas are newer introductions. Prune azaleas immediately after flowering; shear as needed to eliminate rangy shoots. Be prepared for lacebugs on plants in hot locations. The translucent, ¼-inch bugs appear on the undersides of the leaves. Spray to prevent injury; two insecticide applications are needed, one in April and another in September. Yellow foliage may indicate a need for nitrogen, magnesium, or chelated iron. Root rot fungus kills azaleas; avoid poorly drained sites. Invigorate old plantings by transplanting or by reworking the soil.

Companion Planting and Design

Azaleas can be used as specimens or planted in mass groupings. Create displays with small trees like dogwood, Japanese cherry, and redbud. Encore™ azaleas promise two seasons of color and are gaining in popularity for late season color. 'Glen Dale' hybrids form tall hedges and are especially hardy.

Try These

Two Kurume favorites are 'Sunglow' and 'Hershey's Red'. Encore® azaleas have large, bright blooms in myriad colors.

Beautyberry

Callicarpa spp.

Botanical Pronunciation
kal-uh-CAR-puh

Bloom Period and Seasonal Color
Spring blooms in white or pink; showy magenta-purple, lavender, or white fall berries

Mature Height × Spread
4 to 6 feet × 5 to 8 feet

Beautyberry is a "must-have" for gardeners who love time outdoors in autumn. Wisps of berry-laden branches arch lightly when loaded with magenta-purple or white fruit. Persistent clusters of berries last for weeks and can be cut for fall flower arrangements even after frost withers the leaves. American beautyberry, *Callicarpa americana*, is a native, deciduous shrub of Southern woodlands and is ideal for naturalizing. Tiny pinkish lavender blooms appear in spring with medium green, oblong leaves; flowers provide nectar and pollen for many bee and butterfly visits. Blooms are followed by 2-inch dense cymes of pealike berries on the woody stems. Nurseries offer a number of *C. dichotoma* cultivars bearing large quantities of berries that will delight birds discovering their fruit. Tall Japanese beautyberry, *C. japonica* 'Leucocarpa', bears white berries for more interesting autumn contrast.

When, Where, and How to Plant
Plant anytime the soil is workable during fall, winter, or spring. Beautyberry is resilient and holds up well in the planting process though noticeable wilting tells you when to irrigate. It remains densely branched if planted in a sunny location. This woodland shrub can thrive in filtered shade but with fewer berries. Purchase quality container-grown shrubs pruned properly for fullness of form. Prepare a planting hole that is twice the diameter of the rootball or wider. Add soil conditioner to sandy soil, but it generally grows well in average soil. Water thoroughly after planting and weekly for the first month.

Growing Tips
Pay attention to watering for the first month, watering weekly or as needed between rains. The first summer this fast grower will need supplemental watering to prevent wilting. A mulch layer of leaf compost is helpful for establishment. Apply a CFR product every few years to maintain healthy, vigorous leaves for loads of gorgeous berries.

Regional Advice and Care
Being a native of our woods it simply needs very little care. It is one tough cookie for sustainable landscaping. It tends to produce rangy growth where it gets too little sun and is care-free. Full sun plantings for berry production can benefit from routine thinning in the dormant season. Flowers are borne on new growth. Don't shear it into symmetrical form. This plant is practically pest-free and lives for decades once planted in the landscape. Once it's established, there is little to the care of beautyberry other than mulching as needed.

Companion Planting and Design
Add beautyberry to your collection of native plants for the border garden. Chinese beautyberry, *C. dichotoma*, has fine-textured leaves and arching branches lending itself to naturalizing; it's too unwieldy for formal gardens. Use with an evergreen hedge as a foil. White-fruited Japanese beautyberry is wonderful with red fall foliage of Virginia sweetspire, blueberry, and fothergilla.

Try These
Our native American beautyberry is highly ornamental and grows in Zones 7 to 9. Compact 'Issai' is cold hardy in Zone 6. 'Early Amethyst' has lavender berries.

Blueberry

Vaccinium spp.

Botanical Pronunciation
vac-SIN-ee-uh-um

Bloom Period and Seasonal Color
Spring blooms in white; orange-red fall foliage

Mature Height × Spread
5 to 10 feet × 4 to 6 feet

Blueberries can be grown in landscapes and gardens across the Carolinas. Our native wild blueberry is a common understory shrub in woodlands, growing in filtered shade and strongly acidic soils. Blueberries have distinctive light green foliage in spring, which changes to dark green as hot weather arrives. When the summer fruit ripen it is a favorite of songbirds and other creatures. Its open, multistem form is a nice contrast with other landscape plants. Blueberry is well-worth planting for its outstanding fall color in pinks to fiery reds, whether you ever harvest fruit. However, this fine deciduous shrub is popular for edible landscapes and permaculture. For consistent berry crops, rabbiteye blueberry, *Vaccinium ashei*, performs best in the Piedmont. Highbush, *V. corymbosum*, is grown in the mountain region and is a choice commercial species.

When, Where, and How to Plant

Potted blueberries and B&B plants are available in spring. Grow in full or part sun for fruit crops. Select more than one variety to ensure cross-pollination. The rabbiteye type is better adapted to most soils and requires less care. It prefers moist, well-drained soil and will not tolerate soggy soils. Acidic soil is required; do not use limestone. Amend the soil with pine sawdust or peat moss. Set the loosened rootball well above grade. It is best to plant high because of its fibrous roots. Space plants 6 feet apart. Backfill with amended soil, water thoroughly and mulch deeply.

Growing Tips

Water newly planted shrubs directly for ten minutes every other day for two weeks, then irrigate weekly during the growing season providing a minimum of 1¼ inches of water per week. Deep watering is preferred over frequent light watering. Mature shrubs are moderately drought tolerant, but will flourish with a thick mulch layer of pine bark or pine straw. Feed monthly with a liquid fertilizer for the first year, beginning in May and stopping in September. Use an organic fertilizer or CRF product in spring after bloom to boost fruit yield, scattered out at the drip line.

Regional Advice and Care

Blueberries used for their landscape merit are almost carefree. Periodically prune in late winter to remove weak canes or shape plants. Annual stem thinning is helpful for fruit yield; otherwise, leave rabbiteye types alone. Birds will be problematic when berries ripen; bird netting helps. Poorly drained soils will predispose this shrub to root rot disease. Rabbiteye takes heat well, but will not tolerate frigid cold in Zone 6.

Companion Planting and Design

Blueberries offer both fall beauty and tasty berries. Plant as a hedge; add to the garden for foraging honeybees and attracting birds. Clusters can be used in the background of a mixed border for magnificent fall color. Companions are acid-loving shrubs such as camellia, azalea, rhododendron, pieris, and numerous shade-tolerant wildflowers.

Try These

'Premier' and Blue Suede® are self-fruitful varieties for consistent berry crops. Southern highbush blueberries 'O'Neal', 'Sampson', and 'Legacy' are versatile.

Boxwood

Buxus sempervirens

Botanical Pronunciation
BUCK-sus sim-per-VI-renz

Bloom Period and Seasonal Color
Spring blooms tan but non-showy; dark green
foliage year-round

Mature Height × Spread
American (Tree box): 10 to 18 feet × 8 to 14 feet
'Suffruticosa': 3 to 4 feet × 4 feet

"American" boxwood is the aristocrat among shrubs, maturing to 18 feet in height. When used as an evergreen screen, it creates a look of distinction and historical significance. Boxwoods are associated with great estates. They have been used in landscapes from the traditional English garden to Southern plantations. You will find grand old boxwoods all across the Carolinas, from the grandiose Biltmore House in Asheville to Old Salem's colonial gardens to Middleton Place near Charleston. The somewhat hardier, low-growing "English" boxwood 'Suffruticosa' is sought after for foundation plantings of homes with colonial architecture. The dense plants are quite expensive and slow growing, but they make excellent low-maintenance shrubs in sun or shade. At high elevations, common boxwoods are not reliably hardy. Lookalike Korean boxwood makes a good hardy substitute for a low evergreen hedge.

When, Where, and How to Plant

American boxwood can be dug and transplanted or set out as container-grown plants year-round. Plant in full sun to part shade in well-drained soil. Though many are planted in full shade, shade makes "tree" boxwood grow thin and open in its form. English boxwood does fine in shade from afternoon sun. Avoid sites that stay wet constantly, such as near a downspout. Always plant "high" in clay soils. Use organic compost in dry soil sites for hole prep. Water well, then water every three days for the first couple of weeks. Spread mulch to retard weeds and retain moisture.

Growing Tips

Water routinely the first summer, applying water approximately one minute for each inch of diameter of the rootball. No supplementary fertilizer is needed the first year. In the springs that follow, use shrub CRF on an as-needed basis. Some gardeners prefer to use only organic products or a fertilizer mixture of one-half 10-10-10 and one-half cottonseed meal. Spread 1 cup of this mixture around the drip line at bud break in March.

Regional Advice and Care

Shear boxwoods lightly in June after the new growth is fully mature for size control. Overgrown boxwoods can be cut back severely but it is a two-year-process. Begin in February, thinning foliage by 50 percent and keeping leaves on branch tops. Prune back the tops the next spring, shaping plants as you reduce their size. Leafminers are the worst pests of tree box. Treat as new growth emerges in spring. Off-color foliage is symptomatic of soil nematodes or root rot. Consult an Extension agent for advice.

Companion Planting and Design

Shape boxwoods as topiary or grow them as specimen shrubs. Use them to anchor the ends of beds, creating a regal appearance. American boxwood may be planted as hedges or limbed up to tree forms. English boxwood is commonly used in foundations. Avoid overloading your landscape with too many. Pachysandra groundcover complements beds of boxwoods.

Try These

Hybrid 'Green Mountain' has a cone-shaped form. For foundation plantings or to edging walks, try 'Green Velvet', a compact, 3-foot hybrid. Bright 'Elegantissima' rocks!

Butterfly Bush

Buddleia davidii

Botanical Pronunciation
bud-LEE-ah dav-VID-ee-eye

Other Name
Summer lilac

Bloom Period and Seasonal Color
Summer blooms in white, purple, magenta,
or lavender-blue

Mature Height × Spread
3 to 12 feet × 4 to 8 feet

This deciduous flowering shrub is highly attractive to butterflies and bees by day and to moths by night. Long spires of blooms, up to a foot long and mildly fragrant, are what really attract attention. The spires are clusters of tiny flowers that are borne on the ends of the long stems of new growth. They are 2 to 3 inches wide and resemble lilac flowers. Though the flowers of most butterfly bushes are lavender-blue with an orange eye, its colors range from white to magenta to yellow and deep purple. This colorful display continues all summer and into fall provided old blooms are periodically removed. Butterfly bush dons airy, gray-green foliage. The new Lo & Behold® cultivars are compact, suitable for containers. It's a must for the wildlife garden.

When, Where, and How to Plant
Plant spring through fall. Butterfly bush performs best in full sun. Although it is satisfactory in partial shade, it stretches excessively and the thin-stemmed flowers will be weighed down by rain. Butterfly bush thrives in well-drained soil of a neutral pH. When transplanting, don't hesitate to prune extremely long roots. Root-pruning forces production of new feeder roots at the points where the roots are cut. Firm the backfill soil around the roots, and water as you backfill the planting hole. Mulch with bark or pine straw.

Growing Tips
In dry locations, supplemental watering will ensure rapid growth. Be prepared to irrigate during the first growing season. Butterfly bush is basically a low-maintenance plant that seems to bloom better in a soil that is not too rich. Fertilize in spring with a CRF or 10-10-10 analysis when growth starts. Another feeding following a summer shearing should suffice.

Regional Advice and Care
Reports of root sprouts and seedlings escaping to other locations had tarnished the butterfly bush's name. New dwarf releases from NCSU plant breeder Dr. Dennis Werner has restored the namesake. Now everyone is talking about the Lo & Behold™ selections since they are sterile and stay put. One secret to growing butterfly bushes is to prune in early spring and midsummer. The standard species should be pruned to 12 to 20 inches from the ground in late winter. This induces strong new canes that produce a fuller shrub and plenty of large blooms. No further care is needed other than removing spent flowers and twiggy shoots occasionally. No major insects or diseases are known.

Companion Planting and Design
Site near an outdoor sitting area where the butterflies can be observed and the scent of the blooms can be enjoyed. Plant alongside butterfly weed, asters, and Joe-pye weed for a season of entertainment. Place a shallow watering dish containing moist sand close by for thirsty butterflies.

Try These
The dwarf Lo & Behold® cultivars are an amazing horticultural accomplishment. 'Black Knight', 'Attraction', and 'Nanho Blue' are special for gardeners.

Camellia

Camellia spp.

Botanical Pronunciation
ca-MILL-ee-ah

Other Name
Sasanquas

Bloom Period and Seasonal Color
Winter blooms in white, red, and pink

Mature Height × Spread
6 to 15 feet × 5 to 10 feet

Camellias have been grown in China since the ninth century, but American home gardeners didn't catch camellia fever until the 1920s. *Camellia japonica* (often called "japonicas") caused much of the excitement, but in the upper Carolinas, *C. sasanqua* (sasanquas) is more durable in the landscape. It is vigorous, blooming consistently without the devastating loss of flowers from March freezes suffered by japonicas in the Piedmont and westward. Sasanquas adorn many parks and college campuses, where it forms massive hedges. You will see this flowering evergreen espaliered by a wall, or mature specimens limbed up to create a small tree. Delightful single and double blossoms can be enjoyed during fall and winter. The South Carolina Botanical Garden boasts an incredible selection of over 360 cultivars.

When, Where, and How to Plant

Plant sasanquas from March through October to establish roots during warm weather. They tolerate most well-drained soils and grow best in fertile, moist soil. This species is more sun-tolerant than *C. japonica*, but it prefers afternoon shade or high shade all day. Expect winter sunscald on leaves if you plant camellias on a sunny, windswept site. Plant camellia with the rootball above grade. A new sasanqua taller than 3 feet should be tied securely to a single stake. Mulch to protect the roots.

Growing Tips

Water camellias regularly the first summer and fall. It is drought tolerant when mature but will respond to watering during dry periods when it is flowering. Fall-blooming sasanquas can use supplemental water during the fall most years. Fertilize with a specialty camellia fertilizer in spring as needed for leaf color. Apply compost, aged manure, or cottonseed meal for fall fertilization during early September.

Regional Advice and Care

Don't shear camellias unless they are used as a formal hedge. Give plenty of head room for growing them open and full. Prune immediately after flowering. Remove rangy shoots and blighted shoots that die quickly. Keep an eye out for scale insects and spray any with horticultural oil. If voles are a problem, bait mousetraps with slices of apple or peanut butter. Voles (not moles) can kill camellias by eating their roots. The dense root mass of these shallow-rooted shrubs makes it impossible to grow perennials beneath them. Note: Seek advice from Camellia Society or arboreta for *C. japonica* cultivars that thrive in Zones 6 to 7. Flowers and buds are subject to cold snaps.

Companion Planting and Design

Sasanquas are appropriate for hedges along the property line or for training on a trellis. Sasanquas can be used with low spreading shrubs, such as Japanese plum yew, Japanese holly, and loropetalum. There are scores of great japonicas in a plethora of flower colors for Zone 8. Some varieties are low-spreading, and many have improved cold-hardiness.

Try These

Sasanqua favorites in bloom sequence are 'Dawn', 'Yuletide', and 'Setsugekka'. Hybrid cultivars 'Isaribi' and *C.* × 'Crimson Candles' are spring-blooming and sun-tolerant.

Chindo Viburnum

Viburnum awabuki 'Chindo'

Botanical Pronunciation
vi-BUR-num aw-wah-BOO-key

Other Name Japanese viburnum

Bloom Period and Seasonal Color
Spring white flower clusters; year-round black-green foliage

Mature Height × Spread
12 to 20 feet × 8 to 12 feet

Zones 7-8

Lustrous foliage is but one of the many attributes ascribed to this versatile evergreen. Chindo viburnum is a dense, pyramidal shrub with long, dark green leaves to 7 inches. At maturity it has clusters of tiny white flowers that later develop into bright red berries in early autumn. In Piedmont counties it can be found in both sunny and shaded landscapes, though it lacks the pendulous fruit clusters in shade. Veteran gardeners recognize the genus as a family of woody ornamentals that tolerate a wide range of soils. Carolina gardeners in coastal regions know it's difficult to find a better screening plant where the soils deep. Chindo viburnum grows moderately fast and is pest-free. When established, this evergreen withstands dry weather like a champ.

When, Where, and How to Plant
Plant potted plants anytime the ground is workable and you can water, though fall or spring is best. It is pH adaptable and performs well in sun or part shade. Though it tolerants full shade, it gets too leggy. It will grow well in moist soils and survives in dry soils if watered well during early establishment. In sunny locations in the mountain region and foothills, late-season growth and tender shoots are subject to winter injury. Normal planting procedures are fine for chindo viburnum. Use loose soil for the backfill and water thoroughly after setting it.

Growing Tips
Water weekly for the first month after planting. Later, irrigate when the soil is dry to the touch, but water deeply when irrigating. It is quite drought tolerant by the second year. To hold the plant in check, do not overfertilize. Use a controlled-release fertilizer in spring to hurry along growth. Little fertilizer is needed after a few years if mulched well.

Regional Advice and Care
Some large specimens can be found across the northern Piedmont despite 'Chindo' being sensitive to late winter freezes; it's probably too cold sensitive in Zone 6. This evergreen tends to produce sucker growth and develops as a multitrunked shrub; that is okay. Very little pruning is needed, though crowded branches can be removed for grooming. As it matures prune for height control as needed. It can be sheared following flushes of summer growth. Chindo has no serious diseases or insect problems. Brown leaftips may occur in spring from sunscald in winter; remove affected leaves.

Companion Planting and Design
Use it as a specimen shrub in a sunny landscape; its glossy black-green foliage is pleasant to the eye. Space plants closely to make a very dense privacy screen (possibly an alternative to Leyland cypress). Chindo viburnum creates a wonderful foil for perennial flower gardens and beds of azaleas, kerria, spirea, deutzia, and other similar deciduous, spring-flowering shrubs. It's also a nice foil for sweetly fragrant Koreanspice, *V. carlesii*, and doublefile viburnums.

Try These
Chindo viburnum is a fine, cosmopolitan evergreen.

Deciduous Azalea

Rhododendron spp.

Botanical Pronunciation
Row-doe-DEN-drun

Bloom Period and Seasonal Color
Early spring blooms in deep pink and white

Mature Height × Spread
5 to 15 feet × 3 to 10 feet

Most rhododendrons are evergreens, but native azaleas are deciduous. What they lack in foliar character they more than compensate with color. Deciduous azaleas flourish throughout the Carolinas, thriving everywhere from forested upland slopes to river bottoms. Locals refer to woodland species such as pinxterbloom (*Rhododendron periclymenoides*) or Piedmont azalea (*R. canescens*) as "wild honeysuckle." The vivid orange of flame azalea (*R. calendulaceum*) steals the show in mountain gardens. Cold-hardy pinkshell azalea (*R. vaseyi*) occurs naturally at elevations above 3,000 feet. Its blooms are unscented, but what it lacks in fragrance, it compensates with clear apple-blossom-pink petals. Heat-tolerant Exbury cultivars provide vibrant flower trusses and excitement to any spring garden. It is nonsense to say that an azalea must be evergreen to make a statement in the garden.

When, Where, and How to Plant

Plant deciduous azaleas in spring and fall. Set out seedlings and small container-grown plants in spring. Do *not* dig native azaleas from the wild—it's against the law! Site azaleas in morning sun or filtered shade, in well-drained, moist, humusy soil (pH 5.0 to 5.5). Plant in raised beds amended with compost; elevating beds ensures good drainage. Holes dug in poorly drained soils fill with water and hold excess moisture, regardless of the hole's size. Thoroughly loosen the roots of plants grown in pots. For raised beds, mix equal parts soil, compost, and pine-bark soil conditioner. Settle the rootball by watering well, adding 2 to 3 inches of mulch. Avoid fertilizing at planting. See page 150 for planting directions.

Growing Tips

Water deciduous azaleas every three days for the first two to three weeks. Then water weekly as needed until established. Irrigate in our dry summers and maintain an organic mulch layer to encourage root development. Deciduous azaleas that are planted properly and mulched with compost rarely need fertilizer.

Regional Advice and Care

Native deciduous azaleas that thrive in high elevations often languish in lowland summer temperatures. Carefully select species that will naturalize in your garden and zone. Mature plants can be fertilized and pruned if necessary after flowering (during spring). Groom by trimming out weak, crowded branches to maintain a natural appearance. They may be trimmed to keep a desired height. Powdery mildew is not a problem, but treat for lace bugs if this ornamental is planted in a sunny location.

Companion Planting and Design

Deciduous azaleas planted in front of evergreen borders makes a show. In Zones 6 to 7 let pinkshell azalea naturalize alongside early-flowering ornamentals in woodland shade gardens. Exbury hybrids are best for warm, sunny gardens of Zones 7 to 8; 'Pink and Sweet' blooms in late May.

Try These

Piedmont azalea (*R. canescens*) thrives in warmer zones. Swamp azalea (*R. viscosum*) takes wet feet (good for coastal gardens). The orange-red summer blooms of plumleaf azalea (*R. prunifoium*) are always charming in August. 'Homebush' and 'Gibraltar' are favorites.

Deciduous Holly

Ilex spp. and cultivars

Botanical Pronunciation
EYE-lex

Other Name
Winterberry holly

Bloom Period and Seasonal Color
Spring flowers are non-showy; fall berries

Mature Height × Spread
7 to 15 feet × 7 to 15 feet

This native, woody shrub is perfect for winter interest. Deciduous holly can be found growing in swampy areas and flood plains across the Carolinas. Possumhaw, *Ilex decidua*, is a small tree growing 10 to 15 feet at maturity. 'Warrens Red' is valued for its attractive gray bark and deep red, persistent berries that lure migrating birds after fall cold snaps remove the foliage. Winterberry, *I. verticillata*, is the best-behaved deciduous holly with dark green, elliptic-shaped leaves and pea-sized red berries. This species is the darling of nurserymen and its cultivars are widely distributed and planted on residential properties for its distinctive appearance. In the garden, deciduous hollies often fade into the background until fall. However, when the leaves drop, the berries shine in all their glory and garden center inventories are quickly depleted.

When, Where, and How to Plant
Plant deciduous holly throughout the growing season; however, most are purchased in late summer when the berries are shiny red. It is adapted to various soils provided that they are not allowed to get too dry. Find a place where the soil is moist and fertile for the fastest growth. Prepare a planting hole that is wide, and enrich the soil with an organic amendment to help hold moisture. Acidic, clay soils are a natural for this plant. Tree form specimens may need staking for a few months. Water well and add a layer of mulch.

Growing Tips
In soils with an adequate amount of organic matter deciduous holly will establish quickly. Water weekly for two months and irrigate during dry summer months until well-established. Maintain a 3-inch mulch layer. A general garden fertilizer can be used in late fall after berries appear to increase growth in the early years.

Regional Advice and Care
Deciduous holly is "dioecious," meaning this plant has separate male and female flowers. Cross pollination with the male holly varieties 'Jim Dandy' and 'Southern Gentleman' will increase berry production. American hollies in the garden provide pollen too. Your best option is to purchase cultivars that are known to be heavy berry producers. In coastal gardens possumhaw holly will tolerate alkaline soils but grows very large. Winterberry is slow to grow in early years. During periods of drought, drizzle some water on its thirsty roots. Prune in late winter for size control or thin as needed.

Companion Planting and Design
Native possumhaw makes a good specimen tree for naturalizing in the landscape. Winterberry can be used as a winter accent in the border. This deciduous multistem specimen can be underplanted with an evergreen groundcover. Plant several in a group. They're frequently photographed with snow-covered branches laden with red berries.

Try These
Winter Red® and 'Red Sprite' have consistent berry crops. 'Spravy' Berry Heavy® grows to 8 feet.

Distylium

Distylium myricoides

Botanical Pronunciation
dee-STYL-ee-um my-ric-COID-dees

Other Name Blueleaf isu tree

Bloom Period and Seasonal Color
Spring, non-showy maroon flowers

Mature Height × Spread
2 to 10 feet × 4 to 6 feet

Zones 7-8

An evergreen member of the witchhazel family, this broadleaf shrub is being promoted as a replacement for aging hollies and cherry laurels commonly used in older foundation plantings. Distylium is slowly taking its place at garden shops alongside venerable woody shrubs such as boxwood and Japanese holly. The 1½-inch long, oval leaves are dark green and alternate on sturdy, grayish brown stems. Mature specimens of the species distylium are upright, multistemmed shrubs, closely resembling the form of Japanese ligustrum. The spring flowers of 'Vintage Jade' are reddish maroon and must be viewed in close quarters to appreciate. The blooms are followed by small, two-beaked, brown capsules. Nurseries are introducing new, dwarf selections of this Asian plant that hold promise for suburban gardens in dire need of rejuvenation.

When, Where and How to Plant
Distylium prefers moist, acidic soil and will grow in full sun to light shade. Plant container-grown plants throughout the growing season, although spring or fall is the best. This evergreen tolerates heat only after it has established well. Clay soils maintain moisture well, and soil amendments are normally unnecessary with most woody ornamentals. Add compost to sandy soil. Dig a hole that is twice as wide but just as deep as the rootball. Remove the rootball from its pot, and cut vertical slits to free up roots on the perimeter. Backfill and water thoroughly; apply a 3-inch mulch layer.

Growing Tips
Keep its roots moist until the shrub is established. Water daily for a week, then taper off to twice weekly. Water as needed during the root establishment period of three to four months. Distylium performs best in moist conditions and will respond to a generous layer of organic mulch or leaf compost. Watch for signs of wilting during a drought; irrigate deeply and infrequently. Fertilize in spring with a controlled-release shrub fertilizer on established plants.

Regional Advice and Care
Distylium is a relative newcomer to Carolina landscapes, and its cold hardiness was tested in a recent severe winter. Time will tell which cultivars are best adapted to Zones 6 to 7a where the shrub is tender. Few pests have been reported on this broadleaf evergreen. Problems should be reported to Extension agents with Cooperative Extension at N.C. State or Clemson University.

Companion Planting and Design
The cultivar selected will dictate how or where this shrub is best used. The compact, spreading forms can be used in groupings for foundations and low shrub applications. Taller varieties can be used as evergreen screens and in mixed plantings with ornamental trees and deciduous flowering shrubs.

Try These
'Vintage Jade' PPAF and 'Emerald Heights'® are two cultivars showing good cold-hardiness. A special variegated release, 'Spring Frost'™, is low-growing.

Dwarf Crapemyrtle

Lagerstroemia indica Razzle Dazzle®

Botanical Pronunciation
lay-ger-STROM-ee-ah IN-de-ka

Bloom Period and Seasonal Color
Summer blooms in white, pink, red, and lavender; colorful fall foliage

Mature Height × Spread
2 to 3 feet × 2 to 4 feet

Gardeners have a love affair with crapemyrtles because they have a long blooming season and are durable despite our hot summers. Plant breeders have made this excellent landscape plant smaller, thereby expanding its use in borders and formal gardens. Dwarf crapemyrtle is a deciduous shrub with thin 1-inch, dark green leaves on dense horizontal branches. Summer flower clusters in a plethora of colors last can last from summer to fall, snatching the attention from many other ornamentals. As the shrub matures, it takes on a fuller, rounded form with a pleasing texture. The dwarf crapemyrtle will grow slowly to 3 feet. Fall foliage can be vivid. It makes a wonderful summer accent for sunny places when planted in clusters or containers. There are six plants in the Razzle Dazzle® series.

When, Where, and How to Plant

Plant potted shrubs anytime in the growing season, except August. Dwarf crapemyrtle grows well in sun or part sun in ordinary garden soil, although it will not have great fall color without at least a half-day of direct sun. Once established, it tolerates a wide range of moisture conditions. In a border plantings, space shrubs 3 feet apart. Consider preparing a wide bed to accommodate groups of plants, or plant shrubs in wide holes that are equal depth to the rootballs. Form a watering berm, and then water thoroughly to settle the backfill soil.

Growing Tips

Water the planting deeply for the first six weeks. After that, water every ten to fourteen days in summer to encourage new growth and blooming. Maintain a mulch layer of compost or hardwood bark. During the first season use a liquid fertilizer to feed dwarf crapemyrtle. Apply a CRF product in spring the second year and as needed to keep the plants growing vigorously. Apply that at the drip line of plants—not against the stems.

Regional Advice and Care

Late winter is the best time for heavy pruning of overgrown bushes. It is best to do some heavy thinning the first year, then take shrubs down to knee-high height the next winter. Weevils may take bites out of the leaves, but scale insects cause more serious injury. Treat with a fall application of dormant oil and a June insecticide application. Too much shade reduces its vivid fall coloration.

Companion Planting and Design

Mass plant in sweeps for great color displays. Good companions are dwarf shrubs with golden foliage, such as gold mops false cypress, 'Goshiki', and limemound spirea. Use as an accent in a formal garden planting. Ornamental grasses are a good companion for a dazzling autumn display. For height, add mid-sized Dynamite® and 'Red Rocket'.

Try These

Check out the Gardener's Confidence® series, which includes white Diamond Dazzle®, charming Cherry Dazzle®, and petite Sweetheart Dazzle®.

Dwarf Japanese Cedar

Cryptomeria japonica

Botanical Pronunciation
crip-toe-MER-e-ah juh-PON-eh-ka

Other Name Globe Japanese cryptomeria

Bloom Period and Seasonal Color
Spring blooms inconspicuous, year-round evergreen foliage

Mature Height × Spread 3 to 10 feet × 3 to 8 feet

The fine texture of dwarf Japanese cedar makes it a wonderful choice as a dense foundation shrub or low evergreen screen. Fortunately, numerous cultivars are showing up in garden centers alongside the industry standard 'Globosa Nana', which forms a broad cone 6 to 9 feet high. Its awl-like needles curve inward and the foliage appears yellowish green in summer, later assuming a blue-green cast in winter. 'Hino' and 'Elegans Nana' are slow-growing, compact shrubs reaching a height of 3 to 6 feet after many years in the landscape. Japanese cedar prefers moist, fertile soils with good drainage. While most narrowleaf evergreens prefer full sun, this conifer will be happy in the high shade of pine trees or part sun sites. What an exceptional choice for formal gardens!

When, Where, and How to Plant

Plant potted shrubs in late winter, spring, and fall. Transplant field-dug specimens in early spring; avoid planting when the soil is too wet. Dwarf Japanese cedar thrives in full sun or filtered shade in the moist soil that drains well. Amend native soil with 25 percent compost or bark conditioner to enrich the backfill. Use peat moss or compost with sandy loam soils. Form a berm on the edge of the planting hole, and water well. Add a layer of mulch.

Growing Tips

Water new plantings slowly for fifteen minutes every three days for three weeks until the shrub's roots are established. Deep watering is preferred over light watering. When in doubt, check soil wetness with a trowel before watering. Hot weather and dry soils will slow the early growth of your plantings. Water during dry seasons unless the plant gets partial or a half-day of direct sun. Dwarf Japanese cedar does not need regular fertilization if it is kept mulched. For older shrubs, apply a controlled-release nursery fertilizer every few years in mid-spring at the label rate for evergreens; spread it under the canopy of the shrub and a little beyond.

Regional Advice and Care

Shear in spring to shape by removing no more than two years of growth. Brown twigs may be a sign of fungal twig blight; prune those out promptly. Overhead irrigation on dense conifers in evening can predispose plants to leaf disease. Cold injury can lead to canker dieback. Check with an Extension agent for diagnoses.

Companion Planting and Design

Use Japanese cedars to soften the corners of a house or guide the eye to entranceways of private gardens. Plant as a low screen in courtyard, or backdrop for roses or flowering perennials. Place them where garden ornamentals are irrigated in dry summer weather. Dwarf Japanese cedar is not a good selection for naturalizing as it has a somewhat formal look.

Try These

'Globosa Nana' is a fine evergreen for small gardens. Tar Heel landscapers are selecting Chapel View™ for its jade green needles and resistance to winter bronzing.

Dwarf Nandina

Nandina domestica

Botanical Pronunciation
nan-DEE-nuh doe-MESS-tee-ka

Bloom Period and Seasonal Color
Spring blooms are white; fall red foliage

Mature Height × Spread
2 to 3 feet × 2 to 5 feet

Dwarf nandina is hard to beat! It is pest-free; a "no maintenance" ornamental. The winter color of dwarf nandina is superior to that of other shrubs. It maintains the look of the species nandina with the pointed, compound leaves, though they may reach only 2 to 3 feet in height. Unlike the tall, old-garden nandinas that produced clusters of red berries just in time for the holidays, the dwarf cultivars are nearly fruitless—but what they lack in fruit and flowers they make up for in foliage color. The lack of berries should calm the concerns of environmentalists who fear common nadina spreading into Carolina woods. Dwarf nandinas are compact plants with dense foliage that can glow red or chartreuse if you plant cultivars like 'Fire Power' and 'Woods Dwarf'.

When, Where, and How to Plant
Plant dwarf nandinas anytime the ground is workable and in spring before growth begins. Their best winter leaf color appears when they are planted in a sunny spot in well-drained soil. They adapt to shady and dry sites and can be planted near the roots of shade trees, but fine-textured soils like clay loams will literally suck the water out of the rootballs of new plantings. Set the shrub slightly higher than the grade if you're planting in sticky clay. Water thoroughly at planting, then add a layer of mulch.

Growing Tips
The first two to three weeks after planting is critical to the survival of a nandina shrub. Water deeply every third day for the first several weeks in warm weather; don't let the shrubs wilt first. After the new roots catch, dwarf nandinas are on their own. These are tough, low-maintenance shrubs. Fertilize in spring and summer with a general garden fertilizer or CRF using ¼ cup per plant. They are not heavy feeders.

Regional Advice and Care
Prune mature plants in spring by thinning crowded stems. Dwarf nandina is vulnerable to a virus disorder that causes some plants to be stunted and twisted—although the same or another virus may be responsible for the red color we enjoy in the species. In case the plant looks miserable, just dig it out and replace it with a healthy specimen. Rainy seasons can encourage leaf spots; just remove spoiled leaves with a good shearing. Rejuvenate old, lackluster specimens by pruning them back by two-thirds in spring.

Companion Planting and Design
Clusters of these small evergreen shrubs fronted by an edging of variegated liriope or pansies are a car-stopper in winter. New forms 'Gulf Stream' and 'Harbour Belle' create design opportunities for patio containers and colorful winter borders.

Try These
'Harbour Dwarf' and 'Fire Power' give the most winter color. The groundcover variety 'San Gabriel' has delicate, needlelike leaves.

Dwarf Yaupon Holly

Ilex vomitoria 'Nana'

Botanical Pronunciation
EYE-lex vo-my-TORE-ee-ah

Bloom Period and Seasonal Color Spring
blooms are inconspicuous; evergreen foliage

Mature Height × Spread
3 to 4 feet × 4 to 5 feet

Zone 7b-9

Dwarf yaupon holly has remained a top pick for foundation plantings despite grievous cold injury in the Piedmont during a couple of our latest winters. Unlike the Japanese hollies they resemble, dwarf yaupons suffer when a mild fall is followed by a sudden deep freeze (as occurred in 2000). East of Greensboro and south, most recovered after a severe spring pruning. Don't write off this evergreen just yet, because it tolerates drought and neglect. The shiny, dark green foliage and clear gray stems of the species form dense broad shrubs. Dwarf yaupon holly survives coastal conditions, and it does not succumb to pests, root rot, or nematodes. Plant it in sand or clay soil and it will survive adversity. This evergreen species offers great versatility. It is one tough cookie!

When, Where, and How to Plant
Plant potted dwarf yaupon holly from spring to early fall. Site it in full sun to partial shade. This evergreen is tolerant of a wide range of soil types, dry to moist areas. Space shrubs 4 feet apart for clusters. Loosen the roots of this vigorous grower after removing the plant from the pot. Dig a planting hole twice the diameter of the rootball and equal to its depth. There is no advantage to amending the soil unless drainage is poor. Work the native backfill around the roots; water thoroughly.

Growing Tips
Using a 5-gallon bucket or soaker hose water twice weekly between rainfalls for three weeks during the warm months. Taper off to occasional watering to

help your dwarf yaupon hollies through their first summer. Fertilize in spring with a complete garden fertilizer as needed. Mulch yaupons in the warmer months to manage weeds and moisture. Plantings in coastal sands may need monitoring until established.

Regional Advice and Care
These are not recommended for planting in Zones 6 to 7a; stay with a dwarf Japanese holly. Native yaupon shrubs common to the coastal region are can be limbed up for fine-specimen trees. Dwarf yaupon shrubs are tolerant of pruning, but for grooming and size management. Shape into formal "green meatballs" if you like (I prefer boxwoods). Generally, nothing more than an occasional light shearing in spring unless winter injury is severe. There are no serious pests. Legend has it that Native Americans used the leaves to make a black tea for purging (hence the species name "*vomitoria*").

Companion Planting and Design
Dwarf yaupon holly cultivars are terrific foundation shrubs when used in masses. Shear into a low hedge for a formal garden edging. Use in large containers for accent. A cluster at the feet of a mid-sized tree or crapemyrtle is delightful. Weeping yaupon holly, though not dwarf, can be used as specimen accents. The tree form, *Ilex vomitoria* 'Shadow's Hardy Female', has bright red berries and is cold hardy.

Try These
'Schillings Dwarf' and 'Grey's Littleleaf' dwarf yaupons are more compact than 'Nana'.

Eastern Arborvitae

Thuja occidentalis

Botanical Pronunciation
THU-yuh oc-se-den-TAH-less

Bloom Period and Seasonal Color Spring
non-showy blooms; year-round green foliage

Mature Height × Spread
10 to 15 feet × 4 to 5 feet

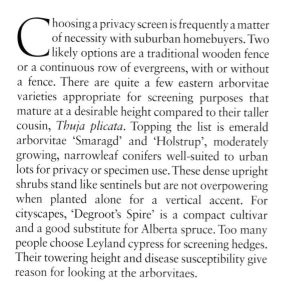

Choosing a privacy screen is frequently a matter of necessity with suburban homebuyers. Two likely options are a traditional wooden fence or a continuous row of evergreens, with or without a fence. There are quite a few eastern arborvitae varieties appropriate for screening purposes that mature at a desirable height compared to their taller cousin, *Thuja plicata*. Topping the list is emerald arborvitae 'Smaragd' and 'Holstrup', moderately growing, narrowleaf conifers well-suited to urban lots for privacy or specimen use. These dense upright shrubs stand like sentinels but are not overpowering when planted alone for a vertical accent. For cityscapes, 'Degroot's Spire' is a compact cultivar and a good substitute for Alberta spruce. Too many people choose Leyland cypress for screening hedges. Their towering height and disease susceptibility give reason for looking at the arborvitaes.

When, Where, and How to Plant
Plant balled-and-burlapped plants or container-grown eastern arborvitae in fall or early spring. Site this evergreen in full sun to partial shade. It can survive in a wide range of soils; however, moist, well-drained soils yield the fastest-growing plants. It is wise to have the soil tested prior to installing an expensive privacy hedge. Apply nutrients accordingly. Prepare a wide planting hole with depth equal to the rootball. Space your plantings 3 to 4 feet apart for a privacy screen. Loosen the roots of potted plants, but handle balled-and-burlapped shrubs with care so as not to break the rootball. Water well after planting and add mulch.

Growing Tips
Water twice during the first two weeks, then taper off to weekly. Irrigate in dry periods. Though these plants don't wilt, a little water during a drought is worth the effort in the early years. Evergreens do not need annual fertilization. An occasional fertilizer application keeps the color sharp. Mulch with 3 inches of pine or hardwood mulch in sandy soils.

Regional Advice and Care
One-gallon pots of arborvitae can grow 6 feet high in five years with no maintenance. You should not concern yourself with topping or shearing these since they rarely break in ice storms or stretch too high. Keep an eye out for bagworms. They don't infest all arborvitae but can seriously weaken those they choose. Deer show no interest in eastern arborvitae, though they roam freely close by.

Companion Planting and Design
Underplant with Japanese garden juniper or carissa holly. Place at the back of perennial borders to make flower colors pop. Use eastern arborvitae freely for privacy screening where western arborvitae, *T. plicata*, would be too tall for a site. The colorful arborvitae 'Rheingold' forms a broad cone that is a striking garden accent shrub.

Try These
'Emerald Green' is the standard. 'Golden Globe' will glow in a sunny location. 'Degroot's Spire' works in large containers. Mr. Bowling Ball™ stays knee high without pruning.

Fig

Ficus carica

Botanical Pronunciation FYE-cuss KAR-ee-ka

Other Name Fig bush

Bloom Period and Seasonal Color
Spring blooms inside green fruit; gold leaves in fall

Mature Height × Spread
8 to 16 feet × 8 to 14 feet

Zones 7b-9

"In the Beginning was the Fig." Adam and Eve accidentally discovered its leaves while desperately searching for the bare necessities of life. Today, scientists have discovered that figs (the fruit) contain high levels of digestible calcium and healthful antioxidants. Cultivars of this temperate plant indigenous to the Middle East are now grown worldwide for their fruit. Subsequently, it is also grown as an ornamental tree, and 'Brown Turkey' has gained the Royal Horticultural Society's Award of Garden Merit. Large lobed, tropical-like leaves appear on multistemmed trunks of mature fig bushes in Zones 7b and southward. Small, immature green fruit can be seen on tender twigs following leaf expansion. Given care in planting, the versatile fig can add beauty, shade, and nutritious fruit to any home landscape.

When, Where, and How to Plant
Plant potted figs in early spring when the soil begins to warm or forsythia is blooming. Also plant in summer and early fall if you're willing to irrigate for a few weeks. Try your hand at layering a neighbor's fig bush; move rooted cuttings to your garden in spring. Find a location that gets a half-day of sun for a fruit crop. Otherwise, any place in sun or partial shade will grow a fig. The best soil is well-drained. Large fig bushes are found on the east side of a house or garage. Spade or till the planting area, and incorporate superphosphate and bark soil conditioner. Remove from the pot and frill out the roots, spread them in the hole before backfilling. Water thoroughly and apply a mulch layer.

Growing Tips
For best growth and fruit crops, keep your fig bush well-watered the first two summers. After well-rooted, they take moderate drought. Late spring fertilization with aged manure or 10-10-10 fertilizer may hurry the bush along. If your goal is a fig tree, remove all but the most vigorous, upright stalk and train to tree form.

Regional Advice and Care
Fig bushes planted even in protected sites are vulnerable to frigid winter weather. Hardy fig varieties are a "must" in the mountain region coupled with cold protection from deep mulch in wire cages. Withhold water in the fall. Fig is care-free, and has no pests, except the four-legged ones that show up at night for fruit. In early spring, prune back cold-damaged twigs; in summer remove basal sucker growth. Rejuvenate old bushes by cutting out oldest trunks only. Consult Extension agents for pruning advice.

Companion Planting and Design
Plant a fig for an accent or small specimen tree. Add for a tropical theme design or near a water feature. Fig makes a good summer screening plant, though it is deciduous. Shouts permaculture; use in sustainable landscapes. Plan with messy fruit drop in mind.

Try These
Small, sweet 'Celeste' figs are my favorite. 'Brown Turkey' reigns supreme in size for the Carolinas. 'Hardy Chicago' and 'Mission' figs show up in backyards everywhere.

Forsythia

Forsythia × intermedia

Botanical Pronunciation
for-SITH-ee-ah in-ter-ME-dee-ah

Other Name
Yellow bells

Bloom Period and Seasonal Color
Late winter blooms in yellow and gold

Mature Height × Spread
6 to 10 feet × 6 to 10 feet

Few shrubs herald the coming of spring like forsythia. Its yellow starlike flowers shine sporadically even during late-winter warm spells. When soil temperatures rise sufficiently, hardy forsythia explodes into bloom, and in a matter of days the leafless branches are aglow with 1-inch, bright flower clusters. Many transplants from "Up North" complain about the poor flowering of our forsythia in the Carolinas. Now, the common, old-garden shrub has been outsourced by new, compact selections such as Gold Tide® and Show Off's™ that are quite showy. Any shrub that is as cold-hardy and resilient as forsythia earns a spot in Carolina gardens. Many traditional gardens feature this spring gem with masses planted in borders or scattered about for their color. Many Southerners have fond memories of forsythia branches cut for early blossoms.

When, Where, and How to Plant
Plant forsythia anytime the soil can be worked. Even the smallest specimens will take off once the roots establish. Provide a sunny location with good drainage. Forsythia adapts to a wide range of soil types and will tolerate dry sites if watered during the first growing season. It will establish more quickly if you first unravel the potbound roots before planting. Some root-pruning is helpful. Space common forsythia 8 feet apart. Water every three days for the first two weeks.

Growing Tips
Water routinely the first season; afterward, these tough shrubs will take dry soil very well. Forsythia benefits from fertilizing with a CRF product in May plantings. Apply a water-soluble fertilizer during the first month after planting. Fertilize annually after the blooming season to encourage strong new growth. Forsythias with plenty of space are low-maintenance shrubs at maturity.

Regional Advice and Care
Prune forsythias immediately after they bloom. For old-timey shrubs, cut the entire plant back to a height of 15 inches to force long, flowing, graceful branches to develop. New compact cultivars may only need occasional thinning to remove old growth. Pests are only a minor concern. Occasionally forsythia will succumb to a bacterial disease known as crown gall; galls occur on the lower half of branches. Prune these away by removing the affected branches. Forsythia is otherwise not bothered by pests and is low maintenance.

Companion Planting and Design
Forsythia has an erect to arching habit and is best planted in masses in borders. Do not use forsythia as a foundation shrub; it can spread to great size. Redbud and Yoshino cherry trees are great companions providing color contrast. Flowering quince, bridal wreath spirea, and daffodils will naturalize together with forsythia for an early spring show.

Try These
New compact cultivars are appearing. For very large, golden flowers plant 'Karl Sax'. The cultivars 'Lynwood Gold' and 'Beatrix Farrand' are great for borders.

Fothergilla

Fothergilla gardenii

Botanical Pronunciation
foth-er-GILL-lah gar-DEN-ee-eye

Other Name
Dwarf witch alder

Bloom Period and Seasonal Color
Spring blooms in white; vivid fall color

Mature Height × Spread
4 to 6 feet × 3 to 6 feet

When azaleas are everywhere during April, "witch alders" offer a breath of fresh air. This native deciduous ornamental boasts showy 2-inch, white, "bottlebrush" flowers and dazzling fall colors from yellow to orange-red. What a terrific break it is to find a native plant nursery or garden center that offers fothergilla. This shrub is a relative of witch hazel and exhibits some of the same traits, particularly pest resistance, shade tolerance, and fall coloration. Dwarf witch alder is a low, multistemmed shrub. Where it gets at least a half-day of sun, dense twigs produce a profusion of oblong, airy blooms in spring. This shrub deserves a place alongside your azaleas to brighten up a woodland garden. Plant fothergillas at the drip line of evergreens and shade trees. They are the perfect choice for naturalizing!

When, Where, and How to Plant
Container-grown fothergilla can be planted in spring, fall, or late winter. It grows relatively fast in moist, acidic soils, tolerating full sun to partial shade. Small container-grown plants are a little slow to take off until they're well established. This species is native to our coastal plains, where it can be found growing by ponds or bogs. Fothergillas require growing conditions similar to those of the azaleas: well-drained, acidic soils. Compost or sphagnum peat moss improves the soil and keeps the roots moist as well. Apply a 3-inch layer of pine-needle mulch. See page 148 in the introduction for planting tips.

Growing Tips
Keep the soil moist but not soggy throughout the first growing season. During extended dry periods, lay out a soaker hose for daily watering. Watering in the driest part of summer will benefit fothergilla, although they are amazingly tolerant of dry conditions. Add mulch annually to keep the soil moist. Apply a specialty organic fertilizer in late winter at the drip line and beyond. For strong growth in the early years, apply a CRF product after flowering. Water the day before you fertilize to avoid injury if soils are dry.

Regional Advice and Care
Thin selectively in the early years to train the shrubs into a pleasing open form. Most pruning should be delayed until after the blooming period. Prune to remove old branches or rangy shoots. Fothergilla is disease-free but will lose a branch occasionally due to stem borer insects. It is a little less cold-hardy than the other native, *Fothergilla major.*

Companion Planting and Design
This plant is a good companion for rhododendrons, deciduous azaleas, and kerria in partial shade. Plant it in front of a golden mops false-cypress, American holly, or other evergreen hedges so the blossoms pop out. Use in masses with other woodland natives.

Try These
'Mt. Airy' and 'Blue Shadow' provide phenomenal fall color and naturalize in woodland settings. What a delightful addition to borders!

Gardenia

Gardenia jasminoides

Botanical Pronunciation
gar-DEE-nee-ah jaz-mine-OY-deez

Other Name
Cape jasmine

Bloom Period and Seasonal Color
Late spring and early summer, pure-white blooms

Mature Height × Spread
3 to 6 feet × 3 to 5 feet

Zones 7-9

However much it may be maligned, there is an advantage to the hot, wet climate in the South: Gardenias will grow here! Gardenia is one of our most valued landscape ornamentals, especially in the eastern half of the Carolinas. It blooms in profusion, emitting a sweet fragrance that brings the ambience of the Old South to our gardens. This delightful evergreen has distinctive dark green, glossy foliage. The beautiful, 3-inch-wide, pristine white flowers resemble the waxy flowers of Southern magnolia. With the introduction of new cold-tolerant varieties and dwarf forms, it isn't unusual to find gardenias in gardens west of the Piedmont. This native of China has found a place in the hearts of Southerners for more than a century. Our grandmothers floated blossoms in bowls to perfume a room.

When, Where, and How to Plant

Plant in spring and early summer. Gardenias grow in a wide range of soils, but they do best in moist, loamy, well-drained soil with a pH of 5.0 to 6.0. Plant in a site protected from cold winter winds and early morning sun, which can cause foliage to sunburn. Sunlight is important for flowering, but modest blooming occurs in a half-day of direct sun. When planting, do not disturb the rootball unless it is potbound, then score it to encourage new roots. Make a backfill of 25 percent organic material and soil. Prepare a wide planting hole, backfilling with this humusy mix. Water thoroughly as you backfill; add a generous layer of pine-straw or ground mulch.

Growing Tips

Gardenias prefer moist soil and benefit from a drip irrigation system or at least a soaker hose. Fertilize twice yearly with a complete garden fertilizer such as 10-10-10 at a rate of 2 tablespoons per foot of height. One application is needed in early April and a second in mid-June. For darker green foliage, an iron-rich specialty fertilizer for roses can be substituted for one of these applications.

Regional Advice and Care

With recent hard winters we have a better feel for the cold-hardiness of gardenias. Prune cold-damaged twigs in spring. Immediately after flowering, prune selectively with hand shears to maintain its natural shape. Dwarf gardenias require little pruning, but sometimes twig thinning or deadheading of faded blossoms is in order. Whiteflies and wax scales may appear. If untreated, leaves turn black from sooty mold fungus. Use horticultural oil sprays or weekly insecticidal soap treatments to manage whiteflies.

Companion Planting and Design

Gardenias make wonderful specimen plants anywhere their fragrance can be appreciated. Groupings of the dwarf, cold-tolerant 'Kleim's Hardy' are great for borders, and single plants make good accents in foundation plantings. Prostrate-growing 'Radicans' is a favorite in Zone 8 and south. Double-flower forms 'Crown Jewel' and 'Double Mint' are charming!

Try These

Heaven Scent® and 'Frostproof' are cold-hardy in protected sites. 'Chuck Hayes' may rebloom in autumn; it's great for cut flowers. 'August Beauty' is also gaining popularity.

Golden Japanese False Cypress

Chamaecyparis pisifera 'Golden Mops'

Botanical Pronunciation
cam-ee-SIP-ah-riss pis-SIF-er-ah

Other Name Golden thread false cypress

Bloom Period and Seasonal Color Spring
bloom inconspicuous; year-round gold foliage

Mature Height × Spread
3 to 4 feet × 4 to 5 feet

Tired of an "all green" landscape and want year-round color from your evergreen plantings? Lucky for you! There are plenty of foliage color options among the Japanese false cypress species. If we held a conifer popularity contest with gardeners, no doubt golden Japanese false cypress would win first place. Following the winter doldrums there are lots of admirers because their soft golden twigs shine compared to leafless deciduous shrubs. Leading the way in Piedmont landscapes is the bodacious 'Golden Mops', a low mounding shrub with a sunny disposition. For decades, home landscapes were decorated with golden threadleaf false cypress with its drooping, deep yellow thin foliage, but over time these grew into 18-foot trees and many were removed. New selections are tighter with dazzling shades of yellow and lemon.

When, Where, and How to Plant

Plant potted golden false cypress late winter to fall. These shrubs are not difficult to transplant; move plants in fall. They adapt to a wide range of soil types. Most prefer moist, slightly acidic soil that drains well. Plant in full sun; it takes part shade as well, but it's less colorful. In sandy or gravelly soils incorporate an organic soil conditioner to increase moisture content and nutrient-holding capability. Water well to settle the backfill soil. Spread a 2-inch layer of mulch. Water twice a week for fall plantings and weekly in spring for the first month.

Growing Tips

Japanese false cypress, *Chamaecyparis pisifera*, is moderate to slow growing compared to its cousin,

C. obtusa. It can suffer in dry soils during the first two summer seasons. The cypress family is native to bog areas, and the plants love moisture. There is no benefit to fertilizing the first year. Apply an organic fertilizer or CRF product if the growth rate needs accelerating. Most evergreens don't need annual feeding. Maintain mulch by re-applying annually.

Regional Advice and Care

Prune in late spring to shape. Proper spacing is dependent on the chosen cultivar. Most Japanese false cypresses reach their mature height within ten years. There are few pests; monitor for bagworms. Handpick cocoons in fall, and spray in mid-spring to control young caterpillars using *B.t.* Mites are common in dry seasons; browning foliage can be a sign of spider mites or sunscald in dry sites. Insecticidal soap makes good miticide.

Companion Planting and Design

The striking color and form is unsurpassed in the winter garden. Plant this cypress in sunny borders or part sun in coastal gardens. Good companions are loropetalum, dwarf crapemyrtle, and liriope groundcover. Use a cluster of three for an accent. Tall cultivars, *C. pisifera* 'Boulevard' or 'Soft Serve', are unique for their bluish gray color and texture contrast; they are also used as hedges.

Try These

'Golden Mops' amd 'Vintage Gold' have vivid color and are foils for many landscape plants. 'Filifera Aurea', threadleaf false cypress, makes a large, pyramidal specimen.

Goshiki False Holly

Osmanthus heterophyllus 'Goshiki'

Botanical Pronunciation
oz-MAN-thus het-ee-ROW-fil-lus

Other Name Holly tea-olive

Bloom Period and Seasonal Color
Late summer sparse fragrant blooms in white;
colorful year-round

Mature Height × Spread 6 feet × 4 to 6 feet

This attractive, variegated shrub may be the most underrated broadleaf evergreen. The *Osmanthus* family hails from Japan but it's perfectly at home in Carolina landscapes. 'Goshiki' is one of the most colorful cultivars of the species and super versatile. Magnificent, upright to oval specimens are found growing in sunny parking lot medians and shaded gardens. It is durable in dry clay and is very hardy in Zones 7-9. Goshiki false holly makes a symmetrical specimen of densely branched foliage. Medium green leaves with spiny-leaf margins are splashed with numerous whitish yellow freckles. Older plants develop character and when set in part shade provide a touch of color. Dr. Michael Dirr provides this description, "A spectral rainbow with new growth tinged pink and bronze, flecked with gold, maturing cream and green."

When, Where, and How to Plant
Container-grown plantings from spring to fall are successful. This evergreen grows in sun or the high shade of pines. Once established, Goshiki osmanthus is more drought tolerant than Japanese holly. Average, well-drained soil is all it needs to thrive; however, moist, fertile soil will increase its growth rate. Loosen the roots of potted plants before planting. In sandy soil, mix bark soil conditioner or compost into the backfill. Most soils in the Carolinas benefit from the addition of phosphate. Create a berm at the edge of the hole. Water thoroughly, then water every three days for three weeks.

Growing Tips
Rootballs of new plantings should not be allowed to dry out. Water when the soil dries during late summer, especially the first two years following planting. Well-mulched evergreen shrubs should not need annual fertilizing after the early years. When fertilizing, use a CRF product or a specialty shrub fertilizer in early spring. It has a slow to moderate growth rate.

Regional Advice and Care
False hollies resemble English holly with their prominent leaf spines. To identify *Osmanthus* species look for opposite leaf arrangement on the stems, while *Ilex* members have alternating leaves. Pruning is seldom needed, which is delightful considering their prickly leaves! Shear lightly in summer to shape or control its height. Sunscald can occur in full sun in dry sites; browning of foliage on the south side can affect the attractiveness of the foliage but is only seasonal. Goshiki is a care-free shrub with no serious diseases. It is insect free and deer-resistant.

Companion Planting and Design
It's an excellent plant for planting in clusters of threes for color accents. Performs well in part shade or on the edge of a woodland garden. Underplant with Japanese plum yew and spreading juniper; use with sun or shade groundcovers depending on the site. Plant on close spacings for a low, impenetrable hedge; the spines keep out unwanted guests.

Try These
'Goshiki' is a winner among ornamental shrubs. Creamy white leaf margins give pyramidal form 'Variegatus' gardening kudos; it is taller at 8 to 10 feet.

Hinoki
False-Cypress

Chamaecyparis obtusa

Botanical Pronunciation
cam-ee-SIP-ah-riss ob-TU-sah

Bloom Period and Seasonal Color
Year-round foliage; no significant flower color

Mature Height × Spread
4 to 16 feet × 3 to 6 feet

If you like dwarf conifers, you will find true diversity among the false-cypress group. The *Chamaecyparis* genus is largely made up of Japanese natives, which include Hinoki and white cedar false-cypress, and numerous varieties of the species *C. pisifera*, which look much different in comparison. Hinoki false-cypress performs exceptionally well in Carolina landscapes. This slow-growing conifer has soft, compressed foliage that can be a rich green to golden color. Dwarf Hinoki, 'Nana Gracilis', has tufted, dark green foliage and a pyramidal shape. It is a choice plant for homeowners who need a vertical accent provided by a pyramidal shrub, or for softening architectural lines and corner beds. Dwarf false-cypress has resilient, evergreen foliage and small stature to qualify it as one of the very few "hug-ables" of the conifer family.

When, Where, and How to Plant

Plant potted false-cypress anytime during the year as soil conditions allow. These shrubs are not difficult to transplant; move established plants in fall. They adapt to a wide range of soil types. Most prefer moist, slightly acidic soil that drains well. Plant in full sun in Zones 6 to 7 and part sun to filtered shade in Zone 8. In sandy or gravelly soils incorporate an organic soil conditioner to increase moisture content and nutrient-holding capability. Water well to settle the backfill soil. Spread a 2-inch layer of mulch, then apply several more gallons of water. Water twice a week for fall plantings and weekly in spring for the first month.

Growing Tips

Dwarf Hinoki false-cypress is slower growing than slender or golden false-cypresses. They take longer to establish and can suffer in dry soils during the first growing season. Cypresses are native to bog areas and like moisture. Apply an organic fertilizer or CRF product occasionally. Most evergreens don't need annual feeding. Maintain mulch by applying annually which enriches the soil.

Regional Advice and Care

Prune in late spring, using hand shears. Proper spacing is dependent on the chosen cultivar. Most Hinoki cypresses reach their mature height within fifteen years. There are few pest problems other than bagworms, which can't be ignored. Handpick bagworm cocoons in the fall, and spray in mid-spring using *B.t.* Mites are common on narrowleaf evergreens in dry seasons. Hold white paper under branch tips and tap them. If little black dots start moving, you have mites.

Companion Planting and Design

Hinoki cypress can be planted in part shade. Hosta and hellebore are good companions. Grow in planters; use as accents in foundation plantings. Some cultivars have a low, spreading habit making them useful in borders. Use tall golden Hinoki 'Crippsii' as an accent specimen with blue rug juniper groundcover.

Try These

'Nana Gracilis' and 'Nana' have dark green color and soft foliage. Fernspray Hinoki 'Filicoides' is a fine pyramidal specimen.

Hydrangea

Hydrangea macrophylla

Botanical Pronunciation
HI-dran-GEE-ah MAC-row-phil-ah

Other Name Mophead

Bloom Period and Seasonal Color Summer blooms in pink, blue, red, and pure white

Mature Height × Spread
3½ to 6 feet × 4 to 8 feet

Carolina gardeners know big-leaf French or florists' hydrangeas as the voluptuous, blue-flowering shrubs found in old gardens or at farmhouses. New cultivars are not only vivid blue but also white or pink, such as 'Forever Pink' and 'Pia'. Reblooming varieties are the rage with 'Endless Summer' and 'Penny Mac' being well publicized. With the mopheads getting so much attention, few gardeners are familiar with the new selections of lacecap hydrangeas. Unlike the large blue mopheads, lacecaps have an umbrella-shaped flower structure with rings of large, showy flowers surrounding a center of bead-shaped blossoms. Royal Majestic® series includes lacecaps that are cold hardy to Zone 6, with coarse texture outstanding for mass plantings. This group offers both a touch of nostalgia and a sleek, contemporary look to the garden.

When, Where, and How to Plant

Only container-grown hydrangeas are available at nurseries. Plant them from spring through summer. Most hydrangeas prefer a part-shade location protected from afternoon sun. To avoid leaf wilt in hot weather, plant in moist soil or where irrigation is available. Though a hydrangea prefers moist soil, it also needs good drainage. Once the plant is set in the hole and the backfill is lightly firmed-in, the top inch or so of the roots should be visible. Cover these roots with 2 inches of loose mulch and water well. In poorly drained conditions, plant above grade in a berm or well-prepared bed containing copious amounts of organic matter.

Growing Tips

Hydrangeas are moderate- to fast-growing shrubs. Irrigation is necessary during summer. In spring when new growth is several inches long, fertilize lacecaps with a general garden fertilizer. Maintain a mulch layer to keep the soil cool and damp.

Regional Advice and Care

Prune hydrangeas immediately following the bloom period. This ensures more flowers and keeps viable young wood actively growing. Hard winter cold may kill the flower buds of hydrangeas formed in fall; groom by removing weak or dead twigs annually. Mophead hydrangea needs a protected location when planted in the western Piedmont or mountains. Protect from cold with a deep mulch of leaves or pine needles laid down by mid-December. Remove this thick mulch later as new growth resumes. There are no insect pests, but a deer repellant will be helpful where they browse. Young plants and rooted cuttings will need protection from rabbits.

Companion Planting and Design

Add variegated hydrangeas to a shade garden for a touch of light. Plant lacecaps in clusters of several shrubs, or use in borders. Choose them as accents with fine-textured perennials and ferns. Interplant with the summer-flowering *Hydrangea arborescens* 'Annabelle' or *H. paniculata* 'Limelight' for extended seasonal color.

Try These

Mopheads 'Penny Mac' and 'Endless Summer' are repeat bloomers. A standard is 'Nikko Blue'. Enjoy airy blooms of lacecaps 'Blue Wave' and 'Midnight Duchess'®. Double blooms of white 'Shooting Star' are unique. Showstopper™ hydrangeas are new.

Indian Hawthorn

Rhaphiolepis spp.

Botanical Pronunciation
raff-ee-o-LEP-sis

Bloom Period and Seasonal Color
Late spring flowers in pink, rose-red, or white; evergreen foliage

Mature Height × Spread
3 to 8 feet × 4 to 6 feet

Zones 7b-9

Gardeners on the coast should not be without Indian hawthorn. This shrub is the coastal equivalent of the Piedmont's Kurume azaleas, as it flourishes in hot locations where azaleas wither. There are cultivars that will survive the harsh winters in the central Piedmont, but in general this shrub is best suited to mild-winter areas. It flowers later than azaleas and can extend the bloom season. It has rounded, dark green, leathery leaves and dense clusters of fragrant pink or white flowers. It forms a compact mound. Its slow to medium growth rate qualifies it for low-maintenance landscapes. Indian hawthorn prefers well-drained, fertile soil but tolerates drought and salt spray. The hybrid hawthorn *Rhaphiolepis × delacourii* is known for having an edge in winter hardiness. Look for cultivars that resist leaf spot.

When, Where, and How to Plant
In coastal regions, plant container-grown Indian hawthorn anytime the ground is workable. The mountain region and foothill area is too cold for this plant. Plant in a sunny location. Indian hawthorn performs best in fast-draining soils. This shrub prefers a slightly alkaline soil, so add limestone if needed to bring the pH to 6. After removing the plant from its container, score the rootball and frill out circling roots. After planting irrigate every three days for two weeks to establish. Mulch well in sandy soils.

Growing Tips
Beginning 5 weeks after planting, apply a water-soluble fertilizer; make two more monthly applications. Irrigate during dry periods in the first growing season. This is especially important in coastal gardens. Drip irrigation and mulching will be necessary where Indian hawthorn is planted in open locations at the beach. Fertilize in May with 10-10-10 fertilizer or CRF.

Regional Advice and Care
In the Piedmont, harsh winters can brown both twigs and foliage in exposed locations of Zone 7. Severe pruning is required to remove cold-damaged foliage; weakened plants may need spring replacement. This shrub flowers on old wood, so delay most of the pruning until blooming is over. If you have Indian hawthorns growing in shade, the plants get leggy and need shaping periodically. Rejuvenate old plants by pruning back to 1 foot in late winter. There are no pests to control, provided you plant in well-drained soils and buy healthy plants to start with.

Companion Planting and Design
Use dwarf Indian hawthorn in raised planters where it will cascade gracefully over the sides or as a low-growing street buffer. Use it as a drought-tolerant, flowering shrub in seaside gardens alongside juniper, oleander, and pittosporum. 'Minor' planted in groups is good for low borders. Tall 'Majestic Beauty' makes a fine privacy screen.

Try These
Choose leaf spot-resistant varieties. Try dwarf selections *R. umbellata* Snowcap® and 'Snow White'. New hybrid cultivars for foundation plantings are coming!

Japanese Holly

Ilex crenata

Botanical Pronunciation
EYE-lex cree-NAD-ah

Bloom Period and Seasonal Color
Spring non-showy whitish flowers;
evergreen foliage

Mature Height × Spread
2 to 8 feet × 2 to 8 feet

Most of the shrubs selected by contractors for new Piedmont homes are likely an assortment of Japanese hollies. This holly adapts well to a wide range of environmental conditions. There are scores of cultivars from which to choose, and new ones appear every year. The flowers of Japanese hollies are rather uninteresting, as are the black berries that follow. But their dark green foliage and a moderate growth rate make them a choice shrub for home landscapes. 'Compacta' is a viable substitute for boxwoods, and in most cases people won't know the difference without a second look. The dwarf mounding forms such as 'Helleri', 'Hoogendorn', and 'Soft Touch' are the most popular with gardeners. They produce symmetrical new growth, and they generally require very little attention.

When, Where, and How to Plant

Healthy Japanese hollies purchased in containers can be planted throughout the growing season. Allow enough time for their roots to establish several weeks before the ground freezes. Plant in sunny to part shade locations; in full shade the shrubs thin out and get leggy. This holly likes moist but not wet sites; give it well-drained soil. Thoroughly loosen the roots of plants grown in pots. Prepare a wide, shallow hole three-fourths as deep and three times as wide as the rootball. Make a mix of one-third organic humus or soil conditioner to native soil. Backfill with the amended soil. Water slowly, applying a several gallons of water to settle the plant. Add 2 to 3 inches of mulch, staying clear of the crown.

Growing Tips

Water in the early years during the dry periods of August into fall. Always water in dry weather, as these hollies appreciate moisture when planted near shade trees. A combination of landscape fabric and mulch can help eliminate drought stress in non-irrigated beds. Once plants establish, use a CRF product in late fall, or apply an organic, specialty holly fertilizer in spring for year-round green color. Mulched plants don't need yearly fertilization; feed when leaf drop is heavy.

Regional Advice and Care

Shear in late winter or early summer to maintain symmetry. Black root rot fungus can kill Japanese hollies ten years old or so. This soil-inhabiting fungus infects plants, especially in heavy clay. Plant hollies high, such as in a raised bed, to prevent fungal attack. Nematodes can wreck Japanese hollies in sandy soils.

Companion Planting and Design

Use an upright form such as 'Hetzii' as a hedge, or 'Sky Pencil' for a vertical accent. Low-growing varieties should be grouped together in mass plantings or used as a groundcover. Dwarf forms, such as 'Soft Touch' and 'Hoogedorn', can be planted as an edging in the flowerbed. In Zone 8 and southward, dwarf yaupon, *Ilex vomitoria*, takes the heat.

Try These

The standard workhorse varieties are 'Compacta' and 'Green Lustre'. I chose 'Helleri' Japanese holly for my semi-shaded foundation planting.

Japanese Plum Yew

Cephalotaxus harringtonia

Botanical Pronunciation
self-oh-low-TAX-us hair-en-TONE-ee-ah

Other Name
Plum yew

Bloom Period and Seasonal Color
Year-round deep green foliage

Mature Height × Spread
2 to 6 feet × 5 to 10 feet

Japanese plum yew has been a favorite of mine since I discovered the giant shrubs in the Sarah P. Duke Gardens at Duke University. Soon afterward, I acquired several specimens for planting in the light shade of my garden. Years later, I found them at the Atlanta Botanical Garden and recognized its suitability as a substitute for yews, *Taxus*, that are so popular in more northerly states. Japanese plum yew is said to be a shrub with an identity crisis. It is neither a yew nor Japanese yew, *Podocarpus*, though all have dark needlelike foliage and upright growth. Their fine-textured and varied forms makes this evergreen a standout in the landscape. The popularity of plum yew will continue to grow as people discover they are care-free and perfectly happy in shady nooks.

When, Where, and How to Plant

Plant Japanese plum yew in spring in Zones 6 to 7 and fall in Zone 8. It prefers a location where there is some shade from the summer sun for better year-round color. Don't be reluctant to plant it in shade gardens. Though growth is best in moist soils, plum yew will survive dry summer conditions. These shrubs don't like wet feet; they prefer well-drained, moist, fertile soil like that preferred by rhododendrons. Plant high to prevent root rot disease, and give them plenty of room to grow. Prepare the soil using one-fourth organic matter by volume for enrichment. Dig a wide planting hole and spread out plum yew's fleshy roots, position it in the hole, backfill, and water as you replace the soil.

Growing Tips

Water well for the first two summers during dry periods. When established, the plants will thrive in dry shaded locations. Fertilize with an organic fertilizer every other spring to keep the best foliage color. Maintain a layer of mulch to help retain moisture. Apply 2 inches of compost annually, and discontinue fertilizing once they're established.

Regional Advice and Care

In Zone 8, give it afternoon shade or plant in filtered shade to maintain the dark leaf color. Remove upright-growing shoots to maintain the spreading form. Prune in late spring to control height or to groom the plant. Browning foliage is a sign of winter wind injury or soil that is too dry. Keep plum yews mulched and watered in periods of drought.

Companion Plant and Design

Prostrate forms of Japanese plum yews are suitable for use foundation plantings. Plant on the edge of a woodland retreat. They are beautiful by a shaded water feature. Good companions are azalea, fothergilla, and upright conifers as a foil. Use as shrub borders.

Try These

My original plants were 'Duke Gardens' yews. 'Fastigiata' is a narrow grower to 10 feet, the perfect fit for a small garden. 'Prostrata' is lovely as a facing plant for border edges.

Lilac

Syringa spp. and hybrids

Botanical Pronunciation
si-RING-guh

Bloom Period and Seasonal Color
Late spring blooms in white, blue, and lavender

Mature Height × Spread
4 to 8 feet × 4 to 6 feet

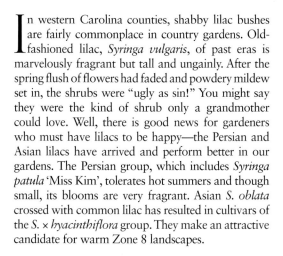

In western Carolina counties, shabby lilac bushes are fairly commonplace in country gardens. Old-fashioned lilac, *Syringa vulgaris*, of past eras is marvelously fragrant but tall and ungainly. After the spring flush of flowers had faded and powdery mildew set in, the shrubs were "ugly as sin!" You might say they were the kind of shrub only a grandmother could love. Well, there is good news for gardeners who must have lilacs to be happy—the Persian and Asian lilacs have arrived and perform better in our gardens. The Persian group, which includes *Syringa patula* 'Miss Kim', tolerates hot summers and though small, its blooms are very fragrant. Asian *S. oblata* crossed with common lilac has resulted in cultivars of the *S. × hyacinthiflora* group. They make an attractive candidate for warm Zone 8 landscapes.

When, Where, and How to Plant

Lilac is usually sold in large containers and planted anytime. Many gardeners buy them in bloom to be sure of the color. Keep them in their pot, watering daily, until the blooms are spent and you can prune them off. Give them plenty of sun with good air circulation to diminish the chance of powdery mildew disfiguring the foliage. It is important to lime the soil before planting. On clay soil, mix 3 cups pelletized dolomitic limestone with the backfill; 2 cups would be sufficient on sandy soils. The ideal soil pH is 6.5. Follow the planting recommendations for shrubs. Water thoroughly and apply a 2-inch mulch layer.

Growing Tips

Trickle water slowly around the rootball of your newly planted lilac approximately one minute for each inch of diameter of the rootball. Repeat three times the first week, twice the second week, and taper to once a week until the shrub's roots are established. In the spring following planting, apply nursery CRF product at a rate of ½ cup per 10 square feet under the canopy and a little beyond. Rake back the mulch, spread the fertilizer, then replace the mulch, keeping it away from the base of the plant.

Regional Advice and Care

In warm Zones 8 gardens, Descanso hybrids and 'Bloomerang' are worth trying. Overgrown lilacs can be pruned back severely in late winter, but doing so removes flower buds for the upcoming season. Powdery mildew presents a problem for Persian lilacs, particularly in shaded areas; select disease-resistant cultivars. Suckers arising anytime from the root collar area should be removed. Lilac hornets chew and remove the plant's bark for their nests; an insecticide spray may be warranted.

Companion Planting and Design

Lilacs with low-growing evergreens hiding their bare legs make a good combination. Plant by a patio window where the fragrance can be enjoyed. As a specimen, a mature Japanese tree lilac, *S. reticulata*, is a show-stopper in Zones 6 to 7.

Try These

'Miss Kim' and 'Blue Skies' are favorites. 'Lilac Sunday' resists powdery mildew and blooms reliably. Purple 'Bloomerang'® reblooms but may be short on fragrance.

Loropetalum

Loropetalum chinense var. *rubrum*

Botanical Pronunciation
lor-o-PET-ah-lum chai-NENSE

Common Name
Fringe flower

Bloom Period and Seasonal Color
Spring blooms in neon pink, light pink and
white; semi- to evergreen burgundy foliage

Mature Height × Spread
2 to 10 feet × 2 to 8 feet

Loropetalum is a showy, semi-evergreen shrub with burgundy leaves. In spring, its wide-spreading branches light up with feathery, hot pink flowers. Blooms occur sporadically during the summer as growth continues. In full sun, the modern cultivars maintain shiny plum-to-ruby colored foliage. It is the perfect substitute for the spiny, red-leaf barberry shrub. This plant is a vigorous grower and will thrive in sun or partial shade. The old garden variety, white-flowering loropetalum, has been used for decades as a hedge or screening plant. In early spring, this Asian cousin bears white blooms resembling the spider-like flowers of witch hazel. New dwarf cultivars, such as 'Crimson Fire' and 'Purple Pixie', are Carolina favorites with gardeners loving them for their sharp color contrast with other ornamental plants.

When, Where, and How to Plant

Loropetalum can be planted anytime it's available and when attention can be given to watering. For winter plantings, allow one month in the ground for root growth before the soil freezes. In the western Carolinas, plant in spring when apple trees begin blooming, and only in protected areas. The mountains are too cold for most loropetalum to retain evergreen foliage, and this shrub's hardiness at upper elevations is not well documented. It thrives in moist, well-drained soil, regardless of type. The plum-to-burgundy foliage will show up best when it is planted in a sunny location, but it will handle partly shady sites just fine.

Growing Tips

Spring plantings need ample water. Water every three days for the first two weeks, then taper to weekly. If no rainfall irrigate when the soil dries during the first two summers. Add a 2-inch mulch layer. Wait three months to fertilize spring-planted shrubs to allow sufficient root growth. If needed, fertilize in spring with a nursery special fertilizer (3-1-2).

Regional Advice and Care

Loropetalum may need pruning after the second season to keep it shaped and to control height. Prune in late spring or after the spring bloom period. Prune to within 1 foot of the ground if a small shrub is desired. Winter in Zones 6 to 7a can be hard on loropetalum and survival rates are not well documented. Groom by removing cold-damaged tips and thinning dense branches. Late-summer fertilization can make it cold-sensitive. It is a care-free shrub with few pests, and little attention from browsing deer.

Companion Planting and Design

This shrub can be espaliered or planted as a standard. Plant it for its shocking pink to neon blooms in spring. Use in clusters to accent coarse-textured evergreens as a foil. Tall 'Sparkling Sangria'™, Ever Red®, and many *Loropetalum chinense* var. *rubrum* cultivars are suitable for screening and hedges. In Zones 7b to 9, loropetalum is magnificent just in time for Christmas.

Try These

Compact 'Crimson Fire' and 'Purple Pixie'® have fabulous burgundy foliage. 'Zhuzhou Fuhsia' is cold hardy with abundant flowers and little dieback. Carolina Moonlight® blooms white.

Oakleaf Hydrangea

Hydrangea quercifolia

Botanical Pronunciation
HI-dran-GEE-ah curs-see-FOIL-e-ah

Bloom Period and Seasonal Color
Late spring blooms in white fading to dusty rose; burgundy with rusty flowerheads in fall

Mature Height × Spread
4 to 8 feet × 4 to 9 feet

Oakleaf hydrangea is one of our finest native shrubs, with large leaves that resemble those of red oak. To some it may appear plain, but to the landscape designer its bold texture has a distinct beauty all its own. During June, oakleaf hydrangea displays large showy panicles of white flowers that later fade to a soft rose color. Coarse, olive green leaves are loosely arranged and provide the woodland garden a lush, almost tropical appeal. This deciduous shrub has outstanding exfoliating, cinnamon-colored bark on spindly, crooked stems. As the plants mature, their wide-spreading branches form an open canopy in light shade. Every gardener with enough space would do well to plant this native shrub in a shade garden. It is easier to grow than the highly hybridized mophead hydrangeas.

When, Where, and How to Plant

Plant potted shrubs year-round as soil conditions and plantings can be irrigated. Oakleaf hydrangea is very durable, even when planted by a novice gardener. Place in a sunny to partially shaded spot in moist, fertile, well-drained soil. Its fibrous root system tends to sucker and spread, making oak leaf hydrangea a candidate for mass plantings on banks. If the native soil is friable (loose like coffee grounds), no soil amendments are necessary. Mulch will encourage rooting and keep the soil cool.

Growing Tips

Water routinely after planting, including three times the first week, twice the second week, and then once a week until the roots are established. Oak leaf hydrangea likes moist soil but not soggy sites. Water generously during the first and second growing season. It is not fussy about fertilizing where it is mulched. If needed in the early years, apply a shrub fertilizer in spring (analysis 12-6-6 or equal) at the rate suggested by the product.

Regional Advice and Care

Oakleaf hydrangea is care-free. Pruning is rarely needed unless space is limited. In spring, prune to remove sucker growth at the base of the plant, and remove the oldest branches every other year. Cut back spent blooms in winter after they deteriorate. Mulch heavily with leaf compost when placed in a woodland garden. Water during a drought only if leaves wilt. This shrub tolerates dryness very well after it's established.

Companion Planting and Design

Plant on the edge of a treeline, or use tall cultivars for screening. Plant compact cultivars if your garden space is limited. Good shrub companions for naturalizing are plum yew, cherry laurel, anise, rhododendron, and sweet shrub. Its exfoliating bark and persistent dried flower panicles add winter interest.

Try These

'Snow Queen' and 'Alice' are tall selections with huge, white, conelike blooms. 'Pee Wee' and 'Sikes Dwarf' are fine compact forms 3 to 4 feet with equal spread. Recent U.S. National Arboretum release 'Munchkin' is small, ideal for planting in masses.

Oleander

Nerium oleander

Botanical Pronunciation
near-EE-um oh-LEE-an-der

Bloom Period and Seasonal Color
Summer blooms in white, yellow, pink, red, purple, and salmon; evergreen foliage

Mature Height × Spread
6 to 12 feet × 6 to 8 feet

Zones 8b-9

Oleander is a gorgeous but cold-sensitive evergreen shrub—commonly seen in the coastal region but rarely elsewhere in the Carolinas. This upright-branched evergreen is from the Mediterranean region. It is hardy throughout Zone 8 and southward, providing a tropical accent as a specimen plant in the landscape. With its lustrous, narrow, green leaves to 6 inches and clusters of 1-inch single or double flowers, oleander blooms heavily spring through summer. Elongated fruit pods form after flowering. Gardeners can grow them in containers to bring them indoors for winter. The dwarf forms are most suited to mass plantings and tall varieties make fine border plants. The wide range of colors and tolerance of droughty conditions make them superb for difficult seaside landscapes.

When, Where, and How to Plant
Plant container-grown oleander in spring or fall. In Zone 7 and northward, it will not survive winter if set outdoors so it's planted in containers for overwintering indoors. This showy ornamental prefers strong sunlight to bloom freely. It is extremely durable and takes the heat. Oleander is not particular about soil, handling beach sands and even tolerating salty conditions. Limestone is not needed, but a small handful of superphosphate is beneficial at planting. Prepare a planting hole with bark soil conditioner or peat moss with sandy soil types.

Growing Tips
Once established, oleanders are drought tolerant and tough as nails. Consistently wet soil encourages lush growth and fewer flowers. Scatter a general garden fertilizer, such as 10-10-10 analysis, six weeks after planting and each spring thereafter. A couple of inches of compost or mulch will conserve moisture and encourage new roots in sandy soils.

Regional Advice and Care
Protect young plants for the first couple of winters in Zone 8a. An application of a wilt-proofing spray and a windscreen constructed around the plant in January can be helpful. Alternatively, protect the crown with a deep mulch of pine straw and depend on new canes to form and bloom. Prune for height control; do this while the plant is dormant and before growth begins in spring. Thinning to maintain form and removing small suckers from the base is recommended. To rejuvenate, cut old canes to the ground. This interesting shrub has virtually no pests other than an occasional caterpillar. In shade, oleander is leggy and produces few flowers. **Warning:** Please warn children not to eat any part of the plant, as it is very poisonous. Be careful that livestock or pets do not have access.

Companion Planting and Design
Plant oleander in coastal gardens where it can be viewed often while in bloom. Use it as a hedge, as a backdrop for perennials. It can be used for a colorful street planting. Single white and double yellow varieties are delightful as accents among dark green evergreens.

Try These
Numerous cultivars include 'Hardy Red', 'Ruby Lace'™, and 'Hardy Pink'.

Paperbush

Edgeworthia chrysantha

Botanical Pronunciation
edge-WORTH-ee-ah cry-SANH-tha

Other Name
Edgeworthia

Bloom Period and Seasonal Color
Spring flower clusters in white and yellow

Mature Height × Spread
5 to 7 feet × 5 to 7 feet

   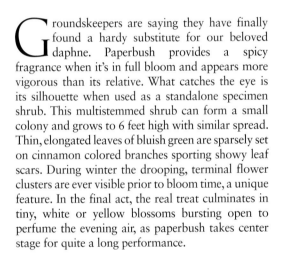

Groundskeepers are saying they have finally found a hardy substitute for our beloved daphne. Paperbush provides a spicy fragrance when it's in full bloom and appears more vigorous than its relative. What catches the eye is its silhouette when used as a standalone specimen shrub. This multistemmed shrub can form a small colony and grows to 6 feet high with similar spread. Thin, elongated leaves of bluish green are sparsely set on cinnamon colored branches sporting showy leaf scars. During winter the drooping, terminal flower clusters are ever visible prior to bloom time, a unique feature. In the final act, the real treat culminates in tiny, white or yellow blossoms bursting open to perfume the evening air, as paperbush takes center stage for quite a long performance.

When, Where, and How to Plant

You will be tempted to purchase and plant potted paperbush year-round. Be advised to avoid planting this gem in the drier months because establishment is better when the soils are cool and moist. An ideal location provides some protection from late afternoon sun. Plant paperbush in an area that drains well. Dig a hole twice as wide but equal depth of the rootball. Incorporate several inches of compost into the backfill soil to help retain moisture. Loosen the fleshy roots but take care not to sever them; spread them throughout the prepared backfill. Water well after planting and follow up a thick mulch layer.

Growing Tips

Keep the roots moist, especially with fall plantings. Water daily for the first week and twice per week for the first month. During the first few summers, irrigate monthly or if the plant shows signs of wilting. They are moderately drought tolerant after maturing. Apply organic fertilizer or a CRF product as necessary to maintain the normal blue-green foliage color.

Regional Advice and Care

The "wow" factor for paperbush is definitely its aromatic charm. Unlike its fragrant cousin, *Daphne odora*, paperbush seems to hold up well across all Carolinas hardiness zones once established. It is a low-maintenance selection, but pay attention to watering during summer droughts. Maintaining a 2-inch mulch layer over time will certainly pay big dividends. To manage the height and spread, some heading back cuts may be in order following the spring bloom. Sucker growth can be rooted to create new plantings for borders.

Companion Planting and Design

This plant screams "specimen plant" to provide a winter accent by a patio or entryway. It is a good foil for a water garden or Asian theme garden. Incorporate paperbush into a border featuring a variety of spring-flowering bulbs. Mass low-growing perennials at its feet, such as hellebores, lungwort, hostas, or cheddar pinks. Place in front of an evergreen background or attractive screen.

Try These

The species variety is a good one, but handsome cultivars to seek out include 'Gold Rush', 'Nanjing Gold', 'John Bryant', and 'Red Dragon'.

Rhododendron

Rhododendron spp.

Botanical Pronunciation
row-do-DEN-drun

Bloom Period and Seasonal Color
Mid-spring blooms in myriad colors;
evergreen foliage

Mature Height × Spread
2 to 10 feet × 2 to 10 feet

Zones 5 - 8a

Rhododendrons have been called the "Crown Jewel of the Garden," the standard by which many gardeners unfairly rate other flowering shrubs. Rhododendrons are members of the same family as mountain laurel, heather, and azaleas (a subclass). One doesn't have to travel to distant estate gardens to see marvelous specimens. There are many fine collections in the mountain regions and throughout the Piedmont. Great numbers of tourists flock to the Smokies annually to see the lavender-pink blooms of our native Catawba rhododendron, *Rhododendron catawbiense*. Since the mid-1800s when the Ironclad hybrids were introduced, gardeners have searched for cultivars for the hot, humid Sunbelt. But a love affair with this evergreen shrub can be bittersweet. Without proper planting and selection, many rhododendrons are destined for a short life.

When, Where, and How to Plant
Plant potted rhododendrons anytime the soil is cool; plant B&B rhodies in late winter and spring. The secret to success is to recreate the plant's native habitat. This means planting in part sun to shade where there is well-drained, moist, acidic soil. An east- or north-facing exposure in a woodland garden or foundation planting is ideal. Rhododendrons do well in our native soils, which are generally acidic. Test soil drainage by digging a foot-deep hole and fill it twice with water. It should drain within twenty-four hours. Otherwise, plant in raised beds. See page 150 for planting tips.

Growing Tips
Water every day for the first week; taper to twice weekly for 2 months. Irrigate as needed using the plant's leaves as an indicator of dryness. Foliage will lose luster and appear wavy as soil dries. Established plants are fairly drought tolerant and durable. Rhodies are not heavy feeders and extract most of their nutrients from natural mulches such as shredded leaves, compost, or pine needles.

Regional Advice and Care
On mountain peaks, rhodies thrive in full sun. Unfortunately, in lower elevations, summer heat is its Achilles' heel. Poorly drained soils can result in root rot, shortening their life expectancy. Prune in late winter by removing entire branches to control height. Avoid shearing. Sudden wilting of a branch in summer may indicate borers or twig dieback fungus. Twig dieback is recognized by curling leaves and off-colored foliage; remove affected twigs immediately. A fungicidal soil drench may be used where there are large numbers of plants in the same bed. Remove rhodies that defoliate. In summer, keep raised beds moist using soaker hoses. Try mounting misting heads above your rhodies in Zone 8 to keep plants cool.

Companion Planting and Design
Use as a background hedge for finer-textured ornamentals. Most rhodies are too large for foundation plantings; dwarf cultivars offer new possibilities. Underrated PJM rhodies are care-free; there are a plethora of colors.

Try These
The lustrous foliage and large flower trusses of 'Scintillation' are simply incredible. Tough cultivars for low elevations are 'Roseum Elegans', 'Nova Zembla', and 'Holden'.

Rose-of-Sharon

Hibiscus syriacus

Botanical Pronunciation
hi-BIS-kus sear-ee-ACT-us

Other Name
Althea

Bloom Period and Seasonal Color
Midsummer blooms in white, lavender, pink, red, and mixed

Mature Height × Spread
8 to 10 feet × 6 to 10 feet

Rose-of-Sharon is a deciduous member of the mallow family, as its funnel-shaped blooms clearly indicate. One of my childhood memories is visiting my grandparents in Statesville, NC, admiring the lavender summer flowers of this multibranched shrub from their porch. I never developed an appreciation for althea until decades later when I spotted a neighbor's flowering in July. Only a precious few shrubs have the stamina to bloom in the twilight of summer. Multitudes of flowers give rise to brown capsules that persist through winter. Rich green foliage and loosely upright branches give it a unique form. Rose-of-Sharon can be grown as a multistemmed shrub or limbed up as a small tree. New hybrid releases have rocked their world with exciting colors from sterile hybrids (no unwanted seedlings).

When, Where, and How to Plant

Plant this deciduous shrub anytime from late fall until spring. Rose-of-Sharon's flowers are single, double, or semidouble; it is best to buy blooming plants to ensure the form you prefer. Althea tolerates half-shade conditions but flowers best in direct sun. It accepts a wide range of soil types but flourishes in moist soil. For hedges, space plants 5 or more feet apart. Plant container-grown shrubs no deeper than originally grown at the nursery. Prepare a wide planting hole with a dusting of limestone. Water thoroughly before mulching.

Growing Tips

Water twice weekly to keep the soil moist for six weeks. Water during prolonged dry periods and keep the plantings mulched for weed control. Irrigate the shrub during the dry periods and while they are blooming. Fertilize with a bloom-booster product or 10-20-20 fertilizer analysis at bud break in late spring.

Regional Advice and Care

This is a vigorous grower with 2 feet of annual growth possible. If it is growing wildly, cut back twigs to four buds in March. Remove large branches at the base with a pruning saw. Rose-of-Sharon can be pruned severely at maturity for height control. Allow specimen shrubs to grow as small trees by limbing up. The large flowers will attract bumblebees and beetles to the huge volume of pollen and nectar; don't apply insecticides unless Japanese beetles appear. Beware—the abundant flowers of the old-fashioned variety can produce legions of seedlings; it's best to choose sterile cultivars from a nursery. Big plus—it's deer resistant.

Companion Planting and Design

Gardeners frequently plant a border or screen of one of the common varieties. Use as an accent specimen for late summer color. Underplant tree-form plantings with low-growing annuals, perennials, or spreading holly shrubs. There are a plethora of colors for garden designs. *Please* don't use this big plant in foundation plantings.

Try These

USDA hybrids are outstanding and have Greek goddess names—'Minerva', 'Aphrodite', and 'Helene'. The pure white, 4-inch flowers of 'Diana' remain open at night. 'Fiji Rose' and Full Blast® are great.

Spirea

Spiraea spp. and hybrids

Botanical Pronunciation
spy-REE-ah

Other Name
Dwarf spirea

Bloom Period and Seasonal Color
Summer blooms in pink

Mature Height × Spread
2 to 4 feet × 3 to 6 feet

Old-fashioned spireas, such as bridal wreath, garland, and baby's breath, can be found around older homes all over the Carolinas. But a new spirea is sweeping the landscape trade. Dwarf spireas are excellent plants for contemporary gardens with limited space. These deciduous shrubs continue to offer flowers and colorful foliage when the old favorites have long since passed their spring glory. *Spiraea japonica* 'Goldmound', for example, provides months of interest. The dense, mounding shrub produces reddish bronze spring foliage that turns to yellow-green by summer, then coppery in fall. Compact shrubs in the *Spiraea japonica* and *S. × bumalda* group have summer blooms, brilliant foliage, and leafless, wiry twigs in winter. Dwarf spireas are responsible for the increased interest in this family of ornamentals.

When, Where, and How to Plant

Plant year-round from containers. Bare-root plants from mail-order nurseries should be planted promptly in spring. Grow in a sunny location in well-drained soil; wet, poorly drained soils kill spirea. Once established, it tolerates dry sites and can be used as a tall groundcover on banks. Plants are pH-adaptable and survive well in ordinary soils. Established plants produce suckers and spread out a bit; give them plenty of room. Spirea planted less than 3 feet apart will ultimately grow together. Plant spirea as you would azalea, butterflying the roots before planting in a hole that is twice as wide as the rootball. Firm-in the backfill, mulch, and water well.

Growing Tips

Water every three days for the first two weeks, then water weekly until they establish. Once established,

they are drought tolerant, as shown by their use in roadway landscaping. The dwarf kinds are not heavy feeders, but they perform better if fertilized once in spring with a general nursery fertilizer.

Regional Advice and Care

Nurseries are growing dwarf spireas all across the Carolinas because they are durable. To encourage reblooming, remove spent summer flowers; the shrubs will look shabby for a few weeks. Eliminate excess twiggy growth by shearing in later winter and increase the flower display. Spirea can be overtaken by weeds but are quite tolerant of pre-emergence herbicides applied to prevent invasive grassy weeds. There are no serious insect or disease pests. Hose down plants if aphids appear in spring.

Companion Planting and Design

Plant dwarf spirea for refreshing summer color in place of, or to complement, perennials. Use in mass plantings, as fillers in the border, tall groundcovers, or as a low cluster in front of evergreens. Though they blend seamlessly with contemporary plants, spireas bring a bit of nostalgia to the landscape. There's a long season of color from leaves and blooms.

Try These

There are numerous species available including taller *S. thunbergii* 'Ogon'. Japanese spireas 'Little Princess' and 'Limemound'® work as groundcovers. 'Shirobana' offers a rainbow of blooms. 'Neon Flash' and 'Ogon' give stellar peformances.

Viburnum

Viburnum spp. and hybrids

Botanical Pronunciation
vi-BURN-num

Bloom Period and Seasonal Color
Spring bloom clusters or snowballs in white; gold fall foliage

Mature Height × Spread
5 to 12 feet × 6 to 12 feet

A mong the fine flora you will discover as you hike through the woodlands of the Carolinas are native species of viburnums. Their berries are important to wildlife, and they are the perfect, deciduous landscape plant, thriving on benign neglect. But some gardeners want more than ruggedness to please songbirds. Koreanspice viburnum, *Viburnum carlesii*, has become one of the most popular species in this huge genus. Its fragrance, graceful shape, and handsome foliage delight gardeners from the coast to the mountains. The 3-inch, rounded flower clusters of pastel pink buds open into tiny, waxy, white blooms with an intoxicating, spicy scent. The hybrid 'Mohawk' offers colorful fall foliage as well. For the peony-lover, Chinese snowball 'Sterile' is a large shrub with spring blooms that resemble softballs. Viburnums are care-free and showy.

When, Where, and How to Plant

Container-grown viburnums can be planted anytime, but late-summer plantings will need frequent watering. The plants prefer full sun or a spot with a few hours of afternoon shade. Many native viburnums grow very tall in woodland gardens where they thrive on slightly acidic, humusy soils and cooler temperatures. Before planting, loosen the roots of potbound plants. Make several vertical slits in the rootball using a shovel and shake potting soil loose. Plant in a hole twice the diameter of the rootball and three-quarters its depth. Cover the roots with native backfill. Form a berm for watering, and water slowly to settle it in.

Growing Tips

During the first growing season, water weekly, then taper to irrigating during dry spells. Well-rooted, established plants tolerate drought. If foliage color is pale, apply chelated iron (found in azalea fertilizer) in late spring.

Regional Advice and Care

Viburnums grow without much pruning—just remove wild shoots in late summer to maintain shape. Groom following spring bloom. In shady sites or during summer rains, leaf spot disease may occur. Raking fallen leaves should help in disease control. Fertilize mature shrubs as indicated by soil tests. Viburnums may be sensitive to sulfur spray as a disease control. Horticultural oils are a good remedy for scale insect infestations. Apply the oils in early autumn.

Companion Planting and Design

Site groupings of viburnum and azalea in the woodland border. Plant fragrant viburnums by a window or patio where you can revel in their fragrance. Though rare in gardens, 'Compactum' and 'Conoy' are dwarf forms. The hybrid 'Eskimo' is a wonderful choice for a flowering border. 'Summer Snowflake' and 'Shasta' are double-file varieties with blooms that are appreciated from high vistas. Use for naturalizing in wildlife gardens.

Try These

Koreanspice, of course. Also consider 'Cayuga', a hybrid bearing abundant blooms and dark green foliage. Try 'Mohican' for berries; 'Sterile', a snowball type, V. × *carlcephalum*, for its plate-sized blooms.

Virginia Sweetspire

Itea virginica

Botanical Pronunciation
eye-TEA-ah vir-GIN-ee-kah

Other Name
Sweetspire

Bloom Period and Seasonal Color
Summer flowers in white to pinkish; reddish purple fall foliage

Mature Height × Spread
2 to 5 feet × 4 to 5 feet

Some plants have to grow on you—pardon the pun, please! Many of the native shrubs are a bit too scraggly for formal foundation plantings, but their innate beauty emerges when they are planted in natural settings. Virginia sweetspire is the epitome of grace and character when interspersed among other native ornamentals. Drooping 6-inch spikes of sweetly fragrant, white flowers appear in midsummer when few shrubs are showy. You will adore the crimson fall foliage of this deciduous shrub. (In coastal gardens it may be semi-evergreen.) Virginia sweetspire grows in swamps and moist woodlands from New Jersey to Florida and is quite adaptable to heavy clay soils. Try this noteworthy species if you prefer the open, informal look of multistemmed shrubs. Little Henry® adds interest to any urban landscape.

When, Where, and How to Plant

Plant Virginia sweetspire in spring or fall in a sunny to partially shady location; too much shade can reduce flower production. Choose a site where the soil is moist and fairly rich. In sandy or poor soils, spade in organic matter. The plant will adjust to almost any soil type or situation, as well as a wide range of light levels. Prepare the site by digging a hole twice the diameter of the rootball (or more) and equal to its depth. Loosen the rootball then position it in the hole. Backfill and water twice before mulching.

Growing Tips

Irrigate the new planting every three days for the first two weeks, and often enough to keep the soil reasonably moist for the first summer. After establishment, this native will appreciate irrigation in late summer during its bloom season. Feed a general fertilizer in spring every few years. Apply a 3-inch mulch layer to ensure plant health and color.

Regional Advice and Care

Once established, sweetspire is a low-maintenance plant. There are no pests to control, and you make a lot of beneficial insects very happy. As the shrub matures, cut the older upright branches back to the ground to stimulate vigorous new canes. The Chinese sweetspire spreads rapidly by suckers and may need periodic root-pruning. Virginia sweetspire is better behaved, but may sucker out in shallow, moist soils.

Companion Planting and Design

Planting sweetspire brings a bonus—it blooms late when our typical spring display is finished. Add the garnet-red fall foliage of 'Henry's Garnet' and you double your pleasure. Groupings of sweetspire will accentuate its cascading form. Plant it in front of evergreen shrubs or with coarse-textured perennials like cannas. Liriope or evergreen groundcovers are a nice complement. Use it as a foil for white-fruited beauty-berry . . . wow!

Try These

The compact varieties 'Sprich', Little Henry®, and 'Merlot' offer great color for small gardens.

Waxmyrtle

Myrica cerifera

Botanical Pronunciation
mah-REE-kah sir-IF-er-ah

Other Name
Southern bayberry

Bloom Period and Seasonal Color
Spring blooms non-showy; evergreen foliage

Mature Height × Spread
4 to 20 feet × 5 to 14 feet

Waxmyrtle may be known best as bayberry since it produces heavy crops of aromatic gray berries used in candle-making and relished by wild birds. This native evergreen grows where most landscape shrubs would fail. Waxmyrtle tolerates a wide range of planting sites from moist clays to sand dunes on the coast. Its scented leaves are olive green, resembling that of willows, and loosely arranged on the stems. It's a strong and fast grower, yielding multitrunked shrubs that can be limbed up to form specimen trees. The upright growth habit serves the gardener well as a windbreak. This native can be found growing throughout the eastern Carolinas in sunny or shady gardens. Too bad it isn't cold hardy in mountain landscapes and is susceptible to ice storm damage.

When, Where, and How to Plant
Plant potted waxmyrtle in spring, summer, or fall. Avoid planting B&B shrubs when the soil is too wet to handle. They tolerate full sun to part shade locations in any type of soil. When planting several plants as a hedge or screen, rototill and plant in a slightly raised bed. Loosen potbound roots and shake off most of the soil. Prepare individual holes three times as wide as the rootball. Firm the backfill soil around the sides of the rootball. Water well before and after mulching to settle the soil. Add a layer of mulch staying clear of the crown.

Growing Tips
Water newly planted waxmyrtle twice weekly for the first month. Taper to weekly until the shrub's roots are established; generally in two months, or when new growth is evident. This plant enjoys moist soil, so be generous with water in dry weather for the first couple of summers. It grows well in clay soil too but will not tolerate "wet feet" from poor drainage. Use a controlled-release nursery fertilizer as in the early years. This native can "fix nitrogen" and is care-free after as it matures.

Regional Advice and Care
Popular for sandy soils of the coastal region. Waxmyrtle does not look good sheared; let it roam free. It tolerates heavy thinning in early spring before new growth emerges and heading back in midsummer. Heavy leaf drop and brown branch tips are common in Piedmont winters and westward. Waxmyrtle produces root suckers from the base; remove them or let it be, if you desire a hedge. Do not use a herbicide to kill sucker growth, prune off unwanted twigs.

Companion Planting and Design
It is the designer's choice for informal, evergreen privacy screens in Zone 8 and south. Use compact variety *M. cerifera* var. *pumila* for borders. The fragrant green foliage can be appreciated in specimen tree form. Waxmyrtle is much too large for foundations.

Try These
Southern waxmyrtle is a nursery mainstay. 'Emperor' is gorgeous where it has room to grow. 'Don's Dwarf', 'Little Bull', and 'Fairfax' are more compact.

TREES

FOR THE CAROLINAS

I t is hard to imagine living in a neighborhood without trees. Trees make our environments more pleasant and add seasonal beauty year-round. Autumn color in the Carolinas is spectacular, particularly in the Piedmont and mountains, and winter snowstorms light up our evergreens. Spring-flowering shrubs are enhanced by the blossoms of trees. Berry-producing trees attract birds and wildlife, and evergreen trees are important nesting sites for birds, doubling as windbreaks and privacy screens.

The color of this Japanese maple in autumn is gorgeous!

The Value of Trees

In studies of residential real estate values, tree-filled lots bring market prices 20 to 30 percent higher than similar lots without trees. Strategically placed trees can significantly reduce the cost of cooling a home by providing much-needed shade during summer. Trees are nature's air-conditioners, reducing ambient heat as they shade homes and transpire moisture.

With increasing concerns for air quality, trees provide a cost-effective way to clean the air in urban communities. Carbon dioxide production is a major factor in global warming. A single mature tree consumes 13 pounds of carbon dioxide yearly. Clearly, trees improve the quality of life in our communities, and frequently lure new businesses to towns earning the "Tree City USA" designation.

Spring announces its arrival in our states with a parade of redbuds, Japanese cherries, saucer magnolias, and dogwoods in full, resplendent bloom. In early summer, 'Royal Purple' smoke tree and 'Forest Pansy' redbuds steal the show with their fabulous burgundy leaf color. Fall echoes the floral display of spring with dazzling colors of other hues. The fall show that envelops the Carolinas begins in early October on the lofty peaks of the Blue Ridge and Great Smoky Mountains and gradually wends its way across the Piedmont to the Coastal Plains. This seasonal spectacle ensures that tourism will always contribute to the economy of the Carolinas.

What Trees Offer

Shade trees can frame a house the way a beautiful frame enhances a lasting work of art. Evergreens block objectionable views and divert strong winds. As a group, evergreens can add color to an otherwise bleak winter landscape, and they generally grow slowly. (But know your plant. Although they never lose them all, pines shed needles each year in spring or fall, gifting you with coveted pine straw mulch. People commonly plant evergreens too close to the house, so ask, "What is the mature spread?" and plant accordingly.)

During winter, many ornamental trees provide colorful berries for our enjoyment and sustenance for birds. Seedpods and berries that follow the handsome flowers are a special treat in the garden. Snow-laden boughs provide a photo-op for gardeners anxious to capture a cardinal feasting near a window. *Prunus mume*, Japanese flowering apricot, is a winter gem that bears fruit in years where no late frosts occur. An often overlooked characteristic of deciduous trees is exfoliating bark. The cinnamon-colored, mottled bark of Japanese crapemyrtle is most appreciated in the winter garden. Research the subtle seasonal characteristics of landscape trees before you plant, and site them where their traits can be appreciated.

Many Carolinians are passionate about dogwoods. Dogwood is a native flowering tree whose spring, fall, and winter beauty is unsurpassed. A fungal disease, dogwood anthracnose, threatens the dogwood's survival in mountain and upper Piedmont. Disease-resistant dogwood hybrids offer hope that this deciduous tree will be planted for many decades to come.

Thinking Ahead

Trees can be big investments. They are relatively expensive, and species with brittle limbs can incur expenses following storm damage. With a little forethought, you can avoid making costly mistakes when selecting and planting trees. Ask yourself why you need a tree for a particular location. Is shade your goal? What about privacy? Are there height restrictions for the space? If a tree produces fruit or drops twigs, would it create a hazard or maintenance concern? Do you desire pretty flowers, or is a conifer acceptable? Many trees attract wildlife, especially squirrels and birds. Are you prepared for the litter that accompanies critters?

Consult with a county forester, city arborist, or Extension agent for lists of trees for special situations. They can guide your selection by considering your particular soil types and environment. Keep in mind that your tree can become a liability for a neighbor or the public. Branches hanging over the property line and into rights-of-way can be pruned without your permission. A hazardous tree can fall, creating insurance nightmares. Many municipalities have tree ordinances that specify which tree species can be planted by streets and that stipulate restrictions for tree protection.

Variety Is the Spice of Life

Not all trees are created equal. There is as much difference between species of trees as there are breeds of dogs, and selecting a tree for the home landscape requires thoughtful preparation. Architect Frank Lloyd Wright said, "Form follows function." This is a good rule to remember when selecting trees. Select the right form (size and shape) to complement the desired function, and you will reduce maintenance costs in the long run. It is sad to see a tree topped or removed at its prime due to poor planning. Worst-case scenarios occur with street plantings where large trees obstruct power lines, requiring utility companies to disfigure specimen trees in order to keep power flowing.

In the mid-1990s, Extension agents across North Carolina participated in an urban tree evaluation program. The evaluation hoped to promote tree planting diversity for difficult sites such as highways and beneath utility lines. Sixty-eight varieties were planted over a three-year period in differing environmental situations. Most were given minimal maintenance and limited irrigation. Notable trees in the original plantings included franklinia, 'Celestial dogwood'™, Chinese wingnut, and Carolina silverbell.

Results from the tree evaluation include the following trees that have since been mainstreamed into nursery trade.

Cornelian cherry dogwood (*Cornus mas*)
Chinese fringetree (*Chionanthus retusus*)
'Autumn Blaze' Freeman maple (*Acer* × *freemanii*)
Lacebark elm (*Ulmus parvifolia*)
Fruitless sweetgum (*Liquidambar rotundiloba*)
'Blieriana' plum (*Prunus blireiana*)

There are literally hundreds of candidates for landscaping purposes. Before you rush out and purchase any tree variety, understand our wide range of environmental conditions. Native trees are not always happy when planted in "urban soils." Some coastal-planted trees suffer from salt spray. Some patented cultivars have limited availability, and a few may have growth habits that will not serve your needs. Nurserymen can advise you on pest-resistant cultivars and new tree releases worthy of planting.

Important Considerations

Though trees are resilient and durable, their durability can be undermined by humans, especially from root disturbance and improper pruning. Most trees don't have taproots. Instead they develop an extensive surface network of lateral and feeder roots. Most of their roots live in the top 18 inches of soil. It is very easy to disturb trees by trenching, grading, backfilling, and landscaping within the drip line of mature specimens. (Now you know why most developers strip building sites up front; conservation comes with a price.)

Proper pruning prevents wood decay and keeps a tree healthy. It is necessary to remove branches or make pruning cuts at a natural juncture, such as the branch collar or another branch union. There is no good reason to top a tree. Proper tree selection and thinning by a certified

Be sure to choose a healthy plant when purchasing trees. The plant on the left is clearly the best choice here.

arborist should keep your tree healthy and attractive. For long-term nutritional needs, it is important to follow soil test recommendations for fertilizing mature trees. While we know that trees can benefit from fertilization when nutrients are deficient, numerous studies provide strong evidence that fertilization decreases a tree's resistance to insect pests. Too much nitrogen can result in a weak branch structure or encourage hungry insects like aphids or scale.

Selecting a Tree

A tree should be selected not only for its form but also for a number of other characteristics. Some varieties grow upright or round. Others are columnar like European hornbeam, pendulous like weeping cherry, or vase-shaped like zelkova. There are deciduous and evergreen species. Deciduous trees, which drop their leaves in autumn, are often selected because they offer summer shade and allow the winter sun to warm our houses. The largest specimens, like the oaks, are known for their long lives and majestic form, while others provide outstanding fall color and ornamental appeal. Still others, like dawn redwood and ginkgo, have an ancient history.

How to Plant a Tree

After you have selected the right tree for the right site, plant it so the tree will establish quickly and grow into a thing of beauty. The planting hole should be wide and shallow rather than deep and narrow. Here's how:

- Kill grass within a circle about 5 feet across and till or spade it to a depth of 8 inches.
- Spread limestone and superphosphate if called for by a soil test.
- Amend clay or sandy soils for potted trees by adding organic soil conditioner (one-fourth the amount of existing backfill) over an area 4 feet across.
- Dig a planting hole to the depth of the rootball for balled-and-burlapped (B&B) specimens. There's no need to add soil amendments for B&B trees. Break up any large clods and remove stones, roots, and debris.
- Inspect the rootball and cut roots that encircle it. If a mat of roots has formed on the bottom of the rootball, prune off the mat.
- Set the tree in the center of the hole, oriented so the best side faces where it will be seen most often. Wire baskets holding rootballs are planted too; cut the top wires once set. (Note: remove wires, straps, nylon cord, and cut burlap from the top of the rootball.)
- Shovel the conditioned soil around the rootball. Gently tamp in soil with a booted foot.
- The backfill should come up to the soil line on the tree and taper down.
- Create a berm of backfill soil on the edge of the hole to facilitate watering. Trickle water around the rootball for an hour or so until it begins to run off.
- Spread a 3-inch layer of mulch over the tilled area.
- Stake trees only if they appear top-heavy or require protection from wind, mowers, or children. Drive two steel fence posts into the soil on opposite sides of the rootball.
- On large trees, use wire cushioned with pieces of water hose or, better still, use canvas straps and tree guying kits available at garden shops. Attach straps at one-half to two-thirds the height of the tree's trunk, leaving a little slack for the tree to flex. Remove guying and support materials in three to six months.
- Water deeply each week for a month, then monthly unless rain does the job for you.

The noteworthy trees on the following pages are personal favorites and by no means comprise an exhaustive list of good-quality trees offered by nurseries. Now, let's get planting!

1. Use a shovel or marking paint to mark the area for the hole. The planting hole should be twice as wide as the tree's rootball.

2. Dig the planting hole. This hole should be just as deep as the rootball—no deeper! If you sharpen the spade before digging, this step will go faster.

3. Set the tree in the planting hole to check the depth. If the top of the rootball is lower than the soil line around the edge of the planting hole, add some soil back into the hole, pull the tree out of the pot, and replace the tree in the hole. You never want the crown of the tree (where the tree trunk meets the tree roots) to be below the soil line.

4. Fill in around the tree with the same soil that you removed from the planting hole. Mulch around the tree, taking care to pull the mulch away from the tree trunk. Do not create a mulch "volcano" around the tree (by piling mulch up high around the trunk)—that just encourages insects and creatures that snack on tree bark to take up residence next to your delicious young tree.

American Holly

Ilex opaca

Botanical Pronunciation
EYE-lex oh-PAY-ka

Bloom Period and Seasonal Color
Spring whitish blooms; red berries in fall and winter

Mature Height × Spread
30 to 45 feet × 15 to 25 feet

Throughout the Carolinas and up the Eastern seaboard, American hollies grow in the wild. This wonderful native evergreen has a rich history, and it has been a symbol of friendship for centuries. The genus *Ilex* has been hybridized repeatedly and offers some of the finest woody ornamentals for landscaping. More than 300 varieties of *I. opaca* have been named, and over sixty of these are commercially available. This is the stately holly that evokes memories of Christmas past with berries on the mantel. Individual trees may be either male or female, and berry production depends upon having both within the range of foraging bees. Small yards call for female trees, but male trees earn the space they occupy in large landscapes by providing season-long foliage color.

When, Where, and How to Plant
Balled-and-burlapped specimens should be planted in late winter and spring. Container-grown trees can be planted in spring and in the fall. Summer planting should be avoided if possible. Plant in full or part sun. American hollies prefer a well-drained, moist soil, though they will tolerate dry sites if irrigated during establishment. Hollies grow relatively slowly in early years, but they need ample space. Rake the mulch twice yearly to kill weeds. Though holly trees are pH-adaptable, add lime to poor soil.

Growing Tips
Fertilize every few years if need is indicated by soil tests. Epsom salts or azalea fertilizer may help deepen foliage color. Add more mulch every summer to established trees to lessen drought stress.

Regional Advice and Care
Prune sparingly only in winter because flowers and berries arise from previous season's growth. Groom and shear after the berries are visible in July. Don't expect berries on a female holly for a couple of years after planting since the plant's energy will go into getting it established. Leafminers are recurring pests on this plant; handpick infested leaves, or use systemic insecticide treatments. Native holly can be transplanted in winter after root-pruning in fall. Winter weather will often temporarily scorch the leaves. Don't be alarmed if your tree loses its leaves in early spring; they are being pushed off by emerging leaves. Fallen leaves from holly trees are slow to decay. You may wish to rake and pile them with green matter to make compost. Remember to wear gloves!

Companion Planting and Design
Plant as a large specimen tree, or in clusters for a dense privacy screen. A woodland setting with half-day sun is a perfect location but requires frequent watering the first year to overcome root competition from older trees. Great foil for spring flowering shrubs.

Try These
Superior selections include 'Jersey Knight' and 'Jersey Princess'. 'Canary' has yellow berries. 'Greenleaf' and 'Carolina No. 2' rank high for the south. Hybrid 'East Palatka' has drooping branches and abundant berries in Zones 8 to 9.

Black Gum

Nyssa sylvatica

Botanical Pronunciation
NISS-ah seal-VAT-ee-ka

Other Name
Black tupelo

Bloom Period and Seasonal Color
Spring flowers are non-showy; rich red fall foliage

Mature Height × Spread
40 to 70 feet × 20 to 30 feet

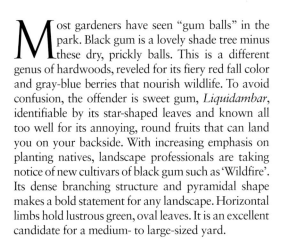

Most gardeners have seen "gum balls" in the park. Black gum is a lovely shade tree minus these dry, prickly balls. This is a different genus of hardwoods, reveled for its fiery red fall color and gray-blue berries that nourish wildlife. To avoid confusion, the offender is sweet gum, *Liquidambar*, identifiable by its star-shaped leaves and known all too well for its annoying, round fruits that can land you on your backside. With increasing emphasis on planting natives, landscape professionals are taking notice of new cultivars of black gum such as 'Wildfire'. Its dense branching structure and pyramidal shape makes a bold statement for any landscape. Horizontal limbs hold lustrous green, oval leaves. It is an excellent candidate for a medium- to large-sized yard.

When, Where and How to Plant

Black gum can be transplanted from the woods but it is challenging, at best, due to its taproot. Planting small B&B selections from autumn to early spring is best. This tree prefers moist, acidic soils that have decent drainage, but adapts well to heavy, clay soils. Prepare a wide planting hole and rough up the sides of the hole. Set the plant with the rootball at ground level and create berm for watering. Water thoroughly after planting; apply mulch.

Growing Tips

Nyssa means "water nymph," a clue that black gum can be found growing naturally in swampy land. Water the tree weekly for two months or as needed. This tree is a slow-grower, so it takes patience and irrigation to watch it mature. Maintain a 3-inch layer of mulch laid on top landscape fabric, stapled to the ground. This combination keeps weeds to a minimum during the establishment period. Water routinely during the first summers; fertilize every four years with a tree fertilizer to maintain good leaf color.

Regional Advice and Care

There is no shortage of black gum seedlings in the Carolinas. However, most naturally occurring trees lack the genetic material to resist leaf diseases and don't transplant for nurserymen. Expect spectacular fall color early in the season when dogwoods begin to change colors, especially where trees were planted in full sun. As it's native, black gum has few pests.

Companion Planting and Design

Because it is a bird-attracting plant, black gum is a good component of a wildlife planting or woodland garden featuring holly, viburnum, wax myrtle, pawpaw, persimmon, and blueberry. It's large enough to form a canopy to shade a house when planted on the west or south side. It can be used to frame the house. Plant tall hardwood trees at least 35 feet from a home's foundation.

Try These

Mature height depends upon the cultivar. The tallest is 'Hayman Red' Red Rage®, to 70 feet; 'Wildfire', to 40 feet; and 'Autumn Cascade', a weeping form to 15 feet with equal spread. Ogeechee tupelo, *N. ogeche*, is native to South Carolina swamps and bears edible fruit.

Chinese Lacebark Elm

Ulmus parvifolia

Botanical Pronunciation
UHL-mus par-VEH-fol-ee-ah

Other Name Lacebark elm

Bloom Period and Seasonal Color
Spring, non-showy blooms; yellowish or reddish purple fall foliage

Mature Height × Spread
20 to 45 feet × 35 to 45 feet

Emerging from a North Carolina Tree Evaluation program with a stellar performance is the Chinese lacebark elm. This medium-sized tree with small, lustrous green leaves has an upright spreading form reminiscent of the American elms that once lined the streets in major cities. Lacebark elm is, however, resistant to the fatal Dutch elm disease that destroyed many of our stately American elms. It is a versatile species suited to residential or municipal plantings. The trunk of mature specimens has an interesting bark pattern that forms as small chips flake away to reveal rusty brown patches. Lacebark elm is destined to be a major player in do-it-yourself home landscaping in the twenty-first century. Ease of care and rapid growth appeals to new homeowners who want a shade in record time.

When, Where, and How to Plant
Plant this container-grown tree any season the soil is workable and the tree can be irrigated. B&B trees should be planted during the dormant season. Chinese lacebark elm is easily transplanted and adapts to extremes in pH and soil type. It thrives in poor soils, and grows as fast as a weed in moist, fertile soil. A sunny location provides the best site, though a half-day of filtered shade is acceptable. Follow the tree planting recommendation for a wide planting pit and hole deep enough to accommodate the rootball. There is no need to amend the soil other than loosen it for better aeration.

Growing Tips
Watering is important during the first two summers to keep a young tree healthy. Irrigate deeply every ten days when the weather is hot and dry. Don't let the new foliage wilt in the early months. Mulch your planting to establish new roots. Fertilize the second spring with 12-4-8 analysis or a CRF product. Fertilize thereafter only as needed for good growth. Maintain a mulch layer to discourage mowing too close to the trunk.

Regional Advice and Care
Lacebark elm is a low-maintenance tree with no serious pests. Flat, greenish white seeds the diameter of garden peas are borne in clusters by late summer. These may self-sow in mulched beds. This could be a minor inconvenience, but they are easily removed by hand or cut down with a string trimmer. (Share the offspring with a friend.) This tree endures urban soil and poor air quality extremely well. All elms sustain branch damage in ice storms.

Companion Planting and Design
Lacebark elm makes a fine specimen shade tree and can be planted in groups for screening. It is fast becoming a staple street tree since its leaves do not scorch during extended dry weather. Unfortunately, it is not a replacement for native American elms though it has a broad crown when it's mature.

Try These
Paired plantings of the cultivar 'Allee' are common. 'Drake' is the most widely planted. 'Athena' has been widely publicized. Cold-hardy 'Dynasty' is for Zone 6.

Chinese Pistache

Pistacia chinensis

Botanical Pronunciation
pis-STASH-she-ah chai-NEN-sis

Bloom Period and Seasonal Color
Spring blooms are non-showy; fall color in red, orange, or yellow

Mature Spread × Height
30 to 40 feet × 20 to 30 feet

Long overlooked as a candidate for the lawn or garden is the Chinese pistache. This medium-sized tree has a rounded form and dense canopy. Its dark green, lustrous leaves are pinnately compound, like an ash tree. In autumn it is a blaze of fiery red to yellow colors, not paling in comparison to sugar maple. The scaly bark turns a gray-brown, eventually flaking off to expose a salmon-colored inner bark for added winter interest. Chinese pistache is dioecious, meaning there are male and female plants, similar to ginkgo and persimmon. At maturity the female produces ¼-inch, red to blue drupe berries; flowers are reddish but not showy, appearing before leaves in spring. This treasured tree will not produce pistachio nuts, but is low-maintenance and virtually pest-free in the Carolinas.

When, Where, and How to Plant
A good time to plant is late fall until spring, which allows root development before its season of active growth. Chinese pistache easily transplants for both container and balled-and-burlapped specimens. Nurserymen offer seedling trees that can vary in fall color; select a tree in fall to ensure the best color and branch structure. This little gem likes full sun locations, is durable, and performs well in a wide range of soil types and pH conditions. However, it won't be happy with wet feet in poorly drained soils, so site it away from swales and low areas in the landscape. Prepare a planting hole that is twice, or better yet, three times the size of the rootball. Plant at the same depth as rootball if the soil is well drained. Form a watering berm around the perimeter of the

hole. Water thoroughly after backfilling to remove air pockets. Mulch the planting in spring.

Growing Tips
Chinese pistache is a tough, drought-tolerant tree useful in planting sites where poor soil conditions and limited irrigation prohibit the use of other trees. It is perfect for warm southern climates considering our dry fall weather. Water twice monthly or as needed until established.

Regional Advice and Care
It's carefree, with limited pressure from insects and diseases. Young seedling selections will need training to develop a single trunk, avoiding multiple leaders too soon. Better still, shop for a plant with a straight trunk.

Companion Planting and Design
Landscape designers have placed this tree in parking lots and used as a street tree. This relatively small tree likes high ground and is great for sustainable landscapes. With its spectacular fall color, use it as an accent specimen. The berries, if they form, can be an interesting conversation piece and food for birds. It is a handsome lawn tree for shade with an underplanting of a drought-tolerant groundcover or hardy perennials, such as toadlily or Lenten rose. For a superb Asian garden, add Chinese fringetree, *Chionanthus retusus*, to your collection.

Try These
Chinese pistache stands alone as the species to select, since grafted varieties are limited.

Crapemyrtle

Lagerstroemia spp. and hybrids

Botanical Pronunciation
lay-ger-STROM-ee-ah IN-dee-ka

Bloom Period and Seasonal Color
Summer blooms in white, lavender, red, and pink; orange or red fall foliage

Mature Height × Spread
15 to 40 feet × 8 to 20 feet

Crapemyrtles make dramatic landscape trees, the glory of summer in the South. Because of their long bloom period, they are called the "flower of one hundred days" in China. In July, their terminal flower clusters are dense with brilliant, ruffled petals. They are most impressive when grown as multi-trunk specimens. Like birches, their peeling bark reveals mottled patterns of tan, twisted, muscle-like wood. The Japanese variety *Lagerstroemia fauriei* 'Fantasy' has outstanding, cinnamon-brown bark and pure white flower clusters. Like clothing, crapemyrtle is available in small, medium, and large. It makes an excellent large shrub for the winter bark color. Crapemyrtles thrive in hot, sunny locations and will grow in almost any type of soil. Their fall coloration is spectacular—but short.

When, Where, and How to Plant
Plant B&B crapemyrtles in early spring and potted specimens in spring or fall. Transplant established plants in late winter or in spring. Sow seeds of dwarf crapemyrtles in late spring. Without ample sun, expect sparse flowering and powdery mildew disease. These trees like moist, slightly acidic soils (pH 5.5) and good soil drainage. In heavy clay soils, plant the rootball one-third above the soil. Pull conditioned soil up around it. Apply a full 5-gallon bucket of water, then layer 3 inches of hardwood or bark mulch. Fertilizer planting tablets can be used with large specimens.

Growing Tips
Until established, crapemyrtles require 1 inch of water per week during their first summer.

Water neglect can result in tree loss. Though drought tolerant when established, crape myrtle needs irrigation during the flowering period and prolonged dry periods. Fertilize in early spring following soil test recommendations. A nursery fertilizer is acceptable; use according to directions.

Regional Advice and Care
For continuous blooming of *L. indica*, remove fading flower clusters before the seedpods form in late summer. Lightly prune to remove the old seedheads in March. Topping, known as "Crape Murder," will *ruin* its natural form. Train a tree into a small single or multi-trunk tree, pruning to expose the attractive trunk; remove basal suckers. Do not prune hard after Labor Day. Blackening leaves in summer indicate aphid infestation, and Japanese beetles crave the new growth. Consider tolerating moderate damage rather than applying insecticides.

Companion Planting and Design
Underplant tall varieties with dwarf evergreen shrubs or groundcovers to accentuate their trunks. For a contemporary look, choose single-trunk specimens for a wide entrance plantings or courtyard garden. Read labels carefully; some crapemyrtles grow into significantly large trees or are dwarf shrubs. There are a plethora of colors for any design plan.

Try These
Select mildew-resistant cultivars. The National Arboretum introduction, the robust and white-flowered 'Natchez', is mildew-resistant. 'Sarah's Favorite' is cold-hardy.

Cryptomeria

Cryptomeria japonica

Botanical Pronunciation
crip-to-MER-ee-ah juh-PON-ee-ka

Other Name
Japanese cedar

Bloom Period and Seasonal Color
Brown male cones in summer; medium green foliage

Mature Height × Spread
40 to 80 feet × 20 to 45 feet

Cryptomeria, or Japanese cedar, a cousin to the giant sequoia, is quite different from our native red cedars. Soft sprays of foliage appear in spirals along drooping branches. The individual needles of juvenile Japanese cedars are prickly. As the tree matures, the older needles, held closely together, look like fingers on the wide-spreading branches. Old specimens have attractive reddish brown bark that peels off in long shreds. Once newly planted trees are established, they will shoot up quickly, producing 2 to 3 feet of tender growth in late summer. Word is out that Japanese cedar makes a fine screening plant and is a good substitute for disease-prone Leyland cypresses. On city lots, gardeners have more possibilities in compact forms like the pyramidal 'Black Dragon'.

When, Where, and How to Plant
Plant cryptomeria anytime the ground can be worked and the tree watered. Cryptomeria thrives in a sunny location with deep, rich, moist soil. In well-drained soils, plant at the same depth the trees were grown in the nursery, slightly higher in clay loam soils. A neutral pH is acceptable for this evergreen, so a little lime or the addition of wood ashes is encouraged. Spread out the loosened roots of container-grown plants in the planting hole. Firm the soil around the roots and pour a 5-gallon bucketful of water over the rootball. To prevent winter winds from toppling the new installation, stake fall-planted Japanese cedars.

Growing Tips
Unlike most conifers, Japanese cedars cannot tolerate long periods of drought. Keep them mulched and watered for the first two years, and you will be amazed at the rich, new growth in the late summer months. Apply slow-release nursery fertilizer as needed.

Regional Advice and Care
Japanese cedars grow moderately fast after establishment. Keep their growth in-bounds with light shearing. Cutting the central leader (trunk) is not recommended; it will ruin the shape of the tree. Cryptomerias are resistant to pests. As they age, the lower branches will die and must be removed. Underplant them with small shrubs at that point. Drought-stressed trees often lose their rich color and may develop twig dieback. In the winter, the needles of cryptomeria may turn bronze, but are replaced by fresh, dark green needles in the spring.

Companion Planting and Design
Cryptomeria is a viable alternative to Leyland cypress, though cryptomeria spreads wider. Plant it as a tall evergreen screen; it makes a fine specimen accent and can survive in partial shade. Cherry laurels and rhododendrons are fine garden companions. There are some marvelous miniature shrub forms for formal designs in small spaces.

Try These
'Yoshino' has blue-green summer foliage and is widely adapted. 'Cristata' is a narrow cone to 24 feet. Plant 'Aurescens' for its dense form and yellow-green foliage.

Flowering Cherry

Prunus spp.

Botanical Pronunciation
PROO-nus

Bloom Period and Seasonal Color
Spring blooms in white and pinks

Mature Height × Spread
15 to 35 feet × 15 to 25 feet

Starting with a few sparse blooms, Japanese flowering cherry quickly bursts into a light-pink wash of color that dominates the April landscape. Except for the grafted weeping cultivars, most Japanese cherry trees are upright in form. Sterile and fruitless, this outstanding ornamental produces either double or single flowers. The large powderpuff pink blooms of 'Kwanzan' are very popular in the Carolinas for its spring display. Tall hybrid cherry 'Yoshino' is the single, white-flowering variety seen at the nation's capitol. Planted alongside evergreen azaleas, flowering cherry is what makes springtime so captivating in the Piedmont region. A landscape with a weeping cherry is special indeed. Higan branches are naturally weeping (pendulous); there's no need for grafting. Popular with landscapers for its heat tolerance and narrow form is hybrid 'Okame'.

When, Where, and How to Plant

Potted flowering cherry trees can be planted in the spring or fall. B&B trees should be planted during the dormant season well before bud swell to avoid decline from heat stress. Find a protected site with filtered afternoon sun where the soil is moist but drains well. Excellent soil drainage is imperative in heavy soils. This tree benefits from being planted on a berm. In friable (loose) soils, dig a hole twice as wide as the rootball and two-thirds as deep. In mass plantings, bury perforated plastic drainpipe every 6 feet for drainage. Keep the soil moist through spring. Give flowering cherry trees plenty of space, 20 feet between them.

Growing Tips

Watering is a must during the early years and during drought; apply 10 gallons of water per week. But, the soil must drain well, or the tree will die from "wet feet." Fertilize in mid-March the second year, and then on an as-needed basis every few years.

Regional Advice and Care

Prune to train a young tree during the dormant season or in early August. Unfortunately, these trees often fail to harden-off properly for winter, resulting in a short-life expectancy in Zone 8. Avoid fertilization or pruning in fall, which may increase the chances of winter injury. Remove sucker growth at the base of the tree and at graft unions during summers. Remove webworms and tent caterpillars by hand. Consult with an Extension agent for advice on controlling borers or Asian ambrosia beetle, and avoid pruning during the early summer borer season. Nongrafted weeping trees appear to be better adapted to mountain climates.

Companion Planting and Design

Flowering cherry is best used as a specimen tree. Plant matching pairs as part of a formal landscape design along a walkway, or soften the lines of a large house. What landscape could not benefit from the unique cascading form of Higan cherry or 'Pendula' (*Prunus* × *subhirtella*)? Use 'Autumnalis' for late fall and winter blooms.

Try These

Who can resist a flowering 'Kwanzan' in a garden nursery? 'Okame' grows quickly, blooms early, and is heat tolerant.

Flowering Dogwood

Cornus florida

Botanical Pronunciation
KOR-nus FLOR-eh-da

Bloom Period and Seasonal Color
Spring blooms in white, pink, ruby-red; red fall foliage

Mature Height × Spread
20 to 30 feet × 20 to 30 feet

Across much of eastern North America, the dogwood may be the most popular flowering tree. In fact, dogwood is the state flower of North Carolina. Dogwood deserves the accolades it receives from its admirers: it makes a beautiful understory tree; when planted in a shady area, it will grow an open framework; and the blooms will have a layered effect. Dogwood flowers can be single or double. Though white or pink-red blooms mean spring to Southerners, we also enjoy the early and intense red fall color they add to our autumn palette, arriving slowly in October with the finale by mid-November. Disease-resistant cultivars are on the market to avoid a fatal fungus—most notably the 'Stellar' series and Rutgers hybrids. Pink flowering dogwood is a springtime favorite, as are ones with variegated leaf forms.

When, Where, and How to Plant

Unlike most deciduous trees, dogwood plants best in spring rather than fall. Purchase healthy grafted trees and leave the seedlings in the woods. Plant in well-drained, highly organic, acidic soil. Nursery-grown dogwood tolerates sun or partial shade. However, planting in full sun where the soil is bone-dry predisposes the tree to borers and other stressers. The top of the rootball should stand 3 inches or more above the soil line, even higher in poorly drained soils. Pull conditioned soil up around it along with several inches of mulch. Water well following planting.

Growing Tips

Use a hose with a slow trickle to water new trees. Repeat twice the two weeks then irrigate monthly thereafter until the tree is firmly established. In full sun, dogwoods will grow a dense, oval canopy and will need mulching and regular watering during periods of drought. Fertilize every few years with a CRF product. Spread the fertilizer in a wide band at the tree's drip line.

Regional Advice and Care

Because of the big scare over the fatal "dogwood blight" (*Discula destructiva*) in Zones 5 to 6, new hybrids are often planted. Dispose of dead and dying branches by pruning immediately following bloom. Remove some inner branches to promote an appealing shape and good airflow. Borers threaten weak or scarred trees under stress; avoid pruning during June and July. Prevent by making proper pruning cuts and avoiding mower injury to trunks. A borer spray treatment in June may be beneficial. Spotted leaves indicate the presence of spot anthracnose, a chronic disease of wild seedlings. Buy mildew-resistant cultivars if possible.

Companion Planting and Design

Plant in clusters for a truly spectacular spring accent. This native understory tree is perfect for the woodland garden. Use dogwood as a small lawn tree or accent specimen among mixed borders of spring-flowering azaleas, late-blooming bulbs, and ornamental shrubs. Double-flowering and variegated cultivars add garden interest.

Try These

'Cherokee Princess' and ruby-red 'Cherokee Brave' or 'Brave' are rock solid. The double-flowered 'Plena' is unique. Variegated forms are different, but delightful.

Ginkgo

Ginkgo biloba

Botanical Pronunciation
GING-ko bi-LO-bah

Other Name
Maidenhair tree

Bloom Period and Seasonal Color
Golden yellow fall foliage

Mature Height × Spread
30 to 70 feet × 8 to 60 feet

Ginkgo is a magnificent, slow-growing tree with straight trunk and brilliant yellow fall color. Its distinctive fan-shaped leaves are 2 to 4 inches wide and are borne in bundles on spur twigs. The leaves drop abruptly in autumn and can be quickly added to the compost pile. Ginkgo is not a flowering plant, but has ancestral ties to conifers. Plant only male ginkgo trees; females produce large, foul-smelling fruit that are messy in a landscape. Young trees are rather gangly, but at maturity are wide-spreading and graceful. Ginkgo tolerates urban conditions and receives acclaim for public parks. The finest old specimens are scattered across the Carolinas from town squares to grand Southern estates. Based on fossil records, we know this primitive tree was once native to North America.

When, Where, and How to Plant

The best time to plant your ginkgo is from November through March. A tree that has been dug while dormant, heeled in, or well-rooted in a container may be planted at any time. Ginkgos like full sun and fertile soils for fastest growth. Once established, they will adapt to poor, dry soils, but they will grow very slowly. On burlap-wrapped rootballs, leave the natural burlap on the ball when you plant. Place the rootball in a wide planting hole. Backfill and water well by pouring on a 5-gallon bucket of water. Apply a layer of mulch.

Growing Tips

Water your ginkgo tree with a slow trickle from a hose for a period of time equal to one minute per inch of diameter of the rootball twice a week for the first month, and every two weeks for two months. Irrigate as needed during its first summer and fall until firmly established. Established trees benefit from irrigation during dry summers in the early years. When in doubt, check the soil moisture before watering by digging down through the mulch into the backfill soil. Fertilize in spring every few years using a CRF for trees.

Regional Advice and Care

The best feature of your new ginkgo is that it is virtually pest- and maintenance-free, succumbing to no diseases. Ginkgo needs very little pruning, but if it is needed, prune in winter or summer. A bonus with ginkgo is that autumn clean-up is not an arduous task.

Companion Planting and Design

Use this large, stately tree as a specimen plant for a formal accent. Their open canopy casts fragmented shadows on the ground below, which is ideal for many shade-loving perennials and groundcovers. A backdrop of tall evergreens and pines is a nice foil. Dwarfs like 'Jade Butterfly' and columnar forms fit well in most cityscapes.

Try These

Ginkgo is no small tree so use the narrow 'Fastigiata' and Goldspire™ on suburban lots. 'Autumn Gold' is symmetrical with fine color; 'Golden Globe' shows promise.

Hornbeam

Carpinus spp.

Botanical Pronunciation
car-PINE-nus

Other Name
Ironwood

Bloom Period and Seasonal Color
Spring blooms are green or whitish; yellow to brown fall foliage

Mature Height × Spread
20 to 40 feet × 15 to 30 feet

The American hornbeam, *Carpinus caroliniana*, is native to the Carolinas. It is no showboat with its small, serrated leaves in spring and pendent non-showy bloom clusters, shaped like rattlesnake buttons, in early summer. Some trees have showier blooms and fall foliage color, but none has the low-growing, dense branching of hornbeam. Our native species' rival is the European hornbeam, *C. betulus* 'Fastigiata'. It grows faster, reaching a height of 25 feet or more, and has a symmetrical habit for formal use in landscape design. It is versatile, finding a place as yard tree specimen or hedge candidate. Both species weather storms well and are care-free. The muscular-looking branches of our native plant earned it the common names musclewood and ironwood. Hornbeam provided strong wood for making golf clubs and primitive hand tools.

When, Where, and How to Plant

Plant container-grown trees in fall or winter for best results. Native hornbeam isn't at all particular about where you plant it; the tree thrives in full sun or all-day filtered shade. In the wild, it is usually found in moist bottomlands. Shaded locations beneath taller trees result in taller and spindlier growth. European hornbeam is dense in a sunny location. Both can be planted in moist, well-drained soil. Dig a hole that is twice the width of the rootball and of equal depth. Free up potbound roots. Use the loose backfill for planting; lightly firm the soil with your foot. Water thoroughly to settle the tree.

Growing Tips

Maintain a 3-inch mulch to the drip line of new trees, avoiding the trunk. During drought, let a sprinkler run beneath your hornbeam; let it trickle for an hour or so each week.

Regional Advice and Care

Don't try to open up young trees by removing branches this first season or two. Hornbeam is a slow-grower in the early years and needs all its foliage to establish. Part of hornbeam's beauty is its remarkable bark. Protect it from damage by antler-rubbing deer, lawnmowers, and string weeders. A single lashing of the tender trunk bark can kill a young tree. Remove all weeds, particularly common bermudagrass, which compete with young trees for nutrients and water within the root zone. Hornbeam has very few insect or disease problems. The variation in seed-grown trees is considerable, so shop carefully for a tree with good form that is not potbound.

Companion Planting and Design

In sunny locations, a fringe of dwarf flowering shrubs and azaleas around a hornbeam can make a pretty composition. The columnar European hornbeam adapts well to small yards, especially as privacy screens and accent specimens. In a woodland edge situation or beneath tall shade trees, hornbeam reaches for the sun and is sparsely branched with smooth, gray bark sculpted like the biceps of a weight lifter.

Try These

There are no named varieties of American hornbeam. Upright European hornbeams 'Fastigiata', 'Pyramidalis', and 'Frans Fontaine' are space-saving cultivars.

Hybrid Holly

Ilex × 'Nellie R. Stevens'

Botanical Pronunciation
EYE-lex

Bloom Period and Seasonal Color
Year-round dark green foliage; red berries

Mature Height × Spread
20 to 25 feet × 10 to 15 feet

A conical hybrid holly, 'Nellie R. Stevens' has become a favorite among landscape designers for formal hedges and screens. This magnificent holly is stately in appearance as it grows rather quickly to 25 feet at maturity. The foliage is compact and glossy dark green like Burford holly. The bright red fruits are not as prominent as they are on some of the American hollies, but the plant's rapid growth rate is a true advantage. 'Nellie R. Stevens' combines the beauty of its English holly parentage and the drought-tolerance of the Chinese holly family. Certainly it is a shrewd choice for a screen or a specimen evergreen tree. It is arguably the most popular of a large group of hybrid hollies that range in height from medium-sized shrubs to tall trees.

When, Where, and How to Plant
Plant container-grown holly anytime the ground permits. Large balled-and-burlapped plants meant for hedges should be planted in late winter through spring. To ensure compact foliage, plant in a full-sun location or one that gets at least six hours of sun. It adapts to clay soils, but avoid poorly drained conditions. Set the rootball slightly higher than the original grade (rootballs often settle in too deeply with large, heavy plants). Backfill halfway, firm-in the soil, and add 5 gallons of water. After the water drains out, finish backfilling, mulch, and water again the next day.

Growing Tips
Water 'Nellie R. Stevens' during dry periods in the first two seasons, setting a sprinkler to deliver 2 inches of water per week over the rootzone. Mulches and soaker hoses are wonderful for irrigating thoroughly in hot summer weather. Once established, the plants tolerate drought extremely well but will grow slowly. Apply a slow-release fertilizer in spring or early fall. Don't overfertilize, or you will be pruning regularly. Keep your holly mulched.

Regional Advice and Care
Stake new specimens over 5 feet tall for four months. Heavy pruning should be done in late winter or early summer. Shaping is important during the early years, particularly if the tree is grown singly as a specimen tree. Old foliage that has dropped should be raked up before reapplying mulch. Few pests other than scale insects bother this holly. Mature specimens can be limbed up to expose the smooth gray trunk.

Companion Planting and Design
Planted 6 to 8 feet apart and left unpruned, a row of 'Nellie R. Stevens' hollies makes a fine impenetrable screen. Plant as an anchor for the corners of a two-story house. When grown as a landscape specimen, give 'Nellie' room to spread out; this is a tree, not a shrub. Homeowners seeking a replacement for ailing Leyland cypresses, choose it.

Try These
'Nellie R. Stevens' is a fine holly. Lusterleaf, *Ilex latifolia*, makes a tall screen. Where smaller specimens are needed for hedges, use 'Mary Nell' or a red holly cultivar.

Japanese Maple

Acer palmatum

Botanical Pronunciation
A-sir pal-MAY-tum

Bloom Period and Seasonal Color
Spring through fall, red foliage

Mature Height × Spread
4 to 25 feet × 6 to 20 feet

Few ornamental trees are as useful for landscaping as the Japanese maple. The outstanding features of this tree are its small size, intricate foliage, and its varying leaf types, colors, and shapes. From the seedlings to the grafted cultivars, the Japanese maples are superb trees. In spring, the leaves burst into color with intense red hues that later fade to green. The grafted cultivars like 'Bloodgood' maintain a steady burgundy color throughout the growing season. The Japanese maple captures the essence of fall color with a brilliance that is unparalleled by other small deciduous trees. The slow-growing threadleaf varieties are the "Rolls Royce" of maples. Though somewhat pricey, a lacy-leaf 'Tamukeyama' is worth every penny. Shop the nurseries in August when true leaf color of red-leaf Japanese maples can be assessed.

When, Where, and How to Plant

Plant Japanese maple anytime from fall to spring. It grows well in a range of soils, provided they are not waterlogged; it prefers moist, rich soils. Filtered shade is preferred to direct sun—some maples will sunburn. Heavy shade will cause the tree to grow spindly and perform poorly. When planting small container-grown trees, free up the roots before planting. Dig a hole and position the rootball to set above grade. Water weekly for the first month, trickling slowly from a garden hose for thirty minutes.

Growing Tips

Irrigate the root zone routinely if there isn't sufficient rainfall; water deeply in the first summer. Until maturity, most trees benefit from irrigation during the dry months of summer. Maintain 2 to 3 inches of mulch across a minimum diameter of 4 feet; increase the size of the ring with time. To speed growth or compensate for nutrient deficiencies, apply a slow-release fertilizer in spring every three to five years to accelerate growth.

Regional Advice and Care

Keep an eye out for Japanese beetles and eliminate them when they first appear. Chronic leaf-tip burn, though not life-threatening, is worse in hot, dry sites. Avoid chronic leaf spot by choosing disease-resistant cultivars; apply fungicide as a last resort. Limb up the trees or thin the interior branches for an open form. Always remove dead twigs. As with all maples, summer pruning minimizes sap "bleeding."

Companion Planting and Design

Plant Japanese maple as an accent or in small groves to create a Japanese garden. Use dwarf forms with gold-leaf groundcovers. Place them in concrete or lightweight containers that can withstand freezing and thawing. Select the cutleaf 'Dissectum' in close quarters where the lacy foliage can be touched. Multicolored leaf forms are hot! When planted at curbside, these low-growing trees will not interfere with power lines.

Try These

Fall color and brilliant spring foliage are features of 'Bloodgood'. Coral bark maple, 'Sango Kaku', has startlingly beautiful reddish bark for close-up viewing. 'Waterfall' is the best green cutleaf for part shade, and 'Butterfly' is best for variegated foliage.

Japanese Snowbell

Styrax japonica

Botanical Pronunciation
STY-rax juh-PON-ee-ka

Bloom Period and Seasonal Color
Late spring blooms in white or pink; yellow
fall foliage

Mature Height × Spread
30 feet × 30 feet

One of the great discoveries by the late Dr. J. C. Raulston while on a plant-collecting expedition to Korea was the *Styrax japonica* cultivar 'Emerald Pagoda' ('Sohuksan'). His glowing description says it all, "a fantastic, phenomenal, unparalleled small flowering tree." This tree has leathery, emerald leaves and pendent, bell-shaped, fragrant white flowers in May. Though relatively unknown by most gardeners, snowbell is now showing up at most full-service garden centers. Its compact form and tolerance of shade give it an edge over many noteworthy candidates. While plantings of the common *Styrax* species have languished in the warmer Carolina climes, the Japanese snowbell has flourished. It is worthy of planting where it can be appreciated close-up during its rather short blooming season in spring.

When, Where, and How to Plant
Plant snowbell in morning sun or filtered shade, especially in Zone 8 gardens. This tree prefers moist, acidic, well-drained soil; spade in copious amounts of organic matter or leaf compost with sandy soils; don't add limestone to the planting hole. Container-grown trees can be planted anytime they can be kept watered, but preferably before summer weather begins. Water thoroughly immediately after planting, and weekly if not provided by nature. Add a generous mulch layer.

Growing Tips
Snowbell may be slow to establish, but after the first year it will do well with little attention if sited properly. It is important to water the tree in summer during the early years and routinely during periods of drought in subsequent seasons. Apply a controlled-release or organic fertilizer in spring. Keep trees mulched with 3 to 4 inches of organic mulch for moisture retention. Do little pruning until its natural form develops.

Regional Advice and Care
This tree has relatively small leaves, and plants growing around it do well in the filtered light cast on the ground. Never remove more than 10 percent of the growth when thinning. Once established, it is practically care-free. Prevent borers by keeping your tree watered in a drought and protecting the lower trunk from lawn mower damage. Diseases are not a problem. However, planting too deeply in poorly drained clay soil can spell trouble if you overwater.

Companion Planting and Design
It's a choice specimen tree for small properties or courtyard gardens where the delicate bell-shaped flowers can be appreciated. Its gray, smooth bark and wide spreading branches are set off well with a background of boxwoods or evergreen shrubs. Good companions are shade perennials, dwarf spirea, and hydrangea. Its blooms give the appearance of fresh snow.

Try These
'Emerald Pagoda' has great qualities. 'Fragrant Fountain' has a weeping habit. 'Pink Chimes' is sweet. In mountain regions, *S. obassia* is used.

Kousa Dogwood

Cornus kousa

Botanical Pronunciation
KOR-nus KU-sah

Other Name
Chinese dogwood

Bloom Period and Seasonal Color
Late spring blooms in white to pink/red; red fall color

Mature Height × Spread
15 to 30 feet × 15 to 25 feet

Little-known Kousa dogwood has come out of obscurity with street tree plantings in suburbia. Homeowners have observed this deciduous, Asian species blooming several weeks after our native flowering dogwood, offering the astute gardener an extended season of spring color once planted. Dark green leaves are 3 to 4 inches long and half as wide with a prominent yellow-green midrib vein on the surface. Mature Kousa dogwoods develop a rounded canopy. Pinwheel flowers appear with spring foliage unlike our flowering dogwood, light green blooms gradually turning to white. Hanging raspberry-like fruit (botanically, "drupes") form on some trees, which adds fall interest. Its resistance to disease and borers makes it a standout. As the smooth bark ages it exfoliates, forming an attractive patchwork of mottled tan and brown, a winter bonus.

When, Where, and How to Plant
Container-grown Kousa dogwood can be planted from late fall to spring. Give it sun for the most blooms, or half-day in afternoon shade in eastern South Carolina. It prefers moist, well-drained soil. It tolerates heavy clays but doesn't like wet feet. Dig a standard planting hole as described on page 194. Add compost or bark soil conditioner to the backfill of dry, poor soil. Set the tree with the rootball slightly above grade. Thoroughly water and mulch with bark or pine straw.

Growing Tips
Irrigate weekly until this shallow-rooted tree is well established. In a dry summer, Kousa dogwood would appreciate a drink in the sweltering heat of Zone 8 since the roots are near the surface. Watch for yellowing foliage as a sign to fertilize an established tree. Apply organic fertilizer or CRF product in late fall or early spring. Maintain a mulch layer to keep the roots cool/moist.

Regional Advice and Care
The National Arboretum has released a series of disease-resistant cultivars with Kousa dogwood in the parentage. The four-petalled flowers bearing pointed bracts help identify the family connection. Whether a rose pink- or white-flowered variety, this dogwood is seldom bothered by borers and chronic leaf diseases of our native tree. Not the best ornamental tree in the coastal region. The tree needs good care in the early years to train to a single trunk. Over time, thin the canopy in late summer as necessary to lift it to increase light penetration to lawns. Never remove more than 15 percent of the foliage when thinning small trees.

Companion Planting and Design
Kousa's a good filler for borders with late spring-flowering perennials. Use it as a small tree accent (but not near walkways); there's no problem planting under power lines. A specimen tree will be adored for its attractive, mottled bark at maturity. Deutzia, butterfly bush, dwarf loropetalum, and shrub roses are good companions.

Try These
'Greensleeves' and 'Milky Way' are good finds. A semi-evergreen hybrid released by NCSU, Little Ruby Dogwood™, has pink/red blooms in single to double (limited quantities). 'Lustgarten' is compact with a weeping habit.

Live Oak

Quercus virginiana

Botanical Pronunciation
KWER-cuss ver-gin-ee-A-nah

Bloom Period and Seasonal Color
No blooms; winter for rich evergreen color

Mature Height × Spread
60 to 80 feet × 100 feet

Zone 8

Live oak is the quintessential tree of coastal landscapes in the South. This signature evergreen has horizontal branches often festooned with Spanish moss and resurrection ferns. Near the coast in large gardens of Charleston, S.C., and Wilmington, N.C., the limbs of old, stately trees are so long and heavy that they touch the ground; but in the lower Piedmont, old live oaks form a dense canopy, broader than tall. Venerable live oaks usually remain sound to a great age, unlike some of the faster-growing oaks. Before you plant, know that within an average life span this tree will have time to grow huge and will change the appearance of your landscape like no other tree. Literally, it will define your home, making it a landmark in the community.

When, Where, and How to Plant

Oaks are relatively difficult to transplant. If you have a live oak nearby, ask the owner for acorns and plant them in the ground or in 1-gallon containers as soon as they ripen. If grown in containers, transplant to a permanent site the following spring. Container-grown trees can be transplanted anytime, but fall and winter are best. The small, spoon-shaped leaves of live oak drop gradually each winter and are replaced by glossy new foliage.

Growing Tips

Water transplanted trees twice weekly for a month, then weekly thereafter. In spring of its second year, use a CRF; then, feed every 3 to 5 years for maintenance.

Regional Advice and Care

Keep string trimmers away from young trees and mulch around them to prevent grass from competing. Don't attempt to train your tree. It will probably lean and branch unpredictably, which adds to its charm. One way to reduce a live oak's need for care is to plant seedlings from trees that have prospered in your area for several generations or in counties to your north. This is important all over the Carolinas, but especially in the Piedmont where winter-cold tolerance is critical. Oak wilt and chestnut blight can affect live oaks near the coast; call a certified arborist at the first sign of decline. *Please* don't top your tree! Seek professional advice from a reputable tree service, or consult with foresters with the State Division of Forest Resources. Established trees may develop girdling roots at the trunk base/root collar; be sure to remove these. Beware of hardscaping projects inside the drip line; these can be fatal to a live oak.

Companion Planting and Design

There's no need for a supporting cast. A live oak is a show in itself. Azaleas thrive beneath its drip line if not too close to the trunk. Inject color into the picture by hanging baskets of variegated foliage plants near branch ends. Darlington and white oaks can be planted in Zone 7 for the same look as live oak with better tolerance of cold and clay soil.

Try These

Any adapted live oak will do. They are always grown from seeds, and variability is inescapable. Seedlings of northern seed stock perform better inland.

Oak

Quercus spp.

Botanical Pronunciation
KWER-cuss

Bloom Period and Seasonal Color
Spring, red buds; late fall, red foliage

Mature Height × Spread
50 to 90 feet × 30 to 60 feet

Oak is an excellent landscape tree and is tolerant of the urban environment. Forty oak species are native to the Carolinas, and are placed in two groups—red and white. Most are deciduous and drop large numbers of acorns seasonally, and a few are semi-evergreen. A leaf blade can be broad or fingerlike, bearing lobes or bristle points. White oaks make significant juvenile growth but slow after a decade to mature a wide-spreading canopy. It is not uncommon for a properly planted red oak to add 2 feet in height annually. Red oaks, particularly northern red oak and pin oak, have tall trunks and narrow crowns at maturity providing high shade if limbed up. Red oak leaves are a lustrous dark green in summer, but they change to a deep red in autumn.

When, Where, and How to Plant

Plant oak from containers in winter to spring. The absence of a taproot makes transplanting easier, especially with smaller trees. Install B&B trees while they are dormant. Oaks like their feet dry; set the rootball high with one-fourth of the rootball above grade and backfill up to the former soil line. Avoid sites with poor drainage or do remedial work prior to planting. Red oak tolerates moist clay soils as well as dry areas. Oak prefers slightly acidic, loamy soils and full sun. Stake larger specimens for six months. Water deeply after planting and mulch out to the drip line.

Growing Tips

Water deeply every ten days the first 2 months and then as needed. In lawns that receive regular fertilization little supplemental feeding is necessary, and is best determined through soil testing. Maintain a mulch ring radiating 3 to 6 feet from the trunk.

Regional Advice and Care

Old, weak trees are best removed since they are subject to windfall. Do not prune young trees except to remove narrow angled branches and broken twigs. Oak has few problems but is subject to oak wilt, consult a certified arborist if crown dieback is observed or there are structural concerns. Double leaders (twin trunks) can be reduced to one central leader. Cankerworms and oakworms can strip foliage; the former insects can be managed with trunk bans and tanglefoot. Protect existing oaks during construction projects so that soil is not compacted beneath them or piled over the root system.

Companion Planting and Design

Rapid-growing red oak species make a good replacement for mature white oak that are in decline. Oaks are good choices for urban landscapes. They offer filtered sunlight for lawns, shade-loving ornamentals, and wildflowers. Plant them 35 feet or more from structures. Given ample space, a mature white oak, *Quercus alba*, adds a majestic touch to any landscape, especially large yards.

Try These

Shumard oak, *Q. shumardii*, is attractive and durable. For fall color try pin oak, *Q. palustris*. Choose nuttall oak, *Q. nuttallii*, and willow oak, *Q. phellos*, for rapid growth.

Palmetto

Sabal palmetto

Botanical Pronunciation SA-bul pal-MET-toe

Other Name
Cabbage palm

Bloom Period and Seasonal Color
Spring, creamy white flowers; black fruits in fall

Mature Height × Spread
20 to 40 feet × 6 to 10 feet

Zone 8

This Southeastern native is one of the hardiest palm species known. Palmetto is known by its straight or slightly curved single trunk covered with persistent leaf bases and rounded crown. Large, fan-shaped leaves expand to 3 to 4 feet long. Once established, it can withstand temperatures of 10 degrees Fahrenheit for brief periods. Palmetto is seldom seen in Piedmont landscapes because the fronds can freeze back, though they typically recover. Juvenile palmettos resemble shrubs, but they can be expected to grow to a height of 40 feet. Dwarf palmetto, *Sabal minor*, is very hardy even into the Piedmont; its blue-green foliage adds a tropical look to landscapes. Both adapt to the drier soils found across the eastern regions. South Carolinians chose this palm as their state tree.

When, Where, and How to Plant
Plant container-grown plants in late spring or summer. They transplant easily from May to July in Zone 8 and south. Give palmetto plenty of space and a sunny location. It will grow in any well-drained soil from clay loam to sand, and it loves moisture. Using a handheld cultivator, carefully loosen the roots of plants grown in pots. Work plenty of aged compost into the planting hole, especially in coarse soil and pure sand. Dig a hole that is two to three times wider but not deeper than the rootball. Create a berm at the edge of the hole so each watering wets the roots. Keep the rootball watered during establishment, and mulch well. Large specimens need bracing to avoid windfall.

Growing Tips
Palmetto must be well watered the first two summers until established; then it requires little attention. Drip irrigation makes this task easier. Fertilize every few years with an 8-2-12 palm fertilizer, or follow a soil test's recommendations. Spread mulch 3 inches deep to form a wide, tree ring circling your planting.

Regional Advice and Care
Palmetto is marginally hardy in the foothills region of the Carolinas. In Zone 8a, deep winter mulch applied within the drip line area will increase survival of seedlings during harsh winters. To protect young plants, place a 2-foot-high cylinder of welded wire fencing around them and fill it with leaves or pine straw; remove it in March. Over time, old leaves deteriorate and stems should be sawed off close to the trunk. Pest problems are minimal, but palmetto weevil and palm leaf skeletonizer may warrant some control. Extremely cold winters cause serious leafburn.

Companion Planting and Design
Tolerant of salt spray, palmetto is an excellent street tree or specimen plant for the seaside. Plant alone or in clusters of three. Use them as a tropical accent in a patio or terrace garden along with ferns, cast-iron plant, hardy ginger, and mandevilla.

Try These
Stately palmetto has durable trunks. Windmill palm, *Trachycarpus fortunei*, is graceful and cold-hardy to 0 degrees Fahrenheit. A less-known hybrid, *S.* × *texensis* 'Brazoria', has appeared locally.

Pine

Pinus spp.

Botanical Pronunciation
PIE-nus

Bloom Period and Seasonal Color
Spring male catkins; evergreen with winter cones

Mature Height × Spread
45 to 80 feet × 25 to 40 feet

Longleaf pine, *Pinus palustris*, is the North Carolina state tree and one of the most distinctive Southern pines. It is appreciated most for its 12-inch needles that provide the marvelous mulching material we southerners call pine straw. As the tree approaches twenty years in age, the mature trunk shows off rough, scaly bark and produces a deep taproot in coastal sands. In the Piedmont, the loblolly pine, *P. taeda*, reigns supreme as a landscaping specimen. They grow straight and tall and provide the filtered shade that many ornamentals appreciate. In the mountain region and east to Winston-Salem, white pine, *P. strobus*, dominates the hills and summits. It will thrive where summer nights are cool, making a fine evergreen and windbreak. Beautiful pines are a Carolina staple.

When, Where, and How to Plant
Plant potted pines anytime soil conditions allow. Position pines 60 feet from your home; a hurricane or strong wind following a soaking rain can knock them over. Bare-root seedlings may be available from State Forestry nurseries for planting woodlots and windbreaks. Plant seedlings immediately upon receipt. Space trees 25 to 35 feet apart unless a privacy screen is desired. Follow recommendations for tree planting as outlined for other potted shade trees. Water plantings thoroughly after backfilling, then mulch. Stake pine trees that are over 6 feet in height to prevent wind from uprooting them.

Growing Tips
Water weekly until a tree is firmly established. On a dry, sandy planting site, water more often during the first growing season. If young trees lack normal color in summer, fertilize with CRF product in spring before new shoots begin to form. Broadcast the fertilizer at the drip line. After a few seasons, these trees rarely need fertilizing, which can produce weak growth.

Regional Advice and Care
The range of white pine is Zones 5 to 7; they are short-lived, succumbing to root rots or borers following dry seasons. Prune pine anytime except when new growth is developing—wait until new candle shoots harden off. It can be limbed up to allow planting under the canopy, but don't cut the leader or a distorted tree will result. Pine cones are a nuisance when the trees are planted in a lawn, but they are easy enough to gather for disposal. Sometimes the pine beetle attacks trees. Promptly remove any trees infested with bark beetles.

Companion Planting and Design
Plant southern indica azaleas in the shade of mature eastern pine species. Longleaf seedlings resemble clumps of ornamental grass. Groupings create a fine screen or windbreak, and single trees are quite handsome. Japanese black pine and mugo pine offer great variety for Carolina gardens that lack space for the larger species.

Try These
Improved seedling selections are available through state-owned nurseries. Plant loblolly pine in the Piedmont and white pine in the mountains. Myriad forms and cultivars, pendulous to columnar, are now found at garden centers.

Redbud

Cercis canadensis

Botanical Pronunciation
SIR-sis can-uh-DEN-siss

Bloom Period and Seasonal Color
Spring blooms in lavender, magenta, rosy-pink, and white; yellow fall foliage

Mature Height × Spread
12 to 25 feet × 12 to 25 feet

Redbuds in full bloom are among the most striking sights of spring. With flowering dogwoods growing alongside them, what a sight! Redbud's lavender pea-like flowers herald the arrival of spring and often burst into bloom slightly before dogwood. This small, vase-shaped tree forms a dense, round canopy of heart-shaped leaves by early summer. 'Forest Pansy' gets high marks for its burgundy spring foliage, and 'Hearts of Gold' for its golden summer leaves. When limbed up, redbud creates a marvelous oasis for outdoor lounging when you want to be shielded from the summer sun. Multi trunk specimens of the outstanding *Cercis reniformis* 'Oklahoma' roundleaf redbud are real showstoppers; this species is rated higher than the Eastern redbud by some authorities. The J. C. Raulston Arboretum in Raleigh has the largest collection of redbuds in the world.

When, Where, and How to Plant
Transplant seedlings during the dormant season before the buds swell. Plant container-grown trees in spring or fall. Redbuds grow in moist soils from clay to loam, and in light shade to full sun. They are at home on the fringes of a woodland garden where they are protected from the afternoon sun. Though they are fairly adaptable, avoid waterlogged locations. Firm backfill lightly around the sides of the rootball. Water well, then cover the exposed roots with a 3-inch layer of mulch.

Growing Tips
Water twice weekly for the first six weeks and, after that, during prolonged dry weather. As long as the leaves are a rich green color, do not be concerned about fertilizing. In spring following the first full growing season, apply an organic fertilizer under the drip line at an estimated rate of 1 cup per 10 square feet. Do not fertilize for another four years. Redbuds are legumes and extract nitrogen from the air with the help of beneficial soil organisms.

Regional Advice and Care
Redbud adapts with little care. Prune wild shoots arising from the trunk, and to shape the young tree. On occasion, a fungal twig dieback may occur; prune out the individual branch promptly. There are no serious pests, but the tree is short-lived. They form hundreds of seedpods that drop and release seeds. Native seedlings by the score follow; discourage them by stirring the mulch or adding a layer.

Companion Planting and Design
A backdrop of evergreens helps redbud flowers to leap out visually. With a height to 25 feet, redbud is recommended as a good choice for planting under power lines. Consider planting a specimen, such as a golden leaf variety or the weeping Texas cultivar 'Traveler'. The white-flowered 'Alba' can brighten a shade garden.

Try These
'Forest Pansy' is the rage because of its burgundy spring leaves. 'Appalachian Red', which has rosy-pink blooms, is special. 'The Rising Sun'™ or 'Merlot', and pendulous 'Ruby Falls' and 'Lavender Twist'®, add variety to landscapes.

Red Maple

Acer rubrum

Botanical Pronunciation
A-sir ROO-brum

Bloom Period and Seasonal Color
Early spring red blooms; brilliant red, yellow or orange-red fall foliage

Mature Height × Spread
35 to 60 feet × 25to 50 feet

Our native red maple is the star of southern maples. Its strong, upright growth habit and broad, spreading crown make red maple a fine shade tree for suburban landscapes. Its striking gray bark and medium-sized, three-lobed leaves with red petioles makes it easy to identify in our forests. Place red maple as a specimen tree where there is ample room, certainly not closer than 30 feet from the house. Homeowners with smaller yards can use the columnar and compact forms such as 'Armstrong'. The latest introductions include exquisite cultivars, such as 'October Glory', with lustrous crimson leaves that hold later than those of most maples. With consistent fall color and ease of establishment, no wonder this is often the tree of choice.

When, Where, and How to Plant

Red maple trees are available as container-grown and balled-and-burlapped (B&B) specimens. Plant B&B trees in late winter or early spring. Plant container-grown trees anytime the soil can be prepared. Red maple grows in a wide range of soil conditions but performs best in moist, well-drained, acidic soils. Give it full sun or light shade. Plant in a wide hole with depth equal to the rootball. Stake it if you have planted it in a windy location or if it is quite large. Mulch with a 3-inch layer of leaf compost or aged hardwood bark. Create a berm on the edge of the planting hole for watering purposes.

Growing Tips

Red maple grows rapidly with summer irrigation. For the first month, irrigate twice a week; taper to monthly. Water regularly during the growing season for the first two years, using a soaker hose or a slow trickle from the garden hose for at least thirty minutes. Fertilize trees in March or November to improve growth rate or foliage.

Regional Advice and Care

It is difficult to garden under red maples due to exposed roots and heavy shade. Try to develop a strong framework with a single trunk and branches growing perpendicular to the trunk. As the tree matures, remove weak branches and limbs or leaders with narrow crotches at the trunk. Prune during in late summer. Pruning while the trees are dormant is also acceptable, but the trees may bleed sap profusely. Chronic leaf spots appear often.

Companion Planting and Design

Some use red maple in an allée to line a driveway. Plant it as a specimen to frame a house or on large lots in clusters of three, spaced 30 feet apart, to make a shaded grove with fall color impact. Maple's shallow root systems may "heave up" walks and driveway pavement. Use upright cultivars, Trident, or Japanese maples for small yards.

Try These

Pyramid-shaped 'Red Sunset' has wonderful orange-red fall color. Hybrid Autumn Blaze® produces fiery red leaves in early autumn. 'October Glory'® is *glorious*.

River Birch

Betula nigra 'Dura-Heat'®

Botanical Pronunciation
BET-you-lah NI-gra

Bloom Period and Seasonal Color
Spring, nonshowy catkins; yellow fall foliage

Mature Height × Spread
25 to 45 feet × 15 to 28 feet

Many people think river birch needs a wet site to flourish, but if you allow enough space for this beautiful native tree, you can enjoy its marvelous features practically anywhere in the home landscape. 'Heritage'® river birch loses tattered bark in slabs to reveal peach-colored inner bark. However, hot, windy locations may cause extensive leafdrop. 'Dura-Heat'®, a vigorous grower, has better retention of its rough-textured, dark green leaves. Most birch trees are grown as multitrunked specimens whose exfoliating bark looks especially nice in the winter landscape. Allow a few growing seasons for peak bark color. The buzz in gardening circles is about weeping 'Summer Cascade'®. Don't waste your time trying to grow European white birch, *Betula pendula*, in the Carolinas; it thrives in cooler climes to the north.

When, Where, and How to Plant
Plant container-grown birches anytime but summer. Small specimens establish quickly and frequently outgrow larger trees in a few years. Winter is the time to plant large B&B trees. Plant at least 25 feet from a structure or patio, and out of septic fields. Provide a moist site with at least a half-day of sun. No soil amendment is necessary. After planting, water at a slow trickle for an hour. Provide a 3-inch layer of mulch to the drip line.

Growing Tips
Water newly planted trees twice the first week, then weekly thereafter for ten weeks. Water during dry periods to avoid heavy leaf drop. In deep, rich soils, fertilizer is not necessary during establishment. In other soils, fertilize every three or four years to keep lush green foliage. Scatter 10-10-10 fertilizer or use fertilizer spikes at the drip line. After the tree reaches desired height, stop fertilizing except for maintenance applications. Young trees grow fast after the second season.

Regional Advice and Care
Unlike white birch, river birch does not have problems with bronze-birch borers. Aphids may cause leaf drop. Winter ice storms are the enemy of their brittle wood. Note: pollen and seed drop occur for a few weeks in spring. Be prepared to remove seedlings in mulched beds. In summer, remove suckers at the base of the trunk. "Limb up" the trees in late summer to maintain easy passage under foliage. Birches' shallow, exposed roots can hinder mowing a lawn. Maintain trees in large mulched beds.

Companion Planting and Design
The graceful branching habit of river birch is most appealing in natural areas and informal settings such as a courtyard. Plant it for winter interest. Use along the perimeter of your property in borders of groundcovers and low-growing, shade tolerant evergreens. This tree sheds limbs and fuzzy seeds; clearly, not what you want at your front door.

Try These
'Dura-Heat'® is an improvement over the standard 'Heritage'® river birch for dry areas. Seedling river birches seldom show the attractive peeling of bark featured by improved cultivars. Weeping river birch 'Summer Cascade'® offers more possibilities.

Saucer Magnolia

Magnolia × soulangeana

Botanical Pronunciation
mag-NO-lee-ah SO-lan-GEE-an-ah

Other Name
Tulip magnolia

Bloom Period and Seasonal Color
Early spring, white, and pink to purplish flowers

Mature Height × Spread
12 to 35 feet × 12 to 25 feet

Saucer magnolias have one major flaw: they don't stay in bloom long enough. When they are at the zenith of their early spring glory, they create a magnificent spectacle, and gardeners rush to nurseries in search of this large-flowered beauty. The latest introductions are quite floriferous and bloom sporadically throughout the growing season, especially with adequate rainfall. During the primary flowering period, the 6-inch white or pinkish purple fleshy flowers burst open before leaves emerge. Unlike the large coarse leaves of evergreen Southern magnolia, the medium-textured leaves of saucer magnolia do not litter the landscape. Multi-trunk specimens have smooth gray bark and make outstanding garden accents. The best thing about cultivars 'Gold Star' and 'Brozzoni' is that they require very little work to stay in full splendor.

When, Where, and How to Plant

Plant potted saucer magnolia from late winter to fall. Plant B&B trees while they are dormant. Avoid planting when the soil is frozen or when the soil is too wet to work. Grow in partial shade or full sun. Moist soil will ensure strong, rapid growth. Trees that are planted in sheltered sites often escape late-spring frosts that periodically spoil the floral display. Thoroughly loosen the roots of plants grown in pots. In a wide planting hole use amended soil as a backfill. Use 5 gallons of water to settle the backfill. Add a 3-inch mulch layer, keeping it away from the trunk.

Growing Tips

Water every three days for three weeks then taper to an as-needed basis. Irrigate saucer magnolias routinely during late summer and fall months for the first growing season. Flower buds form during the summer, and letting the trees go dry can affect the next year's bloom. Apply a shrub fertilizer in spring after flowering commences.

Regional Advice and Care

Late spring frosts can spoil blooms. Train single-trunk specimens in order to develop a strong framework of scaffold branches. Prune saucer magnolias while they are young and keep the basal suckers removed. Any cold-damaged twigs should be pruned off. Multiple-trunk specimens can be limbed up in summer or immediately following bloom. Leaf spots can occur during mild, wet springs. Caution: spent flower petals that drop onto walks can be slippery.

Companion Planting and Design

Saucer magnolia is spectacular in a courtyard or patio garden. It offers seasonal interest with its smooth gray bark that contrasts with the dark green foliage and ostentatious flowers. Saucer magnolias will grow large enough to provide appreciable shade. Underplant with groundcovers or shade perennials, such as hellebore and hosta.

Try These

The 'Jane' hybrid is a repeat-bloomer, along with her sisters, 'Ann' and 'Betty'. Yellow-flowered cultivars 'Butterflies' and 'Yellow Bird' are sweet. New for gardens, shrublike *M. stellata* 'Centennial Blush' has double, pale pink blooms.

Serviceberry

Amelanchier spp. and cultivars

Botanical Pronunciation
am-el-ANK-ee-er

Other Name Shadblow

Bloom Period and Seasonal Color
Early spring blooms; yellow-orange fall color

Mature Height × Spread
15 to 25 feet × 15 to 20 feet

A sure sign of spring in the Carolina forest is serviceberry, a small understory tree. Airy white blooms appearing on leafless branches are easy to spot in March. Early settlers to our region discovered the native *Amelanchier arborea* as a fruit source. Apple serviceberry, *A. × grandiflora* 'Autumn Brilliance'®, a showy hybrid, has thrust the petite deciduous tree into mainstream nursery inventories. This designer plant has larger leaves and flowers than the native serviceberry. Dark green leaves change to red in fall. Clusters of small, edible berries appear like blueberries on branch tips. Though some gardeners relish its fruit for pies or jam, the berries will lure songbirds to your planting. Garden designers are fond of this tree in urban landscapes where space is a premium.

When, Where, and How to Plant
Plant serviceberry from late fall until early April. The hot months make it difficult to establish plantings. Site in sun or afternoon shade; sunlight increases fruit production. It grows naturally in the shadows of a woodland. Apple serviceberry has a rounded form and will need space to mature. When planting, a wide hole is important to break up compact soil, since it has shallow roots. Plant with the rootball placed a couple inches above grade, and stake for the first growing season. Water and apply a generous layer of leaf compost or similar organic mulch.

Growing Tips
Irrigate routinely in late summer during prolonged dry spells. Serviceberries are drought-tolerant natives. Once established, serviceberry can exist with minimal care in woodland gardens. In foundation and exposed plantings, maintain a quality mulch. Fertilize sparingly, only to maintain normal foliage color; use organic fertilizer formulated for azaleas.

Regional Advice and Care
Apple serviceberry is a natural hybrid and a great selection for the edible landscape or wildlife garden. *A. alnifolia* is not recommended for the Carolinas. *A. arborea* is often incorrectly sold as *A. canadensis*, which is a small, suckering shrub. Rust fungus can thin fruit and reduce berry yield, but will not kill the tree. You may need to net the plant by late spring, otherwise you will have to share the harvest with your feathered friends. Compost adds beneficial organisms to the soil and may be the key to success with native plants.

Companion Planting and Design
Serviceberry makes a nice specimen for garden borders, accent beds, or used in clusters of three. Designers will often frame a small house with this diminutive tree near foundation corners. An underplanting of groundcover such as ajuga or pachysandra is a nice touch. They fit nicely into yards with large, shade trees to create a lower layer of vegetation. Combine with waxmyrtle hedge for songbirds.

Try These
'Autumn Brilliance'®, 'Princess Diana'®, and 'Obelisk'® are superior apple serviceberry cultivars for cityscapes. Most serviceberries will do just fine for environmental and wildlife plantings.

Southern Magnolia

Magnolia grandiflora

Botanical Pronunciation
mag-NO-lee-ah grand-dee-FLOR-rah

Bloom Period and Seasonal Color
Late spring blooms in creamy white

Mature Height × Spread
40 to 70 feet × 20 to 50 feet

Southern magnolia is a champion among evergreen trees. In the Carolinas, magnolias are valued for their large, shiny green leaves and 10-inch, creamy white flowers. The sweet fragrance of magnolia blossoms is reminiscent of gardenia flowers. The large conical southern magnolia grows wild from the coastal counties through the Piedmont and foothills. Most urban landscapes are too small for this big tree. For small yards, sweetbay magnolia, a much smaller tree, is a better choice. Many homeowners choose 'Little Gem' southern magnolia, thinking it is a dwarf shrub form—and it is not! It eventually grows into a mid-sized tree. It is precocious and blooms soon after planting. Hand-sized flowers may appear again by September. The leaves and seedpods of magnolias are great for holiday decorating.

When, Where, and How to Plant

Southern magnolia's fleshy roots make it sensitive to cold or dry conditions. Plant container-grown trees in late winter or spring. The foliage looks better when it's grown in partial shade. It grows naturally in rich, moist soil along river swamps or in deep woods, though it will tolerate drier sites. It thrives in high-organic, acidic soils. Break out the cottonseed meal and enrich the ground before planting. Spade in amendments, or till an area four times larger than the rootball for its fleshy roots. Water thoroughly and spread a layer of mulch.

Growing Tips

Water well during the first two seasons. Mulches and soaker hoses perform wonders in establishing your magnolia. It likes organic fertilizers applied at the drip line in spring every few years. Some gardeners mix equal parts by volume of cottonseed meal and 10-10-10 analysis fertilizer. Use 1 pound per inch of trunk diameter.

Regional Advice and Care

Expect burned foliage after hard winters. Selectively prune overgrown trees in March or August. Prune back to make a bushier tree, or train a young magnolia for a full pyramidal shape. Allow lower branches to sweep the ground and hide the spent leaves and seedpods this tree regularly drops. Maintain a deep layer of leaf compost or pine straw. Leaf spots may appear if the tree is stressed by drought.

Companion Planting and Design

Stately southern magnolias add a feeling of grandeur to an estate. These trees are best planted on large properties for screening. On a typical subdivision lot, plant the smaller cultivar Teddy Bear® as a specimen tree. Use as a backdrop for deciduous ornamentals, butterfly bush, Shasta viburnum, and Japanese maple. They combine well with brick structures.

Try These

The fabulous 'Bracken's Brown Beauty' is a dense, upright cultivar. Smaller yards require 'Little Gem', or the columnar form Alta®. For mountain landscapes, check with the North Carolina Arboretum for southern magnolias that are reliable in Zones 6 to 7.

Sugar Maple

Acer saccharum

Botanical Pronunciation
A-sir sac-CAR-um

Bloom Period and Seasonal Color Spring
non-showy blooms; yellow, orange-red in fall

Mature Height × Spread
55 to 80 feet × 35 to 50 feet

Zones 5-8a

For someone raised in the Piedmont or mountain region, it is hard to imagine autumn without sugar maples. Few hardwood trees produce the wonderful, orange-red fall color that is associated with this species. Although this large, deciduous tree can be planted in Zone 8a it prefers the cool summers found in zones northward. With plenty of room to spread, sugar maple develops a dense canopy becoming a focal point on large suburban lots. Leaves are 4 to 7 inches long and wide and dull green in the growing season. After a few frosty nights this showgirl is a blaze of gorgeous foliage, attracting leaf-peepers to our Smoky Mountains from far and wide. Green Mountain®, a more heat-resistant variety, is distinguished by dark gray bark, oval form, and spectacular fall color.

When, Where, and How to Plant
Plant B&B sugar maples during late winter and potted trees in spring or fall. This species grows naturally on the edge of moist hardwood forests. Avoid hot, dry locations; sugar maple prefers moist organic, cool soils. Trees in sunny locations have the most intense fall color. Afternoon shade is important in hot sites of Zone 8. Free up circling roots after removing from the pot. Prepare a planting hole that is at least twice as wide as the rootball and of equal depth. Backfill with loose soil that is amended with compost. Water thoroughly to settle the rootball. Follow up with a layer of mulch.

Growing Tips
Water weekly for thirty minutes for the first several weeks. In nature, this tree grows well in leaf litter so maintain a mulch ring. During the first summer, give supplemental water if rainfall is insufficient to keep the new growth vigorous. Tree fertilizer spikes can be used occasionally in fall for convenience to maintain leaf color. Water is more important in the early years than fertilization.

Regional Advice and Care
New heat -and drought-tolerant cultivars are the best choice for South Carolina landscapes. Southern sugar maple, *Acer barbatum*, occurs naturally in the Carolinas from the foothills to inland coastal plains. Seedlings can be transplanted after being root-pruned in late summer. Train young trees to develop a single trunk. The dense canopy will prevent growing turfgrass beneath sugar maple. At maturity, the tree canopy can be thinned by a certified arborist for better air circulation. Maple worms and aphids are considered minor pests.

Companion Planting and Design
Select this specimen tree for brilliant fall color. It is a tall, dense shade tree with shallow root system, which limits shrub planting within its drip line. Use with shade-loving groundcovers like lamium, vinca, and mondograss. Columnar forms allow for planting in smaller yards. This is not a good choice for a hot, inner-city environment.

Try These
Green Mountain® and Legacy® are better suited to full sun sites without leaf scorch. 'Columnare' and other upright selections are coming for urban gardens.

Sweetbay Magnolia

Magnolia virginiana

Botanical Pronunciation
Mag-NOL-ee-ah ver-JIN-ee-an-ah

Other Name Silver bay

Mature Height × Spread
20 to 50 feet × 10 to 20 feet

Bloom Period & Seasonal Color
Summer blooms in creamy white; conelike
cluster of carmine seeds

When you think magnolia, you imagine a massive tree framing an antebellum house on a Southern plantation. Not this species. Sweetbay magnolia is the lanky cousin that is happy in an urban garden setting or woodland landscape. It has 2- to 4-inch creamy white, cupped flowers with a sweet, lemon fragrance. Bloom time commences in early summer when few ornamental trees flower. Its leaves are narrow, to 5 inches, and medium green, with a silver lower surface. A gentle breeze makes the foliage glisten revealing the light gray bark and multistemmed form. Sweetbay magnolia is reliably cold-hardy but may be evergreen or semi-evergreen depending on the hardiness zone. This native combines well with many fine shrubs and is a perfect specimen tree for tight spaces.

When, Where, and How to Plant

Add container-grown plants during winter and spring for best root growth. Plant in full sun to partial shade. This tree will perform best where the soil is moist and rich, but well drained. In poor soils, backfill using one-third leaf compost or peat moss. Open a planting hole that is wider than the rootball and of equal depth. Use the prepared backfill to firm-in roots. Create a watering berm on the perimeter of the hole. Water thoroughly and apply 3 inches of organic mulch.

Growing Tips

Keep sweetbay's roots moist by following a strict watering schedule for the first season. Irrigate every other day for the first two weeks and taper off to weekly for the first three months. Then water as needed during the first two summers. Large B&B trees can require several years to establish after transplanting. Maintain a generous mulch ring under your tree as a regular practice when planting in a lawn. Controlled-release fertilizers containing iron can improve leaf color and are applied with spring growth.

Regional Advice and Care

Though it is cold-hardy throughout the Carolinas, it can enter spring nearly leafless following a harsh winter. You'll find this tree flourishing in coastal regions where high water tables and rainfall is plentiful. Think moist site! Acidic soils and a plethora of soil types yield quality trees. Plantings in the Piedmont grow 20 feet. Magnolias are host to a number of disease and insect pests. Consult an Extension agent to identify pests and determine action if needed.

Companion Planting and Design

The narrow upright form lends itself to interplanting with moisture-loving groundcovers, such as pachysandra or sweet woodrift. Use in borders where light shade is needed for ferns, wildflowers, and hostas. It's a good choice for a lawn tree, and should be used more often as an accent. Plant in stream bottoms or near rain gardens where moisture is abundant.

Try These

Jim Wilson's Moonglow® is a columnar specimen for smaller yards. Try 'Henry Hicks', 'Green Shadow', and wild swamp magnolia seedlings, *Magnolia virginiana* var. *australis*.

Western Arborvitae

Thuja plicata

Botanical Pronunciation THU-yah ply-KAY-tuh

Other Name Western redcedar

Bloom Period and Seasonal Color
Spring inconspicuous male blooms; year-round grayish green foliage

Mature Height × Spread
40 to 60 feet × 15 to 20 feet

Mention "cedar" in the Carolinas and most residents think of our lanky Eastern redcedars that line farm fence rows or the dark conical evergreens that dot our roadsides. Experienced gardeners are now planting western arborvitae, the long-lived "redcedar" of the Pacific Northwest that reaches towering heights. This narrowleaf evergreen is being added to landscapes as tall hedges to screen off views and provide windbreaks. Western arborvitae 'Green Giant' is a handsome specimen tree frequently used as a substitute for Leyland cypress. These conifers have fine, flattened twigs of scalelike leaves and are soft to the touch, unlike true cedars. Given a sunny site and adequate moisture its grayish green foliage grows relatively fast once established. Western arborvitae has a pyramidal form and is capable of making a punctuation wherever it is planted.

When, Where, and How to Plant

Container-grown specimens can be planted in late winter, spring, and fall. In the coastal region, plant it in late fall or winter to take advantage of sufficient soil moisture. When planted for screening purposes, space 6 to 8 feet apart or wider depending on how quickly you need privacy. Full sun to a half-day of shade in a moderately dry site is ideal. To a wide planting hole add organic soil amendment and ½ cup of superphosphate. Tall specimens set in the fall may need staking until sturdy. Water thoroughly and mulch well.

Growing Tips

Water newly planted western arborvitae three times the first week, twice the second, and weekly for two months when planting in the warm months, until they begin growing strongly. Once fully established they are moderately drought tolerant. Dry summer seasons are their nemesis. Maintain a mulch layer where soils tend to be dry or sandy. A general garden fertilizer can be used the second spring to push them along. This conifer grows relatively fast once it becomes acclimated to a new site.

Regional Advice and Care

Do not prune unless there is good reason. Growing tips can be sheared in early summer for size control but they are best left alone to grow gracefully. Western arborvitae is dense and creates heavy shade as it matures. Forget growing grass inside the drip line of this evergreen—leave it mulched. Bagworms can be problematic on conifers but are easy to manage with biological products and hand-removal in fall.

Companion Planting and Design

Windbreaks and privacy screens are a high priority in urban landscapes. This does both. Unequivocally an evergreen for tall screens; its texture and needlelike leaves are a pleasing backdrop for a broadleaf shrub border. It's the preferred conifer for privacy hedges in lieu of Leyland cypress due to canker disease resistance. Place in mulched beds. Varieties with gold foliage provide accent and year-round color. Plant in clusters.

Try These

'Green Giant', 'Clemson #1', and hybrid Steeplechase® are most notable. In gardens, use a narrow columnar form, such as Hogan arborvitae 'Fastigiata'.

Zelkova

Zelkova serrata

Botanical Pronunciation zel-KO-vah sir-RAH-tah

Other Name Japanese zelkova

Bloom Period and Seasonal Color
Dark green leaves in summer; yellowish bronze to red fall foliage

Mature Height × Spread
70 feet × 50 to 60 feet

The new homebuyer would be well advised to plant a zelkova for fast shade and natural cooling. This large deciduous beauty grows to 70 feet, big enough to thwart the hot afternoon sun. First introduced as a replacement for the disappearing American elm, zelkova has moved from an urban street tree to suburban backyards. Its foliage closely resembles that of American elm with its pointed tips and serrated leaf margins. What it lacks in fall color, zelkova balances with its rich green foliage, sturdy stature, and its tough wood that resists damage from ice and windstorms. This wonderful care-free shade tree is a rapid grower and will reward you with 2 or more feet in height each season. Once established, your prized zelkova will do just fine in drier weather.

When, Where, and How to Plant
Zelkova trees in 2-inch trunk calipers are available at garden centers in large containers. Plant zelkova when the ground is workable in fall or spring, certainly by May. Balled-and-burlapped trees are available during their dormant season, January through March. For maximum growth, plant in moist, deep soil and in sun or partial shade. Follow soil-test recommendations for new homesites. Zelkova's performance depends on its successful transplanting. If zelkova is planted properly, it will grow well with little care. With potted trees free up the major roots when planting in the preferred wide hole.

Growing Tips
Watering during the first two growing seasons is a must if the summers are dry. A soaker hose is a good investment. Plant decline can be related to poorly drained soils. In late September, fertilize to help build a stronger root system, but fertilization is not necessary every year. Maintain a mulch ring out to the outermost branches. This discourages weeds and protects the thin-barked tree from weed-eater or mower injury. Don't heap mulch up on the trunk.

Regional Advice and Care
Expect your zelkova to send out many branches from a short area on the trunk. Where this leads to limb breakage and demise of Bradford pears, the wood of zelkova is so tough that you needn't worry. Light pruning of weak twigs is important as the main scaffold limbs develop. Japanese beetles are occasional zelkova pests in the Carolinas—but even if you don't spray, beetle injury is of minor importance. Elm bark beetles may also show up but seldom cause the fatal Dutch elm disease.

Companion Planting and Design
Plant this specimen tree by a deck or patio to create the perfect place to enjoy a cold drink in the summer. Shade the southeast or southwest roof with Japanese zelkova and save a bundle on your power bill. Underplant with dwarf evergreen shrubs or groundcovers.

Try These
Green Vase® is a Tar Heel favorite. 'Village Green' turns rusty red in the fall.

VINES

FOR THE CAROLINAS

Vines offer diverse visual qualities and are valued for the rich texture of their foliage. Some, like snail vine, perfume the air with delightful fragrances. Others, such as moonvine, evoke mystery and wonder as they open spontaneously in the evening. Crossvine and coral honeysuckle attract hummingbirds and provide food for wild birds. Though most woody vines are deciduous, a few old-fashioned evergreen favorites, like smilax and armand clematis, can be found in many landscapes.

Vines can soften the architecture of a home and cool a harsh leisure area by a patio. Boston ivy is perfectly happy clinging to a hot brick wall. Vines are a must on a decorative arbor or trellis where they can add a vertical dimension as well as seasonal flowers. Lamp posts and mailboxes can serve as supports for a host of showy vines. Even Master Gardeners have gotten hooked on tender vines because of their rampant growth and color. The hyacinth bean vine is a favorite for sunny trellises. Tender mandevilla may show up on fences and mailboxes, or in large containers. Unfortunately, it is not hardy away from the coast, but when grown as an annual it flowers early and continuously.

Being a Carolina resident may affect your opinion of vines. We are all too familiar with the poor examples around us—namely, kudzu and Chinese wisteria. But with these two out of mind, there are some fine native vines that can be found across the state. Carolina jessamine, the state flower of South Carolina, serves both as groundcover and an evergreen vine; its pure yellow flowers are a welcome sight in late winter and early spring.

Get to Know a Vine Fruit

A vine has a mind of its own. One will refuse to climb a trellis in spite of much coaxing, while another will gallop up a tree trunk unaided. Every vine employs a unique mechanism for clinging; many have special plant tissues for this physical attachment. Clematis clings by way of leafy stems that twine around posts and arbors. Climbing hydrangeas and Boston ivy form "roots" on their branches that act like tiny suction cups, giving them an advantage on a brick or stone wall. The native wisteria's twining stem growth ensures a tight hold on anything that crosses its path. Whether twining in a clockwise or counterclockwise direction, a vine has a "plan" to reach its destination and make its presence known.

Get to know a vine's requirements before planting one in the garden. It will save work in the long run. Vines are frequently planted in cramped spaces. Don't be shy about pruning them—they need some handholding. They're like toddlers—give them an inch and they will take a mile. Much like shrubs, perennial flowering vines are best pruned immediately after they finish blooming.

Versatile Vines

If commonplace ornamental vines do not excite you, consider a tender annual vine for the landscape. Annual vines grow quickly and can add marvelous color while inviting bees and butterflies to the garden. If you want edible plants, kiwis and muscadine grapes will be right at home on a sturdy arbor in your garden.

Whether flowering or evergreen, vines are versatile ornamental plants that are still waiting to be discovered. They can be planted in so many wonderful locations. A vine may be just the thing that your garden needs as "icing on the cake."

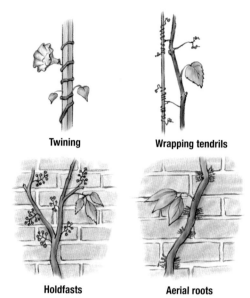

Twining

Wrapping tendrils

Holdfasts

Aerial roots

Planting Vines

Woody or tropical vines are sold in 1- to 5-gallon containers. Loosen the roots of the plant, especially if it is a potbound specimen. Shake part of the soil off the roots and prune back the longest roots to encourage faster establishment. Dig a planting hole as deep as the depth of the rootball and three times as wide. Mix a 5-gallon bucket full of an organic soil conditioner, such as dried cow manure or compost, with the excavated soil. Add 1 cup of pelleted dolomitic limestone and a couple of tablespoons of controlled-release flower fertilizer, or use a phosphorus-rich organic fertilizer. Firm-in the roots with the conditioned backfill soil, and water thoroughly. Put down a 2-inch layer of compost or mulch to enrich the soil. Water twice a week for the first month.

Annual vines such as morning glory or moonvine grow best if direct-seeded where the plants are to remain. There is no advantage to starting with young plants; in fact, annual vine seedlings are difficult to transplant. Soak seeds overnight in tepid water just before planting. In clay soils make low mounds (hills) by mixing a 5-gallon bucket of play sand and a bucket of seed-starting mix soil with an equal volume of clay. (Skip the play sand in sandy soils, of course.) Add an organic garden fertilizer such as cottonseed meal per directions on the packages. Provide strings for the vines to run; they will begin twining within a week of emergence. Annual vines will climb like homesick angels!

Vines Grow in Popularity

The popularity of vines continues to grow as rapidly as the plants themselves. Gardeners are always looking for a quick fix when they need instant shade or want to hide an unsightly area. Vines fit the bill in both cases. Beautiful vines, like the spring-flowering clematis, are the pride of seasoned gardeners. Others, like the tropical mandevilla, render a burst of color in the off-season when there's little else is in bloom.

Carolina Jessamine

Gelsemium sempervirens

Botanical Pronunciation
gel-SEM-ee-um sem-per-VHI-rens

Bloom Period and Seasonal Color
Late winter and spring yellow blooms

Mature Length
20 feet

This native evergreen vine with bright yellow flowers is a great choice for a sunny spot. Though the flowers of Carolina jessamine are small, they appear in clusters, making a great show against the glossy foliage. The dark green leaves are lance-shaped and arranged opposite each other on rich brown stems. In the eastern Carolinas, Carolina jessamine also grows as a groundcover in woodlands where it can make its way up to the very top of understory trees. It is not overly invasive; it has a distinct fragrance and often flowers sporadically in the fall. Certain cultivars were selected for fall blooming. A real novelty is the double-flowered variety. This plant will thrive for many years in the right location. Don't confuse jessamine with jasmine; they are not related in any way.

When, Where, and How to Plant
Carolina jessamine can be planted anytime from containers. If planting in fall, allow time for it to establish to avoid winter injury and burned foliage. Small transplants should be set out in spring. Plant in sunny or shaded locations. It prefers moist, rich soil but grows equally well in sandy soils amended with organic matter. This vine climbs high including, to the consternation of utility company workers, to the tops of power poles, so be mindful of planting next to a utility pole. Water thoroughly at planting and twice weekly for three weeks.

Growing Tips
Water deeply during dry summers, but this vine is very drought-resistant once established. Fertilize with a high-phosphorus 10-20-20 analysis in September. Use water-soluble fertilizers monthly for rapid growth when establishing jessamine. **A word of caution:** All parts of the plant are poisonous to livestock, pets, and people.

Regional Advice and Care
Carolina jessamine has no tendrils for clinging and must be tied to supports. Construct a trellis or use fencing to train this twining vine. Flowers come in spring on new growth, so early summer is the appropriate time to prune. Remove weak or dying twigs anytime. As the plant matures, lower branches will be shaded out and may die off; this is normal for vigorous vines on trellises. Overgrown specimens can be pruned severely in early March to invigorate the wood. Some root-pruning in early fall may help contain rampant growth. No serious pest problems are encountered.

Companion Planting and Design
Carolina jessamine cascading over a wall or fence makes an effective screen. Plant it on fences, arbors, or mailboxes, or next to the trunk of an established tree with open branching to admit light. This glossy vine looks good all year. Jessamine makes a good groundcover if properly maintained, but its tangle of vines complicates leaf-raking.

Try These
'Margarita' is the most cold-hardy and has large flowers. 'Pride of Augusta' has double flowers. Swamp jessamine, *Gelsemium rankinii*, blooms in both fall and spring but is not fragrant; it is not cold hardy in the mountain region.

Clematis

Clematis spp.

Botanical Pronuciation
KLEM-uh-tis

Bloom Period and Seasonal Color
Spring and summer in white, pink, red, mauve, and purple

Mature Length
6 to 25 feet

There is a clematis for every garden. Select from types with cloudbursts of small fragrant flowers or huge blooms 6 inches in diameter. Deciduous clematis needs support for best display. Some species climb better than others, by means of leaf stems that wind around a trellis. The uncommon, spring-blooming *Clematis armandii* has long, leathery leaves that make it a marvelous evergreen vine for the arbor or a wall espalier. Its deep green leaves and 2-inch, fragrant white flowers put on quite a show. Probably the most commonly grown clematis is Jackman, known for its pinwheel-shaped, violet-purple flowers. If pruned properly, the vines may have a second round of flowers in the fall. Another favorite, sweet autumn clematis, perfumes the air with its sprays of sweet-smelling, lacy, white flowers in late summer.

When, Where, and How to Plant
Both fall and spring plantings of container-grown clematis will work fine. The vines like their roots in the cool shade and their foliage in warm sunlight. This is proven; just try planting clematis in full sun without shading its roots and you will get the point. Clematis likes moist, well-drained soil that is very fertile, and it will grow for decades in a good location. Follow the planting instructions on page 225 to ensure quick establishment and long life for your clematis vine. Vigorous sweet autumn clematis can grow in virtually any location and does not benefit materially from special soil preparation.

Growing Tips
Keep the soil moist around your clematis during active growth and bloom periods. Add organic fertilizer in late spring and lime every four years. Withhold fertilizer from October to March. High nitrogen fertilizers can kill them. Replenish mulch annually.

Regional Advice and Care
Vines are easily trained to a trellis with bamboo stakes and plastic (not wire core) "twist-ties" or plastic tape. On a brick or rock wall, use masonry nails and run supporting wires over heavy picture-frame hooks. Prune to thin vines or to confine growth. Prune spring-flowering types immediately after flowering since their buds are formed in fall; cut shoots back to two leaf buds. Late-summer bloomers can be pruned in early spring. Remove rangy twigs to keep the vine groomed, as older plants need thinning. The worst disease is a stem rot fungus that occurs in wet soils. Don't replant in the same spot; move plants to higher ground. Control aphids with horticultural oil.

Companion Planting and Design
Posts on decks serve as a trellis; other possible structures include wooden lattices, arbors, chain-link fences, mailboxes, and lamp posts. Underplant trellised vines with shallow-rooted groundcovers, or shade the roots with a 6-inch mulch of pine straw.

Try These
'Nelly Moser' has huge 7-inch flowers, pale pink with red bars. New clematis Vancouver™ introductions have exceptional color combinations. The native bush clematis, *Clematis ochroleuca*, and bell-shaped *C*. 'Rooguchi' are cutting-edge plants.

Confederate Jasmine

Trachelospermum jasminoides

Botanical Pronunciation
TRAY-key-loh-SPERM-mum jas-men-OID-eez

Other Name
Star jasmine

Bloom Period and Seasonal Color
Summer blooms in white; evergreen foliage

Mature Length 10 to 40 feet

In this diverse genus, many jasmines are shrubby and few are fragrant. True jasmine, the summer-blooming poet's jasmine, *Jasminoides officinale*, is a popular species with fragrant, white flowers but it lacks cold-hardiness. The best choice for most Carolina gardens is a different vining species, Confederate jasmine, *Trachelospermum jasminoides* (meaning "jasmine-like"). It has intensely fragrant white flower clusters and is hardy in protected areas to Zone 7b. Gardeners grow it for the lustrous dark green foliage as a vine and groundcover. Though it's slow to start, it does extremely well as a fast-growing screen, where shrubs planted for privacy would take a long time to mature. Your best bet for finding the right jasmine for your landscape is to check the actual plants for form and fragrance.

When, Where, and How to Plant

In late spring and summer set out container-grown Confederate jasmine that have been staked at the nursery. Plant fragrant species where sweet aromas will waft over decks and patios. In Zone 7, Confederate jasmine survives winter better if it is grown as a groundcover, especially under high shade from evergreen trees. Prepare a planting hole that's as wide and at equal depth of the rootball.

Growing Tips

Do not pinch the tips of the vine to encourage its vertical growth. This plant requires little care other than feeding in spring and again in late summer. It is difficult to determine feeding rates on vines. The safest procedure is to water the soil deeply, wait a day, and drench the area around the plants with liquid fertilizer.

Regional Advice and Care

Serious winter weather with temperatures below 10 degrees Fahrenheit can be too much for Confederate jasmine west of Interstate 85. You will lose top growth to freezing. In the Piedmont it needs deep pine straw mulch in winter. When new growth starts in late spring, prune out dead stems. Groom established vines annually by lightly shearing. Lime these vines every other year, or yearly on sandy soils. Work 1 cup of pelletized dolomitic limestone into the soil around vines. At the same time, apply 2 or 3 cups of organic fertilizer into a furrow encircling the plant 2 feet out from its base. Prune vines to keep them in-bounds.

Companion Planting and Design

Train it to an arbor where the glossy, oval leaves show to good effect after blooms fade. Placing angel's trumpet as a specimen looks good in front of jasmine on arbors. Use as a groundcover with the summer-blooming bulbs of *Lycoris radiata*. Train this vine to a trellis only in a protected spot in Piedmont gardens. To enjoy its fragrance, grow a container plant in a sunroom.

Try These

The evergreen Confederate jasmine is a Carolinas favorite. *J. officinale* 'Frojas' and 'Fiona Sunrise' have gold foliage, hardy in Zones 7b to 8.

Coral Honeysuckle

Lonicera sempervirens

Botanical Pronunciation
lon-NIS-sir-ah sem-per-VHI-rens

Other Name Trumpet honeysuckle

Bloom Period and Seasonal Color
Spring and (sporadic) summer blooms in
reddish orange and yellow

Mature Length 20 to 40 feet

For a native vine that is hardy and attractive to hummingbirds, try coral honeysuckle. Most Southerners are a hard sell for this ornamental vine since the invasive evergreen Japanese honeysuckle has naturalized and overrun fields and woodlands. Unlike its weedy Asian cousin, coral honeysuckle behaves. This semi-evergreen vine features clusters of trumpets or tubular flowers with unmistakable fragrance. Some vines produce ¼-inch, bright red berries in early autumn. In warmer parts of the Piedmont and near the coast, this honeysuckle may be evergreen. It is great for the gardener who has a large area to devote to it. New foliage is tinged with purple and matures to a bluish green. This plant is desirable for its long blooming period, ease of culture, and drawing power for hummingbirds.

When, Where, and How to Plant
Coral honeysuckle can be planted spring through fall. Set out divisions and rooted cuttings after danger of frost in early spring. Plant in sun or a slightly shaded area in well-drained soil. Blooming is reduced in woodland gardens. There is no need to amend well-drained soil, but add peat moss to sandy types. Dig a hole that is several times wider but not deeper than the rootball. Settle the backfill by water thoroughly. Add 2-inch layer of leaf compost or mulch. Construct a trellis for this native or plant by a fence. It can also be espaliered on a building. This plant grows slowly the first year, gallops afterwards.

Growing Tips
Use an open-ended hose to water; deep irrigation is needed twice a week. (Light frequent watering is a waste of time.) Water until the plant's roots are established, generally three to four weeks, or when new growth begins. Fertilize in May, if needed, with an organic or CRF developed especially for flowering plants. Don't overfertilize, or you will have too few blooms and excessive foliage growth.

Regional Advice and Care
Train twining coral honeysuckle during the first season or two. At maturity, prune to control its size on a trellis after the summer blooming period. Avoid severe winter pruning or the next year's flower buds may be eliminated. There are no serious insect problems, though a few aphids may appear in spring. Occasionally, powdery mildew may be observed if honeysuckle vines are planted in shade gardens.

Companion Planting and Design
Plant where you can watch the hummingbirds work the flowers. Train plants to a lamp post, fence, or arbor. This honeysuckle can be grown in a sizable container backed up with a trellis. For a longer bloom season, add the hybrid species *L.* x *heckrottii* and 'Inov'™ cultivars. These are deciduous or semi-green hybrids with native parentage.

Try These
Several selections include yellow blooming 'Sulphurea' and 'John Clayton'. 'Magnifica' has intense red flowers. Cultivars 'Gold Flame' and 'Dropmore' honeysuckle are favorites.

Crossvine

Bignonia capreolata

Botanical Pronunciation
big-NOH-nee-uh KAP-ree-uh-LOT-ah

Bloom Period and Seasonal Color
Spring and early summer, yellow-red, orange-red blooms; evergreen foliage

Mature Length
30 to 50 feet

Crossvine is a native of the Carolinas where it has evergreen to semi-evergreen foliage, depending on minimum winter temperatures. It is a twining plant common to warm, moist woodlands where it can climb to 50 feet. Crossvine gets its name from the cross-shaped pith revealed when its stems are cut. (Leaves also cross over to latch onto things, mind you!) The yellow-red or ruby-orange, trumpet-shaped flowers are mildly fragrant and attractive to hummingbirds. It bears a profusion of 1- to 2-inch blooms, completely obscuring the foliage, when located in full sun. Most homeowners who choose crossvine desire fast growth and will be delighted by the plant's growth rate, especially if shade is wanted for your special garden arbor. It develops "holdfast" disc anchors and is not recommended for running up shingled structures.

When, Where, and How to Plant
Plant crossvine in spring or fall. This vine tolerates a wide range of soil conditions from average dry clays to wet coastal soil. The best site has organically rich, well-drained soil in a sunny location. The addition of a trellised crossvine enhances shade gardens, though you will have to settle for only a few flowers. It is important to follow the soil preparation instructions on page 225 because crossvine is long-lived and needs your help to get off to a strong start from a container.

Growing Tips
Keep the soil moist for the first season. During periods of drought, crossvine benefits from a deep irrigation every couple of weeks. Apply a general garden fertilizer like 10-10-10 in spring during the second season; spread ½ cup of fertilizer in a circle beginning 2 feet out from the basal stem. Apply 3 inches of any organic mulch as hot weather approaches. This native vine is care-free after establishment. No fertilization is required as is matures if mulched with compost.

Regional Advice and Care
Crossvine has little disks at the ends of tendrils and suckers that act as suction cups to help it cling to brick and stone walls. You will need to tie the vine to an arbor or support to prevent it from lying on the ground initially. When growing up a tree, it clings tightly, giving a pleasant appearance. Prune after it flowers and as often as is necessary to train it to a garden structure or support. It is pest-free.

Companion Planting and Design
When it's in bloom, crossvine instantly attracts the attention of all who pass by your garden. Plant it on a trellis for screening and shade. Use it on a fence or place it to nestle up to a masonry or stone wall in the sun. Let it sprawl over an old stump.

Try These
'Tangerine Beauty' is a superb N.C. State University selection bearing rich, ruby-tangerine flowers. 'Shalimar Red' and 'Jekyll' are orange-red cultivars with good vigor in warm climes.

Mandevilla

Mandevilla splendens

Botanical Pronunciation
MAN-deh-vill-ah splend-ENZ

Other Name
Pink allamanda

Bloom Period and Seasonal Color
Summer to frost in pink; tender annual only

Mature Length
15 to 20 feet

The trumpetlike blooms of mandevilla make an attractive accent on trellises, fences, and even mailboxes. Its dark green leaves provide a foil for the vivid pink bloom clusters. It is both drought and salt tolerant, giving it a wide range of growing possibilities. Most gardeners purchase a potted mandevilla each spring in lieu of overwintering a mature landscape specimen indoors. There may be mild winters in coastal South Carolina gardens where this durable vine can return for another year, but gardeners should be prepared to replant with other tropicals. The delightful show a mandevilla delivers makes this vine appealing to brown thumb gardeners as well as veterans. Provide a structure for support and let mandevilla twist and twine without human intervention. There is one negative—all parts of this plant are poisonous.

When, Where, and How to Plant
Mandevilla is best planted in spring when danger of late frost has passed. Plant in full sun or a lightly shaded location. In shaded sites flowering is reduced and plants are more open in growth habit. A trellis or support structure should be intact. Mandevilla tolerates sand, but care may be a bit easier if the planting hole is enriched with organic matter. Dig a hole that is several times wider than the rootball but not deeper. In clay, set the rootball slightly higher than the soil level. Create a watering berm after planting. Delay mulching until strong growth is observed.

Growing Tips
Water daily for the first few weeks after planting. Gradually taper the watering off to an as-needed basis. Mandevilla are drought tolerant once established and require watering only during the driest months. Fertilize every four to six weeks during the growing season by scattering a general garden fertilizer in a wide band beginning 1½ feet from the plant.

Regional Advice and Care
Mandevilla does not survive the cold in most Carolina counties. Prune when the vine fills the trellis and gets out of bounds. In autumn after frost, cut back the spoiled foliage to the ground. Potted specimens can then be overwintered in an unheated garage or crawlspace. During warm months it responds well to trimming to keep it in check. Make cuts back to a node, or set of leaves. No deadheading should be necessary since blooms wither away. Pests are few. Use a strong spray of water or natural insecticide to get rid of aphids.

Companion Planting and Design
Some of the prettiest displays have been on white picket fences enclosing a backyard or to form a backdrop for other annuals. Choose a trellis of mandevilla for vertical accent in perennial borders of garden phlox, perennial salvia and 'Autumn Joy' sedum. Homeowners often train them on and over a mailbox.

Try These
Garden centers offer both mandevilla and dipladenia. They are comparable tender tropicals with a number of hybrids flowering an intense pink or rose red.

GLOSSARY

Alkaline Soil: Soil with a pH greater than 7.0. It lacks acidity, often because it has limestone in it.

All-Purpose Fertilizer: Powdered, liquid, or granular fertilizer with a balanced proportion of the three key nutrients nitrogen N, phosphorus P, and potassium K. It is suitable for maintenance nutrition for most plants. Ex. 10-10-10 or 13-13-13

Annual: A plant that lives its entire life in one season. It is genetically determined to germinate, grow, flower, set seed, and die the same year.

Balled and Burlapped: Describes a tree or shrub grown in the field whose rootball was wrapped with protective burlap and twine when the plant was dug up to be sold or transplanted. Abbreviated as B&B in some nursery catalogs.

Bare Root: Describes plants that have been packaged without any soil around their roots. (Seedlings, shrubs, and trees purchased through the mail arrive with their exposed roots.)

Barrier Plant: A plant that has intimidating thorns or spines and is sited to block access.

Beneficial Insects: Insects or their larvae that prey on pest organisms and their eggs. They may be flying insects, such as ladybugs, parasitic wasps, praying mantis, and soldier bugs, or soil dwellers such as predatory nematodes, spiders, and ants.

Bract: A modified leaf structure on a plant stem near its flower that resembles a petal. Often it is more colorful and visible than the actual flower, as with dogwood.

Branch collar: The point where a branch attaches to a large limb or to the trunk of a tree. When pruning, make the cut outside the branch collar; this ensures the cut will close.

Canopy: The overhead branching area of a tree, usually referring to its extent including foliage. The tip of the branches is referred to as the drip line; location for fertilization.

Cold Hardiness: The ability of a perennial plant to survive the winter cold in a particular area. The USDA Plant Hardiness Zone Map refers to minimum winter temperatures.

Composite: A flower that is actually composed of many tiny flowers. Typically, they are flat clusters of tiny, tight florets, sometimes surrounded by wider-petaled florets. Composite flowers are highly attractive to bees and beneficial insects.

Compost: Organic matter that has undergone progressive decomposition by microbial activity until it is reduced to a spongy, fluffy texture. Added to soil of any type, it improves the soil by adding humus and increasing healthy biological activity.

Controlled-Release Fertilizer: Fertilizer that is water-insoluble and therefore releases its nutrients gradually as a function of soil temperature, particle coating, moisture, and related microbial activity. Typically granular, it may be organic or synthetic.

Corm: The swollen energy-storing structure, analogous to a bulb, under the soil at the base of the stem of plants such as crocus and gladiolus.

Crown: The base of a plant at, or just beneath, the surface of the soil where the roots meet the stems. In trees and shrubs the crown may also be called the root flare or root collar.

Cultivar: A CULTIvated VARiety. It is a naturally occurring form of a plant that has been identified as special or superior and is purposely selected for propagation and production.

Deadhead: To remove faded flower heads from plants to improve their appearance, abort seed production, and stimulate further flowering.

Deciduous Plants: Unlike evergreens, these trees and shrubs lose their leaves in the fall.

Division: The practice of splitting apart perennial plants to create several smaller-rooted segments. The practice is essential to the health and continued flowering of certain plants.

Dormancy: The period, usually the winter, when perennial plants temporarily cease active growth and rest.

Established: The point at which a newly planted tree, shrub, or flower begins to produce new growth, either foliage or stems. This is an indication that the roots have recovered from transplant shock and have begun to grow and spread.

Evergreen: Perennial plants that do not lose their foliage annually with the onset of winter. Needled or broadleaf foliage will persist and continue to function on a plant through one or more winters and drop leaves in cycles of three or four years or more.

Facing Plant: A plant used in the foreground, due to its small size, often with evergreens.

Germinate: To sprout. Germination is a fertile seed's first stage of development.

Graft union: The point on the stem of a woody plant with sturdier roots where a stem from a highly ornamental plant is inserted so that it will join with it. Roses are grafted.

Growth Rate: The pace or speed at which plants develop and increase in size. Plants are described as slow, medium, or fast growers. Among shrub species, hedges are fast growers and dwarf conifers are slow growers. Many groundcovers grow slowly.

Herbaceous: Plants having fleshy or soft stems that die back with frost; the opposite of woody.

Hybrid: A plant that is the result of intentional or natural cross-pollination between two or more plants of the same species or genus.

Liming: The practice of incorporating limestone into acid soil to raise the pH level and increase the calcium level to optimize fertilizer benefits.

Mulch: A layer of material over bare soil to protect it from erosion and compaction by rain and to discourage weeds. It may be inorganic gravel, fabric or organic wood chips, bark, pine needles, chopped leaves.

Naturalize: a To plant bulbs in a random, informal pattern as they would appear in their natural habitat; b to spread throughout natural habitats a tendency of nonnative plants.

Organic Material, Organic Matter: Any material or debris that is derived from plants. It is carbon-based material capable of undergoing decomposition and decay.

Peat Moss: Organic matter from peat sedges or sphagnum mosses Canada, often used to improve water-holding capacity of sandy soil and to create soilless mixes for containers.

Perennial: A flowering plant that lives over three or more seasons. Many die back with frost, but their roots survive the winter and generate new shoots in the spring.

pH: A measurement of the relative acidity low pH or alkalinity high pH of soil or water based on a scale of 1 to 14; 7 is neutral. Individual plants require soil to be within a certain range so that nutrients can dissolve in moisture and be available to them.

Pinch: To remove tender stems and/or leaves by pressing them between thumb and forefinger. This pruning technique encourages branching, compactness, and flowering in plants, or it removes aphids clustered at growing tips.

Rhizome: A swollen stem structure, similar to a bulb, that lies horizontally in the soil.

Rootbound or potbound: The condition of a plant that has been confined in a container too long, its roots having been forced to wrap around themselves and even swell out of the container. Successful transplanting requires untangling and trimming some roots.

Specimen Plant: An ornamental shrub or tree used alone to create a focal point or accent in the landscape. Often, the plant has some unique features, such as showy bark, fragrant flowers, etc.

Sustainable: The ability of a plant to survive on its own with minimal care once established.

BIBLIOGRAPHY

Publications

American Rose Society. *American Rose*. Shreveport, LA. 2014.

Armitage, Allan M. *Herbaceous Perennial Plants*. Varsity Press. Athens, Georgia. 1989.

Bender, Steve and Felder Rushing. *Passalong Plants*. University of North Carolina Press. Chapel Hill, North Carolina. 1993.

Better Homes and Gardens. *Complete Guide to Flower Gardening*. Meredith Books. 1995.

Bost, Toby and Bob Polomski. *Carolinas Gardener's Handbook*. Cool Springs Press. Minneapolis, MN. 2012.

Bost, Toby and Jim Wilson. *The Carolinas Gardener's Guide*. Cool Springs Press. Nashville, TN. 2004.

Bridwell, Ferrell M. *Landscape Plants*. 2nd Edition. Delmar. Albany, NY. 2003.

Carolina Gardener Magazine. Greensboro, North Carolina.

Cathey, H. Marc. *Heat-Zone Gardening*. Time-Life Inc. China. 1998.

Chester-Davis, Leah and Toby Bost. *The Successful Gardener Guide*. John F. Blair Publisher. Winston-Salem, NC. 2011.

Cox, Jeff and Marilyn. *The Perennial Garden*. Rodale Press. Emmaus, Pennsylvania. 1985.

Cutler, Karan and Barbara Ellis. *The Complete Flower Gardener*. John Wiley & Sons. Hoboken, New Jersey. 2007

Dirr, Michael A. *Manual of Woody Landscape Plants, Fifth Ed.* Stripes Publishing Company. Champaign, Illinois. 1998.

Lowe, Judy. *Tennessee Gardener's Guide*. Cool Springs Press. Nashville, TN. 2001.

MacCubbin, Tom and Georgia B. Tasker. *Florida Getting Started Garden Guide*. Cool Springs Press. Minneapolis, MN. 2013.

Meredith Corporation. *Successful Rose Gardening*. Des Moines, Iowa. 1993.

National Wildlife Federation. *Field Guide to Trees of North America*. Sterling Publisher. New York, NY. 2008.

North Carolina Nurserymen and Landscape Assoc. *NCNLA Buyer's Guide*. Raleigh, NC. 2014.

Sabato-Aust, Tracy. *Well-Tended Perennial Garden*. Timber Press. Portland, Oregon. 2006.

Tripp, Kim E. and J. C. Raulston. *The Year in Trees*. Timber Press. Portland, Oregon. 1995.

Wells, B. G. *The Natural Gardens of North Carolina*. UNC Press. Chapel Hill, N.C. 1990.

Nursery Website References

Hawksridge Farms, Inc. Hickory, North Carolina.

Hoffman Nursery. Rougemont, North Carolina.

Monrovia Nursery. Azusa, California.

Nurseries Caroliniana. North Augusta, South Carolina.

Parks Seed Wholesale, Inc. Greenwood, South Carolina.

Plant Delights Nursery. Raleigh, North Carolina.

Riverbanks Botanical Garden. Columbia, South Carolina.

Tinga Nursery. Castle Hayne. North Carolina.

Wayside Gardens. Hodges, South Carolina.

INDEX

PHOTO CREDITS

MEET
TOBY BOST

Born and raised in Piedmont, North Carolina, Toby Bost graduated from North Carolina State University where he holds both Bachelor and Master degrees in Horticulture Science. He studied under the renowned Dr. J. C. Raulston and Dr. Roy Larson, concentrating on a specialty in landscape gardening.

As field faculty emeritus, Toby is best known for his thirty-one years as a horticulturist and Extension Agent with the N.C. Cooperative Extension Service. For more than two decades he recruited and certified more than 400 Master Gardeners in Durham and Forsyth counties, appearing frequently in the media as a gardening educator. He has been a garden writer for several newspapers and magazines, including *Carolina Gardener* and *Our State*. Many landscape professionals have attended his programs developed to assist them with licensure in myriad trade associations. For six years he was director of the Arboretum at Tanglewood Park.

Toby continues to dedicate his time to help gardeners conquer stubborn clay soils and grow healthy lawns and gardens both as a volunteer mentor and garden coach. He is an adjunct instructor at Forsyth Tech Community college in the horticulture department. He is the author of *North Carolina Gardener's Guide, Carolinas Gardener's Guide*, and co-editor of two books, *The Successful Gardeners Guide: North Carolina* and *Carolinas Gardener's Handbook*, most with Cool Springs Press.

Bost has received numerous communication awards, most notable being the Distinguished Service Award from the National Association of County Agricultural Agents, and the Order of the Longleaf Pine presented by the governor's office for public service. Toby is an active member in the Forsyth Master Gardener program and Paul J. Ciener Botanical Garden. He is a supervisor with the Forsyth Soil and Water Conservation Service.

Toby and his wife, Becky, reside in Winston-Salem, NC. They have two adult children, both educators. They serve in leadership at their church, and in his leisure time, Toby enjoys golf, fishing, and, of course, the joys of gardening.